COMMUNICATION IN GLOBAL JIHAD

This book conceptually examines the role of communication in global jihad from multiple perspectives. The main premise is that communication is so vital to the global jihadist movement today that jihadists will use any communicative tool, tactic, or approach to impact or transform people and the public at large. The author explores how and why the benefits of communication are a huge boon to jihadist operations, with jihadists communicating their ideological programs to develop a strong base for undertaking terrorist violence. The use of various information and communication systems and platforms by jihadists exemplifies the most recent progress in the relationship between terrorism, media, and the new information environment.

For jihadist organizations like ISIS and Al-Qaeda, recruiting new volunteers for the Caliphate who are willing to sacrifice their lives for the cause is a top priority. Based on various conceptual analyses, case studies, and theoretical applications, this book explores the communicative tools, tactics, and approaches used for this recruitment, including narratives, propaganda, mainstream media, social media, new information and communication technologies, the jihadisphere, visual imagery, media framing, globalization, financing networks, crime–jihad nexuses, group communication, radicalization, social movements, fatwas, martyrdom videos, pop-jihad, and jihadist nasheeds.

This book will be of great interest to students and scholars of communication studies, political science, terrorism and international security, Islamic studies, and cultural studies.

Jonathan Matusitz is Associate Professor in the Nicholson School of Communication and Media at the University of Central Florida, USA. His research focuses on the role of communication in terrorism, symbolism in terrorism, and the globalization of culture and new media. Previous titles include *Global Jihad in Muslim and Non-Muslim Contexts* (2020), *Online Jihadist Magazines to Promote the Caliphate: Communicative Perspectives* (2019), *Symbolism in Terrorism: Motivation, Communication, and Behavior* (2015), and *Terrorism & Communication: A Critical Introduction* (2013).

POLITICS, MEDIA AND POLITICAL COMMUNICATION

For more information about this series, please visit: https://www.routledge.com/
Politics-Media-and-Political-Communication/book-series/POLMED

COMMUNICATION IN GLOBAL JIHAD

Jonathan Matusitz

R Routledge
Taylor & Francis Group

LONDON AND NEW YORK

First published 2021
by Routledge
2 Park Square, Milton Park, Abingdon, Oxon OX14 4RN

and by Routledge
52 Vanderbilt Avenue, New York, NY 10017

Routledge is an imprint of the Taylor & Francis Group, an informa business

© 2021 Jonathan Matusitz

British Library Cataloguing in Publication Data
A catalogue record for this book is available from the British Library

Library of Congress Cataloging-in-Publication Data
A catalog record has been requested for this book

ISBN: 978-0-367-61707-3 (hbk)
ISBN: 978-0-367-61706-6 (pbk)
ISBN: 978-1-003-10614-2 (ebk)

Typeset in Bembo
by Taylor & Francis Books

CONTENTS

1

INTRODUCTION

This book examines the role of communication in global jihad across 12 chapters and from many perspectives. The main premise is that communication is so vital to the global jihadist movement (GJM)[1] today that jihadists will use any communicative tool, tactic, or approach to impact or transform people and the public at large. For most jihadists, their dream is to fulfill the supposed will of Allah of conquering the world through violence by establishing the Caliphate. Examples of communicative tools, tactics, or approaches described in this book include, but are not limited to, narratives, propaganda, mainstream media, social media, new information and communication technologies, the jihadisphere, visual imagery, media framing, globalization, financing networks, crime–jihad nexuses, group communication, radicalization, social movements, fatwas, martyrdom videos, pop-jihad, and jihadist nasheeds.

In its comprehensive examination of terrorism published in 2019, the U.S. Institute of Peace (USIP)[2] estimates that the number of terrorist attacks has grown by 500% since the 9/11 terrorist attacks. "Terrorism" defines today's international relations and regional politics in many areas of the world. It even influences social and cultural interactions in an increasingly globalizing realm.[3] Jihad, in particular, is arguably the most recognizable Muslim concept to most people across seven continents. The exact meaning of the word has been subject to heated debate for the past few decades. From a contemporary perspective, jihad translates as struggle, which can be personal, spiritual, or metaphoric striving, or it can be religiously inspired war.[4] Jihadism is not a new threat. However, the rapid global influence of jihadist groups is. Before the age of globalization, most jihadist activities were limited to their regional areas. Today, the progress of communication technologies has vastly improved jihadist organizations' global reach. The jihadist threat pervades all sovereign borders. This was evident from attacks in Paris (November 2015), Brussels (March 2016), Orlando (June 2016), Nice (July 2016), Barcelona (August

2017), and Sri Lanka (April 2019), which were all perpetrated by people raised in the countries where they took place.

The purpose of jihadists to exploit communication to the fullest extent is to strengthen currently held attitudes about the importance of jihad or change minds in order to sway public opinion.[5] In this era of globalization, the opportunities for building interconnections are plentiful, but so are the risks of extreme conflicts.[6] Through globalization, particularly the new information environment, jihadist organizations are increasingly able to leverage media technologies to operate in their best interests. New approaches to communication have expanded the horizons of a great many mujahedin; now, they can easily organize and mobilize like-minded people throughout the world to join or contribute to transnational jihadist networks like Al-Qaeda and ISIS. Such jihadist organizations work hard at developing mobilization efforts centered on the communication of messages to audiences. Communication is not merely a process of message transmission; it also constitutes a dialogue with an audience. The interactive opportunities that the internet offers represent an ideal platform for the creation of new global audiences.

We live in a globally mediated world that connects an innumerable number of individuals across global, economic, religious, cultural, and political barriers. Unfortunately, this is a huge boon to jihadist operations. At the simplest level, jihadists can communicate their ideological programs and develop a strong base for undertaking terrorist violence. An example of this is provided in Chapter 7, which explains how, in the age of the coronavirus, Al-Qaeda and ISIS exploited the global pandemic crisis to blame the Muslim world for their neglected duty of jihad and, in the same process, recruit more followers. The use of various information and communication systems and platforms by jihadists exemplifies the most recent progress in the relationship between terrorism, media, and the new information environment.[7] The future of global jihadism looks as dangerous as ever in the wake of globalization. Technological evolution and the escalation of global non-state actions have transformed the theaters of war and conflict across the world. Rather than seeing nation-states opposing each other (or local guerillas clashing with each other), present-day conflict increasingly involves global non-state actors that pursue asymmetrical warfare against states or even against each other. As explained in Chapters 5 and 10, with the rise of new media technologies, jihadist networks are an ever-stronger method of war, allowing rogue players to both diffuse fear and strike in distant locales.[8]

Fighting for the caliphate

Many jihadist groups share the belief that violent jihad should be waged to establish the Caliphate. The Caliphate is a global system of Islamic governance to which all nations on earth (both Muslim and non-Muslim) will be subjected. The ultimate objective of the Caliphate is to follow the Word of Allah, as enshrined in the Quran and hadith, to the letter and establish an Islamic authority over all nations through sharia (a body of Islamic law). The term "Caliph," in its most fundamental sense, means successor and in its historical context signified "the vicegerent of the Prophet" or "Deputy of God." This latter point implied a relinquished power such as that held by Abu Bakr, the first successor to the Prophet Muhammad and, by the same token, the first Caliph.[9]

Enter ISIS's vision of the Caliphate. The terrorist group's global ambition—obvious in the universal, geographically unmarked title of "Islamic State"—was boosted by the online publication of "ISIS takeover maps," fictitious maps displaying re-mapped European, African, Asian, and even American nations as ISIS provinces.[10] The quest for the Caliphate is also predicated upon the idea that the "American–Crusader–Zionist conspiracy" will finally be vanquished. As Thomas Friedman (2009)[11] wrote in *The New York Times*, "propagated by jihadist Web sites, mosque preachers, Arab intellectuals, satellite news stations, and books—and tacitly endorsed by some Arab régimes." As Friedman continues, "this narrative posits that America has declared war on Islam, as part of a grand 'American–Crusader–Zionist conspiracy' to keep Muslims down."[12]

Most jihadists have global objectives that are not confined to a single régime, a single nation, or a single region. For the Caliphate to function according to the jihadist doctrine, international boundaries must be eradicated and a worldwide government established. Major jihadist organizations like Al-Qaeda and ISIS pursue these aims by joining forces with "global affiliates"—groups that can be equally impactful and that pledge allegiance and assistance for Al-Qaeda and ISIS. The latter has found motivated affiliates in Afghanistan, Algeria, Egypt, India, Indonesia, Iraq, Lebanon, Libya, Nigeria, Pakistan, the Philippines, Russia, Saudi Arabia, Somalia, the Sudan, Syria, Tunisia, Uzbekistan, and Yemen.[13] The transnational nature of the Caliphate implies that the GJM will do the utmost to recruit followers so they can sacrifice their lives for the ultimate cause.

Objectives of this book

The **first objective** of this book is to demonstrate how jihadist organizations exploit the myriad benefits of communication to achieve their objectives of establishing the Caliphate and recruiting new jihadists to sacrifice their lives for it. Through a complex, but skillful strategy of global communication tools—like global terrorist networks, online social media, online magazines, martyrdom videos, and even pop music—they communicate their fighting prowess, mass murders, religious zeal, and political goals to the ummah (the global community of Muslim brothers and sisters). Like governments, jihadist groups employ various tools to diffuse their messages to the public. Communicating ideology over the internet is fitting because the information published online is much less likely to be filtered by journalists and editors. Jihadists can disseminate their messages as they see fit. Conflicts involving jihadists are wars of ideas, not just physical violence or military battles.[14] Accessible, low-cost, and interactive global communication networks can make one's voice heard.[15]

Global communication enables Islamist global hegemony to recruit more adherents. *A propos* jihadist recruitment itself, the internet can effortlessly be used to apply marketing-like techniques that target vulnerable demographics. Many marketing models exist on the internet that can help recruiters get in contact with their target demographics of youth, female, and foreign supporters. Without the internet, jihad promoters would have more difficulties roping people in. The internet's ease of accessibility and capacity for users to maintain anonymity are a significant windfall in the GJM because anyone behind a computer screen is susceptible to jihadist recruitment.[16]

To understand the changing world order through a communicative perspective, it is important to understand how communication is essential to how we understand global affairs. Just like government leaders and diplomats, jihadists recognize the power of communication to shape the international order. This phenomenon is exacerbated in the new communication environment characterized by internet and its revolution of how to communicate and with whom.[17] Applying this issue to the context of contemporary global communication, I argue that a common goal of jihadism is global and, most importantly, its single common objective is geographically dispersed with individual climaxes around the planet. The use of online social media has altered the spatial and temporal organization of social life around the concept of jihadism. New forms of extremist action, interaction, and exercise of power surface and push the limits of a physical locale.[18]

The **second objective** is to describe the information and messages disseminated by jihadists. In fact, Chapter 7 is exclusively dedicated to the jihadist narrative. The online media revolution has sparked massive changes in the manner by which information is communicated on a global scale.[19] In this age of instantaneous global communication, every message is quickly conveyable and receivable. The messages behind jihadist communication vary, based on the motives and the type of audience. These messages are framed as informative, galvanizing, and lobbying for support and recruitment. Through deception, these messages are sometimes written in a way to win over audiences through lofty goals, false promises, and flattery. Through coercion, these messages can also intimidate and erode the audience's confidence in their own Muslim governments or leaders. A dangerous corollary is that government officials and security forces become less able to prevent the increase in the number of jihadists in their own countries. Equally dangerous is the ability of jihadist narratives to convince Muslims that individual nations are not as important as the globally unified ummah. Another direct corollary is that such doctrine can impinge on long-established territorial limitations, thereby redefining nationality for both jihadists and would-be jihadists and paving the way for the Caliphate.

The **third objective** is to explain how the power of communication within the radicalization process is amplified through the jihadisphere. In Chapter 10, the notion of jihadisphere makes the point that global communication tools like social media are not only channels or conduits of communication; they are also important media for jihadists' self-promotion and recruitment. The jihadisphere is the internet-based community of jihadists and their supporters who are connected through their shared devotion to the global Salafist/jihadist ideology.[20] The jihadisphere does not consist merely of communication networks. Online social media can also be used by jihadist organizations to inform audiences in a "real time" fashion; Twitter, Facebook, and even interactive online chatrooms can serve as launch pads for new online media products. Examples include video games and musical segments.[21] By posting videos online, jihadist organizations can easily propagate extremist ideologies, attract would-be recruits, radicalize such people, and deepen their narratives. Ultimately, the jihadisphere becomes a borderless and informal platform of organizational learning because it readily provides virtual training that can lead to the imitation of violent attacks—depicted in the jihadist videos—in the real world.

The **fourth objective** is to describe jihadist networks. Though the term "jihad" is imbued with complexities or contradictions, it nevertheless presents a grave threat to global security because it is so easily accessible through global jihadist networks. The faster globalization processes happen, the more powerful networks become. As described in Chapter 5, social network analysis (SNA) is a useful method to understand networks such as centralized networks, horizontal networks, and the all-channel types of networks. Jihad has enormous potential for democratization. It should come to no surprise, then, that networks in the jihadisphere contribute to escalating violence in cities of the Western world.[22] The more presence of jihadist networks, the more opportunities for jihadists to communicate with like-minded others. This presents a threat to the public sphere itself. The public sphere is the public arena—i.e., today, it is cyberspace—where ideas and projects are communicated for and by anyone who participates in that sphere, not just institutions of society.[23] It constitutes "a network for communicating information and points of view."[24]Lazzarich (2015)[25] even talks about a global emotional public sphere when discussing the many groups that come from all corners of the globe. They come into contact in the online public sphere and eventually form revolutionary insurgencies in different parts of the world.

The **last objective** of this book is to explain how youth-oriented channels like Twitter, Facebook, YouTube, and Instagram—in addition to rap videos, martyrdom videos, beheading videos, and even online jihadist magazines—are used to make the GJM look like a "jihad cool" phenomenon. Put differently, social media are only one aspect of the promotion and planning of jihadism. Jihad propagandists have been known to use various tools of popular culture to recruit volunteers in many languages (including Arabic, French, and English, among others). For example, Deso Dogg was a German rapper who uploaded pop-jihad videos on YouTube to promote his pro-Caliphate, anti-Western hatred (see Chapter 11).

Global communication defined

Within the scope of this book, global communication refers to "people-to-people" or "groups-to-groups" interactions on a global scale. More precisely, it encompasses the ways that people connect, share, relate, and mobilize across geographic, social, and cultural borders.[26] When examining communication on a global scale, it is essential to take context into consideration. In the global communication arena, local terrorists can effortlessly exploit international media to communicate their agenda.[27] Information is hardly limited by national borders and, through its high-speech online set-up, it can travel almost faultlessly across communication platforms like the internet and smartphones. Social movements create new values or get old ones to resurface in the communicative spaces occupied by various individuals and groups.

Communication

Communication refers to the exchange and transmitting of information. It is the very enabler of the development of any contact and relationship. Within this perspective, information technologies, media outlets, and media coverage contribute to the formation of such contacts and relationships. Communication plays an important role on the social map. It allows the procurement of new information (as well as the recycling of old information) which is then interpreted through the standpoint or circumstances occupied by the person at any specific time.[28]

Present-day communication includes both mass communication and networked communication. Mass communication spreads information from a principal source through consolidated media, like newspapers, radio, and television. This type of mass-mediated interaction is controlled by huge organizations, some of which are government-owned; it also diffuses mainstream information via conduits of distribution.[29] Networked communication, on the other hand, disseminates information from various sources, including non-traditional sources (e.g., common people on the street) and, as such, expresses multiple different views. It can be seen through an assortment of formats, such as electronic mail, teleconferencing, Twitter, Facebook, and other social media platforms.[30]

Media and technology

People employ different forms of media based on their goals, communication purpose, institutional reasons, and contextual factors. One of the most used tools of global communication are media and technology. The progress of media and technology have played an essential part in globalization and global communication. The global communication sphere is making virtual-global-trespassing practically stress-free. Information society cannot be painlessly controlled either by authorities (that try to regulate the flow of information on text messages or the web) or by moderate religious leaders in their attempt to exert some control over media content.[31] Because of the fluidity and anonymity that the internet offers, it is difficult for law enforcement and security experts to either locate jihadists or fully comprehend their operations. A website or social media platform can have hidden support or transferred to another server in another location (beginning the process again). Additional obstacles also hinder the ability to capture files or intercept communications.

Imagined and indirect relationships

Social ties are relationships that exist among individuals who are in contact with one another (directly or indirectly). Such ties are articulated by a sense of belonging to real or imagined communities. The latter term, "imagined communities," was developed by Anderson (1991).[32] Imagined communities are rooted in the "politics of identification."[33] As Calhoun (1991)[34] continues, "people without direct inter-personal relations with each other are led by the mediation of the world of political symbols to imagine themselves as members of communities defined by common ascriptive characteristics, personal tastes, habits, concerns." They are "imagined" because they are not related to direct or indirect relationships; rather, they pertain to "categorical identities." Calhoun (1991)[35] contends that the diffusion of "indirect relationships" and the creation of "imagined communities" are two traits of modernity. In addition to direct interpersonal relationships (i.e., face-to-face); he considers imagined personal relations that can emerge, for example, *vis-à-vis* political representatives, television figures, but also through tradition.

Communication technologies can expand our social reach in developing direct relationships (e.g., through email or a phone conversation). They can also influence indirect relationships. As such, an activist can cultivate an indirect relationship with an esteemed public figure that one has seen on television or through speeches available online.[36] Such indirect popularity in global jihad was experienced by Anwar al-Awlaki, known as "the bin Laden of the internet" before he was killed in 2011. al-Awlaki was a Yemeni-American jihad propagandist who developed both direct and indirect relationships with countless online users through his captivating sermons—his sermons were disseminated through podcasts on the internet. As a jihadist preacher, he quickly became a dangerously successful online recruiter and motivator. He was also a military strategist for Al-Qaeda.[37]

The network effect

It is abundantly clear that the effects of globalization have improved the inter-connectedness of communities worldwide. As the international community is increasingly globalized, so do jihadist networks. The exponential evolution of technologies in domains such as communication and travel has contributed to the enhancement of prosperity, goods, and services across the international community. However, a darker side to the phenomenon of globalization exists. This darker side is the explosion of international terrorist groups. The technological progress of the twenty-first century has enabled jihadist networks to apply an unprecedented number of communication strategies and applications. Most of those communication strategies and applications have global reach that have brought jihadists closer to one another and more able to accomplish their ultimate goals: the Caliphate.[38] Individuals or groups are more inclined to use a specific channel of communication if other people have used that medium successfully and are now automatically associated with that medium; this phenomenon is referred to as the network effect.[39] Devji (2005)[40] actually calls this network effect "the global media effect," where no single player will have complete control over the effects of other people or actions.

With the network effect, both social and individual narratives can be heard or shared. An actor's identity in cyberspace is molded by a collection of relationships at any given time, leading to a shared vision of the world. From this vantage point, joining a jihadist group is not caused by an external narrative embraced and internalized by a person—as in the case where a collective narrative replaces an individual one. Rather, belonging to a jihadist group is the result of changing patterns of relationships, where a person's narrative aligns with the collective narrative of a group. Here, individual and collective narratives synchronize.[41]

On August 19, 2014, at the height of ISIS's Caliphate era, the beheading video of James Foley, a U.S. journalist and video reporter, became viral through the network effect. When a network effect takes place, the value of an action or element—in this case, the beheading video—increases according to the number of other people using it.[42] Abu Bakr Al-Baghdadi, the former ISIS leader killed on October 27, 2019, was the man who not only championed the practice of publicized beheadings through viral video dissemination; he also cultivated the idea of the network effect of jihadism. The strategy of beheading the Infidels is what set ISIS apart in the GJM; it became a major component of its identity, its brand, and its *raison d'être*.[43] ISIS's objective today remains the same: to terrorize the rest (i.e., the rest of the world, outside their Caliphate) through media practices that are so readily available. In this case, a video of each killing (extremely graphic) is published on every platform. This threat is directed at the international public at large and, unsurprisingly, it becomes news.[44]

Soft power

Soft power is the ability to become more attractive to the audience, to co-opt, and to convince others by avoiding the method of coercion (which would be "hard power").[45] Examples include the psychological, emotional, and intellectual appeal of jihadist narratives that extremist organizations create and disseminate.[46] From this vantage point, global communication denotes a transfer of knowledge and ideas from powerful media sources to local recipients. This is done through various communicative approaches designed to affect the preferences of others and become more appealing.[47] The term "soft power" is also used when discussing the impact of the use of less transparent channels on social and public opinion (through both political and non-political organizations). Such less transparent channels are plentiful in the Information Age.[48]

Propaganda

Propaganda is one of the long-established terms associated with communication. It refers to the "deliberate, systematic attempt to shape perceptions, manipulate cognitions, and direct behavior to achieve a response that furthers the desired intent of the propagandist."[49] It is a tool of persuasion—persuasive processes that can transform people and the public at large, directly or indirectly, through the use of deliberately selected and partial, or even fictitious, disinformation. It has been employed for centuries and impacts communication both nationally and internationally. With the evolution of social media, propaganda is becoming more and more salient, even dangerous.[50] Abundant literature has been published on that topic, but only a fraction of it examines it from a perspective of strategic communication—particularly strategic communication used by an organization to fulfill its dreams.[51] Communication academics and practitioners working in the West consider extremist propaganda a state-of-the-art form of strategic communication.[52] A comprehensive definition of strategic communication is "the practice of deliberate and purposive communication that a communication agent enacts in the public sphere on behalf of a communicative entity to reach set goals."[53]

The propaganda-related objectives of jihadists include enhanced public attention, intensification of demands, the cultivation of sympathy, and legitimacy. The GJM employs a global network of propagandists to promote its ideology, and it is certainly propaganda that attracts most individuals to jihadism.[54] Carruthers (2011)[55] concurs, arguing that an essential element of jihadists' weaponry includes both the need to cause fear and terror and the need to air grievances and diffuse propaganda. To appeal to their global Muslim publics, the widespread dissemination of well-crafted messages by jihad propagandists creates an echo chamber that magnifies the master jihadist narrative through diffusion of loaded language and elimination of competing views. Put another way, by ensuring that the master jihadist narrative is the loudest of all, jihadists' advanced use of social media creates an aura of legitimacy, even if it does not necessarily reflect reality.[56]

Let us look briefly at the case of Al-Qaeda. In addition to using conventional messages of propaganda, the terrorist organization offers library services for more than 3,000 books and monographs from revered "jihadist thinkers" which one can easily download to smartphones.[57] Al-Qaeda's sites contain videos of successful operations against U.S. targets in Iraq, giving rise to the manufacture of jihadist heroes like the "Bagdad Sniper" and the "Sniper of Fallujah."[58] As will be discussed in Chapter 7 (i.e., jihadist narratives), basic propaganda techniques include, among others, high-influence language (by using words that contain highly positive or negative meanings) and the "choice of the majority" technique (that attempts to persuade the audience that the choice of the majority is right).[59]

Competition with other books

In *Understanding Terrorism in the Age of Global Media: A Communication Approach* (2013, Palgrave Macmillan),[60] Cristina Archetti examined the processes of communication that support terrorism in the twenty-first century across eight chapters. Although Archetti conducted her analyses of internet-based radicalization and the role of jihadist narratives thoroughly and admirably, she omitted important communicative components such as terrorist networks, social movements, and mainstream approaches like media framing and media effects. Of equal relevance is the fact that Al-Qaeda was the main case study in her book, which was published before the emergence of ISIS.

In *Online Jihadist Magazines to Promote the Caliphate: Communicative Perspectives*, (2019, Peter Lang),[61] Matusitz, Madrazo, and Udani examine the impact that jihadist magazines like *Inspire* (by Al-Qaeda), *Dabiq* and *Rumiyah* (by ISIS), and *Gaidi Mtaani* (by Al-Shabaab) have on various audiences. Divided into 10 chapters, this book is up-to-date (e.g., the jihadisphere and social media effects) and even includes an applied study based on a content analysis, but specializes mostly on such jihadist magazines. It does not focus on jihadist concepts like fatwas, martyrdom videos, pop-jihad, and jihadist nasheeds, to name a few.

In *Twitter and Jihad: The Communication Strategy of ISIS* (2015, Italian Institute for International Political Studies),[62] Maggioni and Magri put together an edited volume that looked into the videos, Twitter accounts, mainstream media, and viral propaganda tools used by ISIS to promote their self-proclaimed Caliphate. Structured into six chapters, this book does a meticulous analysis of ISIS's internet-driven propaganda. Overall, it is an influential research monograph that can be useful for law enforcement and government officials. However, it fails to capture many other concepts and theories inherent to our understanding of the GJM. The communication of global jihad entails more than social media platforms.

Summary of all chapters

Chapter 2 defines terrorism and argues that communication is inherent to terrorist endeavors. Each attack produces some type of interaction with the public. It is generally an audience beyond the immediate victims; the main targets of influence are those witnessing the attack and the state. Also described are (1) the different types of terrorists, such as lone-wolf actors, non-state actors, and insurgent groups, and (2) the targets of terrorism. Examples are direct victims, indirect victims, and symbolic targets. **Chapter 3** describes jihad in detail. Jihad is a concept that literally means "striving" or "determined effort." Examples of key concepts in this chapter include greater vs. lesser jihad, defensive vs. offensive jihad, vertical vs. horizontal jihad, and neojihadism. Also included are accounts of jihadist leaders such as Abdullah Azzam (Osama bin Laden's mentor and Al-Qaeda's founder). This chapter ends with a large description of Salafism, an ideology that advocates a return to pure, traditional Islam. In other words, Salafism opposes new interpretations or approaches other than those that already exist. Its main concern is about the fundamentals of the faith and doctrinal wholesomeness.

Chapter 4 focuses on the globalization of jihad. Particularly emphasized is glocalized jihad, reflecting the notion that jihad players are connected to the global jihad war, even though they represent countless people who have had no prior contact with fighters for the GJM. As such, in Western countries, second- and third-generation Muslims become passionate about finding their own universal values and truths. Because jihad is so global, the concept of deterritorialization of jihad was discussed. Headquarters are no longer necessary. This chapter ends with a description of social media effects, including the YouTube effect, the global networked effect, and online jihadist magazines. **Chapter 5** deals with global jihadist networks, which can be explained through social network analysis (SNA). SNA is a type of analysis that rests on the principle that nodes (people in the network) are interconnected through clear or unclear relationships. These connections are formed by such interdependent interactions and create a "network." The types of jihadist networks described in this chapter include centralized and decentralized networks, all-channel networks, and crime–jihad networks. Also included are sections on foreign fighters and financial networks.

Chapter 6 is an explanation of the role of mass media in the global communication of jihad. Through mass media, jihadism becomes propaganda of the deed—which allows them to justify their actions and gain public sympathy for their goals. An important part of this chapter is the jihadists' manipulation of mass media by exploiting the symbiotic relationship between the two. It is mutually beneficial. The power of the image and framing techniques are also something to behold: mass media can be cleverly employed to determine the frames of reference for readers or viewers to interpret public events. **Chapter 7** covers the role of narratives in global jihad. In spite of ideological differences between some jihadist organizations, there exists a master jihadist narrative that resonates with a significant minority of Muslims. As such, the Muslim world has been humiliated and discriminated; the Caliphate will be established to replace the secular world; and apocalyptic jihad is the best solution. The master jihadist narrative serves as a platform for Islamic radicalization with the ultimate objective of mobilizing the ummah for violent actions. A specific section on jihadization in the age of the coronavirus is provided in this chapter as well.

Chapter 8 covers the role of fatwas in global jihad. Fatwas are legal decrees issued by an established authority on matters of Islamic legislation. Because the credibility of a fatwa is not universal, Muslims routinely engage in fatwa shopping to search for another scholar to have a second (or even a third or fourth) opinion until they find what they want. Although jihadist fatwas only account for a small percentage of fatwas in general, they have been known to result in the killing of enemies. This is particularly true when fatwas are used as violence against free speech. Examples include jihadist fatwas against the *Jyllands-Posten* cartoonists (i.e., the 12 Muhammad cartoons) and Salman Rushdie. **Chapter 9** describes Islamic revival. In this context, Islamic revival adheres to (1) the Salafist conjecture that the Quran is the perfect, straightforward word of Allah and should be taken literally and (2) the corresponding support of jihad to attain such radical aims. Islamic revival has been heavily influenced by Salafism and Wahhabism. Wahhabism is depicted by the media and public spokespersons as an intolerant, ultra-conservative, militant interpretation of Islam. Just like Salafism, Wahhabism stresses the importance of the holy scriptures and the hadith as the only valid sources of Islam. Also included in this chapter is social movement theory (SMT), a theoretical model that can shed light on the radicalization process and violent extremism inherent to the

Islamic revival movement. A good case study of SMT here is the Arab Spring. This chapter ends with Islamic revival as the "jihad cool" phenomenon.

Chapter 10 details the jihadisphere, the internet-based community of jihadists and their supporters who are connected through their shared devotions. A case study of ISIS's use of Twitter is provided. Twitter plays a huge role in ISIS's operational tactics beyond Syria and Iraq. Twitter streams from ISIS give the group an aura of authenticity, taking the form of a spontaneous activity of a generation clinging to smartphones for self-publication. Case studies are provided on Anwar al-Awlaki, "the bin Laden of the internet," and Abu Musab al-Zarqawi, who also took advantage of cyberspace. **Chapter 11** covers jihad through popular music. An important point is that this matter falls under a category of subculture or counterculture of angry people. An example of this is martyrdom culture. Jihadist videos are turned into music or pop videos to instigate Muslims to become martyrs or heroes dying for the faith. Three music videos, titled *Hijrah, Blood for Blood,* and *My Revenge,* are used as a case study to describe a genre reflecting modern music videos. Hezbollah's martyrdom videos are also used as another case study. The notion of pop-jihad is something to behold. Pop-jihad is a musical genre that glorifies jihad by including intentionally controversial lyrics. This chapter ends with jihadist nasheeds. A nasheed is a spiritual hymn devoted to worship Allah. Nasheeds are an efficient communicative conduit of jihadism as they concentrate on a specific number of radical themes with broad appeal to the ummah.

Chapter 12 is the conclusion of this book. Four major conclusions were drawn from the conceptual analysis conducted across the 11 previous chapters: (1) The more global communication, the more jihadism, (2) a dangerous shrinking world, (3) an emancipating communication environment, and (4) parallel globalization of terror. Chapter 12 also offers solutions in our fight against global jihad. As such, solutions are offered as to what governments and law enforcement agencies can do, what ordinary citizens can do, and what moderate Muslims can do. With regard to the latter, for example, supporting pro-democracy politicians in the Muslim world, supporting citizenship and religious education, and supporting counter-fatwas are presented as steps in the right direction. More importantly, the hermeneutical approach is a solution included in the second half of the chapter. Hermeneutics is a methodological approach to interpretation, particularly the interpretation of scriptures, holy texts, works of wisdom, and philosophical manuscripts. In this discussion, the concept of *ijtihad* (reinterpretation or critical reading of holy texts in Islam) is a possible hermeneutical solution

Notes

1 Maxime Bérubé and Benoit Dupont, "Mujahideen Mobilization: Examining the Evolution of the Global Jihadist Movement's Communicative Action Repertoire," *Studies in Conflict & Terrorism* 42, no. 1 (2019): 5–24. https://doi.org/10.1080/1057610X.2018.1513689

2 United States Institute of Peace, *Preventing Extremism in Fragile States: A New Approach: Final Report of the Task Force on Extremism in Fragile States* (Washington, D.C.: United States Institute of Peace, 2019).

3 Daya Thussu, "(Mis)Representing Terrorism in Global Media," in *Media and Journalism in an Age of Terrorism*, ed. Renaud de la Brosse and Krostoffer Holt (Newcastle: Cambridge Scholars Publishing, 2019): 67–83.
4 Eli Alshech, "The Doctrinal Crisis within the Salafi-Jihadi Ranks and the Emergence of Neo-Takfirism: A Historical and Doctrinal Analysis," *Islamic Law and Society* 21, no. 4 (2014): 419–52. https://doi.org/10.1163/15685195-00214p04; Jacob Høigilt and Frida Nome, "Egyptian Salafism in Revolution," *Journal of Islamic Studies* 25, no. 1 (2014): 33–54. https://doi.org/10.1093/jis/ett056
5 Richard C. Vincent, "Global Communication and Propaganda," in *Global Communication: A Multicultural Perspective*, ed. Yahya R. Kamalipour (Lanham, MD: Rowman & Littlefield, 2019): 239–97.
6 Basyouni Ibrahim Hamada, "Towards a Global Journalism Ethics Model: An Islamic Perspective," *The Journal of International Communication* 22, no. 2 (2016): 188–208. https://doi.org/10.1080/13216597.2016.1205506
7 Levi J. West, "#jihad Understanding Social Media as a Weapon," *Security Challenges* 12, no. 2 (2016): 9–26.
8 Marwan M. Kraidy, "The Projectilic Image: Islamic State's Digital Visual Warfare and Global Networked Affect," *Media, Culture & Society* 39, no. 8 (2017): 1194–209. https://doi.org/10.1177/0163443717725575
9 R. James Ferguson, "Contemporary Political Mobilisation of the 'Caliphate': The Clash of Propaganda and Discontent," *Culture Mandala: The Bulletin of the Centre for East–West Cultural and Economic Studies* 8, no. 1 (2008): Article 1.
10 Kraidy, "The Projectilic Image," 1200–5.
11 Thomas L. Friedman, "America vs. The Narrative," *The New York Times* (2009, November 28): WK8.
12 Ibid., WK8.
13 Barbara F. Walter, "The New New Civil Wars," *Annual Review of Political Science* 20 (2017): 469–86. https://doi.org/10.1146/annurev-polisci-060415-093921
14 Moran Yarchi, "Terror Organizations' Uses of Public Diplomacy: Limited versus Total Conflicts," *Studies in Conflict & Terrorism* 39, no. 12 (2016): 1071–83. https://doi.org/10.1080/1057610X.2016.1184064
15 Gabriel Weimann, *Terror on the Internet: The New Arena, the New Challenges* (Washington, D.C.: United States Institute of Peace Press, 2006).
16 Michael Shaw and Priyantha Bandara, "Marketing Jihad: The Rhetoric of Recruitment," *Journal of Marketing Management* 34, no. 15 (2018): 1319–35. https://doi.org/10.1080/0267257X.2018.1520282
17 Alister Miskimmon, Ben O'Loughlin, and Laura Roselle, *Strategic Narratives: Communication Power and the New World Order* (New York: Routledge, 2014).
18 Johanna Sumiala and Lilly Korpiola, "Mediated Muslim Martyrdom: Rethinking Digital Solidarity in the 'Arab Spring'," *New Media & Society* 19, no. 1 (2017): 52–66. https://doi.org/10.1177/1461444816649918
19 Marshall T. Poe, *A History of Communications: Media and Society from the Evolution of Speech to the Internet* (Cambridge: Cambridge University Press, 2011).
20 Benjamin Ducol, "Uncovering the French-Speaking Jihadisphere: An Exploratory Analysis," *Media, War & Conflict* 5, no. 1 (2012): 51–70. https://doi.org/10.1177/1750635211434366
21 Marco Lombardi, "Islamic State Communication Project," *Sicurezza, Terrorismo e Società* 1 (2015): 99–133.
22 Peter J. Laverack, "What if the Khmer Rouge Had Twitter? Lessons for Today's Online Jihadists on Joint Criminal Liability via Social Media," *Alternative Law Journal* 40, no. 3 (2015): 190–4. https://doi.org/10.1177/1037969X1504000310
23 Manuel Castells, "The New Public Sphere: Global Civil Society, Communication Networks, and Global Governance," *The ANNALS of the American Academy of Political and Social Science* 616, no. 1 (2008): 78–93. https://doi.org/10.1177/0002716207311877
24 Jürgen Habermas, *Between Facts and Norms: Contributions to a Discourse Theory of Law and Democracy* (Cambridge, MA: MIT Press, 1996): 360.

25 Diego Lazzarich, "The Emergence of the Global Emotional Public Sphere," in *Cultures and Languages International Conference Proceedings II*, 2015: 97–106.

26 Daya Thussu, *International Communication: Continuity and Change* (3rd ed.) (New York: Bloomsbury Academic, 2018).

27 Cristina Archetti, *Understanding Terrorism in the Age of Global Media: A Communication Approach* (Palgrave Macmillan, 2013).

28 Cristina Archetti, "Narrative Wars: Understanding Terrorism in the Era of Global Interconnectedness," in *Forging the World: Strategic Narratives and International Relations*, ed. Alister Miskimmon, Ben O'Loughlin, and Laura Roselle (Ann Arbor, MI: University of Michigan Press, 2017): 218–45.

29 Hayley Watson, "Dependent Citizen Journalism and the Publicity of Terror," *Terrorism and Political Violence* 24, no. 3 (2012): 465–82. https://doi.org/10.1080/09546553.2011.636464

30 Gustavo Cardoso, "From Mass to Networked Communication: Communicational Models and the Informational Society," *International Journal of Communication* 2 (2008): 587–630.

31 Haydar Badawi Sadig, Roshan Noorzai, and Hala Asmina Guta, "Communication Technologies in the Arsenal of Al Qaeda and Taliban: Why the West Is Not Winning the War on Terror," in *The Handbook of Global Communication and Media Ethics, I, II*, ed. Robert S. Fortner and P. Mark Fackler (Hoboken, NJ: Blackwell, 2011): Chapter 48.

32 Benedict Anderson, *Imagined Communities: Reflections on the Origins and Spread of Nationalism* (London: Verso, 1991).

33 Craig Calhoun, "Indirect Relationships and Imagined Communities: Large Scale Social Integration and the Transformation of Everyday Life," in *Social Theory for a Changing Society*, ed. Pierre Bourdieu and James S. Coleman (Oxford: Westview Press, 1991): 95–121, 108.

34 Ibid., 108.

35 Ibid., 108–10.

36 Archetti, "Narrative Wars," 222–4.

37 Riyad Hosain Rahimullah, Stephen Larmar, and Mohamad Abdalla, "Understanding Violent Radicalization amongst Muslims: A Review of the Literature," *Journal of Psychology and Behavioral Science* 1, no. 1 (2013): 19–35.

38 Michael S. O'Neil and David H. Gray, "Islamic Terror Networks Implementation of Network Technologies," *Global Security Studies* 2, no. 3 (2011): 10–21.

39 Namkee Park, Jae Eun Chung, and Seungyoon Lee, "Explaining the Use of Text–Based Communication Media: An Examination of Three Theories of Media Use," *Cyberpsychology, Behavior & Social Networking* 15, no. 7 (2012): 357–63. https://doi.org/10.1089/cyber.2012.0121

40 Faisal Devji, *Landscapes of the Jihad: Militancy, Morality, Modernity* (Ithaca, NY: Cornell University Press, 2005).

41 Archetti, "Narrative Wars," 227–30.

42 Kevin J. Boudreau and Lars B. Jeppesen, "Unpaid Crowd Complementors: The Platform Network Effect Mirage," *Strategic Management Journal* 36, no. 12 (2015): 1761–77. https://doi.org/10.1002/smj.2324

43 Lombardi, "Islamic State Communication Project," 105.

44 Ibid., 106.

45 Thomas L. Ilgen, *Hard Power, Soft Power and the Future of Transatlantic Relations* (New York: Routledge, 2016).

46 Ratna Ghosh, W.Y. Alice Chan, Ashley Manuel, and Maihemuti Dilimulati, "Can Education Counter Violent Religious Extremism?" *Canadian Foreign Policy Journal* 23, no. 2 (2017): 117–33. http://doi.org/10.1080/11926422.2016.1165713

47 Majid Tehranian, "Global Communication and International Relations: Changing Paradigms and Policies," *International Journal of Peace Studies* 2, no. 1 (1997): 39–64.

48 Joseph S. Nye, Jr., *Soft Power: The Means to Success in World Politics* (New York: PublicAffairs, 2004).

49 Garth S. Jowett and Victoria O'Donnell, *Propaganda & Persuasion* (7th ed.) (Thousand Oaks, CA: Sage, 2015): 7.
50 Vincent, "Global Communication and Propaganda," 239.
51 Douglas Wilbur, "Propaganda's Place in Strategic Communication: The Case of ISIL's Dabiq Magazine," *International Journal of Strategic Communication* 11, no. 3 (2017): 209–23. http://doi.org/10.1080/1553118X.2017.1317636
52 James P. Farwell, "Jihadi Video in the 'War of Ideas'," *Survival* 52, no. 6 (2010): 127–50. http://doi.org/10.1080/00396338.2010.540787
53 Derina R. Holtzhausen and Ansgar Zerfass, "Strategic Communication—Pillars and Perspectives of an Alternative Paradigm," in *Organisationskommunikation und Public Relations: Forschungsparadigmen und neue Perspektiven*, ed. Ansgar Zerfaß, Lars Rademacher, and Stefan Wehmeier (Wiesbaden, Germany: Springer Verlag, 2013): 73–94, 74.
54 Brigitte Nacos, *Mass-Mediated Terrorism: The Central Role of the Media in Terrorism and Counterterrorism* (New York: Rowman & Littlefield, 2002):
55 Susan Carruthers, *The Media at War* (Basingstoke: Palgrave Macmillan, 2011).
56 Yannick Veilleux-Lepage, "Paradigmatic Shifts in Jihadism in Cyberspace: The Emerging Role of Unaffiliated Sympathizers in Islamic State's Social Media Strategy," *Contemporary Voices: St Andrews Journal of International Relations* 7, no. 1 (2016): 36–51. http://doi.org/10.15664/jtr.1183
57 Jarret Brachman, "High-Tech Terror: Al-Qaeda's Use of New Technology," *The Combating Terrorism Center* 30, no. 2 (2006): 149–64.
58 Cited in Gary Adkins, "Red Teaming the Red Team: Utilizing Cyber Espionage to Combat Terrorism," *Journal of Strategic Security* 6, no. 3 (2013): 1–9, 2. http://doi.org/10.5038/1944-0472.6.3S.1
59 Mahmut Mert Aslan and Muhammet Erbay, "Does Isis's Way of Propaganda Make It a Part of Global Islamophobia?" *Acta Universitatis Danubius* 2 (2017): 32–59.
60 Archetti, *Understanding Terrorism in the Age of Global Media*, 1–5.
61 Jonathan Matusitz, Andrea Madrazo, and Catalina Udani, *Online Jihadist Magazines to Promote the Caliphate: Communicative Perspectives* (New York: Peter Lang, 2019).
62 Monica Maggioni and Paolo Magri, *Twitter and Jihad: The Communication Strategy of ISIS* (Milan: Italian Institute for International Political Studies, 2015).

References

Adkins, Gary, "Red Teaming the Red Team: Utilizing Cyber Espionage to Combat Terrorism," *Journal of Strategic Security* 6, no. 3 (2013): 1–9. https://doi.org/10.5038/1944-0472.6.3S.1
Alshech, Eli, "The Doctrinal Crisis within the Salafi-Jihadi Ranks and the Emergence of Neo-Takfirism: A Historical and Doctrinal Analysis," *Islamic Law and Society* 21, no. 4 (2014): 419–452. https://doi.org/10.1163/15685195-00214p04.
Anderson, Benedict, *Imagined Communities: Reflections on the Origins and Spread of Nationalism.* London: Verso, 1991.
Archetti, Cristina, *Understanding Terrorism in the Age of Global Media: A Communication Approach.* New York: Palgrave Macmillan, 2013.
Archetti, Cristina, "Narrative Wars: Understanding Terrorism in the Era of Global Interconnectedness," in *Forging the World: Strategic Narratives and International Relations*, edited by Alister Miskimmon, Ben O'Loughlin, and Laura Roselle, 218–245. Ann Arbor, MI: University of Michigan Press, 2017.
Aslan, Mahmut Mert, and Muhammet Erbay, "Does Isis's Way of Propaganda Make It a Part of Global Islamophobia?" *Acta Universitatis Danubius* 2 (2017): 32–59.
Bérubé, Maxime, and Benoit Dupont, "Mujahideen Mobilization: Examining the Evolution of the Global Jihadist Movement's Communicative Action Repertoire," *Studies in Conflict & Terrorism* 42, no. 1 (2019): 5–24. https://doi.org/10.1080/1057610X.2018.1513689.

Boudreau, Kevin J., and Lars B. Jeppesen, "Unpaid Crowd Complementors: The Platform Network Effect Mirage," *Strategic Management Journal* 36, no. 12 (2015): 1761–1777. https://doi.org/10.1002/smj.2324.

Brachman, Jarret, "High-Tech Terror: Al-Qaeda's Use of New Technology," *The Combating Terrorism Center* 30, no. 2 (2006): 149–164.

Calhoun, Craig, "Indirect Relationships and Imagined Communities: Large Scale Social Integration and the Transformation of Everyday Life," in *Social Theory for a Changing Society*, edited by Pierre Bourdieu and James S. Coleman, 95–121. Oxford: Westview Press, 1991.

Cardoso, Gustavo, "From Mass to Networked Communication: Communicational Models and the Informational Society," *International Journal of Communication* 2 (2008): 587–630.

Carruthers, Susan, *The Media at War*. Basingstoke: Palgrave Macmillan, 2011.

Castells, Manuel, "The New Public Sphere: Global Civil Society, Communication Networks and Global Governance," *Annals of the American Academy of Political and Social Science* 616, no. 1 (2008): 78–93. https://doi.org/10.1177/0002716207311877.

Devji, Faisal, *Landscapes of the Jihad: Militancy, Morality, Modernity*. Ithaca, NY: Cornell University Press, 2005.

Ducol, Benjamin, "Uncovering the French-Speaking Jihadisphere: An Exploratory Analysis," *Media, War & Conflict* 5, no. 1 (2012): 51–70. https://doi.org/10.1177/1750635211434366.

Farwell, James P., "Jihadi Video in the 'War of Ideas'," *Survival* 52, no. 6 (2010): 127–150. http://doi.org/10.1080/00396338.2010.540787.

Ferguson, R. James, "Contemporary Political Mobilisation of the 'Caliphate': The Clash of Propaganda and Discontent," *Culture Mandala: The Bulletin of the Centre for East–West Cultural and Economic Studies* 8, no. 1 (2008): article 1.

Friedman, Thomas L., "America vs. The Narrative," *The New York Times* (2009, November 28): WK8.

Ghosh, Ratna, W.Y. Alice Chan, Ashley Manuel, and Maihemuti Dilimulati, "Can Education Counter Violent Religious Extremism?" *Canadian Foreign Policy Journal* 23, no. 2 (2017): 117–133. http://doi.org/10.1080/11926422.2016.1165713.

Habermas, Jürgen, *Between Facts and Norms: Contributions to a Discourse Theory of Law and Democracy*. Cambridge, MA: MIT Press, 1996.

Hamada, Basyouni Ibrahim, "Towards a Global Journalism Ethics Model: An Islamic Perspective," *The Journal of International Communication* 22, no. 2 (2016): 188–208. https://doi.org/10.1080/13216597.2016.1205506.

Høigilt, Jacob, and Frida Nome, "Egyptian Salafism in Revolution," *Journal of Islamic Studies* 25, no. 1 (2014): 33–54. https://doi.org/10.1093/jis/ett056.

Holtzhausen, Derina R., and Ansgar Zerfass, "Strategic Communication—Pillars and Perspectives of an Alternative Paradigm," in *Organisationskommunikation und Public Relations: Forschungsparadigmen und neue Perspektiven*, edited by Ansgar Zerfaß, Lars Rademacher, and Stefan Wehmeier, 73–94. Wiesbaden, Germany: Springer Verlag, 2013.

Ilgen, Thomas L., *Hard Power, Soft Power and the Future of Transatlantic Relations*. New York: Routledge, 2016.

Jowett, Garth S., and Victoria O'Donnell, *Propaganda & Persuasion* (7th ed.). Thousand Oaks, CA: Sage, 2015.

Kraidy, Marwan M., "The Projectilic Image: Islamic State's Digital Visual Warfare and Global Networked Affect," *Media, Culture & Society* 39, no. 8 (2017): 1194–1209. https://doi.org/10.1177/0163443717725575.

Laverack, Peter J., "What if the Khmer Rouge Had Twitter? Lessons for Today's Online Jihadists on Joint Criminal Liability via Social Media," *Alternative Law Journal* 40, no. 3 (2015): 190–194. https://doi.org/10.1177/1037969X1504000310.

Lazzarich, Diego, "The Emergence of the Global Emotional Public Sphere," in *Cultures and Languages International Conference Proceedings* II, 2015: 97–106.

Lombardi, Marco, "Islamic State Communication Project," *Sicurezza, Terrorismo e Società* 1 (2015): 99–133.

Maggioni, Monica, and Paolo Magri, *Twitter and Jihad: The Communication Strategy of ISIS*. Milan: Italian Institute for International Political Studies, 2015.

Matusitz, Jonathan, Andrea Madrazo, and Catalina Udani, *Online Jihadist Magazines to Promote the Caliphate: Communicative Perspectives*. New York: Peter Lang, 2019.

Miskimmon, Alister, Ben O'Loughlin, and Laura Roselle, *Strategic Narratives: Communication Power and the New World Order*. New York: Routledge, 2014.

Nacos, Brigitte, *Mass-Mediated Terrorism: The Central Role of the Media in Terrorism and Counterterrorism*. Lanham, MD: Rowman & Littlefield, 2002.

Nye, Joseph S., Jr., *Soft Power: The Means to Success in World Politics*. New York: PublicAffairs, 2004.

O'Neil, Michael S., and David H. Gray, "Islamic Terror Networks Implementation of Network Technologies," *Global Security Studies* 2, no. 3 (2011): 10–21.

Park, Namkee, Jae Eun Chung, and Seungyoon Lee, "Explaining the Use of Text-Based Communication Media: An Examination of Three Theories of Media Use," *Cyberpsychology, Behavior & Social Networking* 15, no. 7 (2012): 357–363. https://doi.org/10.1089/cyber.2012.0121.

Poe, Marshall T., *A History of Communications: Media and Society from the Evolution of Speech to the Internet*. Cambridge: Cambridge University Press, 2011.

Rahimullah, Riyad Hosain, Stephen Larmar, and Mohamad Abdalla, "Understanding Violent Radicalization amongst Muslims: A Review of the Literature," *Journal of Psychology and Behavioral Science* 1, no. 1 (2013): 19–35.

Sadig, Haydar Badawi, Roshan Noorzai, and Hala Asmina Guta, "Communication Technologies in the Arsenal of Al Qaeda and Taliban: Why the West Is Not Winning the War on Terror," in *The Handbook of Global Communication and Media Ethics, I, II*, edited by Robert S. Fortner and P. Mark Fackler, Chapter 48. Hoboken, NJ: Blackwell, 2011.

Shaw, Michael, and Priyantha Bandara, "Marketing Jihad: The Rhetoric of Recruitment," *Journal of Marketing Management* 34, no. 15 (2018): 1319–1335. https://doi.org/10.1080/0267257X.2018.1520282.

Sumiala, Johanna, and Lilly Korpiola, "Mediated Muslim Martyrdom: Rethinking Digital Solidarity in the 'Arab Spring'," *New Media & Society* 19, no. 1 (2017): 52–66. https://doi.org/10.1177/1461444816649918.

Tehranian, Majid, "Global Communication and International Relations: Changing Paradigms and Policies," *International Journal of Peace Studies* 2, no. 1 (1997): 39–64.

Thussu, Daya, *International Communication: Continuity and Change* (3rd ed.). New York: Bloomsbury Academic, 2018.

Thussu, Daya, "(Mis)Representing Terrorism in Global Media," in *Media and Journalism in an Age of Terrorism*, edited by Renaud de la Brosse and Krostoffer Holt, 67–83. Newcastle: Cambridge Scholars Publishing, 2019.

United States Institute of Peace, *Preventing Extremism in Fragile States: A New Approach: Final Report of the Task Force on Extremism in Fragile States*. Washington, D.C.: United States Institute of Peace, 2019.

Veilleux-Lepage, Yannick, "Paradigmatic Shifts in Jihadism in Cyberspace: The Emerging Role of Unaffiliated Sympathizers in Islamic State's Social Media Strategy," *Contemporary Voices: St Andrews Journal of International Relations* 7, no. 1 (2016): 36–51. http://doi.org/10.15664/jtr.1183.

Vincent, Richard C., "Global Communication and Propaganda," in *Global Communication: A Multicultural Perspective*, edited by Yahya R. Kamalipour, 239–297. Lanham, MD: Rowman & Littlefield, 2019.

Walter, Barbara F., "The New New Civil Wars," *Annual Review of Political Science* 20 (2017): 469–486. https://doi.org/10.1146/annurev-polisci-060415-093921.

Watson, Hayley, "Dependent Citizen Journalism and the Publicity of Terror," *Terrorism and Political Violence* 24, no. 3 (2012): 465–482. https://doi.org/10.1080/09546553.2011. 636464.

Weimann, Gabriel, *Terror on the Internet: The New Arena, the New Challenges*. Washington, D. C.: United States Institute for Peace Press, 2006.

West, Levi J., "#jihad Understanding Social Media as a Weapon," *Security Challenges* 12, no. 2 (2016): 9–26.

Wilbur, Douglas, "Propaganda's Place in Strategic Communication: The Case of ISIL's Dabiq Magazine," *International Journal of Strategic Communication* 11, no. 3 (2017): 209–223. http://doi.org/10.1080/1553118X.2017.1317636.

Yarchi, Moran, "Terror Organizations' Uses of Public Diplomacy: Limited versus Total Conflicts," *Studies in Conflict & Terrorism* 39, no. 12 (2016): 1071–1083. https://doi.org/10.1080/1057610X.2016.1184064.

2

DEFINING TERRORISM

In 2017, close to 11,000 terrorist attacks occurred worldwide, causing the deaths of approximately 26,400 people. Even though the number of attacks has declined since its pinnacle in 2014, terrorist attacks happen at much higher rates today than they did in previous decades. Terrorism is not evenly dispersed by world region. Most attacks in 2017 were in the Middle East and North Africa, followed by South Asia and sub-Saharan Africa. A mere 1% of attacks took place in North America. In America specifically, 65 terrorist attacks were perpetrated in 2017, which is 0.5% of the worldwide total.[1] The word "terrorism" became part of the West's vocabulary after French revolutionaries' beheaded their own people in 1793 and 1794. It was used in reference to governmental repression, particularly executions. About 17,000 formal executions were performed during the Reign of Terror, and an additional 23,000 were done illegally.[2] It was not until the 1960s that the study of terrorism became an academic subject—owing to the growing menace of international terrorism. Before, terrorism was mostly considered a tactic of local insurgencies.

Difficulty to define terrorism

Today, terrorism remains a controversial concept. As a complex phenomenon, it must be analyzed from a wide range of perspectives. Hence, there is no universally agreed-upon definition of terrorism. For example, Walter Laqueur, an influential scholar and political commentator, defined it as "the use of covert violence by a group for political ends."[3] His definition points to four essential attributes: (1) terrorism is more of a collective than individual endeavor; (2) it is political, not criminal; (3) it is a type of covert, not conventional, operation; and (4) it is always violent. The aims of terrorism include, but are not limited to, national independence, social justice, and all citizenship rights for minorities. These are often considered legitimate goals and can even garner much popular support. To sum it up in Laqueurian terms, it is covert violence perpetrated by a group for political reasons. What is also unique about terrorism is not only its aims, but also its means; terrorists strike without warning and indiscriminately, thereby targeting and victimizing innocent civilians.

In all cases, terrorism is illegal violence, or threatened use thereof, against human or nonhuman targets.[4] Definitions of terrorism are debatable besides conceptual issues and problems. When equating actions as "terrorism," it automatically labels the actors as "terrorists," which may reveal ideological or political bias.[5] Under these circumstances, all of which can deliberately or inadvertently complicate things and create even more debate, it comes to no surprise that Laqueur (1977)[6] insisted that "a comprehensive definition of terrorism does not exist nor will it be found in the foreseeable future. To argue that terrorism cannot be studied without such a definition is manifestly absurd." We should acknowledge that there are many other definitions, including national and regional ones, but currently there is no universal definition supported by the General Assembly of the United Nations. The one recommended by the Security Council in Res. 1566 (2004) is not legally binding, which weakens legal authority in international law.[7]

Finding a comprehensive definition of terrorism is also challenging because the concept has evolved tremendously since its original designation at the end of the eighteenth century. It can be associated with actions that are not accepted as terrorism by other entities. At the same time, other "terrorist" actions—that have been so labeled by the U.S. government—have been approved as such by other governments or institutions (both past and present). Consider the case of British Malaya. In the 1950s, the most important counter-insurgency manual in British Malaya (from the British Commonwealth) was called "Conduct of Anti-Terrorist Operations in Malaya," suggesting that the two types of offense were similar. In fact, at that time, insurgency and terrorism had to be legally regarded in the same way. The term "terrorism" was only used separately when imbued with politics and propaganda.[8]

Terrorism as a political act

Terrorism has already been defined as "politically motivated violence against non-combatants with the intention to coerce through fear."[9] As Oberschall (2004) contends,[10] "terrorism is an extreme, violent response to a failed political process engaging political régimes and ethnic and ideological adversaries over fundamental governance issues." The political goals of terrorism can be wide-ranging (such as attempting to maintain or remove the existing order) or limited in scope (such as fighting a military "invasion" or a particular law). The word "political" in this context is so broad that it encompasses myriad paradigms such as ideology and religion (among others). Most terrorist groups' political goals are considered dissident and ideological, unlike ordinary criminals, who seek profit or other material interests. In another, equally interesting alternative take of terrorism as a political act, it is generally believed that the "political" character is inherent to terrorism because it involves violence as a tactic to put pressure on governments, regardless of the presence of a political, religious, or ideological agenda to be followed on a large scale.[11]

In his study titled *The Psychology of Terrorism*, John Horgan (2005)[12] corroborates the idea that one trait making terrorism stand out from other types of crime is the political dimension to it. An example is terrorism's distinction between the immediate victim of the attack (e.g., a noncombatant killed in a blast) and the terrorist's ultimate enemy (e.g., the state). Violent deeds like burglary, murder, and kidnapping are performed in the furtherance of personal or criminal objectives. Therefore, they should not be included. This standard stresses that the social and psychological precursors to personal or criminal offenses differ from those of terrorist violence.[13]

Black (1983)[14] interprets terrorism as a particular category of social control aimed at the neutralization of "deviants" (e.g., like Sayyid Qutb's *jahiliyyah*). It threatens the control imposed by the highest state officials—such as monarchs, policymakers, dignitaries, and despots. Walter's (1969)[15] statement about terrorism frames it elegantly: "The proximate aim is to instill terror; the ultimate end is control." Terrorists, then, pursue goals that they see as achievable only through violence. If political mandates are not fulfilled by the enemy, terrorism will operate as a coercive political mechanism to issue a warning of worse actions to come.[16] Terrorism is intense pressure; it is the intentional use or threat of use of immense brutality through intimidation of a large audience. As we have seen, fundamental elements include the political, religious, or ideological purposes and the construction of a climate of fear from which coercion is placed on the powers-that-be to gratify the terrorists' demands.[17]

Terrorism as a threatening act

This section is a direct result of the previous one. The logic of terrorism is grounded in the unpredictability of attacks, which makes terrorism a threatening act because it can happen anywhere and at any time, striking sensitive targets indiscriminately and causing widespread fear. Terrorism is designed to shock the world, making it feel helpless. The objective is to get the average earthling to question the foundations of society and the government's ability to ensure the safety of its people. For terrorists, the bigger the impact of the operation, the more significant the effects. The effects have to be disastrous and reach unprecedented media coverage. The latter is a good measurement of the terrorists' success because it allows them to (1) make their political goals known to the rest of the world and (2) establish the forte of their organizations. At times with coordinated attacks, at other times with simple, low-cost operations, terrorists can hit a much bigger enemy and leave permanent scars by humiliating them. A successful operation can also open opportunities for recruitment of people who are either disaffected or willing to leave everything behind.[18]

As one can see, terrorism is designed to produce an enormously fearful state of mind. This fearful state is not only aimed at the direct victims; it is also targeted at audiences that may, in fact, have no connections to the victims at all.[19] Oots (1990)[20] similarly underlined that terrorism is meant to "create extreme fear and/or anxiety-inducing effects in a target audience larger than the immediate victims." Likewise, the definition of terrorism in the U.S. Army's textbook on military medicine mirrors the idea that terrorism is characterized, in part, by its construction of fear within the hearts and minds of audiences beyond the immediate victims.[21] The Council of the European Union's (2002)[22] definition of terrorism is another useful statement to behold:

> Intentional acts that are committed with the aim of seriously intimidating a population, or unduly compelling a Government or international organization to perform or abstain from performing any act, or seriously destabilizing or destroying the fundamental political, constitutional, economic or social structures of a country or an international organization.

On a similar note, the physical violence inherent in terrorism, or threat thereof, typically includes (1) single-stage actions of deadly violence (as we see in bombings and massive shootings), (2) dual-staged life-threatening attacks (as we see in kidnapping, hijacking, and hostage-taking incidents; i.e., for coercive bargaining), or (3) multi-staged sequences of violence (as we see in forced disappearance, like kidnapping, secret detention, torture, and homicide).[23]

Terrorism as a communicative act

Of equal relevance is the fact that terrorism is a communicative act. Indeed, it is through their utmost violence that terrorists like to communicate. Terrorist violence is largely communicative because it seeks to transmit a message and produce a long-lasting psychological effect. Although strategic violence in military engagements can also involve symbolic or communicative elements, terrorist violence breathes through its communicative components; its chief goal is to send the message that the capabilities of the target ought to be destroyed completely.[24] For example, on September 11, 2001, the 19 Islamist militants were able to promote their agenda thanks to "free publicity." The second aircraft that plunged into the South Tower was witnessed live by about two billion people—which represented almost a third of the world's population at that time.[25] This anecdote reveals how the objectives of a terrorist movement can be easily communicated and framed to the general public through the mass media.[26] Until 9/11, Al-Qaeda was only known to people with vested interest in national security (such as reporters or counterterrorism experts). After that day of infamy, the jihadist network became a household name. Terrorism is inherently linked to communication; each attack produces some type of interaction with the public. It is generally an audience beyond the immediate victims; the main targets of influence are those witnessing the attack and the state. Ultimately, the goal is to get the audience to change their behavior.[27]

Who are the terrorists?

A great many people engage in terrorism. In the eyes of most governments and institutions, individuals become terrorists simply by participating in terrorist activities. The interesting aspect of the issue is that they do not have to be trained to become terrorists. The terrorist may come from a physical and/or psychological terrorist milieu—as is the case in some madrassas in Bangladesh (see Chapter 2)—or he or she may become a terrorist through a context outside terrorist life—in which case, he or she has now "crossed the boundary" of illegal behavior.[28] The following two categories of terrorists (below) are in no way representative of all terrorists today. However, many jihadists would fall under either category.

Nonstate actors

We now know that much—if not all—terrorist violence is inherently political. It is also important to mention that terrorism is characterized by its nonstate nature, even when terrorists acquire military, political, and other sources of support from the state. However, in some cases, entire governments have engaged in terrorism (like the "state terrorism" of the Argentinian administration from 1976 to 1983).[29] States do employ force for political purposes, but when it is used internationally, it should be called an act of war. When it is done domestically, it can be law enforcement, civil war, tyranny, or state terror.[30] The point made in this section is that terrorism is structural violence against randomly chosen targets by nonstate, covert actors. This implies that terrorism is to be differentiated from small-scale types of violence such as inter-clan feuds and from group-based violence such as riots, lynchings, and vigilantism.[31]

Why is covertness so representative of nonstate actors? As nonstate terrorists fall back on extreme violence, they are aware of becoming the subject of surveillance by the police or the military. Various forms of secrecy or camouflage operate as counter-surveillance or counter-control and, thereby, the best hope for the success of terrorist missions. Virtually all international terrorist groups manifest those tactics. State terrorist actors are not concerned about surveillance by the police or the military (as was the case with the leaders of the Nazi régime). Some of them are not even concerned about hiding their personal identity.[32]

Insurgent groups

Many jihadist groups are, or start as, insurgent groups. An insurgent group is a group that rebels against authority through violence. The insurgent group's use of violence is considered terrorism in some cases.[33] However, in all cases, the authorities do not recognize the group as lawful combatants. When insurgent groups use terrorism, they do it because (1) they feel overpowered by the enemy's military force, (2) they find that terrorism is a useful method to air their grievances to those authorities (or even to the rest of the world), or (3) they employ terrorism in order to escalate tensions with the enemy régime (and/or their foreign supporters).[34] Today, terrorism is a tactic used by all jihadist insurgent groups. Conversely, insurgent objectives are behind all jihadists' endeavors, as they spire to upset the status quo through intense violence.[35] For a scholar like Boaz Ganor (2002),[36] an insurgent group is no longer an assembly of "freedom fighters" by the simple virtue of fighting for national liberation or other noble goals. Rather, they are a terrorist organization. Even if its ultimate mission is morally justifiable, an organization that intentionally strikes civilians is now a terrorist organization. There is no value or exculpation in fighting for the rights of a larger group if the existence or wellbeing of others is destroyed in the process. By engaging in terrorism, the perpetrators become the enemies of all humankind.

The targets of terrorism

Terrorist violence is mostly aimed at civilians. Civilians are not members of the military services and/or not actively involved in military combat. This standard identifies terrorism as violence against noncombatants or groups that are not expected to fight against extreme violence. It also includes military targets attacked during a ceasefire. For example, on June 25, 1996, a truck bomb was detonated by jihadists at the Khobar Towers—a U.S. Air Force housing complex—in Dhahran, Saudi Arabia.[37] After the four treaties of the Geneva Conventions were signed in 1949, the world as a community unambiguously condemned violence against civilians.[38] Yet, terrorism continues to target noncombatants and innocent bystanders. Nevertheless, although precision-guided missiles sometimes deviate from their expected trajectory and cause collateral damage (i.e., by inadvertently killing innocent people), it is considered a tragic use of force, not terrorism.[39]

Direct vs. indirect victims

The direct victims of terrorist attacks have rarely been armed forces. Instead, they have been civilians, noncombatants, or other defenseless victims who have no direct connections with the conflict that inflamed the passions of terrorist actors. The direct victims are not the only sought target—unlike the conventional assassination where the intended target *is* the direct victim of the crime. In terrorism, the direct victims serve as message generators, whereby the recipient of the message is the state and/or the entire of the world.[40] In the case of jihadist groups, the entire world remains the enemy until it submits to Islam and the Caliphate. Terrorism and communication go hand in hand, which renders terrorist attacks as acts assisted by the mass media, whereby various audiences and enemy entities can be reached. At the same time, people who sympathize with the terrorist group can identify with the terrorists' professed cause. Terrorists also hope to engender a reaction from the indirect target: the governments, publics, or other enemies—a reaction such as fear, disgust, or overreaction.[41] To conclude this thought, although the direct victims of terrorist violence are not the main target, they remain instrumental to the terrorists' primary objective of frightening the authorities or even the entire world.

Symbolic targets

A bulk of the literature on the role of communication in terrorism has looked at what Gabriel Weimann (2006)[42] calls the "theater of terror." Terrorists want to intimidate audiences. Victims are selected not because they represent the enemy *per se* but because of their symbolic importance. Let us look at the attacks on the World Trade Center: the attacks on the Twin Towers killed nearly 3,000 people, but the ultimate target was a symbolic target: "Some of the primary symbols of America's strength, power, and world status. The World Trade Center stood as the symbol of our financial wealth and enterprise."[43] Audiences of terrorism become intimidated by the communicative power of symbolic violence because they know it is intentional harm. Unlike criminal gangs that routinely employ violence only against parties that directly obstruct their activities, terrorists want to cause fear and terror among the civil masses and the authorities at large. All terrorists need to do is strike single targets that have symbolic value or places frequented by large gatherings of people.

Alex Schmid (2005)[44] included a Chinese proverb in of his works: "Kill one— frighten ten thousands." To accomplish their goals, terrorists have no choice but reach broad audiences. As covert operators, they continue to depend on both traditional and online media to publicize their message. This can come as a catch to many readers, but it drives terrorists' behavior. Their *modus operandi* is to pull off extravagantly violent episodes against symbolic targets, thereby inducing the media to disseminate the message. By flying an aircraft into the Pentagon on 9/11, Al-Qaeda exposed the vulnerability of the U.S. government to the mujahedin world. Likewise, in the beheading videos released by ISIS in August and September 2014, the orange jumpsuits worn by two U.S. journalists were a symbolic reference to the jumpsuits worn by the prisoners in Guantánamo Bay. The recorded executions were acts of revenge against the U.S. government.[45]

Lone-wolf terrorism

The phrase "lone wolf" became popular in the late 1990s when white supremacists Tom Metzger and Alex Curtis inspired racial terrorists to act alone for preemptive security reasons. Other concepts that describe similar or comparable forms of terrorist methods include "leaderless resistance," "individual terrorism," and "freelance terrorism."[46] Lone-wolf terrorism is on the rise across the globe. This tactic is mostly used by right-wing extremists and jihadists and has experienced a conspicuous spike with the advent of the internet.[47] From Nidal Malik Hasan in 2009, who killed 13 of his fellow Americans at the Fort Hood military base in Texas,

Anders Behring Breivik in 2011, who killed a large number of youths in a mass shooting in Norway,[48] to Brenton Tarrant in 2019, who murdered 50 Muslim worshippers in Christchurch, New Zealand,[49] lone-wolf terrorism has left a long and gory trail.

General description

Lone wolves are terrorists who act individually, are not members of a terrorist group, and have been more difficult to identify by authorities. Indeed, unlike conventional terrorist groups or network-based terrorists, lone wolves have the clear advantage of eluding detection before and after their attacks because many of them do not impart their plans publicly. When terrorists work through a cell made up of more than one individual, law enforcement's probability of foiling a terrorist mission increases substantially as "more people" means "more chances of being caught."[50] The growing menace of the self-radicalized lone-wolf terrorist is something to behold. The internet age presents a dilemma in the contemporary security environment. Because a lone wolf is a one-person army, like leaderless resistance. No other human or mentor is needed; rather, the internet becomes his or her companion. The internet, then, constitutes a lethal vehicle for terrorist activities, in addition to other modern information outlets (e.g., smart phones, video games, etc.).[51]

Lone-wolf terrorism has been used as a method by radical actors from a number of ideological backgrounds and by people with mental health problems.[52] Today, this form of terrorism is increasingly popular within religiously radicalized jihadists. For Becker (2014),[53] lone-wolf terrorists symbolize the image of "weak opportunists" whose target choice is mostly driven by ideology. Hampered by their relative weakness, lone-wolf terrorists tend to operate in areas with which they are familiar—thanks to the "nodes, paths and edges" of their physical environment and available spaces. They have more frequently attacked noncombatant targets than government or military ones, and are not too obsessed to attract public support (unlike actors from terrorist groups). However, interpreting the motives of lone wolves can be challenging because of their lack of contact with terrorist networks or even the world at large—or because of possible mental disorders and their predisposition to articulate their own ideologies.[54]

An important point is that the lone-wolf metaphor may educe images of ideologically and socially unaffiliated people (sometimes called "lone nuts"),[55] but it can deflect our attention away from other issues, such as their political narratives[56] or even their radicalization by a remote preacher through internet podcasts. If two or three individuals perpetrate a terrorist attack, then it is no longer a lone-wolf operation because there were multiple perpetrators who were affiliated with one another and who executed the same mission. On the other hand, such an approach can theoretically inflate the incidence of lone-wolf attacks. The amalgamation of lone wolves with terrorist cells or lone-wolf units—because they, too, do not have a hierarchical organizational structure—can obfuscate definitions and concepts pertaining to that subject.[57]

Violent true believer (VTB)

In many cases, before becoming a lone-wolf terrorist, an individual becomes a violent true believer (VTB). A VTB is dedicated to an ideology or doctrine that advocates massacre or suicide terrorism as an ideal method of advancing his or her cause. VTBs have very specific targets and are passionately married to their beliefs; they pay no attention to alternative views. VTBs appreciate like-minded others and those who believe in the same terrorist approach. Evidently, they are found among many lone wolves.[58] Examples of infamous VTBs are Timothy McVeigh, Major Nidal Hasan, and Anders Behring Breivik. For French scholar Jean Baudrillard (1983),[59] VTBs want their belief systems or political platforms to be exposed to the world. Because they embrace their ideology with such steadfastness, they will strike meticulously selected symbolic targets. Depending on the type of damage, VTBs can quickly progress from a stage of nothingness to a stage of worldwide "fame"— the best award they can possibly be granted. From this standpoint, terrorism becomes a sacred activity allowing any resolute individual to achieve his or her 15 minutes of fame.[60]

The violence committed by the VTB is intended to hurt civilians who are the representative culprits and sinners of the larger entity that actually deserves punishment and disdain.[61] As more people access the internet and, ergo, are exposed to extremist ideological content, the number of VTBs or VTB-related beliefs is likely to rise. The big concern is that individuals' attitudes, values, and beliefs can be easily co-opted with existing radical ideologies, often leading to new, unexpected forms of self-radicalization and terrorist violence—sometimes that are completely contrary to the individual's previous life.[62]

Notes

1 Erin Miller, *Global Terrorism in 2017* (College Park, MD: National Consortium for the Study of Terrorism and Responses to Terrorism, 2018). Retrieved on May 3, 2019 from www.start.umd.edu/pubs/START_GTD_Overview2017_July2018.pdf

2 Donald Greer, *The Incidence of the Terror during the French Revolution. A Statistical Interpretation* (Cambridge, MA: Harvard University Press, 1935).

3 Walter Laqueur, *The Age of Terrorism* (Boston, MA: Little, Brown, & Company, 1987): 72.

4 Jack P. Gibbs, "Conceptualization of Terrorism," *American Sociological Review* 54, no. 3 (1989): 329–40. https://doi.org/10.2307/2095609.

5 Ibid, 330–4.

6 Walter Laqueur, *Terrorism* (London: Weidenfeld and Nicolson, 1977): 5.

7 Cited in Alex P. Schmid, "The Revised Academic Consensus Definition of Terrorism," *Perspectives on Terrorism* 6, no. 2 (2012): 158–9.

8 David J. Kilcullen, "Countering Global Insurgency," *Journal of Strategic Studies* 28, no. 4 (2005): 597–617. https://doi.org/10.1080/01402390500300956

9 Thomas A. Marks, "Ideology of Insurgency: New Ethnic Focus or Old Cold War Distortions?" *Small Wars and Insurgencies* 15, no. 1 (2004): 107–28, 107. https://doi.org/10.1080/09592310410001677014

10 Anthony Oberschall, "Explaining Terrorism: The Contribution of Collective Action Theory," *Sociological Theory* 22, no. 1 (2004): 26–37, 26. https://doi.org/10.1111/j.1467-9558.2004.00202.x

11 Richard Jackson, "In Defence of 'Terrorism:' Finding a Way through a Forest of Misconceptions," Behavioral Sciences of Terrorism and Political Aggression 3, no. 2 (2011): 116–30. https://doi.org/10.1080/19434472.2010.512148

12 John Horgan, *The Psychology of Terrorism* (New York: Routledge, 2005).

13 Charles L. Ruby, "The Definition of Terrorism," *Analyses of Social Issues and Public Policy* 2, no. 1 (2002): 9–14. https://doi.org/10.1111/j.1530-2415.2002.00021.x

14 Donald Black, "Crime as Social Control," *American Sociological Review* 48, no. 1 (1983): 34–45. https://doi.org/10.2307/2095143

15 Eugene V. Walter, *Terror and Resistance* (Oxford: Oxford University Press, 1969): 13.

16 Ken Booth and Tim Dunne, *Worlds in Collision: Terror and the Future of Global Order* (New York: Palgrave Macmillan, 2002).

17 Walter Enders and Todd Sandler, "Is Transnational Terrorism Becoming More Threatening? A Time-Series Investigation," *Journal of Conflict Resolution* 44, no. 3 (2000): 307–32.

18 Roland Heickerö, "Cyber Terrorism: Electronic Jihad," *Strategic Analysis* 38, no. 4 (2014): 554–65. https://doi.org/10.1080/09700161.2014.918435

19 Abraham Kaplan, "The Psychodynamics of Terrorism," in *Behavioral and Quantitative Perspectives on Terrorism*, ed. Yonah Alexander and John M. Gleason (New York: Pergamon, 1981): 35–50.

20 Ken L. Oots, "Bargaining with Terrorists: Organizational Considerations," *Terrorism* 13, no. 2 (1990): 145–58, 145. https://doi.org/10.1080/10576109008435821

21 Franklin D. Jones and Yen Hoi Fong, "Military Psychiatry and Terrorism," in *Textbook of Military Medicine*, ed. Franklin D. Jones, Linette R. Sparacino, Victoria L. Wilcox, and Joseph M. Rothberg (Washington, D.C.: Department of the Army, 1994): 264–9.

22 Council of the European Union, *Council Framework Decision of 13 June 2002 on Combating Terrorism* (Brussels: Council of the European Union, 2002): 3.

23 Alex P. Schmid, *Handbook of Terrorism Research* (London, Routledge, 2011).

24 Petter Nesser, "Jihadism in Western Europe after the Invasion of Iraq: Tracing Motivational Influences from the Iraq War on Jihadist Terrorism in Western Europe," *Studies in Conflict & Terrorism* 29, no. 4 (2006): 323–42. https://doi.org/10.1080/10576100600641899

25 Alice M. Greenwald, "'Passion on All Sides': Lessons for Planning the National September 11 Memorial Museum," *Curator: The Museum Journal* 53, no. 1 (2010): 117–25. https://doi.org/10.1111/j.2151-6952.2009.00012.x

26 Pippa Norris, Montague Kern, and Marion R. Just, *Framing Terrorism: The News Media, the Government, and the Public* (New York: Routledge, 2003).

27 Jonathan Matusitz, "Terrorism as Spectacle: It's All for the Audience," *Explorations in Media Ecology* 14, no. 1 (2015): 161–73. https://doi.org/10.1386/eme.14.1-2.161_1; Jonathan Matusitz, "Brand Management in Terrorism: The Case of Hezbollah," *Journal of Policing, Intelligence and Counter Terrorism* 13, no. 1 (2018): 1–16. https://doi.org/10.1080/18335330.2017.1412489

28 Max Taylor and John Horgan, "A Conceptual Framework for Addressing Psychological Process in the Development of the Terrorist," *Terrorism and Political Violence* 18, no. 4 (2006), 585–601. https://doi.org/10.1080/09546550600897413

29 Ruth Blakeley, *State Terrorism and Neoliberalism: The North in the South* (New York: Routledge, 2009).

30 Audrey Kurth Cronin, "Behind the Curve: Globalization and International Terrorism," *International Security* 27, no. 3 (2003): 30–58. https://doi.org/10.1162/01622880260553624

31 Donald Black, "The Geometry of Terrorism," *Sociological Theory* 22, no. 1 (2004): 14–25. https://doi.org/10.1111/j.1467-9558.2004.00201.x

32 Gibbs, "Conceptualization of Terrorism," 338.

33 Peter Paret, *French Revolutionary Warfare from Indochina to Algeria: The Analysis of a Political and Military Doctrine* (London: Pall Mall Press, 1964).

34 Nesser, "Jihadism in Western Europe after the Invasion of Iraq," 324.

35 Kilcullen, "Countering Global Insurgency," 603.

36 Boaz Ganor, "Defining Terrorism: Is One Man's Terrorist Another Man's Freedom Fighter?" *Police Practice and Research* 3, no. 4 (2002): 287–304. https://doi.org/10.1080/1561426022000032060

37 Ruby, "The Definition of Terrorism," 10.

38 Marcello Di Filippo, "Terrorist Crimes and International Co-operation: Critical Remarks on the Definition and Inclusion of Terrorism in the Category of International Crimes," *European Journal of International Law* 19, no. 3 (2008): 533–70. https://doi.org/10.1093/ejil/chn027

39 Cronin, "Behind the Curve," 33.

40 Cronin, "Behind the Curve," 32.

41 Ibid, 32.

42 Gabriel Weimann, *Terror on the Internet: The New Arena, the New Challenges* (Washington, D.C: United States Institute for Peace Press, 2006): 38.

43 Robert Denton, *Language, Symbols, and the Media: Communication in the Aftermath of the World Trade Center Attack* (Piscataway, NJ: Transaction Publishers, 2006): 7.

44 Alex P. Schmid, "Terrorism as Psychological Warfare," *Democracy and Security* 1, no. 2 (2005): 137–46, 138. https://doi.org/10.1080/17419160500322467

45 Jytte Klausen, "Tweeting the Jihad: Social Media Networks of Western Foreign Fighters in Syria and Iraq," *Studies in Conflict & Terrorism* 38, no. 1 (2015): 1–22. https://doi.org/10.1080/1057610X.2014.974948

46 Edwin Bakker and Beatrice de Graaf, "Preventing Lone Wolf Terrorism: Some CT Approaches Addressed," *Perspectives on Terrorism* 5, no. 5 (2011): 43–50.

47 Matthew Feldman, "Comparative Lone Wolf Terrorism: Toward a Heuristic Definition," *Democracy and Security* 9, no. 3 (2013): 270–86. https://doi.org/10.1080/17419166.2013.792252

48 Jeffrey D. Simon, "Lone Wolf Terrorism: Understanding a Growing Threat," in *Lone Actors—An Emerging Security Threat*, ed. Aaron Richman and Yair Sharan (Amsterdam: IOS Press, 2015): 3–10.

49 Joey Garrison, "'Violent Terrorist': Who Is the White Supremacist Suspected in New Zealand Mosque Shootings?" *USA Today* (2019, March 15): A1.

50 Bakker and de Graaf, "Preventing Lone Wolf Terrorism," 46.

51 Rodger A. Bates, "Dancing with Wolves: Today's Lone Wolf Terrorists," *The Journal of Public and Professional Sociology* 4, no. 1 (2012): 10–21.

52 Ramón Spaaij, "The Enigma of Lone Wolf Terrorism," *Studies in Conflict and Terrorism* 33, no. 9 (2010): 854–70. https://doi.org/10.1080/1057610X.2010.501426

53 Michael Becker, "Explaining Lone Wolf Target Selection in the United States," *Studies in Conflict and Terrorism* 37, no. 11 (2014): 959–78, 971. https://doi.org/10.1080/1057610X.2014.952261

54 Mark Juergensmeyer, *Terror in the Mind of God: The Global Rise in Religious Violence* (Berkeley, CA: University of California Press, 2000).

55 Feldman, "Comparative Lone Wolf Terrorism," 281.

56 Lars Erik Berntzen and Sveinung Sandberg, "The Collective Nature of Lone Wolf Terrorism: Anders Behring Breivik and the Anti-Islamic Social Movement," *Terrorism and Political Violence* 26, no. 5 (2014): 759–79. https://doi.org/10.1080/09546553.2013.767245

57 Ramón Spaaij and Mark S. Hamm, "Key Issues and Research Agendas in Lone Wolf Terrorism," *Studies in Conflict & Terrorism* 38, no. 3 (2015): 167–78. https://doi.org/10.1080/1057610X.2014.986979

58 Reid Meloy, Kris Mohandie, Anthony Hempel, and Andrew Shiva, "The Violent True Believer: Homicidal and Suicidal States of Mind (HASSOM)," *Journal of Threat Assessment* 1, no. 4 (2001): 1–14. https://doi.org/10.1300/J177v01n04_01

59 Jean Baudrillard, *Simulations* (New York: Semiotext, 1983).

60 Jonathan Matusitz, *Symbolism in Terrorism: Motivation, Communication, and Behavior* (Lanham, MD: Rowman & Littlefield, 2015).

61 Ernest Becker, *Escape from Evil* (New York: Free Press, 1975).
62 Jeremy G. Carter and David L. Carter, "Law Enforcement Intelligence: Implications for Self-Radicalized Terrorism," *Police Practice and Research* 13, no. 2 (2012): 138–54. https://doi.org/10.1080/15614263.2011.596685

References

Bakker, Edwin, and Beatrice de Graaf, "Preventing Lone Wolf Terrorism: Some CT Approaches Addressed," *Perspectives on Terrorism* 5, no. 5 (2011): 43–50.

Bates, Rodger A., "Dancing with Wolves: Today's Lone Wolf Terrorists," *The Journal of Public and Professional Sociology* 4, no. 1 (2012): 10–21.

Baudrillard, Jean, *Simulations*. New York: Semiotext, 1983.

Becker, Ernest, *Escape from Evil*. New York: Free Press, 1975.

Becker, Michael, "Explaining Lone Wolf Target Selection in the United States," *Studies in Conflict and Terrorism* 37, no. 11 (2014): 959–978. https://doi.org/10.1080/1057610X. 2014.952261.

Berntzen, Lars Erik, and Sveinung Sandberg, "The Collective Nature of Lone Wolf Terrorism: Anders Behring Breivik and the Anti-Islamic Social Movement," *Terrorism and Political Violence* 26, no. 5 (2014): 759–779. https://doi.org/10.1080/09546553.2013.767245.

Black, Donald, "Crime as Social Control," *American Sociological Review* 48, no. 1 (1983): 34–45. https://doi.org/10.2307/2095143.

Black, Donald, "The Geometry of Terrorism," *Sociological Theory* 22, no. 1 (2004): 14–25. https://doi.org/10.1111/j.1467-9558.2004.00201.x.

Blakeley, Ruth, *State Terrorism and Neoliberalism: The North in the South*. New York: Routledge, 2009.

Booth, Ken, and Tim Dunne, *Worlds in Collision: Terror and the Future of Global Order*. New York: Palgrave Macmillan, 2002.

Carter, Jeremy G., and David L. Carter, "Law Enforcement Intelligence: Implications for Self-Radicalized Terrorism," *Police Practice and Research* 13, no. 2 (2012): 138–154. https://doi.org/10.1080/15614263.2011.596685.

Council of the European Union, *Council Framework Decision of 13 June 2002 on Combating Terrorism*. Brussels: Council of the European Union, 2002.

Cronin, Audrey Kurth, "Behind the Curve: Globalization and International Terrorism," *International Security* 27, no. 3 (2003): 30–58. https://doi.org/10.1162/01622880260553624.

Denton, Robert, *Language, Symbols, and the Media: Communication in the Aftermath of the World Trade Center Attack*. Piscataway, NJ: Transaction Publishers, 2006.

Di Filippo, Marcello, "Terrorist Crimes and International Co-operation: Critical Remarks on the Definition and Inclusion of Terrorism in the Category of International Crimes," *European Journal of International Law* 19, no. 3 (2008): 533–570. https://doi.org/10.1093/ejil/chn027.

Enders, Walter, and Todd Sandler, "Is Transnational Terrorism Becoming More Threatening? A Time-Series Investigation," *Journal of Conflict Resolution* 44, no. 3 (2000): 307–332.

Feldman, Matthew, "Comparative Lone Wolf Terrorism: Toward a Heuristic Definition," *Democracy and Security* 9, no. 3 (2013): 270–286. https://doi.org/10.1080/17419166. 2013.792252.

Ganor, Boaz, "Defining Terrorism: Is One Man's Terrorist Another Man's Freedom Fighter?" *Police Practice and Research* 3, no. 4 (2002): 287–304. https://doi.org/10.1080/1561426022000032060.

Garrison, Joey, "'Violent Terrorist': Who Is the White Supremacist Suspected in New Zealand Mosque Shootings?" *USA Today* (2019, March 15): A1.

Gibbs, Jack P., "Conceptualization of Terrorism," *American Sociological Review* 54, no. 3 (1989): 329–340. https://doi.org/10.2307/2095609.

Greenwald, Alice M., "'Passion on All Sides': Lessons for Planning the National September 11 Memorial Museum," *Curator: The Museum Journal* 53, no. 1 (2010): 117–125. https://doi.org/10.1111/j.2151-6952.2009.00012.x.

Greer, Donald, *The Incidence of the Terror during the French Revolution. A Statistical Interpretation.* Cambridge, MA: Harvard University Press, 1935.

Heickerö, Roland, "Cyber Terrorism: Electronic Jihad," *Strategic Analysis* 38, no. 4 (2014): 554–565. https://doi.org/10.1080/09700161.2014.918435.

Horgan, John, *The Psychology of Terrorism*. New York: Routledge, 2005.

Jackson, Richard, "'In Defence of 'Terrorism:' Finding a Way through a Forest of Misconceptions," *Behavioral Sciences of Terrorism and Political Aggression* 3, no. 2 (2011): 116–130. https://doi.org/10.1080/19434472.2010.512148.

Jones, Franklin D., and Yen Hoi Fong, "Military Psychiatry and Terrorism," in *Textbook of Military Medicine*, edited by Franklin D. Jones, Linette R. Sparacino, Victoria L. Wilcox, and Joseph M.Rothberg, 264–269. Washington, D.C.: Department of the Army, 1994.

Juergensmeyer, Mark, *Terror in the Mind of God: The Global Rise in Religious Violence*. Berkeley, CA: University of California Press, 2000.

Kaplan, Abraham, "The Psychodynamics of Terrorism," in *Behavioral and Quantitative Perspectives on Terrorism*, edited by Yonah Alexander and John M. Gleason, 35–50. New York: Pergamon, 1981.

Kilcullen, David J., "Countering Global Insurgency," *Journal of Strategic Studies* 28, no. 4 (2005): 597–617. https://doi.org/10.1080/01402390500300956.

Klausen, Jytte, "Tweeting the Jihad: Social Media Networks of Western Foreign Fighters in Syria and Iraq," *Studies in Conflict & Terrorism* 38, no. 1 (2015): 1–22. https://doi.org/10.1080/1057610X.2014.974948.

Laqueur, Walter, *The Age of Terrorism*. Boston, MA: Little, Brown, & Company, 1987.

Laqueur, Walter, *Terrorism*. London: Weidenfeld and Nicolson, 1977.

Marks, Thomas A., "Ideology of Insurgency: New Ethnic Focus or Old Cold War Distortions?" *Small Wars and Insurgencies* 15, no. 1 (2004): 107–128. https://doi.org/10.1080/09592310410001677014.

Matusitz, Jonathan, *Symbolism in Terrorism: Motivation, Communication, and Behavior*. Lanham, MD: Rowman & Littlefield, 2015.

Matusitz, Jonathan, "Terrorism as Spectacle: It's All for the Audience," *Explorations in Media Ecology* 14, no. 1 (2015): 161–173. https://doi.org/10.1386/eme.14.1-2.161_1.

Matusitz, Jonathan, "Brand Management in Terrorism: The Case of Hezbollah," *Journal of Policing, Intelligence and Counter Terrorism* 13, no. 1 (2018): 1–16. https://doi.org/10.1080/18335330.2017.1412489.

Meloy, Reid, Kris Mohandie, Anthony Hempel, and Andrew Shiva, "The Violent True Believer: Homicidal and Suicidal States of Mind (HASSOM)," *Journal of Threat Assessment* 1, no. 4 (2001): 1–14. https://doi.org/10.1300/J177v01n04_01.

Miller, Erin, *Global Terrorism in 2017*. College Park, MD: National Consortium for the Study of Terrorism and Responses to Terrorism, 2018. Retrieved on May 3, 2019 from www.start.umd.edu/pubs/START_GTD_Overview2017_July2018.pdf.

Nesser, Petter, "Jihadism in Western Europe after the Invasion of Iraq: Tracing Motivational Influences from the Iraq War on Jihadist Terrorism in Western Europe," *Studies in Conflict & Terrorism* 29, no. 4 (2006): 323–342. https://doi.org/10.1080/10576100600641899.

Norris, Pippa, Montague Kern, and Marion R. Just, *Framing Terrorism: The News Media, the Government, and the Public*. New York: Routledge, 2003.

Oberschall, Anthony, "Explaining Terrorism: The Contribution of Collective Action Theory," *Sociological Theory* 22, no. 1 (2004): 26–37. https://doi.org/10.1111/j.1467-9558.2004.00202.x.

Oots, Ken L., "Bargaining with Terrorists: Organizational Considerations," *Terrorism* 13, no. 2 (1990): 145–158. https://doi.org/10.1080/10576109008435821.

Paret, Peter, *French Revolutionary Warfare from Indochina to Algeria: The Analysis of a Political and Military Doctrine*. London: Pall Mall Press, 1964.

Ruby, Charles L., "The Definition of Terrorism," *Analyses of Social Issues and Public Policy* 2, no. 1 (2002): 9–14. https://doi.org/10.1111/j.1530-2415.2002.00021.x.

Schmid, Alex P., "Terrorism as Psychological Warfare," *Democracy and Security* 1, no. 2 (2005): 137–146. https://doi.org/10.1080/17419160500322467.

Schmid, Alex P., *Handbook of Terrorism Research*. London: Routledge, 2011.

Schmid, Alex P., "The Revised Academic Consensus Definition of Terrorism," *Perspectives on Terrorism* 6, no. 2 (2012): 158–159.

Simon, Jeffrey D., "Lone Wolf Terrorism: Understanding a Growing Threat," in *Lone Actors—An Emerging Security Threat*, edited by Aaron Richman and Yair Sharan, 3–10. Amsterdam: IOS Press, 2015.

Spaaij, Ramón, "The Enigma of Lone Wolf Terrorism," *Studies in Conflict and Terrorism* 33, no. 9 (2010): 854–870. https://doi.org/10.1080/1057610X.2010.501426.

Spaaij, Ramón, and Mark S. Hamm, "Key Issues and Research Agendas in Lone Wolf Terrorism," *Studies in Conflict & Terrorism* 38, no. 3 (2015): 167–178. https://doi.org/10.1080/1057610X.2014.986979.

Taylor, Max, and John Horgan, "A Conceptual Framework for Addressing Psychological Process in the Development of the Terrorist," *Terrorism and Political Violence* 18, no. 4 (2006), 588–592. https://doi.org/10.1080/09546550600897413.

Walter, Eugene V., *Terror and Resistance*. Oxford: Oxford University Press, 1969.

Weimann, Gabriel, *Terror on the Internet: The New Arena, the New Challenges*. Washington, D. C.: United States Institute for Peace Press, 2006.

3

DEFINING JIHAD

Before describing jihad in detail, it would be useful to start a conversation on Islam from a number of different perspectives. The youngest of the three major Abrahamic religions, Islam is now the fastest growing religion in the world. With 1.8 billion adherents, or close to a quarter of the global population,[1] Muslims represent the majority of the population in 49 nations. The Asia-Pacific region has approximately 1.2 billion Muslims, or 33% of all Muslim adherents.[2] In Africa, they make up half of the whole population of the continent, representing a majority in 30 nations (out of 56).[3] In fact, in Africa, Muslims have experienced the highest growth in comparison with all other religious groups, including Christians. The number of Muslims born between 2010 and 2015 was 213 million, in contrast to 61 million deaths (a difference of 152 million).[4]

Muslims remain the biggest religious minority group in most Western European countries. The current number of Muslims in Western Europe could be hovering around 25 million. Muslims are generally younger and have more children than non-Muslim Europeans. In 2016, Muslims in Europe were 30.4 years old on average, which is 13 years younger than non-Muslims over there (43.8). On top of everything else, 50% of all European Muslims have not reached the age of 30 yet, unlike one third of non-Muslims in Europe. The fertility rate for the Muslim European woman is 2.6 children in her lifetime, one full point more than her non-Muslim counterpart (1.6 children).[5] For the majority of Muslims, culture may play a more important role than the religion of Islam or sharia-compliant laws. This means that no fixed Muslim identity exists within the ummah; instead, identities are fluctuating and so dissimilar. They are the creation of an ongoing process located within particular contexts or cultures.[6]

Differences within Islam

In line with these contentions, Muslims can be described as an ethno-religious group. Islam is not a religion that comprises only one race or one class. On the contrary, the doctrine presents a set of moral guidelines for all individuals who wish to obey the Prophet Muhammad's teachings.[7] Both "Islam" and "Muslim" are stated many times in the Quran, making Islam the only world religion to employ a built-in name from the outset.[8] As opposed to Catholicism, Islam is a religion with no centralized seat, no hierarchical order, and no single global school of law. The schools of law (i.e., social obligations) clash with each other on multiple issues.[9] For those who identify as Muslims, a wide variety of beliefs and values are to be observed. Although there are expectations—duly enforced in Muslim-majority nations—that sharia (Islamic law) should rule all aspects of life, the way that the word of Allah, cherished in the Quran, is interpreted in a given country or community varies extensively, depending on both cultural and political contexts and on matters of interpretation.[10]

What makes a "true Muslim" remains a bone of contention throughout both the Islamic world and the non-Islamic one. Whereas for Jocelyne Cesari,[11] Professor of Religion and Politics at University of Birmingham (England), Islam is a peaceful religion that has a negligible proportion of extremists (like all major religions, she argues), for Sam Harris,[12] a neuroscientist who is now a champion of the counter-jihad left, to say that Islam is "a peaceful religion hijacked by extremists" would be retrieving into a fantasy world. For Walid Shoebat, a former Palestinian terrorist who has lived in the United States for many years, a true Muslim is inherently a jihadist or a sharia-compliant fundamentalist. In other words, in this train of thought, one cannot be a true Muslim and a moderate Muslim at the same time. These two mental concepts are considered mutually exclusive.[13]

Radical Islam or reactionary Islam?

Radical Islam is advocated by Muslims who aspire to go back to the fundamentals of the Muslim religion. A Muslim may hang on to a radical interpretation of the religion without becoming violent. Some scholars have challenged the conventional routine of associating the term "radical" with Islam. They make a case that the term "radical" is imbued with a sudden, dramatic decision or change in thinking and that "reactionary Islam" is more acceptable than "radical Islam." They further argue that the present-day violent trends of global jihad are the result of actions taken against Islam or Muslims as a whole. On the other hand, there are other scholars who maintain that "radical Islam" is appropriate because it is the perpetuation of a long-established radical interpretation of the Quran and implementation of sharia on Muslims and non-Muslims alike.[14]

Islam vs. Islamism?

According to Bernard Lewis (1994),[15] Islamic worship is not only about personal practice; it is also about public authority and domination, about jihad, and about persuading others that it is the only true religion. Now, it would be interesting to articulate the difference between Islam and Islamism. Moderate Muslims will frame Islam as a religion that traditionally does not consider hatred of non-Muslims as its main focus (although they do acknowledge that the Quran contains violent verses). Nor does it make killing civilian non-combatants its primary goal. On the other hand, the same group of Muslims advance the notion that Islamism is Islamic militancy or fundamentalism. It is not so much a religion as a totalitarian ideology driven by fervent politics, anti-Western and anti-democratic contempt, and a mission to dominate "the world by all means."[16]

The purist Salafists present a different interpretation of Islam. For them, Islam and Islamism should be regarded as one and the same because Islam, in its pure style, is immutable. Human beings were created by Allah for an unconditional religious purpose: to obey their Creator and follow His moral and judicial principles—including waging holy war against the Infidels and Apostates. Purist Salafists advocate a black-and-white religious outlook of the world that seeks to worship and perform the duty of Allah. The Quran, they say, stipulates clearly that obedience to political chiefs must be followed in order to protect Muslim communities from *fitna* (temptation and anarchy).[17] Purist Salafists want to preserve the purity of Islam, in accordance with the requirements of the Quran and the Sunna (the traditional customs and practices of the Islamic community) and with what was prescribed by the *ijma* (the universal and infallible agreement of Muhammad's early companions).[18]

Sunni–Shia relations

In Islam, two major groups exist: the Sunnis and the Shi'ites. Unlike the Sunnis (roughly 85% of all Muslims), the Shi'ites have a centralized and hierarchical structure and account for about 10% of all Muslims, most of whom live in Iran and, to a lesser extent, Iraq.[19] Renard (1998)[20] suggests that an interesting comparison can be made between Protestantism and Sunni Islam, on the one hand, and Roman Catholicism and Shia Islam, on the other hand. Sunni Islam and Protestantism are similar in that the emphasis is laid on the direct relationship between the believer and God—without the existence of an overarching authority structure. Conversely, Shia Islam shares similarities with Roman Catholicism in that both have instituted a hierarchical-legal order of scholars, based on the consensus of the élite who charge themselves with unraveling the Word of God for the disciples.[21] As such, on matters related to faith and morals, authority, dogma, and decisions come from the top: mullahs and priests, *hojat-ul-Islams* and bishops, ayatollahs and archbishops, and grand ayatollahs and cardinals.[22]

In-group identity for political reasons

The most radical jihadist organizations do not think of peace as a possible solution. An agreement with the enemy will only be unfavorable to their reputation as hardliners. As soon as they agree to negotiate, another organization will probably outbid them politically and militarily, thus forming a more robust in-group identity within that organization. An agreement with the enemy may achieve some of their goals, but it would have to be done within the confines of constitutional politics and the rule of law. Most of the time, however, making concessions to the adversary is considered by jihadists an unappealing soft landing. This is why it is hardly ever seen as an ultimate option. These organizations rarely want to become political forces in the electoral field because their own extreme interests are political *per se*.

A brief anecdote about the Muslim Brotherhood points to struggles they had with jihadist competitors in Jordan. The Muslim Brotherhood was more accommodating and opposed the more aggressive tactics promoted by Salafists. Jihadist leaders such as Abu Muhammad al-Maqdisi did not like the ascending popularity of the Muslim Brotherhood, which was more interested in remaining in parliamentary politics and in implicitly acknowledging the peace accord with Israel.[23] Abu Muhammad al-Maqdisi was a Jordanian-Palestinian jihadist and the spiritual mentor of Jordanian jihadist Abu Musab al-Zarqawi, the co-founder of AQI. In actual fact, a political dissent emerged between the two in 2004 when al-Zarqawi was perceived as being too harsh on the Shia populations. More precisely, al-Zarqawi issued threats of public apostasy against Shia groups in Iraq. On the other hand, al-Maqdisi favored a more prudent method of Shia killings, making sure that no radical ideological approach be counter-productive.[24]

Jihadist organizations portray themselves as guardians of in-group identity while everyone else gets shuffled off to the out-group. The out-group consists of enemies responsible for ills that only they—the in-group—can solve. As a result, the more the out-group gives the impression as being the problem-solver, the more people will join the in-group to become heroes and participate in the solution process. In addition, as crises are described by jihadist organizations as more and more threatening and imminent, solutions are also framed as a necessity to be more and more extreme.[25]

Honor cultures

In regard to protecting in-group identity itself, Hafez (2007)[26] describes how long-established notions of masculinity in Arab tribal cultures sometimes require immediate violent actions like holy war. Masculine values like honor, nobleness, and manliness are often measured by one's zealous defense of and control over the female gender. Shame caused by violations of honor and standards of decency can push traditional minds to engage in jihad in order to restore the honor of the violated women. Failure to do so raises questions about one's nobility, notion of masculinity, and standing within the ummah. In like fashion, in the domain of suicide terrorism, Muslim youths are taught, from the cradle, that achieving honor and averting shame are not only expected from true heroes of the faith—i.e., martyrs or, from a Western perspective, suicide bombers—but their ultimate sacrifice will also serve to buttress the identity of the in-group from which they come (even after their death).[27]

Superiority of the ummah

This grooming of in-group mentality causes a change in framing of outside events. The radical ideology turns the in-group into the victimized group, like "a chosen people" (in-group superiority) who have been unfairly treated or stabbed in the back (injustice), and where "no one else cares about them or will help them" (distrust). Their predicament is so "dire" that the in-group or their cause risks being "extinct" (vulnerability).[28] An important element of the radical ideology is the assumed superiority of the in-group: all out-groups are assumed to be inferior.[29] In most religions, a distinction is drawn between adherents and non-adherents. The in-group sees itself as more virtuous than the out-group of unbelievers. From most believers' perspective, that out-group includes those who believe in religions.[30] To this point, in a study conducted by Buijs, Demant, and Hamdy (2006),[31] when an Islamic extremist living in the Netherlands talked about Dutch people, he made it clear that "These people are nothing. Worthless. You cannot trust them." A certain percentage of Muslims consider nationalism a concept antithetical to Islam, which strives for unity and solidarity within the ummah. The feeling of superiority of the ummah can be strengthened by the pilgrimage to Mecca, as well as missionary and educational interests. Millions of Muslims travel every year to pursue higher education in Islamic holy lands. Proselytism is another key component of Muslim life. Dawah is the call to Islam for both the Infidels and the Apostates, as they do not follow the Quran.[32]

Islamic radicalization

Consider the Madrid train bombings perpetrated by Al-Qaeda-inspired terrorists on March 11, 2004. What drove Spanish-speaking Moroccan youths, with a good professional situation, fans of the Real Madrid football club, and living in affluent and cosmopolitan districts (such as Lavapiés)—put simply, well-integrated migrants in a Western nation—to kill close to 200 innocent civilians at a train station? The answer is radicalization.[33] This chapter deems it important to understand and explain Islamic radicalization. Before the internet became popular, programs designed to praise jihad and convince Muslims of its importance in their lives were already in full swing. Let us look at two earlier militant works written in the 1970s and 1980s by Abdullah Azzam (who was described in the previous chapter). His works are the widely celebrated *Defense of the Muslim Lands: The First Obligation after Faith* (originally published in 1979)[34] and *Join the Caravan* (in 1987).[35] In these works, Azzam made it clear that Islamic radicalization was essential to jihad because it was a quick pathway to violence. Therefore, Islamic radicalization was promoted as a chief priority for all Muslims. It became such an international security concern that it alerted law enforcement agencies and authorities across the world.

Radicalization refers to the process of supporting or taking actions perceived (by others) as violating important social norms (e.g., murdering innocent people). From this perspective, radicalization constitutes a subjective judgment expressed by individuals for whom the violated norms appear significant, but not by individuals who have debased or eliminated the norms in question.[36] Based on several assessments, after the September 11, 2001 attacks, more books were published on the subject of radicalization within the subsequent five years than in the six previous decades combined.[37] Between 2005 and 2006 alone, the usage of "radicalization" as a term in the English-speaking mass media more than doubled. Articles in scholarly journals and state- and organization-based reports on that subject have also experienced a significant increase year after year.[38] Academic works on radicalization, in spite of being quite limited, have charged themselves with the mission of answering "why" questions (and, to a lesser degree, "how" questions).

Why do people embrace beliefs and behaviors that support their commitment to subversive and terrorist activities, particularly targeting civilian noncombatants?[39] As far as Islamic radicalization is concerned, the violence and overall narrative of radical Muslims are often accompanied by deep-seated references to the suffering Muslim populations across the world—something that requires revenge against the Oppressor and purification of evil and disbelief. In Western Europe, for example, a significant minority of Muslim youths—some of whom come from wealthy backgrounds—self-radicalize on the internet or face-to-face (e.g., through peer mentorship) and embark on a frenzy of violence, causing indiscriminate deaths and publicizing their elaborate narrative of heroism, fury, and disdain with declarations and photos/videos posted on social media.[40]

What is jihad?

Jihad is a concept that literally means "striving" or "determined effort." A person active in jihad is a *mujahid* (or "someone who strives" or "a participant in jihad").[41] Many Islamic jurists, lawyers, and scholars employ the term "jihad" to refer to "warfare with spiritual significance,"[42] entailing military action with the objective of "Islam's expansion, and defense." In many situations, Islam means "fighting"—though other words in Arabic are used to more unambiguously refer to "making war," such as *qital* or *harb*. The Quran, in its plea for struggle in the path of Allah, laid the foundations for a construction of jihad as struggle for a godly order. In the Quran, jihad is often accompanied by the saying *fi sabil Illah* (or "in the path of Allah").[43]

Jihadism is jihad-driven terrorism. It is considered a "product of a combination of Islamist ideology and the idea of jihad."[44] It is described as extreme manifestations of Islamism, whereas Islamism itself is "activism justified with primary reference to Islam."[45] Jihadist terrorism, an important focus of this book, is directly rooted in jihad, the attempt to "strive or struggle," and encompasses a rigorous system of checks and balances to redress righteousness and justice. In its most radical sense, jihad creates a militant connotation or holy war.[46] Second to the

Quran is the hadith, an essential source of Islamic law (sharia) that describes the sayings and acts of the Prophet Muhammad. A hadith is a collection of texts, in which jihad is defined as "armed action." To this point, the 199 references to jihad in the hadith written by Sahih al-Bukhari—the most standard collection—interpret jihad as warfare.[47]

The typical jihadist has no observable profile. People associated with jihadist organizations come from various backgrounds and countries. Common traits among jihadists have been suggested, such as socioeconomic class, education, and background. Nevertheless, no direct evidence exists as to what traits represent that terrorist population. Hence, identifying and selecting jihadist recruits can be problematic. Radical jihadist groups driven by this ideology are part of a larger movement that could be easily illustrated by social movement theory (see Chapter 9) to better understand the threat it poses to the world.[48] This larger movement is also known as the global jihadist movement (GJM).[49]

Greater jihad vs. lesser jihad

The greater jihad (al-jihad al-akbar) is the struggle or perseverance in leading a life devoid of evil.[50] This type of jihad personifies having a mind that works hard to release evil thoughts and desire out of one's system.[51] It stresses self-control and is a spiritual endeavor to move closer to Allah. Pursuing jihad on oneself is a temporary but required phase to mystical union with the Creator.[52] This concept has been espoused by Western Islamologists (like John Esposito and Carole Hillenbrand) and Muslim reformers who perceive the notion of holy war as not appropriate in the present day.[53] The Prophet reportedly told his war companions that they had come back from the lesser jihad and, from now on, had to struggle against lust (i.e., the greater jihad).[54]

The lesser jihad is a type of jihad that aims at sacrificing oneself for the cause and attack the enemy in order to inflict distress on them. The lesser jihad (jihad al saghir) is militant jihad (i.e., sometimes called "jihad of the sword"). It denotes the obligation to grab a sword to defend the ummah after believing Muslims have had the sword wielded against them.[55] In today's parlance, it continues to be jihad leveraged as "warfare against the kuffar (infidels)." Martin (1987)[56] defines it as "legitimate forms of strife with other human beings through war, violence, and so on." The lesser jihad has two variants: defensive jihad and offensive jihad[57] (described later in this chapter). During the course of its history and legal and theological actions, the lesser jihad has often led to a "just war" under the pretext of purification and proclamation.[58]

The sixth pillar of Islam

Jihad has been referred to as the sixth pillar of Islam,[59] in the same way that jihad is considered one of the ten pillars in Twelver Shia Islam. Twelver Shia Islam is the largest subdivision of Shia Islam. "Twelver" refers to the belief in twelve divinely ordained leaders, identified as the Twelve Imams, and the belief that the last Imam, Muhammad al-Mahdi, will one day come out of the shadow and return as the promised Mahdi or Messiah.[60] A person who does the jihad is a *mujahid* (plural *mujahedin*).[61] In addition to the other five pillars of Islam—shahada (faith); salah (prayer); zakat (charity); sawm (fasting); and hajj (pilgrimage to Mecca)—Islam's sixth pillar necessitates a resolute effort to fulfill Allah's command of dominating the world and recruiting fellow brothers and sisters in the process. This, of course, is to be achieved for the sake of Islam and the ummah at large. The aforementioned jihad *fi sabil illah* (jihad "in the path of God") distinguishes its attribute of struggle as "war" from other struggles conducted for personal reasons such as glory or booty.[62]

Brief note on the Crusades

The Crusades are generally considered a Christian counterpart to jihad. To some extent, this is correct in that both were engaged as "holy wars," and in both cases, those who died in battle were guaranteed an eternal place in Paradise. Yet, it is important to observe that the Crusades happened over a millennium after the birth of Christianity, were waged during a comparatively brief and limited period, and, more importantly, constituted a noteworthy theological deviance from the Gospel scriptures in the New Testament. In the Middle Ages in Europe, Christianity was the most unifying entity and could easily be exploited as a rallying call for diverse purposes. After many previously Christian territories fell to Muslim conquests since the death of the Prophet in 632 AD, the Crusades represented more of a reaction to Muslim aggression. Modern-day Christians interpret the concept of "crusade" as possessing a spiritual meaning, while for Muslims "jihad" does not.[63]

Defensive jihad vs. offensive jihad

Called *jihad al-dafaa*, defensive jihad is a reaction to an enemy's attack on Muslims, pushing them into a defensive position. It is a responsibility incumbent on all Muslims.[64] Offensive jihad is *jihad-e-asghar*. It is an offensive attack on the unbelievers who have been warned about the jihadists' message (to convert to their faith), but who refuse to comply with their demands or quit obstructing the global Muslim expansion.[65] Now, let us further examine defensive jihad but, this time, from a legal perspective. Jihadist thinkers have shaped defensive jihad from a territory-focused strategy into a modern-day global military agenda. In the classical doctrine, the individual obligation is for all those living in the territory that was invaded—or to those who identify with the religion of the attacked (theoretically, it would be all Muslims and those who are devoted to the authentic teachings of Islam).[66]

Jihadist thinkers frame these circumstances as an opportunity to reject the authority of the political world order and, at the same time, apply the classical doctrine of defensive warfare to make it totally legal. The legality of defensive jihad is of critical importance because, otherwise, their actions against Muslim political governments would make them rebels (*bughat*) or dissenters (*Khawarij*). Such labels would legally give political authorities the power to vanquish their rebellions.[67] Hence, thanks to the jihadists' rejection of the authority of national and transnational political rules and establishments, jihadists fall back on the classical legal doctrine of defensive jihad to galvanize the ummah in order to fight for global jihad.[68]

Abdullah Azzam

As Osama bin Laden's mentor and closest friend, Abdullah Azzam played a major role in legalizing defensive jihad across the world to unite Muslims against the Soviet troops in Afghanistan.[69] He theorized defensive jihad as a legal duty for all Muslims, including women and adolescents. In his open call to jump on the jihad bandwagon, Azzam addressed key questions that true Muslims should ask about the viability of implementing the doctrine of defensive jihad in modern times. Among these is a question that relates to the possibility of a universal call to arms (*nafir 'amm*). Some brothers and sisters, he thought, might say that "a general call to arms as required in Islam [stipulates that] a woman should go out to fight without her husband's permission, a boy without his father's permission."

These people, Azzam added, might identify at least three important problems: (1) There is not a single Muslim territory on the planet that could accommodate one tenth of the Muslim population today; (2) a universal call to arms will "lead to violating the ways of Islamic upbringing, which, with God's permission, is considered the hope of the ummah's salvation;" and (3) if all Muslims agreed to take up arms, it would "lead to emptying out all Islamic territories since Muslims would want to go out to fight in Palestine or Afghanistan, leaving these places to the communists, Ba'thists, nationalists, and secularists."[70]

Vertical jihad vs. horizontal jihad

Two categories of violence can illustrate how global jihad operates: vertical jihad (when jihadists challenge the state, either Western or Muslim) and horizontal jihad (when jihadists attack *dar al-harb* because it is the abode of war that is disrespectful to all Muslims). To be more precise, vertical jihad is holy war against Muslim nations and communities, which have become "infamous" for having abandoned the true path of the Prophet. Horizontal jihad is holy war against the Great Satan—a morally depraved, hegemonic, anti-Muslim perpetrator—and the Little Satan (i.e., the State of Israel) that wants to destroy Islam.[71]

Vertical jihad

The concept of vertical jihad was established in a script titled "Knights under the banner of the Prophet" and written by Ayman Al-Zawahiri, the current Al-Qaeda leader. Al-Zawahiri states that it is imperative to gain the support of Muslim populations in order to topple current Muslim governments. The Al-Qaeda leader has proposed a plan to diffuse jihad to the West (particularly the U.S.) in order to, first, attract the sympathy of those Muslims are sitting on the fence and, second, destabilize the Western backing of those Muslim governments considered irreverent. Attacks against Western targets would, by the same token, undermine such immoral régimes. In due course, it would smooth the progress of seizing power and establishing the global Caliphate.[72]

In "Knights under the banner of the Prophet," the point is also made that comprehensive strategic and operational methods must be put in place (both in the short and long term). The fiascos of previous Islamic movements in the twenty-first century are often attributed to the fact that their actions are not well coordinated—at least, this is what extremist thinkers believe. As stated by Sayf Al-Adel, a chief Al-Qaeda military commander in Egypt, "mujahidin should have short-term plans aimed at achieving interim goals and long-term plans aimed at accomplishing the greater objective" (i.e., the institution of the global Caliphate). Throughout his announcement, Al-Adel makes allusions to the existence of a larger program set up by Al-Qaeda's leaders to depose Islamic régimes.[73] On top of putting pressure on Arab-Muslim states, jihad against these countries is waged to get locals to respect their Muslim obligations. When the GIA (the Armed Islamic Group) murdered many civilians in Algeria in the 1990s, they also wanted to punish those populations who, according to them, were acting disobedient to the religious norms.[74]

Horizontal jihad

In the Western world, violence that follows the model of horizontal jihad is designed to challenge the authority and the decisions of Western forces. The sponsorship of European countries provided to Middle-Eastern and Maghrebian régimes is regarded as an impediment to Islam's growth and the prospects for the Caliphate. The terrorist attacks in Madrid on March 11, 2004 did not kill innocent civilians because of their contempt towards Islamic norms. Rather, the objective was to put pressure on Western nations, Spain in this case, to disengage from Iraq. In another unrelated example, the series of bombings on public transport systems (like trains) in Paris and Lyon, perpetrated by the GIA, were meant to coerce France into abandoning its support for the Algerian government. This horizontal type of jihadist violence is different from the jihadism that has exploded in the Arab-Muslim world.[75]

It would also be interesting to explain jihadist terror as a manifestation of the conflict between a secularism-oriented Western civilization (symbolized by the U. S. and allied Muslim nations) and a radical theocracy-oriented civilization (symbolized by Osama bin Laden, Al-Qaeda, and ISIS). The vertical model of a territorial state will conflict with a deterritorialized horizontal model, rooted in the nomadic foundations of Afghan insurgent fighters. The latter create a chaotic campaign inspired by a long-established flow and movement of ideas that strives for destabilizing the hierarchical structure and dogmas of the state. Such regional jihadists are like a "nomadic war machine," conquering the Soviets in Afghanistan and erecting the Taliban régime.[76]

Salafism

The *Salaf* were unique in their classic piety and military conquests. These became the foundations of a vast empire stretching from Spain to India. Salafist theologians and clerics today continue to stress the causal relationship between the faith of the *Salaf* and the required military and political duties.[77] Each time a Muslim community faces a religious, political, or cultural dilemma, Salafists advocate a return to the Islam of the *Salaf*. The first one to have articulated this idea from a religious perspective was Ibn Hanbal (780–855), when the Muslim empire was fighting politico-religious factions. Ibn Taymiyya (1263–1328) echoed this idea when his Damas territory was endangered by the Mongol invasions.[78] Haykel (2009)[79] quotes a fatwa in which Ibn Taymiyya uses the Arabic term *al-salafiyya*, thereby proving that Salafist epithets have existed for many centuries.

Complexities of definitions

The definition of Salafism remains a contentious debate among academics. Upon looking at the classical interpretation in the present-day era, it was codified in the late nineteenth century, when Islamic Reformism (*islah*) developed in the Muslim world.[80] From the standpoint of *islah*, non-Islamic thinking has warped the message of authentic Islam for centuries and this perversion must be discarded for the sake of the religion.[81] At its most fundamental level, the term *salafi* alludes to a Sunni Muslim who models the Prophet Muhammad's behavior and that of his first generation of followers. The paradigmatic and authenticating power of this term has turned it into an appealing label—one that enables intellectuals with vastly different views to stress their commitment to the main religious ideals and disregard for non-Islamic modernization (*bida*).[82]

For the more radical Islamists, Salafism has a more elaborate meaning. It stands for the philosophical system that considers *al-salaf al-salih*, the righteous predecessors (i.e., the aforementioned Prophet's companions), as its only point of reference. To be more precise, Salafists want to model themselves after the Prophet Muhammad and the righteous forefathers in *every* aspect of life. The *al-salaf al-salih* were the Prophet's closest friends and followers (*sahaba*), those who formed the first Muslim community and the two subsequent generations. The Prophet is the absolute role model for a perfect Muslim life as wished-for by Allah. Salafism opposes new interpretations or approaches other than those that already exist. Its main concern is about the fundamentals of the faith and doctrinal wholesomeness.[83]

Under these circumstances, many Salafists believe that democracy must be eradicated and that jihad operations must strike it big.[84] This category of extremists is also referred to as Salafist jihadists.[85] As Husain (2018)[86] puts it elegantly, "not every Salafi is a jihadi, but every jihadi today is a Salafi." Today, Salafism as a global phenomenon is predominantly associated with its hostile stance toward democracy and political pluralism (both pillars of Western political theory). For many Salafist intellectuals, democracy is *bida* (innovation) and a "Western product" of which Muslims should steer clear. Furthermore, they believe that democracy inherently contradicts Islam, like partisan politics (*tahazzub*), which could engender dissent or distress (*fitna*) within the ummah.[87] Salafists' influence in the Islamic revival movement has been enormous. They do not live in isolation or as holy hermits within their own religious communities. In 2017, security experts estimated that the global number of Salafists was 50 million (out of 1.6 billion adherents).[88] In 2015, in Egypt alone, there were five to six million Salafists.[89]

Radical Salafist influences

Such feelings as marginalization, desolation, and embittering resentment can build a pathway toward radicalization. Increasingly, so-called "answers" to burning questions can be found within radical Salafism, which gives alternative ideas about a better world, one built on a global Muslim identity—which has high appeal to alienated Muslims (who find that radical Salafism offers them a sense of belonging in "an imagined worldwide Muslim community").[90] For these disaffected youths, the dream of being a "citizen" of a global Muslim community can be more appealing than it was for first-generation immigrants two to five decades prior. The latter often preserve strong roots in their native lands but do not cling to a global Muslim community for a better world.[91] Radical or purist Salafism is tremendously trendy across communities of Muslim youths, particularly those who do not do well at school or are suspicious of mainstream society. What they are looking for is a type of personal and ideological enhancement, which explains their quest for a religious discourse that validates their choices. Put another way, contextualizing Islam does not create integration, but integration creates a reframing of religious imperatives.[92]

Before following Salafist principles, many Salafists adhered to a Western-oriented lifestyle, such as drinking alcohol and engaging in casual sex. For a multitude of reasons, they often turn over a new leaf and now abide by tenets of Islamic purity. It is like a "Damascus road" conversion and it explains, in part, why they make every effort to avoid associating with their former environment.[93] Essential to the influence of Salafism is the sentiment of grievance induced in regards to the tribulations of Muslims around the globe. The blame is placed directly on the policies of Western states and placed indirectly on pro-West Muslim rulers (who are conniving with them). This feeling of grievance is not necessarily rooted in personal experience but can be "fostered by the narratives of Muslim oppression."[94] These narratives of Muslim oppression can serve as an official explanation for their lack of integration, and their assumed experiences of discrimination regarding social, economic, and political participation, as well as high levels of joblessness and other social issues. To the extent that these narratives lead to jihadization, we know for sure that radical Salafist influences are entrenched within particular Muslim sub-cultures and no-go zones.[95]

Their level of confidence in the merits of Islam's holy scriptures is high. Combined with the promises of a better world, or even Paradise, such confidence stands in sharp contrast to their current situation of insecurity and social alienation. Put simply, they join Islamic terrorist groups for purposes of psychological empowerment. No matter what, it is important to note that those Muslim youths start as vulnerable and impressionable, two ideal factors for indoctrination and radicalization. Jihad recruiters and radical preachers know that fact all too well—not to mention propagandist materials available on the internet.[96] To this very point, the internet has proven to be an ideal pathway out of social alienation. Gathering data compiled by the Internet World Stats, Robin Thompson (2012)[97] contends that the number of internet users in the Middle East and North Africa are surprisingly "above average" (in comparison with other non-Western countries). At the same time, in those nations where internet availability is more prevalent, people are "more likely to be recruited and radicalized via the internet." Therefore, websites and social media networks that offer spaces for radical chat rooms and blogs, lure their users "with a promise of friendship, acceptance, or a sense of purpose." Romero (2007)[98] sums it up elegantly when he writes that jihadist internet links are, indeed, a solution to social alienation because they offer "social backing, meaning to life, and a social or collective identity mainly based on the pride of belonging to the jihad as the only way of reaching the power and glory of Islam."

Religious jihad vs. secular ideologies

In contrast to secular ideologies, jihad is—among many things—a religious ideology because it is inspired by religion in three ways. First, it designates itself and its opponents in religious terms. Jihadists refer to themselves through religious names such as the "Army of Muhammad," the "Lions of Islam," and, obviously, "jihadist." They refer to their foes in religious terms as well. Examples include Crusaders, Apostates, and Infidels. Second, jihadists consider their methods and mission a religious one. Their struggle is a holy war, which they see in religious and military terms, unlike the "internal war" against human sins. One of their principle methods is not the suicide attack but the "martyrdom operation"—a term whose origin is, oddly enough, rooted in Shia Islam, a branch of the religion depicted as apostate by jihadists.[99]

Third, they defend acts of violence as directly inspired by Quranic verses. Martyrs will be with Allah for eternity upon accomplishing their mission successfully. Hence, they rely on a number of verses from the Quran (and hadith) to justify the killing of civilians. An example is Quran 16:126: "And if you take your turn, then punish with the like of that with which you were afflicted."[100] Let us not forget to mention the renowned *Allahu Akbar*, an Arabic phrase meaning "Allah is greater" or "Allah is the greatest." Shouted by innumerable jihadists for centuries, this battle cry continues to express the religious nature of Islamist methods and goals.

Religious identity and dignity

Jihadist organizations are encouraged by deeply entrenched religious identities and the resulting yearning for proving their religious dignity against an enemy whose lifestyle is heinous and unconscionable. Religion makes jihadists unrestrained in their attacks on civilian populations, as the latter are essentialized as the Other. Victims of religion-driven jihadism are considered devoid of human qualities by both the Muslim perpetrators and the sympathizers (or co-jihadists).[101] Owing to this, assaults on soft targets that will probably cause higher numbers of casualties (e.g., in crowded public places) are ideal actions for religious jihadists, who are not even worried about possible backlash from the sympathizers.[102] Religion-sanctioned violence is a "purifying act," a means to make a religious statement, to demonstrate one's fervor and passion to fulfill religious desires. This explains why exceedingly radical tactics like suicide bombings are more widespread among religious terrorists than secular terrorists.[103]

Unlike secular terrorist organizations that conduct terrorist operations to engender sympathy through their actions, religious jihadists are not so much influenced by the desire to "win the hearts and minds" of their constituents. They are less likely to long for popular approval because they anticipate instead an eternal life, like a divine reward. This makes them even less concerned about the ostensible loss of countless innocent lives.[104] Therefore, they declare war on the entire world, not just particular governments (as is generally the case with secular terrorist organizations). For religious jihadists, all members of the enemy group are legitimate targets, including women and children, the most vulnerable. The tactical decision, then, is to inflict as many casualties as possible.[105]

Moral disengagement and neutralization

Albert Bandura (2004),[106] one of the fathers of social cognitive theory, studies the reasons for human behavior. For the Canadian-American psychologist, "self-sanctions play a role in the regulation of inhumane conduct." He remarks, nonetheless, that these self-sanctions are sometimes selectively "activated and disengaged" to simplify behavior that would otherwise contravene one's own moral conduct. This process of removing one's own barriers is called "moral disengagement." It functions on a range of processes, including moral justification, euphemisms and distancing language, placing responsibility on others, minimizing one's own malevolent actions, blaming the victims themselves, and dehumanization of the enemy. The "disengagement" processes described by Bandura have been witnessed in terrorist rhetoric. Invoking "morality" for one's malevolent actions is a method of explaining away one's behavior. It is an explanation for religiously motivated terrorism which, for violent actors, is the path of least resistance, with one's sense of morality now completely disengaged, or perhaps even replaced.[107]

In the sociological school of thought, Sykes and Matza (1957)[108] published a similar theory, which they named "neutralization theory," concerning criminal behavior in general. For the two sociologists, most criminals do acknowledge or care for society's prohibitions of unlawful conduct. What they do is use specific cognitive techniques to rationalize and validate their violent actions, thereby decreasing what social psychologists refer to as "cognitive dissonance." The five main neutralization techniques presented by Sykes and Matza are (1) denying responsibility, (2) denying harm, (3) denying a victim, (4) blaming those in authority, and (5) invoking and pleasing a higher authority. Many of the processes resemble those in Bandura's theory of moral disengagement. It is probably these mechanisms of "disengagement" or "neutralization" that best differentiate radicals who do not resort to violence from those who do.[109]

Neojihadism

Neojihadism is a type of defensive jihad designed to create Islamic states based on strict sharia-compliant laws. Neojihadism is described by Lentini (2008)[110] as,

> A religious, political, paramilitary and terrorist global movement, a subculture, a counterculture and an ideology that seeks to establish states governed by laws according to the dictates of selectively literal interpretations of the Qur'an and the traditions of the Prophet Muhammad, through enacting violence.

Peculiar to the late twentieth and early twenty-first centuries, neojihadism reflects the current multidimensional aspects of the jihad syndrome. It relies on a narrative of victimization that portrays Muslims as an assaulted group and supports violence against both soldiers and civilians as the only methods to end victimization. Neojihadism is undertaken by Sunni jihadists who justify violence through cherry-picked literal interpretations of Muslim texts and the re-appropriation of Shia martyrdom procedures. As a subculture, it glorifies jihadist violence via digital media and global narratives. It is also hostile towards mainstream Islam and the traditions of Muslim-majority states and other countries to which Muslims have migrated. Mainstream Islam, neojihadists say, has become too meek.[111] Neojihadists have a strong presence in southern Thailand, where they act as separatist insurgents who want to restore the Islamic Patani state. They have launched vengeful attacks against the Infidel Siamese persecutor.[112]

Lone-wolf jihad

Occasionally referred to as "freelance jihadism," "solo-actor jihadism," or even "personal jihad," lone-wolf jihad also shares the same features of lone-wolf terrorism. A lone-wolf jihadist is a single individual executing jihadist attacks against noncombatant targets without external leadership or assistance.[113] The entreaty by Al-Qaeda, ISIS, and other jihadist groups for Muslims to carry lone-wolf attacks in the West is often publicized through online jihadist magazines such as *Inspire* (published by Al-Qaeda in the Arabian Peninsula, or AQAP, from January 2010 to November 2016)[114] and *Dabiq* (published by ISIS from July 2014 to July 2016).[115]

Calls for lone-wolf jihad are also made through online videos and podcasts. In September 2014, Abu Muhammad al-Adnani, a courier for ISIS, urged would-be jihadists to "rise and defend your state from wherever you may be," advising them to keep jihadist missions small and simple, and involve as few collaborators as possible.[116]

Characteristics of lone-wolf jihadists

The average lone-wolf jihadist presents the following ten characteristics: (1) A personal discontent and moral outrage toward the Western world (and often Muslim governments as well); (2) the espousal of Islamist dogmas; (3) no personal membership of a jihadist group; (4) the anonymous membership of an online community; (5) a decrease or abandonment of occupational goals; (6) self-radicalization (through the internet, especially today); (7) transformations in thinking and emotion—including cognitive inflexibility and secret excitement about killing others; (8) better creativity and innovation than terrorist organizations; (9) longer and more meticulous planning of a terrorist attack; and (10) intense violence authorized and even encouraged by a moral authority.[117]

With respect to the second and third characteristics, "the espousal of Islamist dogmas" and "no personal membership of a jihadist group," it is important to note that the lone-wolf jihadist will still be cognitively and ideologically affiliated with the GJM, such as the one spearheaded by ISIS. It is a psychological type of affiliation which offers the person a sense of belonging and safety.[118] For the lone-wolf jihadist, this identity with an overarching movement is generally formed in a virtual community in cyberspace, and may have been caused by the rejection from an actual jihadist group with whom he or she had prior physical contact (although this is rare). The present-day macrostructure of jihadist organizations is a centralized command (sometimes on another continent) with decentralization for the accomplishment of jihadist plots. This decentralization has accelerated the occurrence of lone-wolf attacks.[119]

A few statistics

According to a report by the George Washington University's Program on Extremism, between the September 11, 2001 attacks and the end of 2016, about 80 Muslim U.S. citizens were convicted of jihad-related offenses. They all acted alone, with zero affiliation with groups like ISIS, Al-Qaeda, and Al-Shabaab. In all cases, the perpetrators were devoted to the jihadist ideology, but showed no visible signs of allegiance to the aforementioned groups.[120] In like fashion, in a study conducted by Davies (2018),[121] it was found that counterterrorism authorities were more able to uncover group-based jihadist plots (87% in Western Europe and 81% in the United States) than lone-wolf plots (57% in Western Europe and 72% in the United States). More importantly, the highest shift toward lone-wolf jihadist violence occurred around 2009. The reasons are twofold: (1) the emergence and proliferation of social media technologies (e.g., Twitter, among others) occurred around that time and (2) many individual jihadists have been forced to secretly plan and conduct attacks on their own in order to circumvent problems related to detection by counterterrorism agents. The same study reported that, between 2010 and 2015, there was a gradual increase in lone-wolf jihadist attacks and in deaths resulting from these attacks (on both continents). In fact, lone-wolf jihadist attacks accounted for more than 70% of all jihadist violence across both continents.[122]

The lone-wolf suicide bomber

The typical lone-wolf suicide bombing scenario is a single event in which the lone wolf comes out of the woodwork and unsettles an entire community through a singular bombing incident. Suicide bombing can wreak terrible havoc. A single event can be arranged in such a fashion that maximum effect—in terms of victims and public visibility—is accomplished without much effort. This "single event" type of jihadism is a spectacle for a higher cause.[123] The lone wolf suicide bomber is the ultimate altruist, dying for Allah or the Caliphate agenda. By destroying a target or target population, he or she uses his or her body as a weapon—a concept called biopolitics.[124] In fact, by sacrificing his or her life, he or she becomes worthy of great honor and even social status. In many respects, chaos terrorism has much in common with mass murder in the sense that a mass murder event results in the murderer's death at the scene of a spectacular tragedy.[125]

Suicide bombings have been a standard method of lone-wolf jihad at different moments in time and for several reasons: inspired by Hezbollah and Amal in the 1980s, by Hamas and the Palestinian Islamic Jihad in the 1990s, and by the Al-Aqsa Martyrs' brigades after 2001. An important reason for this deadly method lies with the decreased efficiency of skyjackings. Suicide bombings are now the established weapon of the weak, which saw a spectacular rise during the Lebanese Civil War in the 1980s. They could be viewed as low-cost, technological leap, enabling individual jihadists to improve the capabilities of their actions and, at the same time, pursue their agenda-setting objectives without paying tribute or swearing allegiance to actual groups.[126]

Jihobbyists

A jihobbyist is a concept created by Jarret Brachman (2008)[127] to describe an individual who is not actively involved in a jihadist group like Al-Qaeda or Al-Shabaab (a Somali-based jihadist terror group), but who is fascinated or obsessed with jihad and militant Islam. Brachman was previously the director of research at the Combating Terrorism Center (an academic institution at the United States Military Academy in West Point). He invented the term "jihobbyist" to designate people who have had zero contact with Islamic terrorist organizations but who, nevertheless, choose to support the missions of these organizations. For Brachman (2008), a jihobbyist is "an enthusiast of the global jihadist movement, someone who enjoys thinking about and watching the activities of the groups from the first and second tiers but generally they have no connection to Al-Qaeda or any other formal jihadist groups."[128] A case in point is Colleen LaRose, an American woman who was convicted on terrorism-related charges in the mid-2000s. She was known by the nickname of "Jihad Jane" and is the perfect example of a jihobbyist.[129] Adam Gadahn, or "Azzam the American," is another case of an American convert to militant Islam. He was indicted on treason charges for his "services" as media consultant to Al-Qaeda.[130]

Ontological insecurity

Ontological insecurity is an existentialist concept described by Giddens (1990)[131] as the erosion of confidence in the preservation of our self-identity and in the common norms and values of society. In such circumstances of uncertainty and psychological removal, the search for meaning in life becomes anxious.[132] Ontological insecurity is fear. People will make a choice to conquer that fear, the result of which could cause salvation or damnation. The stakes can be enormous, but it might as well be better than living in fear.[133]

Late modernity as a cause of jihadism

The theoretical concept of ontological insecurity concentrates on social changes linked to late modernity. A fundamental hypothesis is that social changes inherent to the evolution from modernity to late modernity lead to a rise in jihadist attacks because late modernity fosters a culture that does not give people a sense of meaning and, consequently, engenders feelings of ontological insecurity. This crucial psychological craving for predictability and continuity is endangered or unsettled for many people by the transition from modernity to late modernity. Part of the reason stems from market-based transformations in both production and consumption.[134]

The growing opportunities, prosperity, and freedom of choice that late modernity provides can come with a hefty price, with respect to profound feelings of vulnerability, insecurity, and instability. Market factors are causing more job insecurity and work pressure at a time where the acceleration of consumerism and the "disembedding of social systems"[135] have engendered more materialistic, ephemeral self-identities (rather than lasting ones). As Garland (2001)[136] explains, "the sense of precariousness, of the strung-out nature of existence, is an important new element in people's lives, even as these lives grow more varied and mobile and exciting."

Ontological insecurity, modernity, and 7/7 jihadist bombers

On July 7, 2005, four British-born Al-Qaeda suicide bombers exploded bombs aboard London subway trains and a double-decker bus (i.e., the 7/7 tragedy). The death toll included 52 people and more than 700 others were injured.[137] In a narrative analysis of martyrdom videos disseminated by the 7/7 Al-Qaeda terrorists (and an additional eight martyrs-to-be in British courts for plotting to bomb passenger aircrafts with explosives), Shaun Best (2010)[138] found a reliable list of altruistic reasons that motivate jihadist martyrs to target symbols of modernity. Modernity seems to be a predominant reason for such martyrs who hold unfettered, postmodern, individualist consumerism in contempt.

On the other hand, for people who appreciate all the perks that modernity offers, such a radical position is inexplicable and irrational. For pro-modernity thinkers, altruistic fundamentalism has no purpose. Nevertheless, the reality is that jihadist martyrs vehemently oppose the self-serving, survival-and-gratification consumerism because they have ulterior goals. Based on the martyrs' narratives, communal goals such as group well-being (e.g., an altruistic form of collectivism) should have precedence over individual satisfaction. Put another way, although the martyrs' collectivist position is inexplicable and irrational for the modernists, the latter's individualist mindset does not resonate with the martyrs themselves.[139]

Jihad as the answer

Overall, the 7/7 tragedy corroborates the idea that ontological insecurity chips away at trust and aggravates the perception of a universal threat from the outside world. Jihad is a pathway to ontological security. Ontological security is an ideal situation where a "person's fundamental sense of safety in the world and includes a basic trust of other people. Obtaining such trust becomes necessary in order for a person to maintain a sense of psychological well-being and avoid existential anxiety."[140] As some Muslims feel vulnerable and suffer from alleged existential anxiety, they will look for answers in jihadism in order to secure a threatened self-identity. Any collective mechanism that can offer such security is an ostensible pole of attraction. Nationalism and religion are two cases for such "identity-signifiers" that can easily provide answers to those in need. Nationalism and religion can offer age-old, powerful narratives and myths because of their power to communicate an image of security, stability, and straightforward answers. Narratives and myths can be framed as message conduits that rest on solid ground, as being true, and as tools that make sense as to what the world really is.[141]

Notes

1 Conrad Hackett and David McClendon, *Christians Remain World's Largest Religious Group, but They Are Declining in Europe* (Washington, D.C.: Pew Research Center, 2017).
2 Michael Lipka, *Muslims and Islam: Key Findings in the U.S. and around the World* (Washington, D.C.: Pew Research Center, 2017).
3 Drew DeSilver and David Masci, *World's Muslim Population More Widespread than You Might Think* (Washington, D.C.: Pew Research Center, 2017).
4 See Hackett and McClendon, *Christians Remain World's Largest Religious Group.*
5 Conrad Hackett, *5 Facts about the Muslim Population in Europe* (Washington, D.C.: Pew Research Center, 2017).

 6 Zygmunt Bauman, *Postmodernity and Its Discontents* (New York: New York University Press, 1997); Richard Jenkins, *Social Identity* (London: Routledge, 1996).
 7 Motamar al-Alam Al-Islami, *Islamic Culture: A Few Angles* (Karachi: Umma Publishing House, 1964).
 8 Dale F. Eickelman, *The Middle East and Central Asia: An Anthropological Approach* (4th Ed.) (London: Pearson, 2001).
 9 Carolyn M. Warner and Manfred W. Wenner, "Religion and the Political Organization of Muslims in Europe," *Perspectives on Politics* 4, no. 3 (2006): 457–79. https://doi.org/10.1017/S1537592706060300
10 Fatima Mernissi, *Women's Rebellion and Islamic Memory* (New York: Saint Martin's Press, 1996).
11 Jocelyne Cesari, *Why the West Fear Islam: An Exploration of Muslims in Liberal Democracies* (New York: Palgrave Macmillan, 2013).
12 Sam Harris, *Letter to a Christian Nation* (New York: Vintage, 2006).
13 John Horgan, "Individual Disengagement: A Psychological Analysis," in *Leaving Terrorism Behind: Individual and Collective Disengagement*, ed. Tore Bjorgo and John G. Horgan (New York: Routledge, 2008): 35–47; Omid Safi, "Who Put Hate in My Sunday Paper? Uncovering the Israeli-Republican-Evangelical Networks behind the 'Obsession' DVD," in *Muslims and Jews in America*, ed. Reza Aslan and Aaron Tapper (New York: Palgrave Macmillan, 2011): 21–32.
14 Tawfik Hamid, *Inside Jihad* (Mountain Lake Park, MD: Mountain Lake Press, 2010).
15 Bernard Lewis, "Legal and Historical Reflections on the Position of Muslim Populations under Non-Muslim Rule," in *Muslims in Europe*, ed. Bernard Lewis and Dominique Schnapper (London: Pinter, 1994): 1–18.
16 Mehdi Mozaffari, "What Is Islamism? History and Definition of a Concept," *Totalitarian Movements and Political Religions* 8, no. 1 (2007): 17–33. https://doi.org/10.1080/14690760601121622
17 Mohamed Ali Adraoui, "Purist Salafism in France," *ISIM Review* 21, no. 1 (2008): 12–3.
18 Stefano M. Torelli, Fabio Merone, and Francesco Cavatorta, "Salafism in Tunisia: Challenges and Opportunities for Democratization," *Middle East Policy* 19, no. 4 (2012): 140–54. https://doi.org/10.1111/j.1475-4967.2012.00566.x
19 Febe Armanios, *Islam: Sunnis and Shiites* (Washington, D.C.: CRS Report for Congress, 2004).
20 John Renard, *Responses to 101 Questions on Islam* (Mahwah, NJ: Paulist Press, 1998).
21 Roy Mottahedeh, *The Mantle of the Prophet* (New York: Pantheon Books, 1985).
22 Warner and Wenner, "Religion and the Political Organization of Muslims in Europe," 460–9.
23 Marc Lynch, "Islam Divided between Salafi-Jihad and the Ikhwan," *Studies in Conflict & Terrorism* 33, no. 6 (2010): 467–87. https://doi.org/10.1080/10576101003752622
24 Ali A. Allawi, *The Occupation of Iraq: Winning the War, Losing the Peace* (New Haven, CT: Yale University Press, 2007).
25 Alastair Reed and Haroro J. Ingram, *Exploring the Role of Instructional Material in AQAP's Inspire and ISIS' Rumiyah* (The Hague: European Counter Terrorism Centre, 2017).
26 Mohammed Hafez, "Martyrdom Mythology in Iraq: How Jihadists Frame Suicide Terrorism in Videos and Biographies," *Terrorism and Political Violence* 19, no. 1 (2007): 95–115. https://doi.org/10.1080/09546550601054873
27 Simon Perry and Badi Hasisi, "Rational Choice Rewards and the Jihadist Suicide Bomber," *Terrorism and Political Violence* 27, no. 1 (2015): 53–80. https://doi.org/10.1080/09546553.2014.962991
28 Clark McCauley and Sophia Moskalenko, "Mechanisms of Political Radicalization: Pathways toward Terrorism," *Terrorism and Political Violence* 20, no. 3 (2008): 415–33, 416. https://doi.org/10.1080/09546550802073367
29 Wagdy Loza, "The Psychology of Extremism and Terrorism: A Middle-Eastern Perspective," *Aggression & Violent Behavior* 12, no. 2 (2007): 141–55. https://doi.org/10.

1016/j.avb.2006.09.001; Michael J. Mazarr, "The Psychological Sources of Islamic Terrorism: Alienation and Identity in the Arab World," *Policy Review* 125 (2004): 39–60.

30 Bertjan Doosje, Annemarie Loseman, and Kees van den Bos, "Determinants of Radicalization of Islamic Youth in the Netherlands: Personal Uncertainty, Perceived Injustice, and Perceived Group Threat," *Journal of Social Issues* 69, no. 3 (2013): 586–604. https://doi.org/10.1111/josi.12030

31 Frank J. Buijs, Froukje Demant, and Atef Hamdy, *Warriors from Own Soil: Radical and Democratic Muslims in the Netherlands* (Amsterdam: Amsterdam University Press, 2006): 28.

32 Emmanuel Karagiannis, "Transnational Islamist Networks: Western Fighters in Afghanistan, Somalia and Syria," *The International Spectator* 48, no. 4 (2013): 119–34. https://doi.org/10.1080/03932729.2013.847696

33 Fidel Sendagorta, "Jihad in Europe: The Wider Context," *Survival* 47, no. 3 (2005): 63–72. https://doi.org/10.1080/00396330500248029

34 Cited in Johannes J. G. Jansen, *The Neglected Duty: The Creed of Sadat's Assassins and Islamic Resurgence in the Middle East* (New York: MacMillan, 1986): 199–200.

35 Cited in Richard C. Martin, "Discourse on Jihad in the Postmodern Era," in *Islamic Ethics of Life: Abortion, War, and Euthanasia*, ed. Jonathan E. Brockopp (Columbia, SC: University of South Carolina Press, 2003): 155–72, 160.

36 Arie W. Kruglanski, Michele J. Gelfand, Jocelyn J. Bélanger, Anna Sheveland, Malkanthi Hetiarachchi, and Rohan Gunaratna, "The Psychology of Radicalization and Deradicalization: How Significance Quest Impacts Violent Extremism," *Advances in Political Psychology* 35, no. S1 (2014): 69–93. https://doi.org/10.1111/pops.12163

37 See publication by Sadeq Rahimi and Raissa Graumans, "Reconsidering the Relationship between Integration and Radicalization," *Journal for Deradicalization* 15, no. 5 (2015): 28–62.

38 Mark Sedgwick, "The Concept of Radicalization as a Source of Confusion," *Terrorism and Political Violence* 22, no. 4 (2010): 479–94. https://doi.org/10.1080/09546553.2010.491009

39 Randy Borum, "Radicalization into Violent Extremism I: A Review of Social Science Theories," *Journal of Strategic Security* 4, no. 4 (2011): 7–36. https://doi.org/10.5038/1944-0472.4.4.1

40 Andrea Mura, "Religion and Islamic Radicalization," in *Routledge Handbook of Psychoanalytic Political Theory*, ed. Yannis Stavrakakis (New York: Routledge, 2019): 316–29.

41 Douglas E. Streusand, "What Does Jihad Mean?" *Middle East Quarterly* 4, no. 3 (1997): 9–17.

42 David Cook, *Understanding Jihad* (Berkeley, CA: University of California Press, 2015): 2.

43 Hanna E. Kassis, *A Concordance of the Qur'an* (Berkeley, CA: University of California Press, 1983).

44 Edwin Bakker, *Jihadi Terrorists in Europe, Their Characteristics and the Circumstances in Which They Joined Jihad: An Explanatory Study* (Wassenaar: Netherlands Institute of International Relations, 2006): 1

45 Thomas Hegghammer, "Should I Stay or Should I Go? Explaining Variation in Western Jihadists' Choice between Domestic and Foreign Fighting," *American Political Science Review* 107, no. 1 (2013): 1–157, 1. https://doi.org/10.1017/S0003055412000615

46 William Adair Davies, "Counterterrorism Effectiveness to *Jihadists* in Western Europe and the United States: We Are Losing the War on Terror," *Studies in Conflict & Terrorism* 41, no. 4 (2018): 281–96. https://doi.org/10.1080/1057610X.2017.1284447

47 Muhammad ibn Isma'il Bukhari, *The Translation of the Meaning of* Sahih al-Bukhari, trans. Muhammad Muhsin Khan, 8 vols. (Medina: Dar al-Fikr: 1981): 4:34–204.

48 Donatella Della Porta, *Social Movements, Political Violence, and the State: A Comparative Analysis of Italy and Germany* (Cambridge: Cambridge University Press, 1995).

49 Maxime Bérubé and Benoit Dupont, "Mujahideen Mobilization: Examining the Evolution of the Global Jihadist Movement's Communicative Action Repertoire," *Studies in Conflict & Terrorism* 42, no. 1 (2019): 5–24. https://doi.org/10.1080/1057610X.2018.1513689

50 Cook, *Understanding Jihad*, 37.

51 Jerrold M. Post, "Reframing of Martyrdom and Jihad and the Socialization of Suicide Terrorists," *Political Psychology* 30, no. 3 (2009): 381–5.

52 Paul L. Heck, "*Jihad* Revisited," *Journal of Religious Ethics* 32, no. 1 (2004): 95–128. https://doi.org/10.1111/j.0384-9694.2004.00156.x

53 Hamdi Muluk, Nathanael G. Sumaktoyo, and Dhyah Madya Ruth, "Jihad as Justification: National Survey Evidence of Belief in Violent Jihad as a Mediating Factor for Sacred Violence among Muslims in Indonesia," *Asian Journal of Social Psychology* 16, no. 2 (2013): 101–11. https://doi.org/10.1111/ajsp.12002

54 Charles W. Amjad-Ali, "Jihad and Just War Theory: Dissonance and Truth," *Dialog* 48, no. 3 (2009): 239–47. https://doi.org/10.1111/j.1540-6385.2009.00467.x

55 Post, "Reframing of Martyrdom and Jihad," 383.

56 Richard C. Martin, "Striving in the Path of Allah: A Fundamentalist Interpretation of *Jihad* in Egypt," *Conflict Quarterly* 7, no. 2 (1987): 5–19.

57 Shireen K. Burki, "Jihad or Qatal? Examining Al Qaeda's *Modus Operandi*," *Defense & Security Analysis* 29, no. 3 (2013): 234–52. https://doi.org/10.1080/14751798.2013.820965

58 Joshua J. Yates, "The Resurgence of Jihad & The Specter of Religious Populism," *SAIS Review of International Affairs* 27, no. 1 (2007): 127–44. https://doi.org/10.1353/sais.2007.0022

59 John L. Esposito, *Islam: The Straight Path* (New York: Oxford University Press, 1988); John L. Esposito, *Islam and Politics* (Syracuse, NY: Syracuse University Press, 1998).

60 Mangol Bayat, *Mysticism and Dissent: Socioreligious Thought in Qajar Iran* (Syracuse, NY: Syracuse University Press, 1999).

61 Lloyd Steffen, *Holy War, Just War: Exploring the Moral Meaning of Religious Violence* (Lanham, MD: Rowman & Littlefield, 2007).

62 Assaf Moghadam, "Mayhem, Myths, and Martyrdom: The Shi'a Conception of Jihad," *Terrorism and Political Violence* 19, no. 1 (2007): 125–43. https://doi.org/10.1080/09546550601079656

63 Bernard Lewis, *The Crisis of Islam: Holy War and Unholy Terror* (London: Weidenfeld & Nicholson, 2003).

64 Sherman Jackson, "Jihad and the Modern World," *Journal of Islamic Law and Culture* 7, no. 1 (2002): 1–26.

65 Ibid, 85–7.

66 Nelly Lahoud, "The Neglected Sex: The Jihadis' Exclusion of Women from Jihad," *Terrorism and Political Violence* 26, no. 5 (2014): 780–802, 782. https://doi.org/10.1080/09546553.2013.772511

67 Majid Khadduri, *The Islamic Law of Nations: Shaybani's Siyar* (Baltimore, MD: Johns Hopkins University Press, 1966): 298.

68 Nelly Lahoud, *The Jihadis' Path to Self-Destruction* (New York: Columbia University Press, 2010).

69 Thomas Hegghammer, *Jihad in Saudi Arabia* (Cambridge: Cambridge University Press, 2010).

70 'Abdallah Azzam, "al-Difa' 'an Aradi al-Muslimin Ahamm Furud al-A'yan," in *Hilf al-Irhab: Tanzim al-Qa'ida*, ed. 'Abd al-Rahim 'Ali (Cairo: Markaz al-Mahrusa, 2004): 116–7, 116.

71 Arshin Adib-Moghaddam, "On 'Islamic' Politics and the Resistance in Iraq," *International Studies Journal* 5, no. 4 (2009): 1–36.

72 Leonard Binder, "Comment on Gelvin's Essay on Al-Qaeda and Anarchism," *Terrorism and Political Violence* 20, no. 4 (2008): 582–8. https://doi.org/10.1080/09546550802257325; Nimrod Raphaeli, "Ayman Muhammad Rabi' Al-Zawahiri:

The Making of an Arch-Terrorist," *Terrorism and Political Violence* 14, no. 4 (2002): 1–22. https://doi.org/10.1080/714005636

73 Cited in Christopher M. Blanchard, *Al Qaeda: Statements and Evolving Ideology* (Washington, D.C.: Congressional Research Service, 2007): 13.

74 Samir Amghar, "Salafism and Radicalisation of Young European Muslims," in *European Islam: Challenges for Public Policy and Society*, ed. Samir Amghar, Amel Boubekeur, and Michael Emerson (Brussels: Centre for European Policy Studies, 2007): 38–51.

75 Ibid, 40–7.

76 Madawi Al-Rasheed, "The Quest to Understand Global Jihad: The Terrorism Industry and Its Discontents," *Middle Eastern Studies* 45, no. 2 (2009): 329–38. https://doi.org/10.1080/00263200802699445

77 Samir Amghar, "Salafism and Radicalisation," 40–4.

78 Ibid, 40.

79 Bernard Haykel, "On the Nature of Salafi Thought and Action," in *Global Salafism*, ed. Roel Meijer (New York: Oxford University Press, 2009): 34–48.

80 Torelli, Merone, and Cavatorta, "Salafism in Tunisia," 141–4.

81 Kamran Bokhari, "Salafism and Arab Democratization," *Geopolitical Weekly* 12 (2012): 10–21.

82 Monica Marks, "Youth Politics and Tunisian Salafism: Understanding the Jihadi Current," *Mediterranean Politics* 18, no. 1 (2013): 104–11. https://doi.org/10.1080/13629395.2013.764657

83 Carmen Becker, "Muslims on the Path of the Salaf Al-Salih," *Information, Communication & Society* 14, no. 8 (2011): 1181–203. https://doi.org/10.1080/1369118X.2011.597414

84 Janis Just, *Jihad 2.0: The Impact of Social Media on the Salafist Scene and the Nature of Terrorism* (Harpswell, ME: Anchor Publishing, 2015).

85 See Alaya Allani, "The Islamists in Tunisia between Confrontation and Participation: 1980–2008," *The Journal of North African Studies* 14, no. 2 (2009): 257–72. https://doi.org/10.1080/13629380902727510; Ayesha Siddiqa, "Jihadism in Pakistan: The Expanding Frontier," *Journal of International Affairs* 63, no. 1 (2009): 57–71.

86 Ed Husain, *The House of Islam: A Global History* (London: Bloomsbury Publishing, 2018): Chapter 10.

87 Khalil al-Anani and Maszlee Malik, "Pious Way to Politics: The Rise of Political Salafism in Post-Mubarak Egypt," *DOMES: Digest of Middle East Studies* 22, no. 1 (2013): 57–73.

88 Andrew Wimhurst, *Shaping Positive Muslim Identity: A Policy Approach to Understanding the Formation of Prejudice—and Building Social Resilience—in Childhood* (Canberra: Centre for Defence and Strategic Studies, 2017).

89 *The Week*, "What Is Salafism and Should We Be Worried by It?" *The Week* (2015, January 19): A1.

90 Angel Rabasa and Cheryl Benard, *Eurojihad: Patterns of Islamist Radicalisation and Terrorism in Europe* (Cambridge: Cambridge University Press, 2015): 192.

91 Thomas Rid, "Cracks in the Jihad," *The Wilson Quarterly* 35, no. 4 (2010): 40–7.

92 Adraoui, "Purist Salafism in France," 12.

93 Ibid, 12–3.

94 Rabasa and Benard, *Eurojihad*, 192.

95 Bart Schuurman, Edwin Bakker, and Quirine Eijkman, "Structural Influences on Involvement in European Homegrown Jihadism: A Case Study," *Terrorism and Political Violence* 30, no. 1 (2018): 97–115. https://doi.org/10.1080/09546553.2016.1158165

96 Daniel E. Agbiboa, "Boko-Haram and the Global Jihad: 'Do Not Think Jihad Is Over. Rather Jihad Has Just Begun'." *Australian Journal of International Affairs* 68, no. 4 (2014): 400–17. https://doi.org/10.1080/10357718.2014.891564

97 Robin L. Thompson, "Radicalization and the Use of Social Media," *Journal of Strategic Security* 4, no. 4 (2012): 167–90. https://doi.org/10.5038/1944-0472.4.4.8

98 J. Antonio Romero, "The Different Faces of Islamic Terrorism," *International Review of Sociology* 17, no. 3 (2007): 443–58. https://doi.org/10.1080/03906700701574364

99   Assaf Moghadam, "The Salafi-Jihad as a Religious Ideology," *CTC Sentinel* 1, no. 3 (2008): 1–3.
100 Ibid, 2.
101 Mark Juergensmeyer, *Terror in the Mind of God: The Global Rise in Religious Violence* (Berkeley, CA: University of California Press, 2000).
102 Eli Berman and David Laitin, "Rational Martyrs versus Hard Targets: Evidence on the Tactical Use of Suicide Attacks," in *Suicide Bombing from an Interdisciplinary Perspective,* ed. Eva Meyerson Milgrom (Princeton: Princeton University Press, 2006): 16–23.
103 Walter Enders and Todd Sandler, "Is Transnational Terrorism Becoming More Threatening? A Time-Series Investigation," *Journal of Conflict Resolution* 44, no. 3 (2000): 307–32.
104 Ibid, 311.
105 James A. Piazza, "Is Islamist Terrorism More Dangerous? An Empirical Study of Group Ideology, Organization, and Goal Structure," *Terrorism and Political Violence* 21, no. 1 (2009): 62–88. https://doi.org/10.1080/09546550802544698
106 Albert Bandura, "The Origins and Consequences of Moral Disengagement: A Social Learning Perspective," in *Understanding Terrorism: Psychosocial Roots, Consequences, and Interventions,* ed. Fathali M. Moghaddam and Anthony J. Marsella (Washington, D.C.: American Psychological Association, 2004): 138–54, 121.
107 Randy Borum, "Radicalization into Violent Extremism I," 10–4.
108 Gresham Sykes and David Matza, "Techniques of Neutralization: A Theory of Delinquency," *American Sociological Review* 22, no. 6 (1957): 664–70. https://doi.org/10.2307/2089195
109 Randy Borum, "Understanding the Terrorist Mindset," *FBI Law Enforcement Bulletin* 72, no. 7 (2003): 7–10.
110 Pete Lentini, "Antipodal Terrorists? Accounting for Differences in Australian 'Global' Neojihadists," in *The Globalization of Political Violence: Globalization's Shadow,* ed. Richard Devetak and Christopher W. Hughes (London: Routledge, 2008), 188–210, 191.
111 Pete Lentini, *Neojihadism: Towards a New Understanding of Terrorism and Extremism?* (Cheltenham: Edward Elgar Publishing, 2013).
112 Virginie André, "'Neojihadism' and YouTube: Patani Militant Propaganda Dissemination and Radicalization," *Asian Security* 8, no. 1 (2012): 27–53. https://doi.org/10.1080/14799855.2012.669207
113 Matthew Feldman, "Comparative Lone Wolf Terrorism: Toward a Heuristic Definition," Democracy and Security 9, no. 3 (2013): 271. https://doi.org/10.1080/17419166.2013.792252.
114 Nuria Lorenzo-Dus, Anina Kinzel, and Luke Walker, "Representing the West and 'Non-Believers' in the Online Jihadist Magazines *Dabiq* and *Inspire*," *Critical Studies on Terrorism* 11, no. 3 (2018): 521–36. https://doi.org/10.1080/17539153.2018.1471081
115 Logan Macnair and Richard Frank, "The Mediums and the Messages: Exploring the Language of Islamic State Media through Sentiment Analysis," *Critical Studies on Terrorism* 11, no. 3 (2018): 438–57. https://doi.org/10.1080/17539153.2018.1447226
116 Cited in Ramón Spaaij, "Lone Wolf Terrorism," in *The SAGE Encyclopedia of Political Behavior,* ed. Fathali M. Moghaddam (Thousand Oaks, CA: Sage, 2017): 453–54.
117 See Nathan González Mendelejis, "Toward a New Typology of Sunni Jihad," *Studies in Conflict & Terrorism* (2019). https://doi.org/10.1080/1057610X.2018.1520797; Valerie Gray Hardcastle, "Lone Wolf Terrorists and the Impotence of Moral Enhancement," *Royal Institute of Philosophy Supplements* 83 (2018): 271–91. https://doi.org/10.1017/S1358246118000395; Jessica Mueller and Ronn Johnson, "Emerging Trends in Technology and Forensic Psychological Roots of Radicalization and Lone Wolf Terrorists," in *Emerging and Advanced Technologies in Diverse Forensic Sciences,* ed. Ronn Johnson (New York: Routledge, 2018): Chapter 1.
118 George Hough, "Does Psychoanalysis Have Anything to Offer an Understanding of Terrorism?" *Journal of the American Psychoanalytic Association* 52, no. 3 (2004): 813–28. https://doi.org/10.1177/00030651040520031101

119 Ramón Spaaij and Mark S. Hamm, "Key Issues and Research Agendas in Lone Wolf Terrorism," Studies in Conflict & Terrorism 38, no. 3 (2015): 170–1. https://doi.org/10.1080/1057610X.2014.986979

120 Sarah Gilkes, Not Just the Caliphate: Non-Islamic State-Related Jihadist Terrorism in America (Washington, D.C.: Program on Extremism, George Washington University, 2016).

121 William Adair Davies, "Counterterrorism Effectiveness to Jihadists," 284–8.

122 Ibid, 281.

123 Gabriel Weimann, "Lone Wolves in Cyberspace," Journal of Terrorism Research 3, no. 2 (2012): 75–90. https://doi.org/10.15664/jtr.405

124 Michael Hardt and Antonio Negri, Multitude: War and Democracy in the Age of Empire (London: Hamish Hamilton, 2005).

125 Alex Thio, Deviant Behavior (10th Ed.) (Boston: Allyn & Bacon, 2010).

126 Luca Ricolfi, "Palestinians, 1981–2003," in Making Sense of Suicide Missions, ed. Diego Gambetta (New York: Oxford University Press, 2005): 77–129.

127 Jarret Brachman, Global Jihadism: Theory and Practice (New York: Routledge, 2008).

128 Ibid, 19.

129 Caroline Joan S. Picart, "'Jihad Cool/Jihad Chic:' The Roles of the Internet and Imagined Relations in the Self-Radicalization of Colleen LaRose (Jihad Jane)," Societies 5, no. 2 (2015): 354–83. https://doi.org/10.3390/soc5020354

130 Bruce Hoffman, "Radicalization and Subversion: Al Qaeda and the 7 July 2005 Bombings and the 2006 Airline Bombing Plot," Studies in Conflict & Terrorism 32, no. 12 (2009): 1100–16. https://doi.org/10.1080/10576100903319896

131 Anthony Giddens, The Consequences of Modernity (Cambridge: Polity, 1990).

132 Zygmunt Bauman, Intimations of Postmodernity (London: Routledge, 1992); Jock Young, The Vertigo of Late Modernity (London: Sage, 2007).

133 Stuart Croft, "Constructing Ontological Insecurity: The Insecuritization of Britain's Muslims," Contemporary Security Policy 33, no. 2 (2012): 219–35. https://doi.org/10.1080/13523260.2012.693776

134 Fenna Van Marle and Shadd Maruna, "'Ontological Insecurity' and 'Terror Management'," Punishment & Society 12, no. 1 (2010): 7–26. https://doi.org/10.1177/1462474509349084

135 David Garland, The Culture of Control: Crime and Social Order in Contemporary Society (Oxford: Oxford University Press, 2001): 154.

136 Ibid, 155.

137 Adam Lankford, The Myth of Martyrdom: What Really Drives Suicide Bombers, Rampage Shooters, and Other Self-Destructive Killers (New York: Palgrave Macmillan, 2013).

138 Shaun Best, "Liquid Terrorism: Altruistic Fundamentalism in the Context of Liquid Modernity," Sociology 44, no. 4 (2010): 678–94. https://doi.org/10.1177/0038038510369355

139 Ibid, 680–3.

140 Anthony Giddens, Modernity and Self-Identity: Self and Society in the Late Modern Age (Cambridge: Polity, 1991): 38.

141 Catarina Kinnvall, "Globalization and Religious Nationalism: Self, Identity, and the Search for Ontological Security," Political Psychology 25, no. 5 (2004): 741–67, 741. https://doi.org/10.1111/j.1467-9221.2004.00396.x

References

Adib-Moghaddam, Arshin, "On 'Islamic' Politics and the Resistance in Iraq," International Studies Journal 5, no. 4 (2009): 1–36.

Adraoui, Mohamed Ali, "Purist Salafism in France," ISIM Review 21, no. 1 (2008): 12–13.

Agbiboa, Daniel E., "Boko-Haram and the Global Jihad: 'Do Not Think Jihad Is Over. Rather Jihad Has Just Begun'." Australian Journal of International Affairs 68, no. 4 (2014): 400–417. https://doi.org/10.1080/10357718.2014.891564.

al-Anani, Khalil, and Maszlee Malik, "Pious Way to Politics: The Rise of Political Salafism in Post-Mubarak Egypt," *DOMES: Digest of Middle East Studies* 22, no. 1 (2013): 57–73.

Al-Islami, Motamar al-Alam, *Islamic Culture: A Few Angles*. Karachi: Umma Publishing House, 1964.

Allani, Alaya, "The Islamists in Tunisia between Confrontation and Participation: 1980–2008," *The Journal of North African Studies* 14, no. 2 (2009): 257–272. https://doi.org/10.1080/13629380902727510.

Allawi, Ali A., *The Occupation of Iraq: Winning the War, Losing the Peace*. New Haven, CT: Yale University Press, 2007.

Al-Rasheed, Madawi, "The Quest to Understand Global Jihad: The Terrorism Industry and Its Discontents," *Middle Eastern Studies* 45, no. 2 (2009): 329–338. https://doi.org/10.1080/00263200802699445.

Amghar, Samir, "Salafism and Radicalisation of Young European Muslims," in *European Islam: Challenges for Public Policy and Society*, edited by Samir Amghar, Amel Boubekeur, and Michael Emerson, 38–51. Brussels: Centre for European Policy Studies, 2007.

Amjad-Ali, Charles W., "Jihad and Just War Theory: Dissonance and Truth," *Dialog* 48, no. 3 (2009): 239–247. https://doi.org/10.1111/j.1540-6385.2009.00467.x.

André, Virginie, "'Neojihadism' and YouTube: Patani Militant Propaganda Dissemination and Radicalization," *Asian Security* 8, no. 1 (2012): 27–53. https://doi.org/10.1080/14799855.2012.669207.

Armanios, Febe, *Islam: Sunnis and Shiites*. Washington, D.C.: CRS Report for Congress, 2004.

Azzam, 'Abdallah, "al-Difa' 'an Aradi al-Muslimin Ahamm Furud al-A'yan," in *Hilf al-Irhab: Tanzim al-Qa'ida*, edited by 'Abd al-Rahim 'Ali, 116–117. Cairo: Markaz al-Mahrusa, 2004.

Bakker, Edwin, *Jihadi Terrorists in Europe, Their Characteristics and the Circumstances in Which They Joined Jihad: An Explanatory Study*. Wassenaar: Netherlands Institute of International Relations, 2006.

Bandura, Albert, "The Origins and Consequences of Moral Disengagement: A Social Learning Perspective," in *Understanding Terrorism: Psychosocial Roots, Consequences, and Interventions*, edited by Fathali M. Moghaddam and Anthony J. Marsella, 138–154. Washington, D.C.: American Psychological Association, 2004.

Bauman, Zygmunt, *Intimations of Postmodernity*. London: Routledge, 1992.

Bauman, Zygmunt, *Postmodernity and Its Discontents*. New York: New York University Press, 1997.

Bayat, Mangol, *Mysticism and Dissent: Socioreligious Thought in Qajar Iran*. Syracuse, NY: Syracuse University Press, 1999.

Becker, Carmen, "Muslims on the Path of the Salaf Al-Salih," *Information, Communication & Society* 14, no. 8 (2011): 1181–1203. https://doi.org/10.1080/1369118X.2011.597414.

Berman, Eli, and David Laitin, "Rational Martyrs versus Hard Targets: Evidence on the Tactical Use of Suicide Attacks," in *Suicide Bombing from an Interdisciplinary Perspective*, edited by Eva Meyerson Milgrom, 16–23. Princeton: Princeton University Press, 2006.

Bérubé, Maxime, and Benoit Dupont, "Mujahideen Mobilization: Examining the Evolution of the Global Jihadist Movement's Communicative Action Repertoire," *Studies in Conflict & Terrorism* 42, no. 1 (2019): 5–24. https://doi.org/10.1080/1057610X.2018.1513689.

Best, Shaun, "Liquid Terrorism: Altruistic Fundamentalism in the Context of Liquid Modernity," *Sociology* 44, no. 4 (2010): 678–694. https://doi.org/10.1177/0038038510369355.

Binder, Leonard, "Comment on Gelvin's Essay on Al-Qaeda and Anarchism," *Terrorism and Political Violence* 20, no. 4 (2008): 582–588. https://doi.org/10.1080/09546550802257325.

Blanchard, Christopher M., *Al Qaeda: Statements and Evolving Ideology*. Washington, D.C.: Congressional Research Service, 2007.

Bokhari, Kamran, "Salafism and Arab Democratization," *Geopolitical Weekly* 12 (2012): 10–21.

Borum, Randy, "Understanding the Terrorist Mindset," *FBI Law Enforcement Bulletin* 72, no. 7 (2003): 7–10.

Borum, Randy, "Radicalization into Violent Extremism I: A Review of Social Science Theories," *Journal of Strategic Security* 4, no. 4 (2011): 7–36. https://doi.org/10.5038/1944-0472.4.4.1.

Brachman, Jarret, *Global Jihadism: Theory and Practice*. New York: Routledge, 2008.

Buijs, Frank J., Froukje Demant, and Atef Hamdy, *Warriors from Own Soil: Radical and Democratic Muslims in the Netherlands*. Amsterdam: Amsterdam University Press, 2006.

Bukhari, Muhammad ibn Isma'il, *The Translation of the Meaning of Sahih al-Bukhari*, trans. Muhammad Muhsin Khan, 8 vols. Medina: Dar al-Fikr, 1981.

Burki, Shireen K., "Jihad or Qatal? Examining Al Qaeda's *Modus Operandi*," *Defense & Security Analysis* 29, no. 3 (2013): 234–252. https://doi.org/10.1080/14751798.2013.820965.

Cesari, Jocelyne, *Why the West Fear Islam: An Exploration of Muslims in Liberal Democracies*. New York: Palgrave Macmillan, 2013.

Cook, David, *Understanding Jihad*. Berkeley, CA: University of California Press, 2015.

Croft, Stuart, "Constructing Ontological Insecurity: The Insecuritization of Britain's Muslims," *Contemporary Security Policy* 33, no. 2 (2012): 219–235. https://doi.org/10.1080/13523260.2012.693776.

Davies, William Adair, "Counterterrorism Effectiveness to *Jihadists* in Western Europe and the United States: We Are Losing the War on Terror," *Studies in Conflict & Terrorism* 41, no. 4 (2018): 281–296. https://doi.org/10.1080/1057610X.2017.1284447.

Della Porta, Donatella, *Social Movements, Political Violence, and the State: A Comparative Analysis of Italy and Germany*. Cambridge: Cambridge University Press, 1995.

DeSilver, Drew, and David Masci, *World's Muslim Population More Widespread than You Might Think*. Washington, D.C.: Pew Research Center, 2017.

Doosje, Bertjan, Annemarie Loseman, and Kees van den Bos, "Determinants of Radicalization of Islamic Youth in the Netherlands: Personal Uncertainty, Perceived Injustice, and Perceived Group Threat," *Journal of Social Issues* 69, no. 3 (2013): 586–604. https://doi.org/10.1111/josi.12030.

Eickelman, Dale F., *The Middle East and Central Asia: An Anthropological Approach* (4th ed.). London: Pearson, 2001.

Enders, Walter, and Todd Sandler, "Is Transnational Terrorism Becoming More Threatening? A Time-Series Investigation," *Journal of Conflict Resolution* 44, no. 3 (2000): 307–332.

Esposito, John L., *Islam: The Straight Path*. New York: Oxford University Press, 1988.

Esposito, John L., *Islam and Politics*. Syracuse, NY: Syracuse University Press, 1998.

Feldman, Matthew, "Comparative Lone Wolf Terrorism: Toward a Heuristic Definition," *Democracy and Security* 9, no. 3 (2013): 270–286. https://doi.org/10.1080/17419166.2013.792252.

Garland, David, *The Culture of Control: Crime and Social Order in Contemporary Society*. Oxford: Oxford University Press, 2001.

Giddens, Anthony, *The Consequences of Modernity*. Cambridge: Polity, 1990.

Giddens, Anthony, *Modernity and Self-Identity: Self and Society in the Late Modern Age*. Cambridge: Polity, 1991.

Gilkes, Sarah, *Not Just the Caliphate: Non-Islamic State-Related Jihadist Terrorism in America*. Washington, D.C.: Program on Extremism, George Washington University, 2016.

González Mendelejis, Nathan, "Toward a New Typology of Sunni Jihad," *Studies in Conflict & Terrorism* (2019). https://doi.org/10.1080/1057610X.2018.1520797.

Gray Hardcastle, Valerie, "Lone Wolf Terrorists and the Impotence of Moral Enhancement," *Royal Institute of Philosophy Supplements* 83 (2018): 271–291. https://doi.org/10.1017/S1358246118000395.

Hackett, Conrad, *5 Facts about the Muslim Population in Europe*. Washington, D.C.: Pew Research Center, 2017.

Hackett, Conrad, and David McClendon, *Christians Remain World's Largest Religious Group, but They Are Declining in Europe*. Washington, D.C.: Pew Research Center, 2017.

Hafez, Mohammed, "Martyrdom Mythology in Iraq: How Jihadists Frame Suicide Terrorism in Videos and Biographies," *Terrorism and Political Violence* 19, no. 1 (2007): 95–115. https://doi.org/10.1080/09546550601054873.

Hamid, Tawfik, *Inside Jihad*. Mountain Lake Park, MD: Mountain Lake Press, 2010.

Hardt, Michael, and Antonio Negri, *Multitude: War and Democracy in the Age of Empire*. London: Hamish Hamilton, 2005.

Harris, Sam, *Letter to a Christian Nation*. New York: Vintage, 2006.

Haykel, Bernard, "On the Nature of Salafi Thought and Action," in *Global Salafism*, edited by Roel Meijer, 34–48. New York: Oxford University Press, 2009.

Heck, Paul L., "*Jihad* Revisited," *Journal of Religious Ethics* 32, no. 1 (2004): 95–128. https://doi.org/10.1111/j.0384-9694.2004.00156.x.

Hegghammer, Thomas, *Jihad in Saudi Arabia*, Cambridge: Cambridge University Press, 2010.

Hegghammer, Thomas, "Should I Stay or Should I Go? Explaining Variation in Western Jihadists' Choice between Domestic and Foreign Fighting," *American Political Science Review* 107, no. 1 (2013): 1–157. https://doi.org/10.1017/S0003055412000615.

Hoffman, Bruce, "Radicalization and Subversion: Al Qaeda and the 7 July 2005 Bombings and the 2006 Airline Bombing Plot," *Studies in Conflict & Terrorism* 32, no. 12 (2009): 1100–1116. https://doi.org/10.1080/10576100903319896.

Horgan, John, "Individual Disengagement: A Psychological Analysis," in *Leaving Terrorism Behind: Individual and Collective Disengagement*, edited by Tore Bjorgo and John G. Horgan, 35–47. New York: Routledge, 2008.

Hough, George, "Does Psychoanalysis Have Anything to Offer an Understanding of Terrorism?" *Journal of the American Psychoanalytic Association* 52, no. 3 (2004): 813–828. https://doi.org/10.1177/00030651040520031101.

Husain, Ed, *The House of Islam: A Global History*. London: Bloomsbury Publishing, 2018.

Jackson, Sherman, "Jihad and the Modern World," *Journal of Islamic Law and Culture* 7, no. 1 (2002): 1–26.

Jansen, Johannes J. G., *The Neglected Duty: The Creed of Sadat's Assassins and Islamic Resurgence in the Middle East*. New York: Macmillan, 1986.

Jenkins, Richard, *Social Identity*. London: Routledge, 1996.

Juergensmeyer, Mark, *Terror in the Mind of God: The Global Rise in Religious Violence*. Berkeley: University of California Press, 2000.

Just, Janis, *Jihad 2.0: The Impact of Social Media on the Salafist Scene and the Nature of Terrorism*. Harpswell, ME: Anchor Publishing, 2015.

Karagiannis, Emmanuel, "Transnational Islamist Networks: Western Fighters in Afghanistan, Somalia and Syria," *The International Spectator* 48, no. 4 (2013): 119–134. https://doi.org/10.1080/03932729.2013.847696.

Kassis, Hanna E., *A Concordance of the Qur'an*. Berkeley: University of California Press, 1983.

Khadduri, Majid, *The Islamic Law of Nations: Shaybani's Siyar*. Baltimore, MD: Johns Hopkins University Press, 1966.

Kinnvall, Catarina, "Globalization and Religious Nationalism: Self, Identity, and the Search for Ontological Security," *Political Psychology* 25, no. 5 (2004): 741–767. https://doi.org/10.1111/j.1467-9221.2004.00396.x.

Kruglanski, Arie W., Michele J. Gelfand, Jocelyn J. Bélanger, Anna Sheveland, Malkanthi Hetiarachchi, and Rohan Gunaratna, "The Psychology of Radicalization and Deradicalization: How Significance Quest Impacts Violent Extremism," *Advances in Political Psychology* 35, no. S1 (2014): 69–93. https://doi.org/10.1111/pops.12163.

Lahoud, Nelly, *The Jihadis' Path to Self-Destruction*, New York: Columbia University Press, 2010.

Lahoud, Nelly, "The Neglected Sex: The Jihadis' Exclusion of Women from Jihad," *Terrorism and Political Violence* 26, no. 5 (2014): 780–802. https://doi.org/10.1080/09546553.2013.772511.

Lankford, Adam, *The Myth of Martyrdom: What Really Drives Suicide Bombers, Rampage Shooters, and Other Self-Destructive Killers*. New York: Palgrave Macmillan, 2013.

Lentini, Pete, "Antipodal Terrorists? Accounting for Differences in Australian 'Global' Neojihadists," in *The Globalization of Political Violence: Globalization's Shadow*, edited by Richard Devetak and Christopher W. Hughes, 188–210. London: Routledge, 2008.

Lentini, Pete, *Neojihadism: Towards a New Understanding of Terrorism and Extremism?* Cheltenham: Edward Elgar Publishing, 2013.

Lewis, Bernard, "Legal and Historical Reflections on the Position of Muslim Populations under Non-Muslim Rule," in *Muslims in Europe*, edited by Bernard Lewis and Dominique Schnapper, 1–18. London: Pinter, 1994.

Lewis, Bernard, *The Crisis of Islam: Holy War and Unholy Terror*. London: Weidenfeld & Nicholson, 2003.

Lipka, Michael, *Muslims and Islam: Key Findings in the U.S. and around the World*. Washington, D.C.: Pew Research Center, 2017.

Lorenzo-Dus, Nuria, Anina Kinzel, and Luke Walker, "Representing the West and 'Non-Believers' in the Online Jihadist Magazines *Dabiq* and *Inspire*," *Critical Studies on Terrorism* 11, no. 3 (2018): 521–536. https://doi.org/10.1080/17539153.2018.1471081.

Loza, Wagdy, "The Psychology of Extremism and Terrorism: A Middle-Eastern Perspective," *Aggression & Violent Behavior* 12, no. 2 (2007): 141–155. https://doi.org/10.1016/j.avb.2006.09.001.

Lynch, Marc, "Islam Divided between Salafi-Jihad and the Ikhwan," *Studies in Conflict & Terrorism* 33, no. 6 (2010): 467–487. https://doi.org/10.1080/10576101003752622.

Macnair, Logan, and Richard Frank, "The Mediums and the Messages: Exploring the Language of Islamic State Media through Sentiment Analysis," *Critical Studies on Terrorism* 11, no. 3 (2018): 438–457. https://doi.org/10.1080/17539153.2018.1447226.

Marks, Monica, "Youth Politics and Tunisian Salafism: Understanding the Jihadi Current," *Mediterranean Politics* 18, no. 1 (2013): 104–111. https://doi.org/10.1080/13629395.2013.764657.

Martin, Richard C., "Striving in the Path of Allah: A Fundamentalist Interpretation of *Jihad* in Egypt," *Conflict Quarterly* 7, no. 2 (1987): 5–19.

Martin, Richard C., "Discourse on Jihad in the Postmodern Era," in *Islamic Ethics of Life: Abortion, War, and Euthanasia*, edited by Jonathan E.Brockopp, 155–172. Columbia, SC: University of South Carolina Press, 2003.

Mazarr, Michael J., "The Psychological Sources of Islamic Terrorism: Alienation and Identity in the Arab World," *Policy Review* 125 (2004): 39–60.

McCauley, Clark, and Sophia Moskalenko, "Mechanisms of Political Radicalization: Pathways toward Terrorism," *Terrorism and Political Violence* 20, no. 3 (2008): 415–433. https://doi.org/10.1080/09546550802073367.

Mernissi, Fatima, *Women's Rebellion and Islamic Memory*. New York: Saint Martin's Press, 1996.

Moghadam, Assaf, "Mayhem, Myths, and Martyrdom: The Shi'a Conception of Jihad," *Terrorism and Political Violence* 19, no. 1 (2007): 125–143. https://doi.org/10.1080/09546550601079656.

Moghadam, Assaf, "The Salafi-Jihad as a Religious Ideology," *CTC Sentinel* 1, no. 3 (2008): 1–3.

Mottahedeh, Roy, *The Mantle of the Prophet*. New York: Pantheon Books, 1985.

Mozaffari, Mehdi, "What Is Islamism? History and Definition of a Concept," *Totalitarian Movements and Political Religions* 8, no. 1 (2007): 17–33. https://doi.org/10.1080/14690760601121622.

Mueller, Jessica, and Ronn Johnson, "Emerging Trends in Technology and Forensic Psychological Roots of Radicalization and Lone Wolf Terrorists," in *Emerging and Advanced Technologies in Diverse Forensic Sciences*, edited by Ronn Johnson, Chapter 1. New York: Routledge, 2018.

Muluk, Hamdi, Nathanael G. Sumaktoyo, and Dhyah Madya Ruth, "Jihad as Justification: National Survey Evidence of Belief in Violent Jihad as a Mediating Factor for Sacred Violence among Muslims in Indonesia," *Asian Journal of Social Psychology* 16, no. 2 (2013): 101–111. https://doi.org/10.1111/ajsp.12002.

Mura, Andrea, "Religion and Islamic Radicalization," in *Routledge Handbook of Psychoanalytic Political Theory*, edited by Yannis Stavrakakis, 316–329. New York: Routledge, 2019.

Perry, Simon, and Badi Hasisi, "Rational Choice Rewards and the Jihadist Suicide Bomber," *Terrorism and Political Violence* 27, no. 1 (2015): 53–80. https://doi.org/10.1080/09546553.2014.962991.

Piazza, James A., "Is Islamist Terrorism More Dangerous? An Empirical Study of Group Ideology, Organization, and Goal Structure," *Terrorism and Political Violence* 21, no. 1 (2009): 62–88. https://doi.org/10.1080/09546550802544698.

Picart, Caroline Joan S., "'Jihad Cool/Jihad Chic:' The Roles of the Internet and Imagined Relations in the Self-Radicalization of Colleen LaRose (Jihad Jane)," *Societies* 5, no. 2 (2015): 354–383. https://doi.org/10.3390/soc5020354.

Post, Jerrold M., "Reframing of Martyrdom and Jihad and the Socialization of Suicide Terrorists," *Political Psychology* 30, no. 3 (2009): 381–385. https://doi.org/10.1111/j.1467-9221.2009.00702.x.

Rabasa, Angel, and Cheryl Benard, *Eurojihad: Patterns of Islamist Radicalisation and Terrorism in Europe*. Cambridge: Cambridge University Press, 2015.

Rahimi, Sadeq, and Raissa Graumans, "Reconsidering the Relationship between Integration and Radicalization," *Journal for Deradicalization* 15, no. 5 (2015): 28–62.

Raphaeli, Nimrod, "Ayman Muhammad Rabi' Al-Zawahiri: The Making of an Arch-Terrorist," *Terrorism and Political Violence* 14, no. 4 (2002): 1–22. https://doi.org/10.1080/714005636.

Reed, Alastair, and Haroro J. Ingram, *Exploring the Role of Instructional Material in AQAP's Inspire and ISIS' Rumiyah*. The Hague: European Counter Terrorism Centre, 2017.

Renard, John, *Responses to 101 Questions on Islam*. Mahwah, NJ: Paulist Press, 1998.

Ricolfi, Luca, "Palestinians, 1981–2003," in *Making Sense of Suicide Missions*, edited by Diego Gambetta, 77–129. New York: Oxford University Press, 2005.

Rid, Thomas, "Cracks in the Jihad," *The Wilson Quarterly* 35, no. 4 (2010): 40–47.

Romero, J. Antonio, "The Different Faces of Islamic Terrorism," *International Review of Sociology* 17, no. 3 (2007): 443–458. https://doi.org/10.1080/03906700701574364.

Safi, Omid, "Who Put Hate in My Sunday Paper? Uncovering the Israeli-Republican-Evangelical Networks behind the 'Obsession' DVD," in *Muslims and Jews in America*, edited by Reza Aslan and Aaron Tapper, 21–32. New York: Palgrave Macmillan, 2011.

Schuurman, Bart, Edwin Bakker, and Quirine Eijkman, "Structural Influences on Involvement in European Homegrown Jihadism: A Case Study," *Terrorism and Political Violence* 30, no. 1 (2018): 97–115. https://doi.org/10.1080/09546553.2016.1158165.

Sedgwick, Mark, "The Concept of Radicalization as a Source of Confusion," *Terrorism and Political Violence* 22, no. 4 (2010): 479–494. https://doi.org/10.1080/09546553.2010.491009.

Sendagorta, Fidel, "Jihad in Europe: The Wider Context," *Survival* 47, no. 3 (2005): 63–72. https://doi.org/10.1080/00396330500248029.

Siddiqa, Ayesha, "Jihadism in Pakistan: The Expanding Frontier," *Journal of International Affairs* 63, no. 1 (2009): 57–71.

Spaaij, Ramón, "Lone Wolf Terrorism," in *The SAGE Encyclopedia of Political Behavior*, edited by Fathali M. Moghaddam, 453–454. Thousand Oaks, CA: Sage, 2017.

Spaaij, Ramón, and Mark S. Hamm, "Key Issues and Research Agendas in Lone Wolf Terrorism," *Studies in Conflict & Terrorism* 38, no. 3 (2015): 167–178. https://doi.org/10.1080/1057610X.2014.986979.

Steffen, Lloyd, *Holy War, Just War: Exploring the Moral Meaning of Religious Violence*. Lanham, MD: Rowman & Littlefield, 2007.

Streusand, Douglas E., "What Does Jihad Mean?" *Middle East Quarterly* 4, no. 3 (1997): 9–17.

Sykes, Gresham, and David Matza, "Techniques of Neutralization: A Theory of Delinquency," *American Sociological Review* 22, no. 6 (1957): 664–670. https://doi.org/10.2307/2089195.

Thio, Alex, *Deviant Behavior* (10th ed.). Boston, MA: Allyn & Bacon, 2010.

Thompson, Robin L., "Radicalization and the Use of Social Media," *Journal of Strategic Security* 4, no. 4 (2012): 167–190. https://doi.org/10.5038/1944-0472.4.4.8.

Torelli, Stefano M., Fabio Merone, and Francesco Cavatorta, "Salafism in Tunisia: Challenges and Opportunities for Democratization," *Middle East Policy* 19, no. 4 (2012): 140–154. https://doi.org/10.1111/j.1475-4967.2012.00566.x.

Van Marle, Fenna, and Shadd Maruna, "'Ontological Insecurity' and 'Terror Management'," *Punishment & Society* 12, no. 1 (2010): 7–26. https://doi.org/10.1177/1462474509349084.

Warner, Carolyn M., and Manfred W. Wenner, "Religion and the Political Organization of Muslims in Europe," *Perspectives on Politics* 4, no. 3 (2006): 457–479. https://doi.org/10.1017/S1537592706060300.

The Week, "What Is Salafism and Should We Be Worried by It?" *The Week* (2015, January 19): A1.

Weimann, Gabriel, "Lone Wolves in Cyberspace," *Journal of Terrorism Research* 3, no. 2 (2012): 75–90. https://doi.org/10.15664/jtr.405.

Wimhurst, Andrew, *Shaping Positive Muslim Identity: A Policy Approach to Understanding the Formation of Prejudice—and Building Social Resilience—in Childhood*. Canberra: Centre for Defence and Strategic Studies, 2017.

Yates, Joshua J., "The Resurgence of Jihad & The Specter of Religious Populism," *SAIS Review of International Affairs* 27, no. 1 (2007): 127–144. https://doi.org/10.1353/sais.2007.0022.

Young, Jock, *The Vertigo of Late Modernity*. London: Sage, 2007.

4

THE GLOBALIZATION OF JIHAD

The global jihad phenomenon is not only a conveyor of ethno-national alternatives; it is also an indicator of alternative spaces in which various new actors and overlapping national, regional, and global processes are present.[1] Globalization theory is often used to describe shifts in financial systems, trade dealings, transnational governance institutions, and so forth. This chapter advances the argument that globalization has changed the institution of terrorism, an idea that sparked an academic trend in the late twentieth century and has continued until today. The goals of international terrorism have been transformed through globalization. Foreign interferences and increasing awareness of shrinking global spaces have given more incentives to resort to the supreme asymmetrical weapon, terrorism, for more efficient results.[2]

Definitions

By and large, globalization denotes the ever-expanding, deepening, and facilitating of global interconnections,[3] which happen through social relations across space and time.[4] Explained differently, it is the mechanism of interaction and integration among individuals, groups, and institutions worldwide. As a complex and multidimensional phenomenon, globalization goes beyond the realm of technology to include cultural and ideological expansion as well.[5] Though there is a propensity to liken globalization to improvements in technology, particularly those pertaining to communication and capitalism, the term should be looked at as a more sweeping occurrence, distinguished by the growing pace of modern social life, what Harvey (1989)[6] calls "time-space compression" and the heightened importance of "rapidly developing and ever-densening networks of interconnections and interdependences."[7] Without a doubt, technology has been a chief stimulus of globalization. However, to reduce the phenomenon to the domain of technology is a gross oversight.

Sociologist and communication specialist Manuel Castells (2000)[8] considers globalization a type of "network society" rooted in and emboldened by new information and communication technologies. In particular, he contends that a network society driven by information technology is a domain in which "the space of flows—flows of information, technology, and finance—replaces the space of places, the rootedness of industrial work, the fixity of urban and rural life."[9] Globalization has witnessed significant transformations with respect to scale, speed, and cognition.[10] In regards to scale, the volume of economic, political, and social connections between people is greater than at any other time in history. In terms of speed, globalization is compressing time and space in an unparalleled fashion. In regards to cognition, the globe is perceived to be a smaller place (smaller by the day), so much so that any event on the planet can have an impact on our daily political, social, and economic life, affecting our wellbeing. This deterritorialization of time and space influences our everyday life; in a place of decreasing territorial barriers, the quest for continuous time- and space-bound identities can help individuals cope with the upshots of modern life.[11]

Critics of globalization

It is important to discuss globalization and jihad in ample detail. For Salafists and jihadists, globalization does not elicit positive feelings when it is perceived as a global Western product. The backlash against globalization symbolizes the objection to the way it homogenizes non-Western cultures and expunges their uniqueness. Globalization originates from and is fueled by U.S. institutions and technological advances. To Salafists and jihadists, globalization is Americanization, a perception that stokes the flames of the already-existing hostilities between the U.S. and the Muslim world. While a great many are impressed by America's prosperity, another great many look at it with resentment. This feeling is predicated on the belief that America has a monopoly over so many areas of life.[12] Those communities that feel bullied by globalization think that it is unremitting and unstoppable—a force that endangers their traditional, cultural identity. Fathers and mothers are concerned that their children will be raised as McDonald's-munching Americans in an ever-increasing imperialist world. As a result, violent acts of jihad against symbols of globalization and Western imperialism should come to no surprise.[13]

Globalization has been profoundly examined since the 1970s as a phenomenon that has the potential to unite people and, at the same time, tear them apart. In the contemporary world, there are many examples of such uniting and the fragmenting traits of globalization. Among critics in the West, some of whom are activists of the anti-globalization movement, globalization is portrayed as an adversary of social progress—the roots of poverty—and the foe of literacy, cultural independence, diversity, gender equality, the environment, etc. Outside the Western world, globalization is held in contempt because it is the driver of social progress with an undermining effect on traditional culture and religion.[14] From this vantage point, globalization is equated with Westernization, secularization, democratization, consumerism, and the unfettered expansion of the marketplace, all of which constitute an offensive on the downtrodden in conservative cultures. Such people become deterred by the fundamental changes inherent to globalization. They get frustrated by the problems and uneven distributions of the so-called benefits of globalization.[15]

Zygmunt Bauman (2001)[16] indicates that the contemporary era is mostly the perpetuation of capitalism's development, rather than a new phenomenon whose purpose is to unite people. The present-day globalized epoch of capitalism is, for Bauman, "sorely distorted, one-sided, and incomplete, suffering the consequences of blatantly uneven development."[17] Put another way, a highly developed global marketplace can be thoroughly felt, and it works side-by-side with an underdeveloped cultural and social network of helpless people or entities. Various categories of people from all corners of the globe come together and offer assistance in the event of a natural disaster in Myanmar or New Orleans, while others strongly resist the application of neo-liberal policies in Bolivia and the Westernization of India. What it is important to understand is that globalization is not integrally good or bad. The way we handle or guide it will determine what it becomes.

Global divergence

Global divergence reflects the notion that certain cultural and religious groups—no matter how large—are gradually deviating from beliefs or practices that differ from theirs. What such cultural and religious groups do is fashion a more cohesive identity that reduces their antagonistic relations with other groups to a minimum, regardless of geographic locations.[18] An important corollary of the current clash of civilizations is that many groups in the world have returned to a mentality characterized by global religious and cultural conflict. For example, certain global movements like jihadism have convinced millions of followers that differences in religion, politics, and culture are not—and should not be—subject to compromise or negotiation. This phenomenon can be called "global divergence." A minor theme in Huntington's (1996)[19] work is the prevalence of "core" or dominant states within civilizations that seek to attract communities of similar culture (e.g., diasporas) and outright reject those that are culturally and religious dissimilar in order to guarantee collective security or launch a new world order.

Globalization and jihadism

Chua (2003)[20] claims that globalization, the free marketplace, and the attempt at diffusing democracy have led to economic instability, explosive social situations, and, in some cases, economic desolation, ethnic hatred and genocides across the developing world. For Chua (and others), the market is not fair or unbiased: it is detrimental and engenders radical, violent change. Mousseau (2002)[21] concedes that a fundamental root cause of terrorism is "the deeply embedded anti market rage brought on by the forces of globalization." In another example, politico-religious factions in Pakistan receive financial support and policy recommendations from the United States as well as from Iran and Saudi Arabia. In a parallel manner, the consolidation of Hindu communalism in India corroborates the mindset that "Islam is under threat." Both cases of Pakistan and India can be interpreted as reactions to the rampant global hegemony of modernity. This type of situation is exploited by politico-religious groups to promote violence (e.g., to be a "true" Pakistani Muslim, one should join the GJM).[22]

Removal of borders

Moving more freely across borders allows jihadists to execute more attacks and ostensibly avoid capture. At the same time, it sets hurdles to prosecution if they are caught (i.e., because of the intricate web of extradition laws that vary from state to state). The rising porousness of the global system has also improved the ability of non-state terrorists to gather intelligence (or even avoid it). Governments are no longer the only players interested in gathering, disseminating, and/or applying such information. In some ways, terrorism is akin to an international criminal enterprise—a gloomy development, indeed.[23]

Globalization allows terrorist groups to reach across international borders in the same way that commerce and business interests are interconnected—often using the same channels. The decrease of barriers under the North American Free Trade Agreement (NAFTA) and the European Union (EU) has simplified the flow of many practices, good and bad, among nations. This has enabled jihadist organizations like Hezbollah, Al-Qaeda, and the Egyptian al-Gama'at al-Islamiyya to travel freely and form cells on other continents. A clear illustration of this occurred in December 2001, with the dismantling of a multinational plot in Singapore by the international jihadist group Jemaah Islamiyah. The plan was to detonate explosives at key Western targets, including the U.S. embassy. A video recording of the intended targets (that came with an explanation of the plans in Arabic) was found in Afghanistan after Al-Qaeda members had escaped. As one can see, clear connections between these organizations exist. It is strong evidence of collaboration and coordination of attacks.[24]

A facilitator of jihadist identity politics

Globalization has expedited the growth of identity politics by linking up unrelated people and allowing them to mutually reinforce each other across space and time, and also across ethnic and religious boundaries—even when, in some cases, those people aspire to reinforce these boundaries to their own benefit. Radicalization is also taking place outside the mosque. The corollary is a deterritorialization of religious tradition, belief, and identity. The images that Western jihadists absorb give shape to events from many different regional angles. This helps understand how and why European, Australian, Canadian, and American Muslims have found common ground with their Muslims from Chechnya, Egypt, and Pakistan in the face of great differences in their everyday lives and historical experiences.[25]

Many of the cultural characteristics that are commonplace in the Muslim migrants' countries of origin do not always make sense in a Western urban and cosmopolitan environment. The web of institutions, social relations, and values that strictly guides how people should lead their lives and belief systems in their place of origin is not necessarily replicated in their new place of residence. Although the original philosophy of migrants barely survives the first generation, the search for identity continues. Defying a Western culture which fails to truly represent universal values and truths, second- and third-generation Muslims become passionate about finding their own universal values and truths. Religion is a key identity marker. In the neo-fundamentalist mind, it has to be cleansed of all its dishonorable cultural attributes. Such Islamic neo-fundamentalism has managed to emerge from the capitalism and modern lifestyle without completely discarding the latter.[26]

Considering that jihad propagandists convey their message in perfectionistic and global terms, it should not be surprising that the ideology has attracted enthusiasts from outside the Middle East and Central Asia. These include Muslims and converts from the E.U., with whom the jihadist message resonated at a more profound level and convinced them to join the jihad caravan. The United States has witnessed a number of homegrown celebrity jihadists, including Anwar Al-Awlaki—considered by many as a rising star in jihadist circle until he died in September 2011 by a U.S. drone strike. Several jihadist terrorists who executed operations in the United States traced their activism to his online sermons and written communiqués.[27]

Glocalized jihad: think globally, act locally

What is unique about the present-day environment is that, owing to the links offered by tools of globalization like the internet, social media, and satellite communications, a more dangerous category of local and regional players has emerged. These players are connected to the global jihad war. They operate as regional allies or affiliates of organizations like Al-Qaeda, and take advantage of local groups and events to advance jihadism. Virginie André (2013)[28] has called this phenomenon "glocalized jihad." The term stems from the theoretical concept of glocalization, the practice whereby international organizations or institutions adapt their merchandise, practices, or traditions to local cultures (i.e., in order to cater to them).[29]

Glocalized jihad is characterized by a mélange of global jihad ideas, which are adapted locally, but remain true to the overarching cultural and historical aspects of holy war. It is a distinctive type of hybridized jihad catered specifically to a certain locality.[30] For example, two jihadist groups in Southern Thailand, the Islamic Liberation Front of Patani and the Patani Islamic Mujahideen Movement, are believed to have affinities with Al-Qaeda and the creation of the global Caliphate. Nevertheless, they apply their own local versions of jihad recruitment in the south of the country (to recruit more insurgents or militants).[31] Likewise, Jemaah Islamiyah, the regional Al-Qaeda affiliate in Indonesia, has sparked sectarian conflicts in Sulawesi to produce more recruits, anti-Western propaganda, financial backing, and "tribulations" that can be used for jihad purposes. On the whole, Al-Qaeda rarely has direct engagement with local insurgents or militants, but it still deals with its regional affiliates in an indirect manner. This is why regional-level players are a critical link in global jihad.[32]

The deterritorialization of jihad

By "territory," we mean a bordered space that has had "something done to it"—that "has been acted upon."[33] Territoriality, on the other hand, is the social and spatial mechanism that gives rise to identities; collective subjects interacting within structures of power that can join forces if they are attacked or forcibly removed.[34] Territoriality takes advantage of this bordered space, or "territory," to create and maintain the control, categorization, symbolic representation, communication, inclusion, and exclusion of individuals and objects.[35] Territoriality can also be a dangerous tool that serves as an ideological guise for the interests of the dominant class.[36] Territoriality generates socio-spatial identities supported by political or religious ideologies.[37]

Deterritorialization: definition

A large part of the current chaos in the Muslim world and the hostilities between Islam and the West can be attributed to the process of deterritorialization. Deterritorialization is the erosive bond between culture and place.[38] With respect to jihad, the term refers specifically to the removal of the boundaries between militant Islam and the West through the process of globalization. Like globalization, deterritorialization is rooted in historical events, but the level and scope at which it is taking place are now extraordinary. A type of geography of uncertainty is quickly surfacing, particularly with regard to national borders. That is the typifying aspect of jihad in its terroristic structure, because it is global and it transcends state borders; because of this, each Western nation can be a target of terrorism.[39]

Deterritorialization of ISIS

Jihadists' aggressive push for Islamic States (IS) defies the very concept of territoriality. ISIS opposes nationalism and tribalism in support of the ummah of Islam. Its image of the ummah as an "imagined community" signals a transition from the predominant conception of the nation and the nation-state to a religious conception that challenges the nationalist movements from the colonial and postcolonial eras. The revival of this "imagined ummah" provides Muslims across the world a dream for the golden past—a dream of going back to the Muslim empire and the first Caliphate after the Prophet Muhammad's death.[40]

Since its self-identified Caliphate in June 2014, ISIS has modified its internal structure, making its territorial dimension unclear. The name of the organization itself speaks to its tendency to "stretch" its borders. In the beginning, it was ISIS (Islamic State of Iraq and Sham) or ISIL (Islamic State of Iraq and Levant). Now, it is just IS, without a clear geographical location, although many of the current media reports still call it ISIS or ISIL (to avoid confusion, the ISIS label will be used throughout the present book). This last change seems to be of significance as it points to the global inclination toward the Caliphate, which covers the entire globe (not particular territories). This is an important trait of ISIS, which seeks the approval of the whole ummah—the community of believers and the heart of Islam. It is a community grounded in religious doctrines, not territorial links.[41]

ISIS considers the borders created by Western powers (in the past two centuries) in Central Asia, the Middle East, and Africa as "imaginary borders" that should be dismantled or removed. The progress toward the Caliphate brings about two main outcomes: (1) geographical uncertainty and (2) the attempt to institute a new political and geographical model. Indeed, it is no longer a certainty rooted in Western principles, but in religious principles. ISIS aggressively wants to reign supreme. Hence, it has a natural tendency to expand and to affirm its own universal "geographical certainty." In the process, the tearing apart of Western political and geographical assumptions would certainly allow this to happen.[42]

In comparison with modern states, the Islamic State presents a threat to the territory and territoriality in both theory and practice. ISIS's proclamations about the defeat of Rome and other Western cities expose a propensity toward globalization of jihad because they are, put simply, purely founded on the concept of jihad. The concept of borders and limitations is not mentioned at all; in jihad, the enemy is not created in territorial terms, but only in religious and ideological terms. For this reason, global jihad today is particularly a non-territorial idea.[43] In its radical vision of the Caliphate, ISIS's message is that, the more Islamic States are created, the closer the ummah becomes to the perfect realization of Allah's will. Anyone who endeavors for this realization meets the essential condition of Islam: to be in active submission to Allah.[44]

Losing territory, not losing combat

On March 23, 2019, ISIS was at its worst point, in almost five years, since its declaration of its Caliphate in June 2014. Today, the group has zero territory in Iraq and Syria. Although the loss of territories has given a huge black eye to the jihadist group, the conditions that nurtured the insurgency in war-torn Iraq and Syria remain very dangerous.[45] To this point, experts who are constantly studying ISIS are worried that the group has become far more powerful and threatening today than in 2011, during which the Coalition forces were disengaging from Iraq. Many of ISIS's leaders are still alive and ISIS-inspired lone wolves continue to carry out attacks. ISIS is adapting to its losses, falling back on guerilla tactics that it employed in the past—examples include bombings, martyrdom operations, targeted killings, ambushes, and raids. According to U.S. Army General Joseph Votel, there are still thousands of ISIS fighters dispersed all over Iraq and Syria.

Territory that is now ISIS-free remains unsafe, as sleeper cells are emerging. From summer 2018 to March 2019, the jihadist group perpetrated no fewer than 250 attacks outside its territories in Syria. The move toward hit-and-run methods, which use close surveillance and clandestine networks to execute targeted attacks, has allowed ISIS to remain operational in Syria despite the huge black eye it received.[46]

In addition to the Middle East, the group's adherents continue to carry out attacks outside that region. For instance, ISIS claimed responsibility for the bombing of a Roman Catholic church in the Philippines on January 27, 2019 (at least 20 people were killed).[47] An analysis conducted by the Institute for the Study of War in early March 2019 reported that "ISIS's post-caliphate insurgency in Iraq is accelerating faster than efforts to prevent it by the U.S."[48] More importantly, ISIS remains a wealthy terrorist organization that can finance its global operations. According to a February 2019 report by the United Nations, it is worth between $50 million and $300 million in cash; the money is hidden in either Iraq and Syria. It may have been smuggled into bordering countries for safekeeping.[49] According to Colin P. Clarke, a senior fellow at the Soufan Center (a U.S. nonprofit organization dedicated to research), ISIS has invested in businesses like fish farming, car dealing, and cannabis growing. Military intelligence and spy agencies are closely watching ISIS fighters who have migrated from and returned to North Africa, Europe, and the Middle East. Analysts said that approximately 1,200 of the extremists have gone back to Europe alone.[50]

The ISIS affiliate in Afghanistan has engulfed entire units of Taliban fighters. In the Democratic Republic of Congo, ISIS-affiliated fighters established a new "province" by recruiting soldiers of the Allied Democratic Forces rebel organization, which benefited from cash transactions from an ISIS financier. These groups have felt virtually no impact from the territorial losses in Iraq and Syria. Nor do they need to have direct contact with ISIS to apply its Caliphate-driven ideology, which the terrorist group transmits through regular audio recordings. According to Colin P. Clarke, the aforementioned senior fellow at the Soufan Center, "when combined with ISIS's technical know-how and expertise, the combination with the local knowledge of more parochial groups can have devastating effects."[51] The group's late leader, Abu Bakr al-Baghdadi, who was killed by U.S. Forces on October 27, 2019, was hiding underground in Syria. He was believed to send his communications only by personal courier. At the same time, ISIS fighters can still easily communicate through encrypted apps.[52]

Social media effects

The internet and social media are a central factor in globalization and the evolving jihadist space. For Wu (2015),[53] social media is an innovation that permits individuals to "share information ideas, personal messages, and other content around the world." Today's computer-mediated technologies have greatly changed the manner by which we share information and develop connections with others.[54]

Internet users from all corners of the planet can work together to create data on social media platforms such as Facebook, YouTube, and Twitter.[55]

YouTube effect

Among possible sources of jihadization, observers cite online spaces as a chief concern, underlining that video-sharing sites like YouTube can be exploited as radicalizing environments. In these environments, youths are exposed to pro-jihadist messages, can bond with others who have similar views, and, in some cases, recruit others to join.[56] YouTube is a cornerstone of jihadist activities. Jihadist radicalization is facilitated by such "YouTube effect," the phenomenon whereby videos posted by registered members (acting on their own) are rapidly circulated across the world through video-sharing websites like YouTube, Google Video, and others.[57] As a supreme global medium, video-sharing and social media sites can easily disseminate the "Jihad Cool" message by suppressing differences between cultures worldwide (i.e., jihad can unify people from disparate cultures and geographical locations).

Many neojihadists are members of the Millennial Generation (or Millennials), a generation who were raised using digital communication technologies like smartphones, social media, and computer networks. Social networking platforms like Facebook and YouTube remain the main source of information for Millennials.[58] In essence, the YouTube effect is the "viral video effect." The potential corollaries of such a popular fever can be far-reaching. In particular, the jihadist threat will grow even further. It is anticipated that online interactions for millions of users will be become easier and more accessible.[59] Pictures of jihadists in balaclava masks standing behind to-be-decapitated Western hostages have been a common phenomenon on video-sharing sites. The purpose of this action is to cause fear in the hearts of the unbelievers.[60] As quoted in Quran 8:12, "I shall cast terror into the hearts of the unbelievers and you will strike their heads and limbs."[61]

Global networked affect

Similarly, Kraidy (2017)[62] uses the term "global networked affect" to explain how videos disseminated by ISIS function as projectiles—like images as weapons[63] or image munitions.[64] ISIS's graphic images produce terror as affect. Affect is defined as "bodily intensity that precedes its representation in language and culture."[65] Affect is essential in reconsidering "power after ideology" because ideology "is now [only] one mode of power in a larger field that is not defined, overall, by ideology."[66] In early 2015, the spectacle of ISIS's war machine was exemplified by the release of a graphic video showing the immolation of a Jordanian pilot.[67] The global networked affect is akin to the YouTube effect in the sense that every time ISIS propagates terror through its images, videos, or tweets, it contributes to an escalated effect of terror. As Kraidy (2017)[68] continues, ISIS's images "can become important weapons that convey projectilic affect—a feeling of bodily harm and violation. After all, a projectile entails movement toward, presence in proximity of, and finally touching its target."

Online jihadist magazines

To further circumvent the hindrances of distance and language, jihadist organizations have produced multiple types of online magazines in various languages spoken in Western nations. Much content of these magazines, however, is in English, making it the lingua franca for communicating a bellicose version of Islam.[69] The ease to publish those magazines allows Al-Qaeda, ISIS, and Al-Shabaab to propagate their messages to millions of people who have had no prior contact with jihadists. To begin, Al-Qaeda launched its *Inspire* magazine in 2010 to attract the youth and pre-existing target audiences like jihadist fighters, jihad supporters, and would-be lone wolves (from both the Western and non-Western world). *Inspire* offers recipes as to how to make a bomb. Also included are guidelines on how to perpetrate attacks based on other homemade devices, traditional weapons of war (e.g., guns, knives, and grenades), and low-cost but innovative techniques like vehicular attacks.[70] *Inspire* ceased to be published in 2016.

Like Al-Qaeda, ISIS began publishing its first major online magazine in 2014: *Dabiq*. *Dabiq* was originally a conduit for declaring ISIS as a separate entity from Al-Qaeda. The magazine urges readers to abandon their lands, leave their jobs and homes, and join the jihad bandwagon in the Middle East. This straightforward appeal to ISIS has attracted a great many new followers. In 2016, *Dabiq* was replaced by *Rumiyah*, another ISIS magazine. *Rumiyah* was meant to assist ISIS even more. This magazine described the ease to travel across the world and how to best take control of the locations that followers call home. *Rumiyah* provided many details as to how to engage in violence in the name of Allah. It glorified jihadist power as a scare tactic to non-Muslims.[71] *Rumiyah* ceased to be published in 2017. Al-Shabaab, the Somali Islamic terrorist organization, also followed in the path of Al-Qaeda and ISIS by publishing its own magazine: *Gaidi Mtaani*. Founded in 2012, *Gaidi Mtaani* is still in circulation today. The magazine includes state-of-the-art graphics to convey an image of modernity and sophistication to draw the youths and present the terrorist group as a special entity chosen by Allah.[72]

Taken as a whole, all four magazines have posed a colossal threat to people who identify as non-Muslims or Muslims who left the faith. Despite having different titles or different formats, these magazines have the same objective: to recruit as many new followers as possible for jihad and establish the Caliphate. Those four online jihadist magazines are highly dangerous because (1) they are the most important official publications of Al-Qaeda, ISIS, and Al-Shabaab and (2) they have had an extraordinary impact on readers across the world. For example, the two Boston Marathon bombers—aka, the Tsarnaev brothers—were influenced by *Inspire* for detonating their homemade bomb at a public event.[73] Owing to cyberspace, those magazines can replace some of the traditional practices and endeavors of the three-dimensional world. One useful technique to assist in the production of all four magazines is the pdf format. A pdf format not only reduces straightforward digital footprint; it also evades the cat-and-mouse chase from law enforcement.[74]

Notes

1 Arolda Elbasani and Olivier Roy, "Islam in the Post-Communist Balkans: Alternative Pathways to God," *Southeast European and Black Sea Studies* 15, no. 4 (2015): 457–71. https://doi.org/10.1080/14683857.2015.1050273

2 Audrey Kurth Cronin, "Behind the Curve: Globalization and International Terrorism," *International Security* 27, no. 3 (2003): 30–58. https://doi.org/10.1162/01622880260553624

3 David Held, David Goldblatt, Anthony McGrew, and Jonathan Perraton, *Global Transformations* (Cambridge: Polity, 1999).

4 Paul James, "Arguing Globalizations: Propositions towards an Investigation of Global Formation," *Globalizations* 2, no. 2 (2005): 193–209. https://doi.org/10.1080/14747730500202206

5 Manfred B. Steger, *Globalization: A Very Short Introduction* (New York: Oxford University Press, 2017).

6 David Harvey, *The Condition of Postmodernity: An Enquiry into the Origins of Cultural Change* (Oxford: Blackwell, 1989): 240.

7 John Tomlinson, *Globalization and Culture* (Cambridge: Polity, 1999): 2.

8 Manuel Castells, "Materials for an Exploratory Theory of the Network Society," *British Journal of Sociology* 51, no. 1 (2000): 5–24. https://doi.org/10.1111/j.1468-4446.2000.00005.x

9 Manuel Castells, *The Information Age: Economy, Society, and Culture. Vol. 1. The Rise of the Network Society* (Oxford: Blackwell, 1996): 1.

10 Catarina Kinnvall, "Analyzing the Global–Local Nexus," in *Globalization and Democratization in Asia: The Construction of Identity*, ed. Catarina Kinnvall and Kristina Jönsson (London: Routledge, 2002): 3–18.

11 Catarina Kinnvall, "Globalization and Religious Nationalism: Self, Identity, and the Search for Ontological Security," *Political Psychology* 25, no. 5 (2004): 741–67, 742. https://doi.org/10.1111/j.1467-9221.2004.00396.x

12 Thomas L. Friedman, *The Lexus and the Olive Tree: Understanding Globalization* (New York: Farrar, Straus and Giroux, 1999).

13 Ibid., 382–3.

14 Joseph F. Pilat, "The Causes of Terrorism," *Journal of Organisational Transformation & Social Change* 6, no. 2 (2009): 171–82. https://doi.org/10.1386/jots.6.2.171_1

15 Cronin, "Behind the Curve," 45.

16 Zygmunt Bauman, "Wars of the Globalization Era," *European Journal of Social Theory* 4, no. 11 (2001): 11–28. https://doi.org/10.1177/13684310122224966

17 Ibid., 13.

18 Eric Neumayer and Thomas Plümper, "International Terrorism and the Clash of Civilizations," *British Journal of Political Science* 39, no. 4 (2009): 711–34. https://doi.org/10.1017/S0007123409000751

19 Samuel P. Huntington, *The Clash of Civilizations and the Remaking of World Order* (New York: Free Press, 1996): 155.

20 Amy Chua, *World on Fire: How Exporting Free Market Democracy Breeds Ethnic Hatred and Global Instability* (New York: Doubleday, 2003).

21 Michael Mousseau, "Market Civilization and Its Clash with Terror." *International Security* 27, no. 3 (2002): 5–29, 5. https://doi.org/10.1162/01622880260553615

22 Cassandra Balchin, "The Network 'Women Living under Muslim Laws:' Strengthening Local Struggles through Cross-Boundary Networking," *Society for International Development* 45, no. 1 (2002): 126–31.

23 Cronin, "Behind the Curve," 49.
24 Ibid., 49.
25 Alex S. Wilner and Claire-Jehanne Dubouloz, "Homegrown Terrorism and Transformative Learning: An Interdisciplinary Approach to Understanding Radicalization," *Global Change, Peace & Security* 22, no. 1 (2010): 33–51. https://doi.org/10.1080/14781150903487956
26 Olivier Roy, *Globalised Islam: The Search for a New Ummah* (London: Hurst, 2004)
27 Mark Mazzetti, Eric Schmitt, and Robert F. Worth, "Two-Year Manhunt Led to Killing of Awlaki in Yemen," *The New York Times* (2011, September 30): A1.
28 Virginie André, "From Colonialist to Infidel: Framing the Enemy in Southern Thailand's 'Cosmic War'," in *Culture, Religion and Conflict in Muslim Southeast Asia: Negotiating Tense Pluralisms*, ed. Joseph Camilleri and Sven Schottmann (London: Routledge, 2013): 109–25.
29 Roland Robertson, "Glocalization: Time-Space and Homogeneity-Heterogeneity," in *Global Modernities*, ed. Mike Featherstone, Scott Lash, and Roland Robertson (Thousand Oaks, CA: Sage, 1995): 25–44; Demi Simi and Jonathan Matusitz, "Glocalization of Subway in India: How a US Giant Has Adapted in the Asian Subcontinent," *Journal of Asian and African Studies* 52, no. 5 (2017): 573–85. https://doi.org/10.1177/0021909615596764
30 Virginie André, "The Janus Face of New Media Propaganda: The Case of Patani Neo-jihadist YouTube Warfare and Its Islamophobic Effect on Cyber-Actors," *Islam and Christian–Muslim Relations* 25, no. 3 (2014): 335–56. https://doi.org/10.1080/09596410.2014.900948
31 Duncan McCargo, *Tearing Apart the Land: Islam and Legitimacy in Southern Thailand* (Ithaca, NY: Cornell University Press, 2015).
32 David J. Kilcullen, "Countering Global Insurgency," *Journal of Strategic Studies* 28, no. 4 (2005): 597–617. https://doi.org/10.1080/01402390500300956
33 Deborah Cowen and Emily Gilbert, *War, Citizenship, Territory* (London: Routledge, 2008): 16.
34 Yosef Jabareen, "The Emerging Islamic State: Terror, Territoriality, and the Agenda of Social Transformation," *Geoforum* 58 (2015): 51–5. https://doi.org/10.1016/j.geoforum.2014.10.009
35 Robert D. Sack, *Human Territoriality: Its Theory and History* (Cambridge: Cambridge University Press, 1986).
36 James Anderson and Ian Shuttleworth, "Fixing Capitalism and Europe's Peripheries: West European Imperialism," in *Geopolitics of European Union Enlargement: The Fortress Empire*, ed. Warwick Armstrong and James Anderson (London: Routledge, 2007): 125–41.
37 Neil Brenner, "Beyond State-Centrism? Space, Territoriality, and Geographical Scale in Globalization Studies," *Theory and Society* 28, no. 1 (1999): 39–78; Henri Lefebvre, *The Production of Space* (Oxford: Blackwell Publishing, 1991).
38 Linda Basch, Nina Glick Schiller, and Christina Szanton Blanc, *Nations Unbound Transnational Projects, Postcolonial Predicaments, and Deterritorialized Nation-States* (London: Routledge, 2005).
39 Kabir Sethi, "The Allure of the Radical: Understanding Jihadist Violence in the West," *Macalester International* 22 (2009): 201–25.
40 Jabareen, "The Emerging Islamic State," 53.
41 Ibid., 51.
42 Ibid., 53.
43 Greg Barton, "Understanding Key Themes in the ISIS Narrative: An Examination of *Dabiq* Magazine," in *Contesting the Theological Foundations of Islamism and Violent Extremism*, ed. Fethi Mansouri and Zuleyha Keskin (New York: Palgrave Macmillan): 139–61; Tyler Welch, "Theology, Heroism, Justice, and Fear: An Analysis of ISIS Propaganda Magazines *Dabiq* and *Rumiyah*," *Dynamics of Asymmetric Conflict* 11, no. 3 (2018): 186–98. https://doi.org/10.1080/17467586.2018.1517943

44 Cited in Paul Kamolnick, "On Self-Declared Caliph Ibrahim's December 2015 Speech: Further Evidence for Critical Vulnerabilities in the Crumbling Caliphate," *Small Wars Journal* 11 (2015): 10–21.
45 Sune Engel Rasmussen, "Islamic State's Caliphate Is Gone, But Not Its Violent Extremism," *The Wall Street Journal* (2019, March 24): A1.
46 Jin Wu, Derek Watkins, and Rukmini Callimachi, "ISIS Lost Its Last Territory in Syria. But the Attacks Continue," *The New York Times* (2019, March 23): A1.
47 Jason Gutierrez, "Philippines Cathedral Bombing Kills 20," *The New York Times* (2019, January 27): A4.
48 Brandon Wallace, "ISIS Re-establishes Historical Sanctuary in Iraq," *Institute for the Study of War* (2019, March 7). Retrieved on March 24, 2019 from http://iswresearch.blogspot.com/2019/03/isis-re-establishes-historic-sanctuary.html
49 United Nations Security Council, *Eighth Report of the Secretary-General on the Threat Posed by ISIL (Da'esh) to International Peace and Security and the Range of United Nations Efforts in Support of Member States in Countering the Threat* (New York: United Nations Security Council, 2019, February 1). Retrieved on March 24, 2019 from www.un.org/sc/ctc/wp-content/uploads/2019/02/N1901937_EN.pdf
50 Eric Schmitt, "Its Territory May Be Gone, but the U.S. Fight Against ISIS Is Far From Over," *The New York Times* (2019, March 24): A1.
51 Cited in Rukmini Callimachi and Eric Schmitt, "Sri Lanka Attack Signals an ISIS Shift Beyond Middle East," *The New York Times* (2019, April 25): A1.
52 Ibid., A1.
53 Paulina Wu, "Impossible to Regulate? Social Media, Terrorists, and the Role for the U.N.," *Chicago Journal of International Law* 16, no. 1 (2015): 281–311, 283.
54 Yochai Benkler, *The Wealth of Networks: How Social Production Transforms Markets and Freedom* (New Haven, CT: Yale University Press, 2006); Manuel Castells, *The Network Society: A Cross-Cultural Perspective* (Northampton, MA: Edward Elgar, 2004); Hyunjin Seo and Dennis F. Kinsey, "Meaning of Democracy around the World: A Thematic and Structural Analysis of Videos Defining Democracy," *Visual Communication Quarterly* 19, no. 2(2012): 94–107. https://doi.org/10.1080/15551393.2012.682890
55 Hyunjin Seo, "Visual Propaganda in the Age of Social Media: An Empirical Analysis of Twitter Images during the 2012 Israeli–Hamas Conflict," *Visual Communication Quarterly* 21, no. 3 (2014): 150–61. https://doi.org/10.1080/15551393.2014.955501
56 Mia Bloom, "In Defense of Honor: Women and Terrorist Recruitment on the Internet," *Journal of Postcolonial Studies* 4, no. 1 (2013): 150–95; Tim Stevens and Peter Neumann, *Countering Violent Online Radicalisation: A Strategic for Action* (London: International Centre for the Study of Radicalisation and Political Violence, 2009).
57 Moises Naim, "The YouTube Effect: How a Technology for Teenagers Became a Force for Political and Economic Change," *Foreign Policy* 158 (2007): 104–5.
58 Jonathan Matusitz, *Symbolism in Terrorism: Motivation, Communication, and Behavior* (Lanham, MD: Rowman & Littlefield, 2015).
59 Justin Nix and Justin T. Pickett, "Third-Person Perceptions, Hostile Media Effects, and Policing: Developing a Theoretical Framework for Assessing the Ferguson Effect," *Journal of Criminal Justice* 51 (2017): 24–33. https://doi.org/10.1016/j.jcrimjus.2017.05.016
60 Yinka Olomojobi, *Frontiers of Jihad: Radical Islam in Africa* (Sebastopol, CA: Safari Books, 2015).
61 Available at http://corpus.quran.com/translation.jsp?chapter=8&verse=12
62 Marwan M. Kraidy, "The Projectilic Image: Islamic State's Digital Visual Warfare and Global Networked Affect," *Media, Culture & Society* 39, no. 8 (2017): 1194–209. https://doi.org/10.1177/0163443717725575
63 Neville Bolt, *The Violent Image: Insurgent Propaganda and the New Revolutionaries* (New York: Columbia University Press, 2012).
64 Nathan Roger, *Image Warfare in the War on Terror* (New York: Palgrave Macmillan, 2013).
65 Kraidy, "The Projectilic Image," 1199.

66 Brian Massumi, *Parables for the Virtual: Movement, Affect, Sensation* (Durham, NC: Duke University Press, 2002): 42.
67 Alexandra A. Siegel and Joshua A. Tucker, "The Islamic State's Information Warfare: Measuring the Success of ISIS's Online Strategy," *Journal of Language and Politics* 17, no. 2 (2018): 258–80. https://doi.org/10.1075/jlp.17005.sie
68 Kraidy, "The Projectilic Image," 1199.
69 Jonathan Matusitz, Andrea Madrazo, and Catalina Udani, *Online Jihadist Magazines to Promote the Caliphate: Communicative Perspectives* (New York: Peter Lang, 2019).
70 Anthony Celso, "Al Qaeda's Post 9–11 Travails," *Terrorism and Political Violence* 30, no. 3 (2018): 553–61. https://doi.org/10.1080/09546553.2018.1440046
71 Logan Macnair and Richard Frank, "Changes and Stabilities in the Language of Islamic State Magazines: A Sentiment Analysis," *Dynamics of Asymmetric Conflict* 11, no. 2 (2018): 109–20. https://doi.org/10.1080/17467586.2018.1470660
72 Seth G. Jones, Andrew M. Liepman, and Nathan Chandler, *Counterterrorism and Counterinsurgency in Somalia: Assessing the Campaign against Al Shaba'ab* (Santa Monica: RAND, 2016).
73 Richard Serrano, "Boston Bombing Indictment: Dzhokhar Tsarnaev Inspired by Al Qaeda," *Los Angeles Times* (2013, June 27): A1.
74 Peter Wignell, Sabine Tan, Kay L. O'Halloran, and Rebecca Lange, "A Mixed Methods Empirical Examination of Changes in Emphasis and Style in the Extremist Magazines *Dabiq* and *Rumiyah*," *Perspectives on Terrorism* 11, no. 2 (2017): 2–20.

References

Anderson, James, and Ian Shuttleworth, "Fixing Capitalism and Europe's Peripheries: West European Imperialism," in *Geopolitics of European Union Enlargement: The Fortress Empire*, edited by Warwick Armstrong and James Anderson, 125–141. London: Routledge, 2007.

André, Virginie, "From Colonialist to Infidel: Framing the Enemy in Southern Thailand's 'Cosmic War'," in *Culture, Religion and Conflict in Muslim Southeast Asia: Negotiating Tense Pluralisms*, edited by Joseph Camilleri and Sven Schottmann, 109–125. London: Routledge, 2013.

André, Virginie, "The Janus Face of New Media Propaganda: The Case of Patani Neojihadist YouTube Warfare and Its Islamophobic Effect on Cyber-Actors," *Islam and Christian–Muslim Relations* 25, no. 3 (2014): 335–356. https://doi.org/10.1080/09596410.2014.900948.

Balchin, Cassandra, "The Network 'Women Living under Muslim Laws:' Strengthening Local Struggles through Cross-Boundary Networking," *Society for International Development* 45, no. 1 (2002): 126–131.

Barton, Greg, "*Understanding Key Themes in the ISIS Narrative: An Examination ofContesting the Theological Foundations of Islamism and Violent Extremism*, edited by Fethi Mansouri and Zuleyha Keskin, 139–161. New York: Palgrave Macmillan.

Basch, Linda, Nina Glick Schiller, and Christina Szanton Blanc, *Nations Unbound Transnational Projects, Postcolonial Predicaments, and Deterritorialized Nation-States*. London: Routledge, 2005.

Bauman, Zygmunt, "Wars of the Globalization Era," *European Journal of Social Theory* 4, no. 11 (2001): 11–28. https://doi.org/10.1177/13684310122224966.

Benkler, Yochai, *The Wealth of Networks: How Social Production Transforms Markets and Freedoms*. New Haven, CT: Yale University Press, 2006.

Bloom, Mia, "In Defense of Honor: Women and Terrorist Recruitment on the Internet," *Journal of Postcolonial Studies* 4, no. 1 (2013): 150–195.

Bolt, Neville, *The Violent Image: Insurgent Propaganda and the New Revolutionaries*. New York: Columbia University Press, 2012.

Brenner, Neil, "Beyond State-Centrism? Space, Territoriality, and Geographical Scale in Globalization Studies," *Theory and Society* 28, no. 1 (1999): 39–78.

Callimachi, Rukmini, and Eric Schmitt, "Sri Lanka Attack Signals an ISIS Shift Beyond Middle East," *The New York Times* (2019, April 25): A1.

Castells, Manuel, *The Information Age: Economy, Society, and Culture. Vol. 1. The Rise of the Network Society*. Oxford: Blackwell, 1996.

Castells, Manuel, "Materials for an Exploratory Theory of the Network Society," *British Journal of Sociology* 51, no. 1 (2000): 5–24. https://doi.org/10.1111/j.1468-4446.2000.00005.x.

Castells, Manuel, *The Network Society: A Cross-Cultural Perspective*. Northampton, MA: Edward Elgar, 2004.

Celso, Anthony, "Al Qaeda's Post 9-11 Travails," *Terrorism and Political Violence* 30, no. 3 (2018): 553–561. https://doi.org/10.1080/09546553.2018.1440046.

Chua, Amy, *World on Fire: How Exporting Free Market Democracy Breeds Ethnic Hatred and Global Instability*. New York: Doubleday, 2003.

Cowen, Deborah, and Emily Gilbert, *War, Citizenship, Territory*. London: Routledge, 2008.

Cronin, Audrey Kurth, "Behind the Curve: Globalization and International Terrorism," *International Security* 27, no. 3 (2003): 30–58. https://doi.org/10.1162/01622880260553624.

Elbasani, Arolda, and Olivier Roy, "Islam in the Post-Communist Balkans: Alternative Pathways to God," *Southeast European and Black Sea Studies* 15, no. 4 (2015): 457–471. https://doi.org/10.1080/14683857.2015.1050273.

Friedman, Thomas L., *The Lexus and the Olive Tree: Understanding Globalization*. New York: Farrar, Straus and Giroux, 1999.

Gutierrez, Jason, "Philippines Cathedral Bombing Kills 20," *The New York Times* (2019, January 27): A4.

Harvey, David, *The Condition of Postmodernity: An Enquiry into the Origins of Cultural Change*. Oxford: Blackwell, 1989.

Held, David, David Goldblatt, Anthony McGrew, and Jonathan Perraton, *Global Transformations*. Cambridge: Polity, 1999.

Huntington, Samuel P., *The Clash of Civilizations and the Remaking of World Order*. New York: Free Press, 1996.

Jabareen, Yosef, "The Emerging Islamic State: Terror, Territoriality, and the Agenda of Social Transformation," *Geoforum* 58 (2015): 51–55. https://doi.org/10.1016/j.geoforum.2014.10.009.

James, Paul, "Arguing Globalizations: Propositions towards an Investigation of Global Formation," *Globalizations* 2, no. 2 (2005): 193–209. https://doi.org/10.1080/14747730500202206.

Jones, Seth G., Andrew M. Liepman, and Nathan Chandler, *Counterterrorism and Counterinsurgency in Somalia: Assessing the Campaign against Al Shaba'ab*. Santa Monica, CA: RAND, 2016.

Kamolnick, Paul, "On Self-Declared Caliph Ibrahim's December 2015 Speech: Further Evidence for Critical Vulnerabilities in the Crumbling Caliphate," *Small Wars Journal* 11 (2015): 10–21.

Kilcullen, David J., "Countering Global Insurgency," *Journal of Strategic Studies* 28, no. 4 (2005): 597–617. https://doi.org/10.1080/01402390500300956.

Kinnvall, Catarina, "Analyzing the Global–Local Nexus," in *Globalization and Democratization in Asia: The Construction of Identity*, edited by Catarina Kinnvall and Kristina Jönsson, 3–18. London: Routledge, 2002.

Kinnvall, Catarina, "Globalization and Religious Nationalism: Self, Identity, and the Search for Ontological Security," *Political Psychology* 25, no. 5 (2004): 741–767. https://doi.org/10.1111/j.1467-9221.2004.00396.x.

Kraidy, Marwan M., "The Projectilic Image: Islamic State's Digital Visual Warfare and Global Networked Affect," *Media, Culture & Society* 39, no. 8 (2017): 1194–1209. http s://doi.org/10.1177/0163443717725575.

Lefebvre, Henri, *The Production of Space*. Oxford: Blackwell Publishing, 1991.

Macnair, Logan, and Richard Frank, "Changes and Stabilities in the Language of Islamic State Magazines: A Sentiment Analysis," *Dynamics of Asymmetric Conflict* 11, no. 2 (2018): 109–120. https://doi.org/10.1080/17467586.2018.1470660.

Massumi, Brian, *Parables for the Virtual: Movement, Affect, Sensation*. Durham, NC: Duke University Press, 2002.

Matusitz, Jonathan, *Symbolism in Terrorism: Motivation, Communication, and Behavior*. Lanham, MD: Rowman & Littlefield, 2015.

Matusitz, Jonathan, Andrea Madrazo, and Catalina Udani, *Online Jihadist Magazines to Promote the Caliphate: Communicative Perspectives*. New York: Peter Lang, 2019.

Mazzetti, Mark, Eric Schmitt, and Robert F. Worth, "Two-Year Manhunt Led to Killing of Awlaki in Yemen," *The New York Times* (2011, September 30): A1.

McCargo, Duncan, *Tearing Apart the Land: Islam and Legitimacy in Southern Thailand*. Ithaca, NY: Cornell University Press, 2015.

Mousseau, Michael, "Market Civilization and Its Clash with Terror." *International Security* 27, no. 3 (2002): 5–29. https://doi.org/10.1162/01622880260553615.

Naim, Moises, "The YouTube Effect: How a Technology for Teenagers Became a Force for Political and Economic Change," *Foreign Policy* 158 (2007): 104–105.

Neumayer, Eric, and Thomas Plümper, "International Terrorism and the Clash of Civilizations," *British Journal of Political Science* 39, no. 4 (2009): 711–734. https://doi.org/10. 1017/S0007123409000751.

Nix, Justin, and Justin T. Pickett, "Third-Person Perceptions, Hostile Media Effects, and Policing: Developing a Theoretical Framework for Assessing the Ferguson Effect," *Journal of Criminal Justice* 51 (2017): 24–33. https://doi.org/10.1016/j.jcrimjus.2017.05.016.

Olomojobi, Yinka, *Frontiers of Jihad: Radical Islam in Africa*. Sebastopol, CA: Safari Books, 2015.

Pilat, Joseph F., "The Causes of Terrorism," *Journal of Organisational Transformation & Social Change* 6, no. 2 (2009): 171–182. https://doi.org/10.1386/jots.6.2.171_1.

Rasmussen, Sune Engel, "Islamic State's Caliphate Is Gone, But Not Its Violent Extremism," *The Wall Street Journal* (2019, March 24): A1.

Robertson, Roland, "Glocalization: Time-Space and Homogeneity-Heterogeneity," in *Global Modernities*, edited by Mike Featherstone, Scott Lash, and Roland Robertson, 25–44. Thousand Oaks, CA: Sage, 1995.

Roger, Nathan, *Image Warfare in the War on Terror*. New York: Palgrave Macmillan, 2013.

Roy, Olivier, *Globalised Islam: The Search for a New Ummah*. London: Hurst, 2004.

Sack, Robert D., *Human Territoriality: Its Theory and History*. Cambridge: Cambridge University Press, 1986.

Schmitt, Eric, "Its Territory May Be Gone, but the U.S. Fight against ISIS Is Far From Over," *The New York Times* (2019, March 24): A1.

Seo, Hyunjin, and Dennis F. Kinsey, "Meaning of Democracy around the World: A Thematic and Structural Analysis of Videos Defining Democracy," *Visual Communication Quarterly* 19, no. 2 (2012): 94–107. https://doi.org/10.1080/15551393.2012.682890.

Seo, Hyunjin, "Visual Propaganda in the Age of Social Media: An Empirical Analysis of Twitter Images during the 2012 Israeli–Hamas Conflict," *Visual Communication Quarterly* 21, no. 3 (2014): 150–161. https://doi.org/10.1080/15551393.2014.955501.

Serrano, Richard, "Boston Bombing Indictment: Dzhokhar Tsarnaev Inspired by Al Qaeda," *Los Angeles Times* (2013, June 27): A1.

Sethi, Kabir, "The Allure of the Radical: Understanding Jihadist Violence in the West," *Macalester International* 22 (2009): 201–225.

Siegel, Alexandra A., and Joshua A. Tucker, "The Islamic State's Information Warfare: Measuring the Success of ISIS's Online Strategy," *Journal of Language and Politics* 17, no. 2 (2018): 258–280. https://doi.org/10.1075/jlp.17005.sie.

Simi, Demi, and Jonathan Matusitz, "Glocalization of Subway in India: How a US Giant Has Adapted in the Asian Subcontinent," *Journal of Asian and African Studies* 52, no. 5 (2017): 573–585. https://doi.org/10.1177/0021909615596764.

Steger, Manfred B., *Globalization: A Very Short Introduction.* New York: Oxford University Press, 2017.

Stevens, Tim, and Peter Neumann, *Countering Violent Online Radicalisation: A Strategic for Action.* London: International Centre for the Study of Radicalisation and Political Violence, 2009.

Tomlinson, John, *Globalization and Culture.* Cambridge: Polity, 1999.

United Nations Security Council, *Eighth Report of the Secretary-General on the Threat Posed by ISIL (Da'esh) to International Peace and Security and the Range of United Nations Efforts in Support of Member States in Countering the Threat.* New York: United Nations Security Council (2019, February 1). Retrieved on March 24, 2019 from www.un.org/sc/ctc/wp-content/uploads/2019/02/N1901937_EN.pdf.

Wallace, Brandon, "ISIS Re-establishes Historical Sanctuary in Iraq," (2019, *March 7).* Retrieved on March 24, 2019 from http://iswresearch.blogspot.com/2019/03/isis-re-establishes-historic-sanctuary.html.

Welch, Tyler, "Theology, Heroism, Justice, and Fear: An Analysis of ISIS Propaganda Magazines *Dabiq* and *Rumiyah,*" *Dynamics of Asymmetric Conflict* 11, no. 3 (2018): 186–198. https://doi.org/10.1080/17467586.2018.1517943.

Wignell, Peter, Sabine Tan, Kay L. O'Halloran, and Rebecca Lange, "A Mixed Methods Empirical Examination of Changes in Emphasis and Style in the Extremist Magazines *Dabiq* and *Rumiyah,*" *Perspectives on Terrorism* 11, no. 2 (2017): 2–20.

Wilner, Alex S., and Claire-Jehanne Dubouloz, "Homegrown Terrorism and Transformative Learning: An Interdisciplinary Approach to Understanding Radicalization," *Global Change, Peace & Security* 22, no. 1 (2010): 33–51. https://doi.org/10.1080/14781150903487956.

Wu, Jin, Derek Watkins, and Rukmini Callimachi, "ISIS Lost Its Last Territory in Syria. But the Attacks Continue," *The New York Times* (2019, March 23): A1.

Wu, Paulina, "Impossible to Regulate? Social Media, Terrorists, and the Role for the U. N.," *Chicago Journal of International Law* 16, no. 1 (2015): 281–311.

5

GLOBAL JIHADIST NETWORKS

Examining jihadist organizations' use of network technologies and tactics offers insights into the motives and abilities of the GJM. Global jihadist networks are multifaceted entities on the rise. The repertoire of jihadist insurgencies expands day by day. Sources of jihadist violence can be lone wolves, small cells (affiliated or unaffiliated), diffuse global networks, and even state actors or state-sponsored clandestine operatives (e.g., death squads and hit groups). Unless carried out by individual perpetrators or unaffiliated cells, these attacks are often the outcome of painstaking preparation and coordination with committed individuals who have numerous connections in different countries. A global jihadist network is a network consisting of (1) nodes of jihad soldiers or sympathizers and (2) the links created by these nodes. The global jihadist network is akin to a swarm; it is extremely decentralized, with individual and autonomous elements that, nevertheless, establish and preserve cohesion. Lacking a solid hierarchal and leadership arrangement, a massive motivator within the network is peer-to-peer influence by friends, kinsfolks, neighbors, and other compatible people—both in the three-dimensional world and on the internet.

Global jihadist networks can be compared with other popular waves or movements which, through publicity and propaganda, can activate a rapid mobilization that can have an online and offline impact.[1] As Leiken (2005)[2] continues,

> Jihadist networks span Europe from Poland to Portugal, thanks to the spread of radical Islam among the descendants of guest workers once recruited to shore up Europe's postwar economic miracle. In smoky coffeehouses in Rotterdam and Copenhagen, makeshift prayer halls in Hamburg and Brussels, Islamic bookstalls in Birmingham and "Londonistan," and the prisons of Madrid, Milan, and Marseilles, immigrants or their descendants are volunteering for jihad against the West.

Taken as a whole, the GJM is made up of a loosely affiliated confederation of autonomous networks and activities. It is more than just a single unified framework of terrorists fighting in the name of Salafism. Terrorist networks are centralized when a leading command exerts control over the network, like issuing operational orders and directing its ideology. In this case, decisions flow from top to bottom, and levels in the hierarchy do not intermingle. A clear separation exists between the leader(s) and rank-and-file members.[3] This was the exact model of the Provisional Irish Republican Army. What counterterrorism agencies recognize is that, today, the central headquarters of jihadist organizations like Al-Qaeda and ISIS are not that significant. Indirect jihadist actors across the world can become nodes in the network, espouse the same ultra-violent doctrine, receive or donate monies, and strike targets at any time.

Social network analysis

Networks have become a central channel of jihadist activities as they function as recruitment tools, interactive forums, psychological warfare, and platforms for sharing various forms of information. Networks allow anyone to get in contact with radicalized individuals, thereby initiating their own radicalization process. There are a multitude of vulnerability indicators associated with socio-economic and demographic conditions that render (would-be) jihadist fighters ideal targets for network-based radicalization.[4] Terrorist networks are often clandestine and not so open to public inquiry. Therefore, law enforcement agencies spend a great deal of time and effort to identify hidden connections between distinct terrorist groups that make the flow of information and resources easy.

A description

The implementation of social network analysis (SNA) to examine terrorism was developed by Krebs's (2002)[5] analysis of the terrorist network behind the September 11, 2001 attacks in New York and Washington, D.C. SNA is used to understand terrorist networks in regards to density, connections, hierarchy, and shape.[6] SNA enables scholars to represent the hidden dynamics within terrorist networks. Such analysis rests on the principle that nodes (people in the network) are interconnected through clear or unclear relationships. Nodes and their actions are considered interdependent (instead of independent). These connections are formed by such interdependent interactions and create a "network." The network is mapped through a diagram and can be examined in its own right.[7]

Although most nodes within the network are connected and dependent on each other, it is crucial to acknowledge that a certain number of them accomplish roles that are more essential to the tasks of the network than others. Inside a network, a particular type of individual is charged with fulfilling the role of facilitator. This type of individual is often more visible, less prudent, and with many and varied interconnections with the other nodes or hubs (i.e., important nodes of the network). The position of facilitator is of utmost importance as it connects the network with other networks (or the outside world). It also gets other isolated parts to become interconnected within a network. As the adage goes, "no man is an island." Instead of being islands of non-interacting cells, there is a broad inter-connected network of people that goes beyond operational cliques. Facilitators also want to guarantee that certain parts of the world participate disproportionately in the network through their simple presence.[8]

The centralized network

"Centrality" reflects the state of being the key node in the network, like a go-to individual. It is expected to wield influence. This denotes a high advantage of contacts and access. According to the principles of SNA, the metric determines the frequency with which a node is on the shortest path between other nodes. Nodes with high scores become hubs, meaning that they are the most central to the net-work. This postulation explains that being the key node in the network is more important than being on the margin, even if the simple number of connections remains the same. Put another way, social capital is contingent on having friends. Having friends who also have friends is best.[9]

Harris-Hogan and Barrelle (2018)[10] examined networks of Australian jihadists in ample detail. The two authors concluded that the overwhelming majority of jiha-dists identified in Australia since the dawn of the twenty-first century form an interconnected network with clear leadership and directives, transcending time and geographic locations. Close-knit relationships seem to be key to identifying how Australian jihadists recruit and how their network develops. Based on the principles of SNA, some nodes are well connected and, therefore, influential, whereas others find themselves between pairs of other actors, a strategically beneficial rank of broker. This type of analysis can lead to conclusions as to which nodes are central within a network.[11]

The decentralized network

Decentralized networks are the most likely to attain efficiency because they include many direct communication lines among actors. Horizontal networks strive to balance the need to act cooperatively and the need to preserve trust and secrecy within collaborative endeavors (i.e., to efficiently resist law enforcement interven-tions).[12] Such networks do not typically precipitate their plans or amplify the probability of their attack; rather, they eschew frequent communication and keep a low profile.[13] Players with many connections to other players are often seen as powerful. Just like the centralized network, however, those who perform the roles of brokers between disparate groups will exert substantial control over the amount of information (and/or resources) within the network.[14]

De Bie, de Poot, Freilich, and Chermake (2017)[15] used SNA to examine the organizational structures and roles of three Dutch jihadist networks. The authors relied on a longitudinal Dutch police database published during the 2000–2013 period. This study revealed how the jihadist organizational structures evolved from a hierarchical cell formation (with a clear division of roles) to decentralized networks with a much more ambiguous orientation on tasks. This case also illustrates how the core members of the jihadist movement can evolve from global jihadists with clear leadership roles to homegrown mujahedin with lower status and less expertise.

The "all-channel" network

Arquilla, Ronfeldt, and Zanini (1999)[16] regard modern terrorist organizations like Al-Qaeda as "all-channel" networks. Their definition of the all-channel network is a decentralized entity with wide-ranging global communication configurations that enable them to "coordinate across considerable distances." Such networks may not benefit from formal vertical influence, but through the density of their communication conduits, they are still integrated and able to organize actions in different regions of theaters of war. They combine "central ideational, strategic, and operational coherence" with "tactical decentralization."

In their study of Australian jihadist networks, Kelly and McCarthy-Jones (2019)[17] examined how six jihadist cells, over a 14-year timespan, formed an interconnected network of individuals linked by local and global kinships. For example, the authors found that the Sydney cell formed an all-channel network. The inner circle of the Sydney cell was made up of two key men: Mohamed Ali Elomar and Khaled Cheikho. Their central location placed both men as crucial to the network's structure on a local and global scale. This was largely due to the high volume of personal connections to other players. The all-channel network enables (virtually) unrestricted communication between all actors. The density of connections can reach a maximum level. This network model can guarantee maximum efficiency if each actor exchanges information with all the others.[18]

In a similar fashion, ISIS's extensive use of social media platforms (particularly Twitter) has highlighted the importance of the all-channel network within the GJM. This heralds a clear shift from the previous organization-centric model espoused by Al-Qaeda. In that model, unrelated sympathizers interacted with one another and produced propaganda content in real-time by actively contributing to its further dissemination. With ISIS today, SNA can help shed light on the most important part of ISIS's improved use of the social media—particularly regarding its initial ways of distribution and the role of sympathizers who further diffuse content (instead of the content itself) with just a few mouse clicks away.[19]

Before ISIS became a major actor in global jihad, the creation of jihadist media was organized hierarchically and controlled strictly (in spite of moving to online forums). For example, a few years after the War in Afghanistan started, top Al-Qaeda leaders increasingly attempted to deliver readily accessible information about the organization on the internet, including its membership, agenda, and strategy. This aimed at compensating for its decreased ability to perpetrate terrorist attacks successfully.[20] The problem is that this approach remained intrinsically one-directional, as places for interaction between global jihadists and Al-Qaeda's top leadership were limited. Although messages were created, distributed, and received, no clear feedback method was available. With its all-channel network, ISIS has changed all that.[21]

The crime–jihad network

Basra, Neumann, and Brunner (2016)[22] describe a phenomenon whereby the criminal and jihadist worlds can intersect. It is a situation in which both types of groups "have come to recruit from the same pool of people, creating (often unintended) synergies and overlaps that have consequences for how individuals radicalise and operate." Jihadism has two separate functions for street criminals: (1) To validate criminal activity (e.g., harming or killing enemies in *dar al-harb*—"the lands of war"—is still considered jihad); and (2) jihadism can also be used as a type of redemption for segregated or ostracized street criminals.[23] Crime–jihad networks can be centralized or decentralized. In the case of the latter, they can take the form of a composite network that consists of discrete cells communicating across geographic locations and time periods.

Enter the network around Khalid Zerkani. Born in Morocco in 1973, Zerkani migrated to Belgium in the 1990s. First involved in petty crime and theft, he quickly evolved into a talented recruiter for ISIS. He pushed Muslim youths of Moroccan backgrounds to engage in petty crimes and robberies in Brussels (as a way to join the GJM later).[24] His argument for encouraging people to do so was rooted in the Muslim religion: as a witness in his trial said, Zerkani told recruits that "to steal from the infidels is permitted by Allah."[25] The proceeds were soon divided amongst the group, earning Zerkani the moniker of Papa Noël (Father Christmas).[26] Before his arrest in 2014, Zerkani was already a hugely powerful personality within the Brussels jihadist network. In fact, he was responsible for the recruitment of up to 72 foreign fighters. His best-known disciple was Abdelhamid Abaaoud, a key player of the network that committed the November 13, 2015 attacks in Paris and the March 22, 2016 attacks in Brussels. His tactical and operative approach illustrates how the new crime–terror nexus in Belgium worked, and it created an effective merger of two milieus.[27]

To cite another example, the Norwegian Police Security Service examined a sample of 137 people suspected of being dangerous jihadists. The sample ranged from people involved in extreme pro-jihad milieus to others coordinating terrorist attacks or traveling to Syria to join ISIS. The relatively small sample of women were usually law-abiding, but 68% of the men had been suspected, charged, or condemned for criminal acts before their radicalization. More precisely, 43% were drug abusers, 42% were implicated in drug-related crimes, and 46% were accused of non-political violent offenses.[28] Similar numbers can be found in neighboring Sweden, where about 60% of jihadist foreign fighters have a history of at least one crime on their record.[29]

Jihadist networks of foreign fighters

Foreign fighters are "noncitizens of conflict states who join insurgencies during civil conflicts."[30] Particularly in the twenty-first century, these volunteers have undertaken direct combat roles and even engaged in suicide bombing.[31] Other people who migrate to conflict zones undertake not combat roles, but auxiliary roles within insurgent groups. For this reason, we need to consider such individuals as foreign combatants because it is not always possible to know the extent or nature of their roles once they move to a conflict zone (or how their roles change over time).[32] When it comes to Islamic foreign fighters, they often depict themselves as heroes being called upon to fight the "enemies of Islam" in territories with tyrannical régimes and conditions that subjugate Muslims, subdue their movements, and do not allow them to be in control of their destiny. They call on the ummah to jump on the global jihad bandwagon. It becomes a global fight framed as a religious obligation to uphold the principles of pan-Islamic unity.[33] The majority of Western Muslim fighters embark on foreign missions because they perceive the fight in Muslim lands as a legitimate defensive measure, not as an offensive or aggressive move.[34]

Western foreign fighters in global jihad

Although this phenomenon is not new, the flux of jihadist foreign fighters into Syria and Iraq is unparalleled. It has been estimated that, between 2011 and 2017, a whopping 30,000 jihadist foreign fighters landed in Syria and Iraq from more than 100 nations. About 20% of these people came from the West. This is dangerous because, besides their roles in conflict areas, some of them return to their home countries and, in turn, commit or support jihadist attacks, exploiting the connections, the experience, and the prominence they gained in the Near East. To this point, many severe jihadist attacks in Europe were coordinated or perpetrated by returned foreign fighters. Examples range from Mohammed Merah's shootings in Montauban and Toulouse in March 2012 to the aforementioned attacks in Paris on November 13, 2015.[35]

In addition to the Near East, Western Muslims have also joined the GJM in Afghanistan, Pakistan, and Somalia to protect Islam from its perceived enemies. Global jihadist networks have played a crucial role in bringing them to conflict areas by accomplishing three objectives: (1) The radicalization through mosques, jihadist sermons, and the internet, (2) the recruitment of would-be or potential jihadists (either physically or digitally), and (3) the identity formation that offers the radicalized recruits more justification to fight as members of the ummah, often an imagined global community.[36] In Somalia, Al-Shabaab has attracted support from the Somali diaspora in the United States and Europe, as well as newly converts to the religion. Western law enforcement agencies are concerned that Muslims are returning home with new terrorist skills. Foreign experiences would potentially increase the skills and efficiency of Western jihadist fighters if they opt for domestic jihadism.[37]

Making the jihadist foreign fighter

In their examination of 99 profiles of foreign Muslim fighters from Germany, Reynolds and Hafez (2019)[38] developed a dataset of profiles by looking at the national news magazines *Der Spiegel, Die Welt, BILD, Frankfurter Allgemeine Zeitung*, and *Süddeutsche Zeitung*. Based on SNA, the two researchers found that it is not so much a lack of integration with German society or pure self-radicalization through social media that led those 99 German Muslims to leave their land and fight in Syria and Iraq. Rather, most of the data suggests that close ties within jihadist networks have motivated the phenomenon of foreign fighters from Germany. Recruitment is often based on clustered mobilization within interconnected radical milieus, implying that peer-to-peer networks are a massive motivator for German foreign fighters.

By 2016, Belgium was the European nation with highest number of foreign fighters per capita (with almost 400 confirmed cases). The government of the Netherlands estimated the number of their jihadists in Syria and Iraq at 220, including one third of females.[39] In most cases, close-knit affiliations played a crucial role in the radicalization and recruitment of both Belgian and Dutch foreign fighters in global jihad. They were highly connected to one another through family bonds and friendships. Friendship primarily included both larger groups—even networks of radicals—and smaller groups or a handful of friends.[40] Such groups often insist that it is the duty of every true Muslim to travel to holy Muslim lands (now or in the future) to fight for the ummah.[41]

Jihadist financing networks

Jihadist financing networks represent a highly dynamic form of sustained jihadism across the planet. They incessantly evolve and mold themselves to new realities. Globalization enables jihadists to move money in large or small quantities, complicating the task of security agencies to track the direct or indirect flow of currency. Jihadists rely on international banks, Islamic banks, or channels of informal exchange.[42] So far, governments' approaches to fight terrorism financing are not too innovative, partly because they get entangled in red tape or policies that are still obsolete. After the September 11, 2001 attacks, the bureaucratic complications experienced by countries to implement global strategies to fight terrorism financing prohibited a genuine understanding of the financial networks of organizations like Al-Qaeda. This, in turn, stalled the possibility to sue its financiers to court. When such policies are ready to be put in place, the jihadist financing network has already evolved and their bank accounts (and money trail) have disappeared.[43]

Financial support of global jihad

Financial support of global jihad has been a legitimate concern for several decades. Jihadist organizations have been known to fund one another's activities. An elaborate network of clandestine patronage and mutual commitment connects groups financially across dispersed regions in the world. Non-governmental organizations (NGOs)—including *hawala* transfer systems, charitable organizations, and religious fundraising groups—become direct or indirect channels for funding. *Hawala* is an informal banking network (mostly in the Muslim world). Many of such NGOs are headquartered in the Arabian Peninsula.[44] Middle Eastern oil has, to some degree, contributed to terrorist and insurgent funding, making the Peninsula the nucleus of financial links feeding various movements.[45]

The financing of global jihad depends largely on visibility in the media, which unknowingly or indirectly advertises the centrality of jihadist propaganda efforts. The actual size of the international financing of jihad is impossible to assess, but a modicum of evidence suggests that it is substantial, even for organizations that already have colossal amounts of money and material resources. It is, indeed, hard to estimate the extent to which "market leaders" benefit from more funds than others, but the influx of foreign fighters is a clear sign that the global jihad business is a multi-million dollar business.[46] We know that ISIS built a 262-room luxury hotel in Mosul (Iraq) in 2015.[47] Jihad market leaders embody the far-reaching networks of finance and recruitment that link, for instance, the aforementioned "indirect jihadist players" with the outside world. Foreign fighters carry large amounts of money and materials upon their arrival, and are often "nurtured" by fundraising cartels of supporters in their homelands. The flow of foreign fighters to ISIS surpasses, by large measures, previous global migrations of mujahedin. ISIS, then, not only has a highly motivated force, but it also enjoys unmatched resources through its global network. This validates ISIS's success in outperforming other jihadist organizations and becoming the definite "market leader" of jihad.[48]

Al-Qaeda, too, uses modern communication channels for financing and recruiting reasons. Other jihadist groups like Hamas, Lashkar e-Taiba, and Hezbollah rely on the internet to raise and wire funds to support their own activities or other groups'. Modern communication tools like the internet present many advantages, such as global reach, time efficiency, and a certain level of anonymity and security for both benefactors and recipients.[49] Jihadist groups are also notorious for using charity as a smokescreen to gather funds through a gamut of community support or social programs. In a sense, through their donations, individual Muslims wittingly or unwittingly finance the work of charities that, in turn, finance jihadist operations, even when they oppose these groups' agenda.[50] They donate funds to charities that subsidize jihadist causes for reasons such as social pressure and zakat (a 2.5% tax on savings to be bequeathed to the Muslim poor and disadvantaged).[51]

Case study: Bangladesh

Enter jihadism in Bangladesh. Global networks and financiers of jihad support Bangladeshi militancy in large amounts. It is estimated that, every year, devoted followers of militant Islam in Bangladesh provide an astounding Tk120 billion (about $1.5 billion) to Islamic NGOs in that nation. These NGOs' fraudulent use of money in the name of religious and charitable activities eludes government's control, a practice that ultimately facilitates the rise of jihad. Radical religious schooling has progressed by leaps and bounds since parts of the secular constitution were discarded. Among the more than 80,000 Bangladeshi villages, there are about 74,000 madrassas.[52] A madrassa is a Muslim religious school or seminary. Although accurately determining the ideology imparted in those madrassas remains a challenge, it should come to no surprise that they encourage students to participate in jihad. Additional concerns in this Bangladeshi case are that (1) many textbooks in state madrassas are in Arabic,[53] (2) Tk5,000 is spent on each student in these madrassas (vs. Tk3,000 in state schools), and (3) the government barely oversees the syllabi, curricula, and financial proceedings within those educational institutions.[54]

Case study: Bitcoins

There is a solid body of data indicating that Bitcoins and other crypto-currencies have financed a series of jihadist attacks in Europe and Indonesia. Bitcoin is a decentralized digital currency that has no a central bank.[55] Both jihad operatives and supporters are continuing to look for new and emerging technologies like Bitcoin to alleviate some of the risks involved with financial transactions in the three-dimensional world or those of conventional online banking. Some terrorist websites are already collecting funds through Bitcoins. Many Bitcoin ATMs and Bitcoin trades can be found in places in the Middle East that have experienced a massive number of foreign fighters who trained for ISIS. In fact, such ATMs and transactions are also located in many cities across Western nations.[56]

Mutual aid

Mutual aid refers to the deliberate and reciprocal exchange of resources within a global system.[57] Included in mutual aid networks are Judaic Tzedakah, Islamic Zakat, and a multitude of Christian associations of charity, as recommended in the Acts of the Apostles.[58] Berman's (2009)[59] work, titled *Radical, Religious, and Violent: The New Economics of Terrorism*, uses a rational choice model to examine jihadization, proving that the existence of mutual aid networks makes extremist organizations even stronger. When these organizations resort to violence, they wreak more lethal damage and are shielded from defection and other forms of intervention by external entities.

Every time religious organizations offer mutual aid to numerous groups of adherents across the world, they incur economic risks. Although theological acquiescence is cheap, action can be expensive. In the case of Islamist organizations, by enforcing strict social rules, such as limits on tolerable styles of dress, diet, language, and interactions with other groups (or members of the other gender), such organizations shrewdly select the best groups that should enter into a mutual aid partnership, thereby decreasing the possibilities of free riding. These limitations present a dual effect in jihadist groups. Not only can Islamist organizations be more certain that a group is committed to the cause, but they also limit people's access to consumption opportunities and any action that might convince them to dissociate themselves from the cause. As people become more implicated in jihadist activities, their social circles encounter more restrictions which, in turn, reduce contact with would-be opponents and further reinforce radical thinking.[60]

Resource mobilization theory

Resource mobilization theory is another theory that explains the motivation of participants in a group or social movement to organize themselves in order to acquire additional or more valuable resources for their collective purposes.[61] The theory rests on the premise that members of a movement will increase their abilities to (1) acquire resources and to (2) mobilize as many potential recruits as possible to achieve the movement's goals. As opposed to the long-established collective behavior theory that regards social institutions as deviant and irrational, resource mobilization considers them rational social movements because they are produced and filled by social participants with the mission of taking a political action.[62]

According to the main tenets of resource mobilization theory, an important obstacle to an organization's success is a lack of resources. The mobilization of resources—i.e., workforce, supplies, amenities, facilities, and money—for collective action is often a challenge.[63] Although people may follow particular social or political goals, no effective collective action can be taken in support of those group goals unless they have enough resources. Flourishing social movements are always the ones that conquer the barriers to collective action. What these successful movements have in common are (1) a talented team of leaders who can materialize the group's set of ideas into political capital, and (2) a solid institutional foundation from which group leaders pull resources to create new organizations. Thanks to these internal workings, leaders can manage to cultivate resources and attract new members to a social movement.[64]

Within the context of jihad, the most certain and cost-efficient method to mobilize a militant movement is to apply tactics of an already-existing infrastructure and fine-tune them to new uses. For example, as a reaction to Iranian and Shia pressure, the Saudis adapted some of the approaches used by the Iranian-sponsored religious infrastructure in the Middle East by turning them to their own diversity of Islamist organizations and activities. Likewise, the Pakistani military régime endorsed jihadist militants and their madrassas through an already-employed low-cost structure. Their objective was to support terror in Kashmir and the Taliban group in Afghanistan. For the military government in Pakistan, the result today is a culture of terror that has turned against itself.[65]

Inside Western lands

A universal mujahedin method of organization was promoted by Osama bin Laden for Al-Qaeda in the 1990s. A key novelty was the expansion of recruitment and funding of terrorists from Islamic lands to Western Europe and the United States—two continents where a small component of Muslim immigrants had already set up an infrastructure of fundamentalist clerics, community leaders, and resource providers through institutions that could be camouflaged as schools and charitable organizations. For many years, in light of the exceptionally lenient controls on travel, communications, financial deals, study abroad programs, visa and ID documentation, and religious activities—in addition to the constitutional limits on social control of all these—it was very easy to disguise unlawful, criminal, and terrorist behaviors and actions in many nations of the Western hemisphere. Entire terrorist units could actually board a plane and fly to remote locations while these terrorists' local affiliates were providing them with vital information on targets, weapons, and safe houses.[66]

It has been confirmed by many sources that jihadists are often recruited within Western lands, in addition to would-be terrorists recruited in the Maghreb, Central Asia, and other places. In the case of Western Europe, data on recruitment patterns suggests that they more often consist of a bottom-up recruitment model than a top-down one.[67] A recurring situation is a situation in which alienated Muslim youths in European nations feel like "newborn Muslims" and take proactive steps to learn more about jihad. They attend radical mosques, get acquainted with extremist preachers, or encounter charismatic gatekeepers on the internet. In this context, a "gatekeeper" is a militant with combat experience (like the Arabs or Afghans fighting the Soviets in the 1980s). It can also be a radical with jihadist camp training in the Maghreb, Central Asia, or the Middle East. Such jihad veterans possess invaluable knowledge about jihad indoctrination and joining the GJM. As gatekeepers, they also have many contacts as to where those Muslim youths can train to become holy warriors.[68] This is exactly how jihadist battle veterans have contributed to the radicalization of thousands of youths in Western Europe. Some veterans are more open or renowned than others; they can release recorded sermons in which they preach anti-Western hatred and glorify groups like Al-Qaeda.[69]

Other group kinships in jihad

In the 1980s and 1990s, the background and personal life of individuals across the GJM were similar in multiple ways. Many combated the Soviet troops in Afghanistan. Many received religious education from Wahhabi clerics in Saudi Arabia and maintained contact with them. Later generations of jihadists waged holy battles in Kosovo, Bosnia, and Chechnya. Many went to the same madrassas (or even secular schools) together, were in the same military units, or trained together in jihadist camps. Networks of friendship or mutual obligation expanded worldwide, and some of them made mutual friends. Many fighters in global jihad were related by blood, and partnerships between groups were glued by marriage. This was the case with the marriage of Osama bin Laden with Mullah Omar's daughter (he was a Taliban leader). And let us not forget follow-on leadership, whereby sons followed their fathers. Widows took revenge for their husbands' death that they became suicide bombers. This occurrence is still so common in Chechnya today that the Black Chechen Widows have gained notoriety as a distinctive sub-category of jihadists.[70]

In line with these contentions, romantic and familial entanglement is a factor in jihad that is overlooked. Certain violent extremist groups got their start through tightly knit friendship circles with mutual religious, financial, social, and sexual bonds. While this example may be true in more extreme situations, it is also relevant to radicalization in non-religious environments. Love can create a potent bond between influential people, connecting their webs of followers through a mix of attraction and loyalty.[71] People can join an existing jihadist group because their loved ones—husband, wife, boyfriend, girlfriend, another family member, or a close friend—asked them to, or because they need to assist and shield a loved one. The reverse is also true. In some cases, a member of a jihadist organization may develop a personal attraction with a new recruit.[72]

Notes

1 Rik Coolsaet, *What Drives Europeans to Syria, and to IS? Insights from the Belgian Case* (Brussels: Royal Institute for International Relations, 2015).
2 Robert S. Leiken, "Europe's Angry Muslims," *Foreign Affairs* 84, no. 4 (2005): 120–35, 120.
3 Daveed Gartenstein-Ross and Kyle Dabruzzi, "Is Al-Qaeda's Central Leadership Still Relevant?" *Middle East Quarterly* 15, no. 2 (2008): 27–36.
4 Raúl Lara-Cabrera, Antonio González Pardo, Karim Benouaret, Noura Faci, Djamal Benslimane, and David Camacho, "Measuring the Radicalisation Risk in Social Networks," *IEEE Access* 5 (2017): 10892–900. https://doi.org/10.1109/ACCESS.2017.2706018
5 Valdis E. Krebs, "Unlocking Terrorist Networks," *First Monday* 2, no. 4 (2002): 10–21.
6 David Bright, Chad Whelan, and Shandon Harris-Hogan, "On the Durability of Terrorist Networks: Revealing the Hidden Connections between Jihadist Cells," *Studies in Conflict & Terrorism* 43, no. 7 (2020): 638–56. https://doi.org/10.1080/1057610X.2018.1494411
7 Shandon Harris-Hogan, "Australian Neo-Jihadist Terrorism: Mapping the Network and Cell Analysis Using Wiretap Evidence," *Studies in Conflict & Terrorism* 35, no. 4 (2012): 298–314. https://doi.org/10.1080/1057610X.2012.656344
8 Ibid., 302.
9 Eliane Tschaen Barbieri and Jytte Klausen, "Al Qaeda's London Branch: Patterns of Domestic and Transnational Network Integration," *Studies in Conflict & Terrorism* 35, no. 6 (2012): 411–31. https://doi.org/10.1080/1057610X.2012.675551
10 Shandon Harris-Hogan and Kate Barrelle, "Young Blood: Understanding the Emergence of a New Cohort of Australian Jihadists," *Terrorism and Political Violence* (2018). https://doi.org/10.1080/09546553.2018.1473858
11 John Scott, *Social Network Analysis* (4th ed.) (Thousand Oaks, CA: Sage, 2017).
12 Carlo Morselli, Cynthia Giguère, and Katia Petit, "The Efficiency/Security Trade-off in Criminal Networks," *Social Networks* 29, no. 1 (2007): 143–53. https://doi.org/10.1016/j.socnet.2006.05.001
13 Valdis E. Krebs, "Mapping Networks of Terrorist Cells," *Connections* 24, no. 3 (2002): 43–52; Efstathios D. Mainas, "The Analysis of Criminal Terrorist Organizations as Social Network Structures: A Quasi-Experimental Study," *International Journal of Police Science & Management* 14, no. 3 (2012): 264–82. https://doi.org/10.1350/ijps.2012.14.3.285

14 Stephen P. Borgatti, Martin G. Everett, and Jeffrey C. Johnson, *Analyzing Social Networks* (2nd ed.) (Thousand Oaks, CA: Sage, 2018).
15 Jasper L. de Bie, Christianne J. de Poot, Joshua D. Freilich, and Steven M. Chermake, "Changing Organizational Structures of Jihadist Networks in the Netherlands," *Social Networks* 48 (2017): 270–83. https://doi.org/10.1016/j.socnet.2016.09.004
16 John Arquilla, David Ronfeldt, and Michele Zanini, "Networks, Netwar, and Information-Age Terrorism," in *Countering the New Terrorism*, ed. Ian O. Lesser, Bruce Hoffman, John Arquilla, David Ronfeldt, Michele Zanini, and Brian Michael Jenkins (Santa Monica, CA: RAND Corporation, 1999): 39–81. 41, 45.
17 Mitchel Kelly and Anthea McCarthy-Jones, "Mapping Connections: A Dark Network Analysis of Neojihadism in Australia," *Terrorism and Political Violence.* https://doi.org/10.1080/09546553.2019.1586675
18 Chad Whelan, *Networks and National Security: Dynamics, Effectiveness and Organization* (Farnham: Ashgate Publishing, 2012).
19 Yannick Veilleux-Lepage, "Paradigmatic Shifts in Jihadism in Cyberspace: The Emerging Role of Unaffiliated Sympathizers in Islamic State's Social Media Strategy," *Contemporary Voices: St Andrews Journal of International Relations* 7, no. 1 (2016): 36–51. http://doi.org/10.15664/jtr.1183
20 Jarret M. Brachman, *Global Jihadism: Theory and Practice* (New York: Routledge, 2008).
21 Veilleux-Lepage, "Paradigmatic Shifts in Jihadism in Cyberspace," 38–9.
22 Rahan Basra, Peter R. Neumann, and Claudia Brunner, *Criminal Pasts, Terrorist Futures: European Jihadists and the New Crime–Terror Nexus* (London: The International Centre for the Study of Radicalisation and Political Violence, 2016): 3.
23 Ibid., 26.
24 Rajan Basra and Peter R. Neumann, "Criminal Pasts, Terrorist Futures: European Jihadists and the New Crime–Terror Nexus," *Perspectives on Terrorism* 10, no. 6 (2016): 25–40.
25 Andrew Higgins and Kimiko De Freytas-Tamura, "A Brussels Mentor Who Taught 'Gangster Islam' to the Young and Angry," *The New York Times* (2016, April 11): A1.
26 Pieter Van Ostaeyen, "Belgian Radical Networks and the Road to the Paris Attacks," *CTC Sentinel* (2016, June 16): 10–4.
27 Ibid., 29.
28 Jonathan Ilan and Sveinung Sandberg, "How 'Gangsters' Become Jihadists: Bourdieu, Criminology and the Crime–Terrorism Nexus," *European Journal of Criminology* 16, no. 3 (2019): 278–94. https://doi.org/10.1177/1477370819828936
29 Amir Rostami, Joakim Sturup, Hernan Mondani, Pia Thevselius, Jerzy Sarnecki, and Christofer Edling, "The Swedish Mujahideen: An Exploratory Study of 41 Swedish Foreign Fighters Deceased in Iraq and Syria," *Studies in Conflict & Terrorism* 43, no. 5 (2020): 382–95. https://doi.org/10.1080/1057610X.2018.1463615
30 David Malet, *Foreign Fighters: Transnational Identity in Civil Conflicts* (New York: Oxford University Press, 2013), 9.
31 Mohammed Hafez, *Suicide Bombers in Iraq: The Strategy and Ideology of Martyrdom* (Washington, D.C.: United States Institute of Peace, 2007).
32 Sean C. Reynolds and Mohammed M. Hafez, "Social Network Analysis of German Foreign Fighters in Syria and Iraq," *Terrorism and Political Violence* 31, no. 4 (2019): 661–86. https://doi.org/10.1080/09546553.2016.1272456
33 Thomas Hegghammer, "The Rise of Muslim Foreign Fighters: Islam and the Globalization of Jihad," *International Security* 35, no. 3 (2010): 53–94. https://doi.org/10.1162/ISEC_a_00023
34 Thomas Hegghammer, "Should I Stay or Should I Go? Explaining Variation in Western Jihadists' Choice between Domestic and Foreign Fighting," *American Political Science Review* 107, no. 1 (2013): 1–157. https://doi.org/10.1017/S0003055412000615
35 Francesco Marone, "Ties that Bind: Dynamics of Group Radicalisation in Italy's Jihadists Headed for Syria and Iraq," *The International Spectator* 52, no. 3 (2017): 48–63. https://doi.org/10.1080/03932729.2017.1322800

36 Emmanuel Karagiannis, "Transnational Islamist Networks: Western Fighters in Afghanistan, Somalia and Syria," *The International Spectator* 48, no. 4 (2013): 119–34. https://doi.org/10.1080/03932729.2013.847696
37 Ibid., 120.
38 Reynolds and Hafez, 661.
39 Edwin Bakker and Roel de Bont, "Belgian and Dutch Jihadist Foreign Fighters (2012–2015): Characteristics, Motivations, and Roles in the War in Syria and Iraq," *Small Wars & Insurgencies* 27, no. 5 (2016): 837–57. https://doi.org/10.1080/09592318.2016.1209806
40 Ibid., 844.
41 Ibid., 846.
42 Osman Antwi-Boateng, "The Rise of Pan-Islamic Terrorism in Africa: A Global Security Challenge," *Politics & Policy* 45, no. 2 (2017): 253–84. https://doi.org/10.1111/polp.12195
43 Loretta Napoleoni, "Terrorist Financing," *The RUSI Journal* 151, no. 1 (2006): 60–5. https://doi.org/10.1080/03071840609442004
44 Chris Chaplin, "Imagining the Land of the Two Holy Mosques: The Social and Doctrinal Importance of Saudi Arabia in Indonesian Salafi Discourse," *Austrian Journal of South-East Asian Studies* 7, no. 2 (2014): 217–36.
45 Erika Solomon, Guy Chazan, and Sam Jones, "ISIS Inc: How Oil Fuels the Jihadi Terrorists," *Financial Times* (2015, October 14): A1.
46 Brynjar Lia, "Understanding Jihadi Proto-States," *Perspectives on Terrorism* 9, no. 4 (2015): 31–41.
47 Heather Saul, "ISIS Opens 262-Room Luxury Hotel in Mosul," *The Independent* (2015, May 6): A1.
48 Lia, "Understanding Jihadi Proto-States," 32–8.
49 Michael Jacobson, "Terrorist Financing and the Internet," *Studies in Conflict & Terrorism* 33, no. 4 (2010): 353–63. https://doi.org/10.1080/10576101003587184
50 Tolga Koker and Carlos L. Yordan, "Microfinancing Terrorism: A Study in Al Qaeda Financing Strategy," in *State of Corruption, State of Chaos: The Terror of Political Malfeasance*, ed. Michaelene Cox (Lanham, MD: Lexington Books, 2008): 167–82.
51 Matthew Levitt, *Hamas: Politics, Charity, and Terrorism in the Service of Jihad* (New Haven, CT: Yale University Press, 2006).
52 Asim Roy, *Islam in History and Politics: Perspectives from South Asia* (New York: Oxford University Press, 2006).
53 Qandeel Siddique, *Weapons of Mass Instruction? A Preliminary Exploration of the Link between Madrassas in Pakistan and Militancy* (Kjeller, Norway: Norwegian Defence Research Establishment, 2009).
54 Roy, *Islam in History and Politics*, 12.
55 Dirk G. Baur, Ki Hoon Hong, and Adrian D. Lee, "Bitcoin: Medium of Exchange or Speculative Assets?" Journal of *International Financial Markets, Institutions and Money* 54 (2018): 177–89. https://doi.org/10.1016/j.intfin.2017.12.004
56 Angela S. M. Irwin, "The Use of Crypto-Currencies in Funding Violent Jihad," *Journal of Money Laundering Control* 19, no. 4 (2016): 10–21. https://doi.org/10.1108/JMLC-01-2016-0003
57 Alex Gitterman, *Mutual Aid Groups, Vulnerable and Resilient Populations, and the Life Cycle* (3rd Ed.) (New York: Columbia University Press, 2005); Peter Kropotkin, *Mutual Aid: A Factor of Evolution* (Charleston, SC: Forgotten Books, 2008).
58 Meredith Gould, *Deliberate Acts of Kindness: Service as a Spiritual Practice* (New York: Doubleday, 2002).
59 Eli Berman, *Radical, Religious, and Violent: The New Economics of Terrorism* (Cambridge, MA: MIT Press, 2009).
60 Berman, *Radical, Religious, and Violent*, 10–4.
61 John D. McCarthy and Mayer N. Zald, "Resource Mobilization and Social Movements: A Partial Theory," *American Journal of Sociology* 82, no. 6 (1977): 1212–41. https://doi.org/10.1086/226464

62 Steven M. Buechler, *Social Movements in Advanced Capitalism* (Oxford: Oxford University Press, 1999).
63 Bert Klandermans, "Mobilization and Participation: Social-Psychological Expansions of Resource Mobilization Theory," *American Sociological Review* 49, no. 5 (1984): 583–600. http://dx.doi.org/10.2307/2095417
64 Daniel M. Cress and David A. Snow, "Mobilization at the Margins: Resources, Benefactors, and the Viability of Homeless Social Movement Organizations," *American Sociological Review* 61, no. 6 (1996): 1089–109. https://doi.org/10.2307/2096310
65 Jessica Stern, "Pakistan's *Jihad* Culture," *Foreign Affairs* 79 (2000): 115–26.
66 Anthony Oberschall, "Explaining Terrorism: The Contribution of Collective Action Theory," *Sociological Theory* 22, no. 1 (2004): 26–37. https://doi.org/10.1111/j.1467-9558.2004.00202.x
67 Michael Taarnby, *Recruitment of Islamist Terrorists in Europe* (Aarhus: Danish Ministry of Justice, 2005).
68 Olivier Roy, *Globalised Islam: The Search for a New Ummah* (London: Hurst, 2004).
69 Petter Nesser, "Jihadism in Western Europe after the Invasion of Iraq: Tracing Motivational Influences from the Iraq War on Jihadist Terrorism in Western Europe," *Studies in Conflict & Terrorism* 29, no. 4 (2006): 323–42, 326. https://doi.org/10.1080/10576100600641899
70 David J. Kilcullen, "Countering Global Insurgency," *Journal of Strategic Studies* 28, no. 4 (2005): 597–617. https://doi.org/10.1080/01402390500300956
71 Donatella Della Porta, *Social Movements, Political Violence, and the State: A Comparative Analysis of Italy and Germany* (Cambridge: Cambridge University Press, 1995).
72 Christian Leuprecht, Todd Hataley, Sophia Moskalenko, and Clark Mccauley, "Containing the Narrative: Strategy and Tactics in Countering the Storyline of Global Jihad," *Journal of Policing, Intelligence and Counter Terrorism* 5, no. 1 (2010): 42–57, 49. https://doi.org/10.1080/18335300.2010.9686940

References

Antwi-Boateng, Osman, "The Rise of Pan-Islamic Terrorism in Africa: A Global Security Challenge," *Politics & Policy* 45, no. 2 (2017): 253–284. https://doi.org/10.1111/polp.12195.

Arquilla, John, David Ronfeldt, and Michele Zanini, "Networks, Netwar, and Information-Age Terrorism," in *Countering the New Terrorism*, edited by Ian O. Lesser, Bruce Hoffman, John Arquilla, David Ronfeldt, Michele Zanini, and Brian Michael Jenkins, 39–81. Santa Monica, CA: RAND Corporation, 1999.

Bakker, Edwin, and Roel de Bont, "Belgian and Dutch Jihadist Foreign Fighters (2012–2015): Characteristics, Motivations, and Roles in the War in Syria and Iraq," *Small Wars & Insurgencies* 27, no. 5 (2016): 837–857. https://doi.org/10.1080/09592318.2016.1209806.

Barbieri, Eliane Tschaen, and Jytte Klausen, "Al Qaeda's London Branch: Patterns of Domestic and Transnational Network Integration," *Studies in Conflict & Terrorism* 35, no. 6 (2012): 411–431. https://doi.org/10.1080/1057610X.2012.675551.

Basra, Rajan, and Peter R. Neumann, "Criminal Pasts, Terrorist Futures: European Jihadists and the New Crime–Terror Nexus," *Perspectives on Terrorism* 10, no. 6 (2016): 25–40.

Basra, Rajan, and Peter R. Neumann, and Claudia Brunner, *Criminal Pasts, Terrorist Futures: European Jihadists and the New Crime–Terror Nexus.* London: The International Centre for the Study of Radicalisation and Political Violence, 2016.

Baur, Dirk G., Ki Hoon Hong, and Adrian D. Lee, "Bitcoin: Medium of Exchange or Speculative Assets?" *Journal of International Financial Markets, Institutions and Money* 54 (2018): 177–189. https://doi.org/10.1016/j.intfin.2017.12.004.

Berman, Eli, *Radical, Religious, and Violent: The New Economics of Terrorism*. Cambridge, MA: MIT Press, 2009.

Borgatti, Stephen P., Martin G. Everett, and Jeffrey C. Johnson, *Analyzing Social Networks* (2nd ed.). Thousand Oaks, CA: Sage, 2018.

Brachman, Jarret, *Global Jihadism: Theory and Practice*. New York: Routledge, 2008.

Bright, David, Chad Whelan, and Shandon Harris-Hogan, "On the Durability of Terrorist Networks: Revealing the Hidden Connections between Jihadist Cells," *Studies in Conflict & Terrorism* 43, no. 7 (2020): 638–656. https://doi.org/10.1080/1057610X.2018.1494411.

Buechler, Steven M., *Social Movements in Advanced Capitalism*. Oxford: Oxford University Press, 1999.

Chaplin, Chris, "Imagining the Land of the Two Holy Mosques: The Social and Doctrinal Importance of Saudi Arabia in Indonesian Salafi Discourse," *Austrian Journal of South-East Asian Studies* 7, no. 2 (2014): 217–236.

Coolsaet, Rik, *What Drives Europeans to Syria, and to IS? Insights from the Belgian Case*. Brussels: Royal Institute for International Relations, 2015.

Cress, Daniel M., and David A. Snow, "Mobilization at the Margins: Resources, Benefactors, and the Viability of Homeless Social Movement Organizations," *American Sociological Review* 61, no. 6 (1996): 1089–1109. https://doi.org/10.2307/2096310.

de Bie, Jasper L., Christianne J. de Poot, Joshua D. Freilich, and Steven M. Chermake, "Changing Organizational Structures of Jihadist Networks in the Netherlands," *Social Networks* 48 (2017): 270–283. https://doi.org/10.1016/j.socnet.2016.09.004.

Della Porta, Donatella, *Social Movements, Political Violence, and the State: A Comparative Analysis of Italy and Germany*. Cambridge: Cambridge University Press, 1995.

Gartenstein-Ross, Daveed, and Kyle Dabruzzi, "Is Al-Qaeda's Central Leadership Still Relevant?" *Middle East Quarterly* 15, no. 2 (2008): 27–36.

Gitterman, Alex, *Mutual Aid Groups, Vulnerable and Resilient Populations, and the Life Cycle* (3rd ed.). New York: Columbia University Press, 2005.

Gould, Meredith, *Deliberate Acts of Kindness: Service as a Spiritual Practice*. New York: Doubleday, 2002.

Hafez, Mohammed, *Suicide Bombers in Iraq: The Strategy and Ideology of Martyrdom*. Washington, D.C.: United States Institute of Peace, 2007.

Harris-Hogan, Shandon, "Australian Neo-Jihadist Terrorism: Mapping the Network and Cell Analysis Using Wiretap Evidence," *Studies in Conflict & Terrorism* 35, no. 4 (2012): 298–314. https://doi.org/10.1080/1057610X.2012.656344.

Harris-Hogan, Shandon, and Kate Barrelle, "Young Blood: Understanding the Emergence of a New Cohort of Australian Jihadists," *Terrorism and Political Violence* (2018). https://doi.org/10.1080/09546553.2018.1473858.

Hegghammer, Thomas, "The Rise of Muslim Foreign Fighters: Islam and the Globalization of Jihad," *International Security* 35, no. 3 (2010): 53–94. https://doi.org/10.1162/ISEC_a_00023.

Hegghammer, Thomas, "Should I Stay or Should I Go? Explaining Variation in Western Jihadists' Choice between Domestic and Foreign Fighting," *American Political Science Review* 107, no. 1 (2013): 1–157. https://doi.org/10.1017/S0003055412000615.

Higgins, Andrew, and Kimiko De Freytas-Tamura, "A Brussels Mentor Who Taught 'Gangster Islam' to the Young and Angry," *The New York Times* (2016, April 11): A1.

Ilan, Jonathan, and Sveinung Sandberg, "How 'Gangsters' Become Jihadists: Bourdieu, Criminology and the Crime–Terrorism Nexus," *European Journal of Criminology* 16, no. 3 (2019): 278–294. https://doi.org/10.1177/1477370819828936.

Irwin, Angela S. M., "The Use of Crypto-Currencies in Funding Violent Jihad," *Journal of Money Laundering Control* 19, no. 4 (2016): 10–21. https://doi.org/10.1108/JMLC-01-2016-0003.

Jacobson, Michael, "Terrorist Financing and the Internet," *Studies in Conflict & Terrorism* 33, no. 4 (2010): 353–363. https://doi.org/10.1080/10576101003587184.

Karagiannis, Emmanuel, "Transnational Islamist Networks: Western Fighters in Afghanistan, Somalia and Syria," *The International Spectator* 48, no. 4 (2013): 119–134. https://doi.org/10.1080/03932729.2013.847696.

Kelly, Mitchel, and Anthea McCarthy-Jones, "Mapping Connections: A Dark Network Analysis of Neojihadism in Australia," *Terrorism and Political Violence* (2019). https://doi.org/10.1080/09546553.2019.1586675.

Kilcullen, David J., "Countering Global Insurgency," *Journal of Strategic Studies* 28, no. 4 (2005): 597–617. https://doi.org/10.1080/01402390500300956.

Klandermans, Bert, "Mobilization and Participation: Social-Psychological Expansions of Resource Mobilization Theory," *American Sociological Review* 49, no. 5 (1984): 583–600. http://dx.doi.org/10.2307/2095417.

Koker, Tolga, and Carlos L.Yordan, "Microfinancing Terrorism: A Study in Al Qaeda Financing Strategy," in *State of Corruption, State of Chaos: The Terror of Political Malfeasance,* edited by Michaelene Cox, 167–182. Lanham, MD: Lexington Books, 2008.

Krebs, Valdis E., "Mapping Networks of Terrorist Cells," *Connections* 24, no. 3 (2002): 43–52.

Krebs, Valdis E., "Unlocking Terrorist Networks," *First Monday* 2, no. 4 (2002): 10–21.

Kropotkin, Peter, *Mutual Aid: A Factor of Evolution.* Charleston, SC: Forgotten Books, 2008.

Lara-Cabrera, Raúl, Antonio González Pardo, Karim Benouaret, Noura Faci, Djamal Benslimane, and David Camacho, "Measuring the Radicalisation Risk in Social Networks," *IEEE Access* 5 (2017): 10892–10900. https://doi.org/10.1109/ACCESS.2017.2706018.

Leiken, Robert S., "Europe's Angry Muslims," *Foreign Affairs* 84, no. 4 (2005): 120–135.

Leuprecht, Christian, Todd Hataley, Sophia Moskalenko, and Clark Mccauley, "Containing the Narrative: Strategy and Tactics in Countering the Storyline of Global Jihad," *Journal of Policing, Intelligence and Counter Terrorism* 5, no. 1 (2010): 42–57. https://doi.org/10.1080/18335300.2010.9686940.

Levitt, Matthew, *Hamas: Politics, Charity, and Terrorism in the Service of Jihad.* New Haven, CT: Yale University Press, 2006.

Lia, Brynjar, "Understanding Jihadi Proto-States," *Perspectives on Terrorism* 9, no. 4 (2015): 31–41.

Mainas, Efstathios D., "The Analysis of Criminal Terrorist Organizations as Social Network Structures: A Quasi-Experimental Study," *International Journal of Police Science & Management* 14, no. 3 (2012): 264–282. https://doi.org/10.1350/ijps.2012.14.3.285.

Malet, David, *Foreign Fighters: Transnational Identity in Civil Conflicts.* New York: Oxford University Press, 2013.

Marone, Francesco, "Ties that Bind: Dynamics of Group Radicalisation in Italy's Jihadists Headed for Syria and Iraq," *The International Spectator* 52, no. 3 (2017): 48–63. https://doi.org/10.1080/03932729.2017.1322800.

McCarthy, John D., and Mayer N. Zald, "Resource Mobilization and Social Movements: A Partial Theory," *American Journal of Sociology* 82, no. 6 (1977): 1212–1241. https://doi.org/10.1086/226464.

Morselli, Carlo, Cynthia Giguère, and Katia Petit, "The Efficiency/Security Trade-off in Criminal Networks," *Social Networks* 29, no. 1 (2007): 143–153. https://doi.org/10.1016/j.socnet.2006.05.001.

Napoleoni, Loretta, "Terrorist Financing," *The RUSI Journal* 151, no. 1 (2006): 60–65. https://doi.org/10.1080/03071840609442004.

Nesser, Petter, "Jihadism in Western Europe after the Invasion of Iraq: Tracing Motivational Influences from the Iraq War on Jihadist Terrorism in Western Europe," *Studies in Conflict & Terrorism* 29, no. 4 (2006): 323–342. https://doi.org/10.1080/10576100600641899.

Oberschall, Anthony, "Explaining Terrorism: The Contribution of Collective Action Theory," *Sociological Theory* 22, no. 1 (2004): 26–37. https://doi.org/10.1111/j.1467-9558.2004.00202.x.

Reynolds, Sean C., and Mohammed M. Hafez, "Social Network Analysis of German Foreign Fighters in Syria and Iraq," *Terrorism and Political Violence* 31, no. 4 (2019): 661–686. https://doi.org/10.1080/09546553.2016.1272456.

Rostami, Amir, Joakim Sturup, Hernan Mondani, Pia Thevselius, Jerzy Sarnecki, and Christofer Edling, "The Swedish Mujahideen: An Exploratory Study of 41 Swedish Foreign Fighters Deceased in Iraq and Syria," *Studies in Conflict & Terrorism* 43, no. 5 (2020): 382–395. https://doi.org/10.1080/1057610X.2018.1463615.

Roy, Asim, *Islam in History and Politics: Perspectives from South Asia*. New York: Oxford University Press, 2006.

Roy, Olivier, *Globalised Islam: The Search for a New Ummah*. London: Hurst, 2004.

Saul, Heather, "ISIS Opens 262-Room Luxury Hotel in Mosul," *The Independent* (2015, May 6): A1.

Scott, John, *Social Network Analysis* (4th ed.). Thousand Oaks, CA: Sage, 2017.

Siddique, Qandeel, *Weapons of Mass Instruction? A Preliminary Exploration of the Link between Madrassas in Pakistan and Militancy*. Kjeller, Norway: Norwegian Defence Research Establishment, 2009.

Solomon, Erika, Guy Chazan, and Sam Jones, "ISIS Inc: How Oil Fuels the Jihadi Terrorists," *Financial Times* (2015, October 14): A1.

Stern, Jessica, "Pakistan's Jihad Culture," *Foreign Affairs* 79 (2000): 115–126.

Taarnby, Michael, *Recruitment of Islamist Terrorists in Europe*. Aarhus: Danish Ministry of Justice, 2005.

Van Ostaeyen, Pieter, "Belgian Radical Networks and the Road to the Paris Attacks," *CTC Sentinel* (2016, June 16): 10–14.

Veilleux-Lepage, Yannick, "Paradigmatic Shifts in Jihadism in Cyberspace: The Emerging Role of Unaffiliated Sympathizers in Islamic State's Social Media Strategy," *Contemporary Voices: St Andrews Journal of International Relations* 7, no. 1 (2016): 36–51. http://doi.org/10.15664/jtr.1183.

Whelan, Chad, *Networks and National Security: Dynamics, Effectiveness and Organization*. Farnham: Ashgate Publishing, 2012.

6

THE MASS MEDIA

The mass media play a critical role through the production of news in influencing how citizens have their perceptions and opinions shaped. "The entire study of mass communication," McQuail (1994)[1] wrote, "is based on the premise that the media have significant effects." In this chapter, "mass media" is used to include traditional news media, such as independent and government-controlled radio and television broadcasts, wire agencies, newspapers, and online news publications, all operated by trained or skilled journalists.[2] The global penetration of the mass media and the values, images, and tastes they purvey, have a powerful impact upon myriad cultures. The phrase "mass media" does not include self-proclaimed jihadists who post only on Twitter, Facebook, or other social media platforms. Chapter 10, titled The Jihadisphere, is exclusively devoted to cyberspace and online media platforms used by jihadists.

Jihadists' relentless combat-driven rise has been fueled by a savvy media-driven war, fought not with bullets but with bulletins, not with rockets but with reports, not with tanks but with timely theological thought-pieces. Jihadists' high-order production skills involved in mediated bloodletting seem very effective in reaching the predominantly young Muslim target audiences.[3] Jihadists' success in alarming the international community is largely contributed to by their use of the mass media. Jihadist leaders have utilized the ability to promulgate change through the use of social engineering and mass media outlets to further advance agendas and causes. For instance, Juergensmeyer (2002)[4] claims that terrorism is being increasingly performed for a televised global audience, "as vivid as the globalised forms of entertainment and information that crowd satellite television channels and the internet." The increasing use of global media by jihadists reaffirms that the "indeterminate" nature of jihadism poses a more serious threat to global insecurity than sovereign states.[5] This desire to engage with and mobilize the Muslim masses in order to combat the grave existential threat posed by obsolescence has been the principal underlying factor behind the rise of the media jihad.[6] Global jihadists have focused on the media as the primary vehicle to avert failure, in much the same way as the doctrine of "winning hearts and minds" has been deployed to shore up counter-terror efforts.[7]

Surprisingly dangerous outreach

The media outreach of certain jihadist organizations is astonishingly effective and dangerous. For example, from 2014 to 2016, the central organization of ISIS's media output was handled by the Ministry of Media, which operated through four divisions, each of which had a different brief.[8] Each Islamic State province (over 30 of them in 2015) also had "its own regional media bureau, all of which could produce and distribute their own content."[9] With online content, there is a multiplier effect from the activities of sympathizers (known as "disseminators") who repost and transmit material to their own networks. Jihadist media should be seen as a form of outreach designed to advance the cause of an extremist religious ideology and framed as Islamic. This outreach is based on dynamic integration of messaging on multiple media platforms, along with careful communication analysis and strategizing.[10]

Prominent jihadist media platforms include Global Islamic Media Front or Al-Fajar Media Center, which not only dedicated to reproducing material produced by others; they are also, in a rather imaginative manner, motivated to produce their own content in support of jihadist discourse. "Media platform" is understood to be those "virtual" organizations whose principal mission is to edit, reproduce, and support the propagandistic actions of jihadist groups immersed in terrorist violence.[11] Al-Qaeda's media strategy is central to its military strategy in its fight against the West. Ayman Al-Zawahiri, the current leader of the organization, has argued that "more than half of this battle is taking place in the battlefield of the media. We are in a media battle in a race for the hearts and minds of our ummah."[12] In fact, jihadists have been remarkably prescient in recognizing the centrality of the media to this battle—and indeed to their very existence—arguably far more so than their opponents.[13]

Propaganda of the deed

Propaganda of the deed includes extremists employing political violence or terror as well as the mass media to justify their deeds and gain public sympathy for their goals. The main idea is that "terrorists strikes would drive fear into targeted societies and make them amenable to the revolutionary changes they sought."[14] In this realm, fear becomes part and parcel of the terrorist rhetoric targeting audience that both the terrorists and the governmental leaders claim to represent. The mass media inflates fear via exaggerating threats of perceived enemies. Political violence or terror, especially when supported with live coverage, shows off the ability to supersede the other apparently powerful side. The mass media are important in shaping public agendas by influencing what people think about and how events and issues are packaged and presented. Hence, both state and non-state actors, thus, exploit the mass media to rationalize their deeds and legitimize their perpetual violence, recommend actions or counteractions, and clarify their ethical virtue and efficacy.[15]

Galloway (2016)[16] talks about "media jihad." As the GJM battles on the ground, it advances its media strategies with a constant on- and offline output merging pre-modern religious ideology with twenty-first-century communication management. A particular jihadist method of propaganda of the deed consists of providing a video narrative, using social media such as YouTube, as a pre-packaged broadcast content for further dissemination through the mainstream media. Jihadists disseminate videos through websites while a copy is given to mass media outlets such as Al Jazeera for further amplification to sympathetic audiences. "Media jihad" is propaganda of the deed that targets both local and international audiences.[17] It complements an on-the-ground, battlefield-based "offensive jihad."[18] An example occurred on September 13, 2011, when the Taliban attacked the U.S. Embassy and NATO headquarters in Kabul, Afghanistan, which was preceded by the 10th anniversary of 9/11. On September 12, 2011, Al-Qaeda's leader, Ayman Al-Zawahiri, released a one-hour video to jihadist websites and Al Jazeera marking the 10th anniversary of 9/11. Such coordination between the Taliban and Al-Qaeda is routine for organized transnational extremists projecting their utopian theocracies and political advocacy in unstable regions of the world such as Pakistan and Yemen.[19]

Functions of jihadist mass media

The functions of jihadist mass media are manifold; they include communication, mobilization, recruitment, training, media production, and dissemination. An important function of jihadist mass media, and indeed its *raison d'être*, has always been news provision or propaganda: to furnish information about Muslim oppression and grievances, and document the activities of the mujahedin in order to mobilize the masses and rally others to the cause.[20] Communication and transmission of ideological discourse are of paramount importance to collective mobilization.[21] Such communication is critical to "how entities are formed, how people come to share a political cause and mobilize around it, as well as how political action can turn to violence."[22] Any attempt at recruitment makes use of persuasive instruments, direct (e.g., a face-to-face invitation to participate in paramilitary training) or indirect (e.g., political pronouncements and exhortations posted on a Web site). These instruments include every form of mass media in use today (e.g., newspapers, radio, television, and the web) as well as interpersonal social influence (e.g., sermons, rumors, education, and training).

The media productions of jihadist organizations have something in common with Western notions of propaganda, such as exploiting bandwagon effects.[23] Already in the 1980s, powerful jihadist mass media to emerge did precisely this during the Afghan jihad against the USSR. The *al-Jihad* magazine edited by Abdullah Azzam, for example, focused on the humanitarian plight of Afghan civilians, denouncing the atrocities committed by Soviet forces and simultaneously extolling the virtues of jihad in defense of Muslim lands—all of which greatly facilitated the steady influx of donations, equipment, and volunteers, particularly from within the Arab world.[24] Especially in the twenty-first century, the jihadist movement seeks to gain traction from many alleged "anti-Muslim" incidents. For example, in December 2009, Al-Qaeda's media wing *al-Sahab* released a missive titled "Letter to My Muslim Sisters" from Ayman al-Zawahiri's wife Umayma, in which she stated, "The campaign against the veil represents the most intense battle between Islam and unbelief," no doubt seeking to influence the sentiments of European Muslim women.[25]

Osama bin Laden's take on the media

In November 2002, Osama bin Laden, upon speaking to the ummah, declared that the media was an essential tool in disseminating the "truth" about the enemy. His following statement[26] exemplifies this:

> The time has come to have the media take its rightful place, to carry out its required role in confronting this aggressive campaign and the open declared Crusader war by all means that can be seen, heard, and read. It is upon the media people, whether writers, journalists, analysts or correspondents, to exercise responsibility in reporting events, and to carry out their required role by showing the Ummah the reality of the events, and to announce the real intentions of the enemy, to reveal his plans and his tricks, and to stand unified in one line regardless of their different attitudes, for the enemy today doesn't differentiate between one group of people and another, for his aim is to get rid of everyone who's related to the Arab nation and Islam

Today, even after bin Laden's death, Al-Qaeda continues to encourage open and clandestine distribution of propaganda through diverse media channels. The spectacular character of jihadist global communication has led to global media attention that other jihadist groups envy and emulate. For example, it drew massive global media attention through its beheading videos. Since the late 1980s, Al-Qaeda has perfected a media campaign that allows potential recruits to indoctrinate themselves and encourages their transformation from consumers to producers of jihadist rhetoric. However, Al-Qaeda operates on a fine line between wanting to be seen as a legitimate Islamic social movement and employing religious justifications for mass murder. Al-Qaeda believes that preceding Jihadi groups were unsuccessful in overthrowing oppressive régimes because they could not control their own media spin.[27]

Abu Bakr Al-Baghdadi's take on the media

Until his death in late 2019, Abu Bakr Al-Baghdadi remained a key ideologue and propagandist for ISIS, going as far as claiming that he was a descendant of the

Prophet Muhammad. Al-Baghdadi believed it was important to adroitly exploit the media to (1) flaunt the group's successes on the battlefield and in its suicide missions, (2) publicize its genocidal campaigns in Syria and Iraq, (3) record its beheadings and stonings, and (4) diffuse its jihadist agenda to audiences worldwide.[28] In August 2018, in a fiery audio-recorded speech, he urged his followers to wage holy war against Westerners "in the countries of the crusaders, in Canada, Europe, and elsewhere," equating one attack in the West to 1,000 in Iraq or Syria. Mujahedin, he said, should "rip them apart, either with gunfire, or a stab to their bodies, or a bombing."[29] A few months earlier, he ordered pro-ISIS media sources to issue a series of threats against the 2018 FIFA World Cup in Russia, calling for active supporters to murder players and fans at the tournament.[30]

Al-Baghdadi knew that exploiting the media is the underpinning process of getting individuals—though most of them do not even know each other—to identify and connect with a group. It contributes to the development of social identification. Starting in 2014, ISIS's clever use of the media honed and accelerated the metamorphosis of individual Muslims into psychological members of a jihadist group. This effortless radicalization was due to ISIS's propagandist ability to exploit the communicative affordances of the media (particularly online media) to construct a shared social identity.[31]

Jihadists' manipulation of the mass media

Jihadist groups appreciate the media attention that allows them to diffuse their political message. Today, they benefit from many social media and mass media outlets. This way, they can frame their messages as they please. Because a great deal of the media establishment seeks to cover terrorism-related news, and terrorists are keenly aware that they can produce media focus on a "shocking and sensational"[32] act, the outcome is uninterrupted coverage of a terrorist incident that creates an atmosphere of fear.[33] It is often contended that those perpetrating terrorist attacks who are Muslim are driven more by the aspiration to belong to a historic epic struggle, which is underscored even more by media coverage.[34]

Symbiotic relationship

The relationship that the media and terrorists share has been called symbiotic or mutually beneficial. Their motive in exploiting the media includes the ability to reach nearly "every corner of the globe almost instantaneously."[35] In sociological terms, *symbiosis* is a relation of mutual dependence among groups in a community; these groups have to be different from one other and share complementary relations. Terrorism, in and of itself, is a psychological mechanism that serves to convey a threat to the larger society. This explains why terrorism and the media have a symbiotic relationship. By and large, they mirror the underlying principles of the democratic society. Nevertheless, media outlets vie for visibility in the open marketplace of ideas; they are frequently under pressure to keep abreast with the news and offer new, fresh information, eagerness, and entertainment. Therefore, they are made to knee-jerkingly respond to terrorist propaganda of the deed with attention-grabbing "bad news" articles.[36]

With increasingly clever technology and media controllers, government censorship has become useless. The media is no longer monolithic; modern-day coverage of terrorist incidents highly differs from that of newspapers.[37] Terrorism, as opposed to other war strategies and criminal acts, is primarily a "means to win media attention and news coverage,"[38] particularly by amateur non-state actors with limited or no access to mainstream media outlets and craving for publicity, visibility, and legitimacy. From 2014 to 2017, the growing attention on ISIS's terrorism and cruelty made it gain further ground, which was often seen through the coverage of terrorist acts that stressed the symbiotic relationship between terrorism and media.[39]

Because the two are increasingly co-dependent, there would be an inseparable love–hate relationship. In the past, mainstream mass media would regulate terrorism's public presence.[40] As a communicative act, terrorism seeks publicity to reach and inflict terror on targeted publics, but mass media has the power to magnify and contain this process. News and entertainment media intensify terror by (1) increasing the seriousness of threats by large amounts, (2) connecting threats to others, or (3) depicting threats in broad terms through rumors, linguistic vagueness, or unskilled use of numerical, quantitative metrics of "terror."[41]

Power of the image

Present-day jihadist organizations have charged themselves with video-recording many of their own missions to amplify the entertainment value of terrorism. Chechen insurgents have flaunted the power of the image to both recruit and intimidate enemies. They have done so by producing their own propaganda video series called "Russian Hell," which incorporated dreadful acts against Russian troops with Arab music in the background.[42] For Al-Qaeda, the importance of visuals has led the group to publish many more videos and photographs (in addition to writing texts). By extension, Al-Qaeda has increased the effects of mass media through a series of images extolling the virtues of martyrdom and abducting Westerners using graphic materials.[43]

Until 2017, ISIS's extreme terrorist images engendered unprecedented global media coverage so as to intimidate enemies of Islam. At the same time, ISIS also diffused messages of recruitment, propaganda, and calls for action.[44] In a specific example, less than one day after eight ISIS members attacked Paris on November 13, 2015, an ISIS recruitment video (initially released in November 2014) reappeared and gained wide circulation. The video "starred" three French men burning their passports and imploring French Muslims to leave their land for Syria and Iraq or perpetrate jihad inside France.[45] ISIS's spectacles of extreme brutality are frequently accompanied by pleas for recruitment, particularly targeting nationals interested in the terrorist act. For example, ISIS's beheading videos excessively stress the diversity of the slaughterers, "ensuring that the foreign fighters [are] clearly visible and sparking a rush [by the media] to identify them."[46] As Lesaca (2015)[47] explains,

> ISIS is following an unprecedented and sophisticated audiovisual strategy, consisting on the massive elaboration and distribution of audiovisual images that are highly salient and resonant in the culture of their targeted audiences. ISIS's audiovisual campaigning is massive in scale.

This demonstrates that these beheadings allow ISIS to attract more foreign fighters or sympathizers, simultaneously reinforcing its gloomy and terrifying image.[48] Public beheadings have been a symbolic method used by many groups, but ISIS brought this monstrous act to astronomical heights, thereby (1) reintegrating it within its propaganda framework, (2) over-sensationalizing it with state-of-the-art production and storytelling approaches, (3) diffusing it profusely through online social media, and (4) aligning it efficiently with its brand to fulfill its public diplomacy objectives of touching the hearts and minds of foreign supporters.[49]

Media framing

The ability of mass media to structure and present information is powerful in diffusing ideologies through framing.[50] Framing is a technique of arranging information into news stories published for an audience that identifies with certain events and values through a specific focus or lens.[51] Developed further by Entman (1993),[52] media framing is akin to social constructivism: mass media can be cleverly employed to determine the frames of reference for readers or viewers to interpret public events. For Entman, selection and salience are two key concepts: "To frame is to select some aspects of a perceived reality and make them more salient in a communicating text, in such a way as to promote a particular problem definition, causal interpretation, moral evaluation, and/or treatment recommendation."[53] The framing and portrayal of news in mass media can systematically determine how news consumers eventually comprehend these events.[54]

Much of this is also analogous to propaganda. Marlin (2002)[55] defines propaganda as "the organized attempt through communication to affect belief or action or inculcate attitudes in a large audience in ways that circumvent or suppress an individual's adequately informed, rational, reflective judgment." Jihadist organizations like ISIS use communication to influence beliefs and actions. Ultimately, their goal is to propagate and maintain the value system of the ummah. As Abu Bakr Al-Baghdadi, the late leader of ISIS, framed it in 2014, when addressing the ummah: "Today, you have a state and caliphate that will renew your dignity and strength, that will recover your rights and your sovereignty."[56] Under such circumstances, information is not a commodity but, instead, it communicates a moral and ethical imperative.[57]

Jihadist organizations make the most of media channels and technologies to create robust, networked organizations that try to influence how Muslims perceive events and the Western political "agenda." To achieve this, they add an anti-Western spin to news events.[58] Gamson and Modigliani (1987)[59] define such framing practice as "a central organizing idea or story line that provides meaning to an unfolding strip of events. The frame suggests what the controversy is about, the essence of the issue." Jihadist organizations have refined their media management approaches to the point of "spin doctoring," explaining away their violent deeds and then pressing others to join them.[60] In fact, it is not uncommon for terrorist groups to promote their own television and radio stations in order to fully control the reporting of events. It is also necessary to discuss framing of jihadist groups' image management. For instance, although ISIS was a focal politico-religious entity in the territories it governed in Syria and Iraq until 2019, the group wanted to not only broadcast its cruelties and triumphs, but also to position itself as a welfare state to its constituents. It achieved this through impression management techniques to prove how qualified the organization was when maneuvering the apparatus of a state, such as health and social programs.[61]

Distrust of Western news

Within a significant minority of Muslim immigrants and citizens in Europe and elsewhere, the consumption of alternative media is often caused by distrust of Western news.[62] Charges of insincerity and double standards against Western media— despite the advantages of freedom of expression and the press promoted by various U.S. administrations—have been an efficient tactic used by jihad propagandists to radicalize people. Often, the bad reputation of the mass media makes it difficult for journalists to set up interviews. When Swedish Television called a representative of a youth organization in Stockholm to ask about its alleged tributes to deceased jihadists, he simply retorted: "Why should I answer when I know that you have evil intentions?"[63]

"Collusion" between mainstream media and coalition

Many news sites have disparaged the so-called "collusion" between the mainstream media and Coalition Forces.[64] Doubts about the true reasons for the Iraq War, and condemnation of U.S. and Coalition Forces *vis-à-vis their* treatment of detainees at camps like Guantánamo Bay, Abu Ghraib, and elsewhere have eroded trust. Some news sites have published "evidence" of fabrication, concealment, or subversion of untrue "news" into the mass media. Examples include (1) the Pentagon's fabricated story about the "heroic rescue" of Jessica Lynch during the Battle of Nasiriyah, (2) the questionable claims about the uprising in Basra (during the First Gulf War in 1991), (3) the dubious claim that white phosphorus (an efficient smoke-generating agent that burns quickly) was only used to illuminate the sky during the Fallujah Offensive of November 2004 (and the subsequent confession that it was used indiscriminately against personnel and civilians), and (4) the refutation that napalm was employed in Iraq (and the subsequent acknowledgment that MK77 bombs were used; the deadliest of all forms of napalm).[65]

Case study: Al-Shabaab and alternative news media

Al-Shabaab, the Somali jihadist organization, dedicates considerable resources, time, and energy to radicalize local Muslims in Somalia and Kenya. One of its tools of radicalization is the publication of alternative news media to update followers on the organization's progress. Al-Shabaab also publishes online and offline magazines aimed at Western Muslim audiences. Like many jihadist affiliates, it understands the value of finding alternative sources to the Western mainstream media. Since the introduction of the internet, jihadist movements have managed their own media production to disseminate alternative narratives to their audiences.[66]

Time after time, Al-Shabaab has gotten better at producing such alternative news material. Its media production unit is called al-Kataib, which follows the public relations model used by renowned jihadist groups like Al-Qaeda and ISIS. The Somali organization has published English-language videos through both news reports and press releases. Highly dependent on digital videos and Twitter, the organization brands itself as a state-of-the-art media-oriented jihadist group that can fulfill Allah's will by implementing sharia and combating the enemies of Islam. Twitter allows Al-Shabaab to do this interactively, giving supporters instant updates on events and offering them to post rebuttals or critiques. While the mainstream media sometimes report losses, Al-Shabaab only extoll victories. In fact, to radicalize viewers or new recruits, Al-Shabaab posts articles that exaggerate their victories over the Somali or Kenyan government and present their own versions of events.[67]

Notes

1 Denis McQuail, *Mass Communication Theory: An Introduction* (3rd ed.) (Thousand Oaks, CA: Sage, 1994): 327.
2 Robyn Kriel, "TV, Twitter, and Telegram: Al-Shabaab's Attempts to Influence Mass Media," *Defence Strategic Communications* 4 (2018): 11–48.
3 Chris Galloway, "Media Jihad: What PR Can Learn in Islamic State's Public Relations Masterclass," *Public Relations Review* 42, no. 4 (2016): 582–90. https://doi.org/10.1016/j.pubrev.2016.03.014
4 Mark Juergensmeyer, "Religious Terror and Global War," *Global & International Studies Program* (Paper 2. University of California, 2002): 3. Retrieved on October 1, 2019 from http://repositories.cdib.org/gis/2
5 Arthur Saniotis, "Re-enchanting Terrorism: Jihadists as 'Liminal Beings'," *Studies in Conflict & Terrorism* 28, no. 6 (2005): 533–45. https://doi.org/10.1080/10576100500236907
6 Akil N. Awan, "Jihadi Ideology in the New-Media Environment," in *Contextualising Jihadi Thought*, ed. Jeevan Deol and Zaheer Kazmi (London: Hurst & Co., 2012): 99–119.
7 Ibid., 103–5.
8 Galloway, "Media Jihad," 586.

9 Monica Maggioni and Paolo Magri, *Twitter and Jihad: The Communication Strategy of ISIS* (Milan: Italian Institute for International Political Studies, 2015).

10 Galloway, "Media Jihad," 582, 586.

11 Manuel R. Torres Soriano, "Spain as an Object of Jihadist Propaganda," *Studies in Conflict & Terrorism* 32, no. 11 (2009): 933–52. https://doi.org/10.1080/10576100903259977

12 Letter from Ayman al-Zawahiri to Abu Musab al-Zarqawi.

13 Steve Tatham, *Losing Arab Hearts and Minds: The Coalition, Al Jazeera and Muslim Public Opinion* (London: Hurst & Co., 2006).

14 Brigitte Nacos, Yaeli Bloch-Elkon, and Ropert Y. Shapiro, "Post 9/11 Terrorism Threats, News Coverage, and Public Perceptions in the United States," *International Journal of Conflict and Violence* 1, no. 2 (2007): 105–26, 107. https://doi.org/10.4119/UNIBI/ijcv.10

15 Rasha El-Ibiary, "Mediatisation of Terror in Cyberspace: Scrutinizing Al-Qaeda's Media Strategy," in *The Real and the Virtual*, ed. Daniel Riha and Anna Maj (Oxford: Inter-Disciplinary, 2009): 193–202.

16 Galloway, "Media Jihad," 583.

17 Marco Lombardi, "IS 2.0 and Beyond: The Caliphate's Communication Project," in *Twitter and Jihad: The Communication Strategy of ISIS*, ed. Monica Maggioni and Paolo Magri (Milan: Italian Institute for International Political Studies, 2015): 83–122, 98.

18 Cited in Cole Bunzel, *From Paper State to Caliphate: The Ideology of the Islamic State* (Washington D.C.: Brookings Institution, 2015): 10.

19 Andrew C. Kim, "Weapons of Mass Destruction: Communicating Ethical Solutions," in *Applying the Professional Military Ethic across the Spectrum of Operations*, ed. Mark H. Wiggins and Larry Dabeck (Fort Leavenworth, KS: Command and General Staff College Foundation Press, 2012): 129–44.

20 Awan, "Jihadi Ideology," 106–7.

21 Charles Tilly, *Stories, Identities, and Political Change* (Lanham, MD: Rowman & Littlefield, 2002); Maxime Bérubé and Benoit Dupont, "Mujahideen Mobilization: Examining the Evolution of the Global Jihadist Movement's Communicative Action Repertoire," *Studies in Conflict & Terrorism* 42, no. 1 (2019): 5–24. https://doi.org/10.1080/1057610X.2018.1513689

22 Cristina Archetti, *Understanding Terrorism in the Age of Global Media: A Communication Approach* (New York: Palgrave Macmillan, 2013): 33.

23 Randal Marlin, *Propaganda and the Ethics of Persuasion* (Peterborough, ON: Broadview Press, 2002).

24 Awan, "Jihadi Ideology," 107–9.

25 Andrew Hoskins, Akil Awan, and Ben O'Loughlin, *Radicalisation and the Media: Connectivity and Terrorism in the New Media* (New York: Routledge, 2011).

26 Osama bin Laden, *Statement on Occasion of One-year Anniversary of the Beginning of the U.S. War in Afghanistan*, November 10, 2002.

27 Jeremy White, "Virtual Indoctrination and the Digihad: The Evolution of Al-Qaeda's Media Strategy," *Small Wars Journal* 8 (2012): 10–21.

28 Adam Schreck and Zeina Karam, "Islamic State Leader Al-Baghdadi Leaves a Legacy of Terror," *The Associated Press* (2019, October 27): A1.

29 Rukmini Callimachi, "ISIS Leader Baghdadi Resurfaces in Recording," *The New York Times* (2018, August 22): A1.

30 Michael Munoz, "Selling the Long War: Islamic State Propaganda after the Caliphate," *CTC Sentinel* 1, no. 10 (2018): 10–8.

31 Laura Wakeford and Laura Smith, "IS' Propaganda and the Social Media: Dissemination, Support, and Resilience," in *ISIS Propaganda: A Full-Spectrum Extremist Message*, ed. Stephane J. Baele, Katharine A. Boyd, and Travis G. Coan (New York: Oxford University Press, 2019): 155–87.

32 Joseph S. Tuman, *Communicating Terror: The Rhetorical Dimensions of Terrorism* (Thousand Oaks, CA: Sage, 2010): 196.

33 Kimberly A. Powell, "Framing Islam/Creating Fear: An Analysis of U.S. Media Coverage of Terrorism from 2011–2016," *Religions* 9, no. 257 (2018): 1–15, 2. https://doi.org/10.3390/rel9090257

34 Ibid., 2.

35 Walter Enders and Todd Sandler, *The Political Economy of Terrorism* (Cambridge: Cambridge University Press, 2005): 37.

36 Paul Wilkinson, "The Media and Terrorism: A Reassessment," *Terrorism and Political Violence* 9, no. 2 (1997): 51–64. https://doi.org/10.1080/09546559708427402

37 Christopher Hewitt, "Public's Perspectives," in *Terrorism and the Media*, ed. David L. Paletz and Alex P. Schmid (Newbury Park, CA: Sage, 1992): 170–207.

38 Brigitte Nacos, *Mass-Mediated Terrorism: The Central Role of the Media in Terrorism and Counterterrorism* (New York: Rowman & Littlefield, 2002): 14.

39 Wilkinson, "The Media and Terrorism," 53–5.

40 Andrew Hoskins and Ben O'Loughlin, *Television and Terror: Conflicting Times and the Crisis of News Discourse* (New York: Palgrave Macmillan, 2007).

41 Mina Al-Lami, Andrew Hoskins, and Ben O'Loughlin, "Mobilisation and Violence in the New Media Ecology: The Dua Khalil Aswad and Camilia Shehata Cases," *Critical Studies on Terrorism* 5, no. 2 (2012): 237–56. https://doi.org/10.1080/17539153.2012.692509

42 White, "Virtual Indoctrination and the Digihad," 14–8.

43 Manuel R. Torres Soriano, "The Road to Media Jihad: The Propaganda Actions of Al Qaeda in the Islamic Maghreb," *Terrorism and Political Violence* 23, no. 1 (2010): 72–88. https://doi.org/10.1080/09546553.2010.512839

44 Jad Melki and May Jabado, "Mediated Public Diplomacy of the Islamic State in Iraq and Syria: The Synergistic Use of Terrorism, Social Media and Branding," *Media and Communication* 4, no. 2 (2016): 92–103. https://doi.org/10.17645/mac.v4i2.432

45 Kukil Bora, "New ISIS Video Released Showing French Jihadists Burning Passports, Calling for Terror in France," *International Business Times* (2014, November 20): A1.

46 Jessica Stern and J. M. Berger, *ISIS: The State of Terror* (New York: HarperCollins, 2015): 76.

47 Javier Lesaca, *On Social Media, ISIS Uses Modern Cultural Images to Spread Anti-Modern Values* (Washington, D.C.: Brookings Institution, 2015).

48 Melki and Jabado, "Mediated Public Diplomacy," 93.

49 Ibid., 93.

50 Todd Gitlin, *The Whole World Is Watching: Mass Media in the Making & Unmaking of the New Left* (Berkeley, CA: University of California Press, 1980).

51 Erving Goffman, *Frame Analysis: An Essay on the Organization of Experience* (New York: Harper & Row, 1974); Charlotte Ryan, *Prime Time Activism: Media Strategies for Grassroots Organizing* (Boston, MA: South End Press, 1991); Fred Shook, *Television Field Production and Reporting* (Boston, MA: Allyn & Bacon, 2000).

52 Robert M. Entman, "Framing: Towards Clarification of a Fractured Paradigm," *Journal of Communication* 43, no. 4 (1993): 51–8. https://doi.org/10.1111/j.1460-2466.1993.tb01304.x

53 Ibid., 52.

54 Dietram A. Scheufele, "Framing as a Theory of Media Effects," *Journal of Communication* 49, no. 1 (1999): 103–22. https://doi.org/10.1111/j.1460-2466.1999.tb02784.x

55 Marlin, *Propaganda and the Ethics of Persuasion*, 22.

56 Cited in Bunzel, *From Paper State to Caliphate*, 41.

57 Hamid Mowlana, "Theoretical Perspectives on Islam and Communication," *China Media Research* 3, no. 4 (2007): 23–33.

58 Timothy D. Bailey and Michael R. Grimaila, "Running the Blockade: Information Technology, Terrorism, and the Transformation of Islamic Mass Culture," *Terrorism and Political Violence* 18, no. 4 (2006): 523–43. https://doi.org/10.1080/09546550600880518

59 William Gamson and Andre Modigliani, "The Changing Culture of Affirmative Action," in *Research in Political Sociology*, ed. Richard G. Braungart and Margaret M. Braungart (Greenwich, CT: JAI Press, 1987): 137–77, 143.

60 Michele Zanini, Sean Edwards, Phil Williams, John Sullivan, Tiffany Danitz, Warren Strobel, Paul de Armond, Dorothy Denning, and Luther Gerlach, "The Networking of Terror in the Information Age," in *Networks and Netwars: The Future of Terror, Crime, and Militancy*, ed. John Arquilla and David Ronfeldt (Santa Monica: RAND, 2001): 29–60, 42.
61 Galloway, "Media Jihad," 582.
62 Sameera Ahmed, "The Media Consumption of Young British Muslims," in *Muslims and the News Media*, ed. Elizabeth Poole and John E. Richardson (New York: I. B. Tauris, 2006): 167–75.
63 Cited in Marco Nilsson, "Interviewing Jihadists: On the Importance of Drinking Tea and Other Methodological Considerations," *Studies in Conflict & Terrorism* 41, no. 6 (2018): 419–32. https://doi.org/10.1080/1057610X.2017.1325649
64 Akil N. Awan, "Radicalization on the Internet?" *RUSI* 152, no. 3 (2007): 76–81. https://doi.org/10.1080/03071840701472331
65 Ibid., 79.
66 Alexander Meleagrou-Hitchens, Shiraz Maher, and James Sheehan, *Lights, Camera, Jihad: Al-Shabaab's Western Media Strategy* (London: International Centre for the Study of Radicalisation and Political Violence, 2012).
67 Ibid., 29.

References

Ahmed, Sameera, "The Media Consumption of Young British Muslims," in *Muslims and the News Media*, edited by Elizabeth Poole and John E. Richardson, 167–175. New York: I. B. Tauris, 2006.
Al-Lami, Mina, Andrew Hoskins, and Ben O'Loughlin, "Mobilisation and Violence in the New Media Ecology: The Dua Khalil Aswad and Camilia Shehata Cases," *Critical Studies on Terrorism* 5, no. 2 (2012): 237–256. https://doi.org/10.1080/17539153.2012.692509.
Archetti, Cristina, *Understanding Terrorism in the Age of Global Media: A Communication Approach*. New York: Palgrave Macmillan, 2013.
Awan, Akil N., "Radicalization on the Internet?" *RUSI* 152, no. 3 (2007): 76–81. https://doi.org/10.1080/03071840701472331.
Awan, Akil N., "Jihadi Ideology in the New-Media Environment," in *Contextualising Jihadi Thought*, edited by Jeevan Deol and Zaheer Kazmi, 99–119. London: Hurst & Co., 2012.
Bailey, Timothy D., and Michael R. Grimaila, "Running the Blockade: Information Technology, Terrorism, and the Transformation of Islamic Mass Culture," *Terrorism and Political Violence* 18, no. 4 (2006): 523–543. https://doi.org/10.1080/09546550600880518.
Bérubé, Maxime, and Benoit Dupont, "Mujahideen Mobilization: Examining the Evolution of the Global Jihadist Movement's Communicative Action Repertoire," *Studies in Conflict & Terrorism* 42, no. 1 (2019): 5–24. https://doi.org/10.1080/1057610X.2018.1513689.
Bora, Kukil, "New ISIS Video Released Showing French Jihadists Burning Passports, Calling for Terror in France," *International Business Times* (2014, November 20): A1.
Bunzel, Cole, *From Paper State to Caliphate: The Ideology of the Islamic State*. Washington D.C.: Brookings Institution, 2015.
Callimachi, Rukmini, "ISIS Leader Baghdadi Resurfaces in Recording," *The New York Times* (2018, August 22): A1.
El-Ibiary, Rasha, "Mediatisation of Terror in Cyberspace: Scrutinizing Al-Qaeda's Media Strategy," in *The Real and the Virtual*, edited by Daniel Riha and Anna Maj, 193–202. Oxford: Inter-Disciplinary, 2009.
Enders, Walter, and Todd Sandler, *The Political Economy of Terrorism*. Cambridge: Cambridge University Press, 2005.

Entman, Robert M., "Framing: Towards Clarification of a Fractured Paradigm," *Journal of Communication* 43, no. 4 (1993): 51–58. https://doi.org/10.1111/j.1460-2466.1993. tb01304.x.

Galloway, Chris, "Media Jihad: What PR Can Learn in Islamic State's Public Relations Masterclass," *Public Relations Review* 42, no. 4 (2016): 582–590. https://doi.org/10.1016/j. pubrev.2016.03.014.

Gamson, William, and Andre Modigliani, "The Changing Culture of Affirmative Action," in *Research in Political Sociology*, edited by Richard G. Braungart and Margaret M. Braungart, 137–177. Greenwich, CT: JAI Press, 1987.

Gitlin, Todd, *The Whole World Is Watching: Mass Media in the Making & Unmaking of the New Left*. Berkeley, CA: University of California Press, 1980.

Goffman, Erving, *Frame Analysis: An Essay on the Organization of Experience*. New York: Harper & Row, 1974.

Hewitt, Christopher, "Public's Perspectives," in *Terrorism and the Media*, edited by David L. Paletz and Alex P. Schmid, 170–207. Newbury Park, CA: Sage, 1992.

Hoskins, Andrew, and Ben O'Loughlin, *Television and Terror: Conflicting Times and the Crisis of News Discourse*. New York: Palgrave Macmillan, 2007.

Hoskins, Andrew, Akil Awan, and Ben O'Loughlin, *Radicalisation and the Media: Connectivity and Terrorism in the New Media*. New York: Routledge, 2011.

Juergensmeyer, Mark, "Religious Terror and Global War," Global & International Studies Program (Paper 2. University of California, 2002): 3. Retrieved on October 1, 2019 from http://repositories.cdib.org/gis/2.

Kim, Andrew C., "Weapons of Mass Destruction: Communicating Ethical Solutions," in *Applying the Professional Military Ethic across the Spectrum of Operations*, edited by Mark H. Wiggins and Larry Dabeck, 129–144. Fort Leavenworth, KS: Command and General Staff College Foundation Press, 2012.

Kriel, Robyn, "TV, Twitter, and Telegram: Al-Shabaab's Attempts to Influence Mass Media," *Defence Strategic Communications* 4 (2018): 11–48.

Lesaca, Javier, *On Social Media, ISIS Uses Modern Cultural Images to Spread Anti-Modern Values*. Washington, D.C.: Brookings Institution, 2015.

Lombardi, Marco, "IS 2.0 and Beyond: The Caliphate's Communication Project," in *Twitter and Jihad: The Communication Strategy of ISIS*, edited by Monica Maggioni and Paolo Magri, 83–122. Milan: Italian Institute for International Political Studies, 2015.

Maggioni, Monica, and Paolo Magri, *Twitter and Jihad: The Communication Strategy of ISIS*. Milan: Italian Institute for International Political Studies, 2015.

Marlin, Randal, *Propaganda and the Ethics of Persuasion*. Peterborough, ON: Broadview Press, 2002.

McQuail, Denis, *Mass Communication Theory: An Introduction* (3rd ed.). Thousand Oaks, CA: Sage, 1994.

Meleagrou-Hitchens, Alexander, Shiraz Maher, and James Sheehan, *Lights, Camera, Jihad: Al-Shabaab's Western Media Strategy*. London: International Centre for the Study of Radicalisation and Political Violence, 2012.

Melki, Jad, and May Jabado, "Mediated Public Diplomacy of the Islamic State in Iraq and Syria: The Synergistic Use of Terrorism, Social Media and Branding," *Media and Communication* 4, no. 2 (2016): 92–103. https://doi.org/10.17645/mac.v4i2.432.

Mowlana, Hamid, "Theoretical Perspectives on Islam and Communication," *China Media Research* 3, no. 4 (2007): 23–33.

Munoz, Michael, "Selling the Long War: Islamic State Propaganda after the Caliphate," *CTC Sentinel* 1, no. 10 (2018): 10–18.

Nacos, Brigitte, *Mass-Mediated Terrorism: The Central Role of the Media in Terrorism and Counterterrorism*. Lanham, MD: Rowman & Littlefield, 2002.

Nacos, Brigitte, Yaeli Bloch-Elkon, and Ropert Y. Shapiro, "Post 9/11 Terrorism Threats, News Coverage, and Public Perceptions in the United States," *International Journal of Conflict and Violence* 1, no. 2 (2007): 105–126. https://doi.org/10.4119/UNIBI/ijcv.10.

Nilsson, Marco, "Interviewing Jihadists: On the Importance of Drinking Tea and Other Methodological Considerations," *Studies in Conflict & Terrorism* 41, no. 6 (2018): 419–432. https://doi.org/10.1080/1057610X.2017.1325649.

Powell, Kimberly A., "Framing Islam/Creating Fear: An Analysis of U.S. Media Coverage of Terrorism from 2011–2016," *Religions* 9, no. 257 (2018): 1–15. https://doi.org/10.3390/rel9090257.

Ryan, Charlotte, *Prime Time Activism: Media Strategies for Grassroots Organizing*. Boston, MA: South End Press, 1991.

Saniotis, Arthur, "Re-enchanting Terrorism: Jihadists as 'Liminal Beings'," *Studies in Conflict & Terrorism* 28, no. 6 (2005): 533–545. https://doi.org/10.1080/10576100500236907.

Scheufele, Dietram A., "Framing as a Theory of Media Effects," *Journal of Communication* 49, no. 1 (1999): 103–122. https://doi.org/10.1111/j.1460-2466.1999.tb02784.x.

Schreck, Adam, and Zeina Karam, "Islamic State Leader Al-Baghdadi Leaves a Legacy of Terror," *The Associated Press* (2019, October 27): A1.

Shook, Fred, *Television Field Production and Reporting*. Boston, MA: Allyn & Bacon, 2000.

Soriano, Manuel R. Torres, "Spain as an Object of Jihadist Propaganda," *Studies in Conflict & Terrorism* 32, no. 11 (2009): 933–952. https://doi.org/10.1080/10576100903259977.

Soriano, Manuel R. Torres, "The Road to Media Jihad: The Propaganda Actions of Al Qaeda in the Islamic Maghreb," *Terrorism and Political Violence* 23, no. 1 (2010): 72–88. https://doi.org/10.1080/09546553.2010.512839.

Stern, Jessica, and J. M. Berger, *ISIS: The State of Terror*. New York: HarperCollins, 2015.

Tatham, Steve, *Losing Arab Hearts and Minds: The Coalition, Al Jazeera and Muslim Public Opinion*. London: Hurst & Co., 2006.

Tilly, Charles, *Stories, Identities, and Political Change*. Lanham, MD: Rowman & Littlefield, 2002.

Tuman, Joseph S., *Communicating Terror: The Rhetorical Dimensions of Terrorism*. Thousand Oaks, CA: Sage, 2010.

Wakeford, Laura, and Laura Smith, "IS' Propaganda and the Social Media: Dissemination, Support, and Resilience," in *ISIS Propaganda: A Full-Spectrum Extremist Message*, edited by Stephane J. Baele, Katharine A. Boyd, and Travis G. Coan, 155–187. New York: Oxford University Press, 2019.

White, Jeremy, "Virtual Indoctrination and the Digihad: The Evolution of Al-Qaeda's Media Strategy," *Small Wars Journal* 8 (2012): 10–21.

Wilkinson, Paul, "The Media and Terrorism: A Reassessment," *Terrorism and Political Violence* 9, no. 2 (1997): 51–64. https://doi.org/10.1080/09546559708427402.

Zanini, Michele, Sean Edwards, Phil Williams, John Sullivan, Tiffany Danitz, Warren Strobel, Paul de Armond, Dorothy Denning, and Luther Gerlach, "The Networking of Terror in the Information Age," in *Networks and Netwars: The Future of Terror, Crime, and Militancy*, edited by John Arquilla and David Ronfeldt, 29–60. Santa Monica, CA: RAND, 2001.

7

THE NARRATIVE

Narrative is a method of reasoning to interpret the world. As a medium of representation, narrative allows us to "tell" about the world.[1] It can be used as a discourse that offers logic and consistency to the people, situations, and concepts for
showing the moral conduct of an environment. It gives meaning to the lives of
members of society and is essential to the process of framing policy.[2] Therefore,
narratives are structures of communication thanks to which we are expected to
interact. They are "compelling storylines which can explain events convincingly
and from which inferences can be drawn."[3]

In like fashion, a narrative comprises a sequence of events (true or false) described during a course of narration (by way of discourse or in writing). It is a phenomenon whereby events are selected and organized in a specific order (the plot).[4]
A narrative offers a coherent system of interconnected and sequential stories that
share the mutual rhetorical aspiration to solve a conflict by creating audience
expectations based on the known paths of its literary and rhetorical form.[5] As
Vlahos (2006)[6] tells us, "'narrative' may sound like a fancy literary word, but it is
actually the foundation of all strategy, upon which all else—policy, rhetoric and
action—is built."

Narratives can also be exploited to direct people on appropriate behavior, cultural history, and establishment of communal identities and values. They help
reinforce the cultural identity of a collective. Cultural identity is inherently related
to group identity because it contributes to an individual's self-concept and self-
image, and it is rooted in national origin, ethnicity, faith, social status, generation,
or any type of social group with its own unique culture. In this manner, cultural
identity is characteristic of both the person and the culturally identical group of
individuals who have a cultural identity or upbringing. Ultimately, narratives create
communal frames, which are social constructions of the world by a group, leading
to the construction of what is right and wrong that people should live by.[7]

The master jihadist narrative

Many different types of jihadist narratives have been articulated and published by various jihadist organizations. Indeed, a close examination of geographically dispersed organizations that apply jihadist principles demonstrates that there are disparities (and similarities) in narratives that ought to be ascribed to differing ideological concerns on which those organizations focus.[8] However, there exists a grand, overarching narrative—that we can call "master narrative"[9]—that captures the essence of the global jihad. Schmid (2014)[10] defines this master jihadist narrative as a "unifying framework of explanation that provides vulnerable Muslims with an emotionally satisfying story to make sense of the world in which they live and their role in it." The jihadist narrative today transcends the Muslim world and resonates with a significant minority of Western Muslims who, out of political, financial, or educational motives, left their lands where they, oddly enough, faced various forms of intolerance and discrimination.[11] As Schmid (2014)[12] continues, the main elements of the master jihadist narrative are set to inspire the ummah to join the GJM, as explained below:

1.   The Muslim world is in shambles because of the Zionist–Christian alliance being the culprit of all the ills experienced by Muslims: humiliation, discrimination, and/or mistreatment in the world.
2.   The Caliphate will be established to supplant the corrupt, apostate leaders of the Muslim world who are pro-West. This will be achieved by imposing sharia to fulfill Allah's will and restore order.
3.   Violent jihad is the only solution to eradicate Western impact in the Muslim world. For this reason, great sacrifices are necessary to accomplish this mission. Every devout Muslim must wage holy war against the oppressing Crusaders to defend Islam and its holy lands from both the near enemy and the far enemy.

Master narratives supersede narratives in importance because they are an essential element or reason for jihadists' *raison d'être*. The master jihadist narrative represents a universal alternative narrative that transcends local borders. It has become the predominant political, ideological, and religious glue that binds jihadists and would-be jihadists together in their search of a common identity.[13] It is a comprehensive message that strives to inspire its adherents into action.

In their perpetual message that "the West is at war with Islam," modern-day jihadists combine aspects of Islamic history with myths and symbols to foster a narrative developed on the perception that (1) Muslims have been dehumanized (which is also their own "fault" because they follow those pro-West Muslim leaders), (2) they have completely kowtowed to Western values and lifestyles, and (3) they must seek redemption through faith and sacrifice.[14] As one can see, a chief purpose of the master jihadist narrative is to create a clear separation between Muslims and non-Muslims. The impact of such type of extremist discourse can quickly bear fruit. For example, Amble and Meleagrou-Hitchens (2014)[15] note that, in Kenya, jihad ideologues have employed the jihadist narrative so successfully that it resonates with a significant minority of the country's Islamic population as well as Swahili-speaking majority ethnic enclaves. In fact, thousands of newly jihad converts have already joined the Somali-based Al-Shabaab terrorist group.

Exploiting the Muslim religion as a rallying cry

There is nothing surprising about the exploitation of religion as a battle cry to launch a global revolution in the quest of a new world order. Through a clever use of symbols, collective memories, mythologies, folklores, and heritage, contemporary framers can draw attention to the forefathers of a religious group to develop an ideology and a guide for future actions. Religion can be manipulated as a powerful source; religious revelations are transformed into sacred shrines, religious miracles are now national feasts, and holy texts are re-framed as global epics.[16] Under these circumstances, by spinning religion into a collective trauma or selected glory, many opportunities abound for religious leaders to propagate rhetoric and particular holy verses to form and influence an identity group. The mélange of empiricist verification of purported "facts" and the diffusion of online social media has played a pivotal part in this process.[17]

Islamic terrorism is inherently linked to Islamic fundamentalism. Jihadists opt for violent actions (directly or indirectly) to fulfill the perceived guidelines prescribed by Allah. This carries with it a number of alarming implications: The instructions of a deity may not be as evident to those outside the religion. Hence, the actions taken by jihadist organizations can be unpredictable. More importantly, religious terrorists are rarely inhibited by worries about the reactions of their supporters or constituents. Their primary mission is to fulfill religious goals for their deity, not necessarily to please their audience(s). Of course, religious terrorists are also uninhibited by profane values and laws. Often, a prime target of the attacks is the man-made, secular society symbolized by modern-day lifestyles. A massive motivator is to abolish the current post-Westphalian state system in favor of the Caliphate.[18] The post-Westphalian state system is a secular order of the United Nations according to which superpowers like the United States can intervene against human rights abuses in other nations.[19]

Kitab al-Jihad

Abdallah ibn al-Mubarak (726–797) was a pioneer of Islamic thought, famous for his enthusiasm to publish his knowledge and hadith. He wrote *Kitab al-Jihad*, meaning "Book of Struggle" or "Book of Jihad." It is a collection of sayings by the early Muslim fighters. His *Kitab al-Jihad* traces the evolution of Muslim interpretation of holy war during the early Muslim conquests and combats against the

Infidels. The spiritual approach to jihad is much more manifest than verses about jihad in the Quran.[20] Below is an excerpt of his collection:

> The martyr (*shahid*) is tested, and is in the camp of Allah under His throne; the prophets do not exceed him in merit except by the level of prophecy. A believer, committing offenses and sins against himself, who struggles with himself and his possessions in the path of Allah, such that when he meets the enemy (in battle), he fights until he is killed. This cleansing wipes away his offenses and his sins—behold the sword wipes away sins—and he will be let into heaven from whatever gate he wishes.[21]

A few centuries later, in 1105, Ali ibn Tahir al-Sulami also published a treatise of the same name: *Kitab al-Jihad*. Ali ibn Tahir al-Sulami (who died in 1106) was a legal expert and philologist from Damascus. He was the first to advocate jihad against the Crusaders after the First Crusade in 1095. In his version of *Kitab al-Jihad*, al-Sulami communicated his ideas from the Great Mosque of Damascus.[22] He warned about the Christian invaders, citing examples of their relentless conquests—like those of Sicily and Spain. He was concerned about Muslims' departure from jihad and other religious obligations, and requested the Caliphs to reinstate the old rule of waging war on the Christian enemy once a year, a rule they had not followed for many years. Allah, he wrote, was admonishing Muslims for their religious deviance. To triumph over the Crusaders, al-Sulami argued that Muslims had to observe the inner jihad—through the inner transformation of the self—in order to successfully embark on jihad against the enemy.[23]

Narratives of Islamic radicalization

The master jihadist narrative is designed to radicalize both Muslims from Muslim lands and those living in the Western hemisphere (such as Europe and North America). It serves as a platform for Islamic radicalization with the ultimate objective of mobilizing the ummah for violent actions. What is considered radical varies in accordance with the diverse social, cultural, religious, and political contexts.[24] Within the Western context, narratives of Islamic radicalization often tackle the problems associated with democratic values, including human rights, women's rights, civil liberties, diversity, secular sources of law, and peaceful transitions of political power. In turn, such narratives will resonate within radicalized Muslim communities in the West and deepen their support of jihadist violence, their endorsement of the implementation of sharia-based laws, their rejection of other social groups (particularly those enjoying those Western lifestyles), and their aspirations to the global Caliphate.[25] Such narratives can be effective because, when repeated over and over again, they can solidify like water and ice and lead people to commit atrocities such as mass killing.[26]

Four narratives of global jihad

Leuprecht, Hataley, Moskalenko, and Mccauley (2010)[27] interpret global jihad as a meta-narrative that can be divided into four distinct narratives. The political narrative concentrates upon the evils of the West, including the neo-Marxist approach to global injustices and the destructive force of Western hegemony and exploitation. Such narrative was introduced by the most famous cultural historian in Islam: Ibn Khaldun (1332–1406). The moral narrative deals with the internal "illogicalities" of liberal democracies, which promote freedom as their core value, but equal treatment of all as their secondary values. For global jihadists, these values are unrealistic and contribute to Islam's moral decay. The religious narrative advocates jihad against the Crusader West. The social-psychological narrative uses the traditional "in-group vs. out-group" model to shuffle the Infidels off to the out-group category, at the same time promoting the ummah, the brotherhood of arms, to the in-group category. The "us v. them" dichotomy, so cherished by global jihadists, is what will galvanize "true believers" into joining the global jihad against the rest of the world.

Eschatological narratives

Eschatology is a category of theology dealing with the final days of history, or the supreme destiny of humankind. This notion is also called the "end of the world" or "end times" philosophy.[28] Islamic eschatology is complex; significant differences of interpretation exist between the Shia and Sunni eschatological traditions. The two groups sometimes violently conflict over this, and both agree and contradict with conventional Jewish and Christian eschatology.[29] Apocalyptic Muslim authors relate their interpretations to the world's current events, like the creation of the State of Israel in 1948 as the beginning of the End Times. Some also argue that the Six-Day War in 1967 or the U.S. invasion of Iraq in 2003 heralded the end of the world. Muslim scholars have been adapting their apocalyptic narratives to their own epoch for centuries, including the Fall of Constantinople in 1453 and the Westernization of Turkey in 1924 (which abolished the Ottoman Empire, or the last Caliphate).[30]

Muslim apocalyptic narratives are mostly rooted in the hadith (not the Quran itself).[31] These eschatological narratives nevertheless continue to rely on contemporary events, not just the hadith. In addition to emphasizing the importance of Islamic radicalization in the entire world, the eschatological narrative is the same: "The West is engaged in a millennial battle against Islam and Muslims must defend themselves—Islam is under attack and Muslims have an obligation to rise to its defence."[32] This narrative champions a "global jihad" and its potency "is rooted in the fundamental precept that superior political will, when properly employed, can defeat greater economic and military power."[33]

Consider Abu Musab al-Zarqawi, the late Jordanian jihadist is established training camps in Afghanistan and instigated many terrorist attacks during the Iraq War. al-Zarqawi devoted his time and energy to disseminate a jihadist and apocalyptic narrative in Iraq. The U.S. invasion of Iraq in 2003 was a catalyst for many radical

Muslims because it would herald the Hour of Judgment, a notion that al-Zarqawi popularized.[34] He likened the fight in Iraq to three historical Muslim battles: the Arab battle with the Persians in the seventh century, the Shi'ites' alleged alliance with Mongols in the later centuries (and related betrayal of Baghdad), and conflicts between the Byzantines and Arabs or Turks. In due course, al-Zarqawi's apocalyptic narratives laid the foundations for ISIS's establishment of the Caliphate in 2014 and the bombastic language of the jihadist group.[35] A detailed case study of al-Zarqawi is provided in Chapter 10 (though on a different subject).

ISIS and the Apocalypse

In *The ISIS Apocalypse: The History, Strategy, and Doomsday Vision of the Islamic State*, McCants (2015)[36] explains how ISIS has fused two dangerous notions in Salafist Islam: the desire to return to the Golden Age of Islam (i.e., as witnessed through the early violent Islamic conquests) and the end of the world (that will herald the Islamic supreme rule over the earth). Combined, these two ideas forge a mission and a narrative that have motivated Muslim youths around the world to join an army of fervent warriors. This type of doomsday prophecy will be fulfilled with the coming of the Mahdi, the redeemer of Islam who will appear and rule for a number of years before the Day of Judgment and purge the world of evil. In many Muslim interpretations, the Mahdi will be accompanied by Isa (Jesus) to defeat the false Messiah or Antichrist.

It is important to discuss how ISIS interprets the events heralding the arrival of the Mahdi. ISIS mentions the apocalypse based on one particular hadith, which makes reference to Dabiq, a small town in northern Syria. The name *Dabiq* was eventually selected as ISIS's first online jihadist magazine (published from 2014 to 2016) to unambiguously cultivate the apocalyptic prophecy of the final battle between Good and Evil, and the terrorist organization predicts that the battle will take place in Dabiq.[37] ISIS described the entire process of the prophecy in the very first issue of the magazine in 2014:

> Battles between the Muslims and the crusaders will take place near Dabiq. Abu Hurayrah reported that Allah's Messenger (…) said [here follows the hadith], "The Hour will not be established until the Romans land at al-A'maq or Dabiq [two places near each other in the northern countryside of Halab]."[38]

In this quote, ISIS brought up apocalyptic phrases that are all too familiar: "battles between the Muslims and the crusaders," "Allah's Messenger," and "the Hour." In the following excerpt, ISIS ended the paragraph with the notion of *fitna*, which refers to trial or distress. The group made it clear that, in the end times, Allah's chosen army will not be afflicted by such trial or distress:

> An army from al-Madinah (…) will leave for them… [and] will fight them. Then one third of them will flee; Allah will never forgive them. One third

will be killed; they will be the best martyrs with Allah. And one third will conquer them; they will never be afflicted with *fitna*.[39]

ISIS fighters and sympathizers generally regard "Rome" as the Judeo-Christian world. In a subsequent issue of *Dabiq*, ISIS explains how the "battle ends the era of the Roman Christians, as the Muslims will then advance upon Constantinople and thereafter Rome, to conquer the two cities and raise the flag of the Khilafah [Caliphate] over them."[40]

Differences between ISIS and Al-Qaeda

After the September 11, 2001 terrorist attacks, Al-Qaeda lived through an episode of stagnation which it sought to alleviate by reinventing and rebranding itself. Disapproving of this strategy, ISIS regarded Al-Qaeda as an elitist group that had caused the stagnation of the Salafist-jihadist movement as a whole. In order to secure dominance over global jihad, ISIS propagandists openly discredited Al-Qaeda's existence and mission by portraying it as ideologically flawed. More importantly, ISIS attempted to improve its standing within the ummah by focusing heavily on Islamic eschatology, sectarian activism, extreme violence, and, of course, the Caliphate. To these points, differences can be noticed between ISIS's and Al-Qaeda's vision of the apocalypse.[41]

   To begin, Novenario (2016)[42] looked at dissimilarities in their propaganda tactics for advocating Allah-ordained control through jihadist violence. On the one hand, Al-Qaeda favored (and continues to favor) slow destruction of the enemy to induce politico-religious changes in the West; on the other hand, ISIS concentrates on outbidding and intimidation of the enemy to not only attract as many followers as possible but, also, to increase the number of Muslims overall so as to fulfill their Caliphate dream. By way of outbidding, ISIS wants to gain legitimacy to its claim to the Caliphate and dominate the entire world. After incurring severe losses, particularly in early 2019, and after experiencing heightened pressure (e.g., from Coalition airstrikes and ground combat),[43] ISIS's eschatological propaganda departed from Al-Qaeda even more. As such, ISIS continues to provide much effort, via videos and online social media posts, to convince fighters to abandon the West—and other jihadist groups in the process—and pledge allegiance to ISIS leaders because the latter claim that they are the only ones who can pave the way for the Mahdi.[44] Lastly, spoiling is a frequent tactic used by the terrorist organization to erode moderate interpretations of Islam and bolster the feeling that apocalyptic holy war for the Caliphate is a politico-religious obligation for *all* Muslims.[45]

Teaching of hatred

Global jihadism can be appealing to a shockingly diverse set of individuals. It is a heterogeneous cohort whose ideological cohesion is solidified by a simple fact regarding the jihadist narrative: its teaching of hatred. As a profound and penetrating human feeling, hatred brings up sentiments of rancor, anger, and dis-like, often directed against the Other—in the case of jihadists, it is the whole world that should be hated.[46] Jihadist hatred is channeled into a conduit of propaganda to incite intimidation or violence against civilians, which is both illegal (e.g., behead-ing, burning, or cage-drowning videos) or deeply concerning (e.g., framing the Infidels as "worthless dogs").[47]

In the jihadist narrative, dehumanization of the enemies is pivotal. The enemies are subhuman. The perception is that their lack of humanity does not elicit feelings of empathy when committing violence against them.[48] The teaching of hatred "essentializes" the self and the Other as good and evil entities. One kills the ene-mies because they are evil. The jihadist use of *takfirism* (i.e., apostasy) to rationalize the killing of non-Muslims and nonbelievers (*Kuffar*) is a testimony to this.[49] This type of hatred is both religious and political.[50] As Sternberg (2003)[51] continues,

> The second basis is the desire for revenge over injustices and humiliations one (or one's group) has experienced, especially when threatened egotism has been involved. The third basis is greed, lust, ambition, and other forms of self-interest in instances in which a rival is standing in the way of what one wants. The fourth root, sadism, can precipitate brutal violence but typically may be less relevant to hate.

Those who produce narratives of hatred seek to transform the thought processes of the favored population (i.e., the in-group) so that its members regard the targeted group (i.e., the out-group) in a repulsive fashion—i.e., because of the "injustices and humiliations one (or one's group) has experienced." This situation can be further explained through the three-part model of hatred:[52]

- **Exclusion of intimacy in hate**: hatred increases when repulsion and disgust increase. This works by marking an emotional and cognitive distance between the hater and the victim—as in dehumanization. This way, psychological bar-riers to violence are eroded too. Hate narratives generally portray the enemies as subhumans who cannot receive, give, or even understand feelings of proximity, warmth, concern, compassion, and respect. For Sternberg (2003),[53] normally, these feelings are slow to form and slow to wane.
- **Passion for hatred**: to love to hate the enemy is in reaction to a threat—like an imminent threat to society, and one whereby the enemy should be hated forever because of this threat. These feelings develop and disappear rapidly.
- **Decision and devaluation**: decision is profound dedication to hatred and devaluation is degrading of the enemy through contempt. The hater expresses contempt toward the victim, considering the target as subhuman and, conse-quently, naturally contemptible.

Similarly, Gartenstein-Ross and Grossman (2009)[54] described six elements of jihadist radicalization, three of which deal with radical interpretations of religious doctrines, and three with expressions of hatred. Such hatred is felt toward two types of enemies: the "near enemy" and the "far enemy." For most jihadist groups, the "far enemy" is the United States (and Western nations as a whole); the "near enemy" refers to autocratic régimes in the Muslim world or Muslim governments that are in bed with the West.[55]

Jihadist language to avenge the ummah

The communal and supranational character of the jihadist discourse is something to behold. One of the foundations of the jihadist discourse is the disapproval of a social construct of community built upon the traditional spheres of ethnicity or nationalism. Rather, leaders of the GJM want a global community of belief, a belief shared by the entire ummah.[56] As a case for the advocacy of this global community of belief, the Global Islamic Media Front, a well-known media body of Al-Qaeda, stated in 2005, "The [battle]front does not belong to anyone. It is the property of all zealous Muslims and knows no geographical boundaries."[57] This official support of the ummah as the only source of identity and belonging is also mirrored in the rhetoric of individual jihadist martyrs themselves. Shahzad Tanweer, one of the 7/7 bombers, attempted to justify his actions by pointing to British tacit support for injustices perpetrated against the ummah, as shown in the excerpt from *The Guardian* (2006)[58] below:

> To the non-Muslims of Britain you may wonder what you have done to deserve this. You have those who have voted in your government who in turn have and still continue to this day continue to oppress our mothers, children, brothers and sisters.

By the same token, Mohammed Siddique Khan, in his posthumously published "martyrdom" testament, constantly brought up the "communal identity" that subjugated the brothers and sisters of his community as being a major reason for perpetrating his martyrdom mission. The excerpt below came from his pre-recorded testament and was released by BBC News (2005):[59]

> Your democratically elected governments continuously perpetuate atrocities against my people all over the world. And your support of them makes you directly responsible, just as I am directly responsible for protecting and avenging my Muslim brothers and sisters. Until we feel security, you will be our targets. And until you stop the bombing, gassing, imprisonment and torture of my people we will not stop this fight.

Khan and Tanweer expressed a complex and melodramatic sense of obligation to the vague and disparate members of the ummah ("my Muslim brothers and sisters," "our children in Palestine," "our mothers and sisters in Kashmir"). Ultimately, these people became the object of their sacrifice in the London terrorist attack.[60]

The neglected duty: Muslim neglect in the past

Abd al-Salam Faraj (1954–1982), who ran the Cairo division of the Egyptian Islamic Jihad and who wrote a seminal book for the GJM, *The Neglected Duty*, considered jihad the sixth pillar of Islam. Jihad had become the "neglected duty" and should be put on the same pedestal as the other five pillars of the faith.[61] This revolutionary plea to defensive jihad became even more popular when Abdullah Azzam took the same *Neglected Duty* doctrine at the international level. Soon after, Al-Qaeda ideologues and strategists implemented it to launch jihadist attacks. Thanks to the support of classical *fiqh* scholars of the established Sunni schools of law, Azzam determined that the doctrine of defensive jihad was more than applicable in contemporary times.[62] Under these circumstances, when a Muslim territory is invaded, a "call to arms" (*nafir 'amm*) is to be done and jihad becomes a legal duty for all Muslims:

> If, however, the enemy attacks a port or enters into a Muslim town, jihad becomes an individual obligation (*fard 'ayn*), incumbent upon the people of that town, and the people in the surrounding towns. In such a case, [the requirement] to seek permission becomes void.[63]

In the excerpt above, jihad is a duty for all Muslims when enemies of Islam invade Muslim territories. In fact, "to seek permission becomes void;" jihad must be waged at all costs. As Azzam continued,

> A boy is permitted to go out to fight without his father's permission, a wife without the permission of her husband, and he who is in debt without the permission of his creditor. This situation (i.e., the suspension of traditional authority structures) continues until the removal of the enemy from Muslim land.[64]

All jihadists concur that defensive jihad provides a sound rationale for embracing global jihad. In light of the political conditions that influence the Islamic world, there is no shadow of a doubt that jihadists are using defensive jihad profusely. After all, as they see it, their actions are both legitimate and legalized. In defensive warfare, classical jurists insist that no Muslim is required to obtain permission of another to fight, in the same way that he or she does not have to seek the approval of another before conducting the five daily prayers.[65]

The neglected duty: Muslim neglect in the age of the coronavirus

COVID-19, also called coronavirus disease 2019 or, simply, coronavirus, is an infectious disease caused by critical respiratory problems. Frequent symptoms include fever, cough, fatigue, shortness of breath, and loss of smell and taste. The coronavirus was identified in December 2019 in China and began to diffuse rapidly across the world, resulting in a pandemic in 2020.[66] Jihadists took advantage of the coronavirus pandemic to wage new attacks, attract new members, and boost their credibility as the ideal leaders in unstable territories across the Middle East, Asia, and Africa. This is reflected through their narratives. For example, in early April 2020, Al-Qaeda issued a six-page commentary on the coronavirus, making it clear that the affliction of the pandemic on the Muslim world was a result of their "own sins and the obscenity and moral corruption… widespread in Muslim countries." The group continued by saying that the crisis presented a chance "to spread the correct creed, call people to jihad in the way of Allah and revolt against oppression and oppressors." A more detailed excerpt of the neglected duty of Muslims to uphold violent Salafist standards can be found below:

> Before this great disaster struck, obscenity and moral corruption had already become widespread in Muslim countries. In fact, this phenomenon had extended its dirty tentacles to the vicinities of the purest site on the face of the earth, the Haram in Makkah.[67]

In the quote above, Al-Qaeda points the finger at the "obscenity and moral corruption" of the Muslim people. In the below, "the despots ruling over the Muslim world" have been so neglectful of their duty that they even have perpetrated "the most unimaginable forms of torture and rights abuses:"

> The despots ruling over the Muslim world, specifically in the Arab World, have been guilty of committing the most unimaginable forms of torture and rights abuses against Muslim scholars and Mujahideen in secret torture cells that have become a norm across the Muslim World.[68]

Likewise, the March 2020 issue of ISIS's *Al-Naba* newsletter referred to the deserved "plague" as a "torment sent by God on whomsoever He wills," adding that "illnesses do not strike by themselves but by the command and decree of God."[69] Global security experts worry that natural disasters or health crises like the coronavirus pandemic offer a boon for jihadist organizations to spread such extremist narratives to gain support because corrupt, ineffective, and poorly resourced governments across the Middle East, Asia, and Africa tend to have substandard care for already suspicious or skeptical populations. Hardly any nation severely harmed by extremism has valuable healthcare systems. Such levels of precarity can increase the risks that the afflicted and disadvantaged join the global jihad movement.[70]

Destroying America (and the West)

The political aspect of global jihad often begins with an assemblage of like-minded extremists who seek to upset the status quo. In the twenty-first century, the United States remains a major spearhead of the current world order, an order mostly driven by man-made decisions (not by Allah). The first logical step to destroy this world order is by neutralizing the United States, after which they will be more capable of replacing local leadership with a new Islamic world order. To some extremists, "neutralizing" means annihilating the United States completely; others would be content with eroding or disciplining the United States enough to get it expelled from the Muslim world. "Destroying America"—the aggressor and illegal occupant of the Muslim world—also resonates as a rallying cry within Muslim communities.[71]

The operational stratagem to neutralize the United States rests on a combination of active and passive tactics. Active jihad consists of launching military strikes that directly target U.S. interests (at home and abroad) in order to affect U.S. policy. Besides the physical damage produced, these attacks chip away at the illusion that America is unconquerable. In the eyes of global jihadists, invasions by U.S. and Coalition Forces into Muslim territories should be encountered with violent attacks on Western interests at home and abroad. These jihadist operations have been diverse: from small-scale ones (e.g., political murders) to large-scale ones like the September 11, 2001 attacks. On the other hand, passive jihad consists of stealth jihad; that is, destroying America from within by getting democracy to work against itself, by getting laws passed that censor freedom of speech, by Islamizing America, and, ultimately, by gradually replacing or tweaking the U.S. Constitution and adopting Islamic law.[72]

Al-Qaeda security chief Sayf Al-Adel confirms that the 9/11 attacks were designed to elicit a military response from the U.S. government, in addition to wreaking havoc on the immediate targets of the attack:

> Our main objective, therefore, was to deal a strike to the head of the snake at home to smash its arrogance. The second objective of this strike was the emergence of a new virtuous leadership for this world. Third, our ultimate objective of these painful strikes against the head of the serpent was to prompt it to come out of its hole. This would make it easier for us to deal consecutive blows to undermine it and tear it apart. It would foster our credibility in front of our nation and the beleaguered people of the world.[73]

What this statement shows is that Al-Qaeda was determined to entangle U.S. forces into hostile territories. The ultimate objective was to make the U.S. vulnerable to attrition. At the same time, assaults on U.S. interests are aimed at inciting a military response. A blatant U.S. invasion—rather than the usual guise of magnanimity concealing a political, cultural, and economic attack—provokes Muslim anger against the invaders.[74] Over and above targeting America, jihadist leaders urge Muslims to make their world unfriendly to the Western world at large—Western commerce, tourism, and other activities. In the tactical application of this strategy, jihadists from all corners of the planet execute local unrelated strikes against Western interests, turning the occurrence of random or opportunistic violence into an ostensible massive campaign of coordination and direction.[75]

Territorial invasions

Like nations, institutionalized religions are often territorially defined. In Islam, there is a principle called *fard ayn*, according to which every Muslim is obligated to join his or her co-religionists through jihad after a holy territory has been invaded. An attack on one Muslim territory is an attack on the entire *dar al-Islam*.[76] Today, jihadists also interpret jihad as the outcome of a long history of Western suppression of Islam that includes the invasion of Muslim lands by the Infidels and apostate régimes of the Middle East.[77] Osama bin Laden and other jihadist champions of defensive jihad were motivated by both their love of Allah and their hatred of U.S. geopolitical actions and policies that have devastated the Muslim world. In a statement released on October 6, 2002, Osama bin Laden stated that defensive jihad had to stand because the United States was showing no expressions of regret for its "previous crimes" against the ummah. Rather, the "criminal gang at the White House" was intensifying its attack on the Muslim world. Consequently:

> I am telling you, and God is my witness, whether America escalates or dees-calates the conflict, we will reply to it in kind, God willing. God is my wit-ness, the youth of Islam are preparing things that will fill your hearts with fear. They will target key sectors of your economy until you stop your injustice and aggression or until the more short-lived of us die.[78]

As Scheuer (2007)[79] explains, from the jihadists' perspective, they are simply fol-lowing the rules of defensive jihad. It was not Western secular culture that so irri-tated Osama bin Laden, but U.S. actions and policies that defied Allah's word, attacked the ummah, and invaded Muslim lands. Scheuer's work drew our atten-tion on the beliefs and principles of those groups that we tried to conquer in a military campaign.

Notes

1 Patricia Geist-Martin, Eileen B. Ray, and Barbara Sharf, *Communicating Health: Personal, Cultural, and Political Complexities* (Belmont, CA: Wadsworth Press, 2003).
2 Richard Jackson, "Language, Policy and the Construction of a Torture Culture in the War on Terrorism," *Review of International Studies* 33, no. 3 (2007): 353–71. https://doi.org/10.1017/S0260210507007553
3 Lawrence Freedman, *The Transformation of Strategic Affairs* (London: International Insti-tute for Strategic Studies, 2006): 22.
4 James A. Holstein and Jaber F. Gubrium, *The Self We Live By: Narrative Identity in a Postmodern World* (New York: Oxford University Press, 2000).
5 Jeffry R. Halverson, H. L. Goodall, Jr., and Steven R. Corman, *Master Narratives of Islamist Extremism* (New York: Palgrave Macmillan, 2011).
6 Michael Vlahos, "The Long War: A Self-defeating Prophecy," *Asia Times* (2006, Sep-tember 9): A1.
7 Laura K. Guerrero, Peter A. Andersen, and Walid Afifi, *Close Encounters* (5th Ed.) (Thousand Oaks, CA: Sage, 2017).

8 Dina Al Raffie, "Whose Hearts and Minds? Narratives and Counter-Narratives of Salafi Jihadism," *Journal of Terrorism Research* 3, no. 2 (2012): 13–31.

9 Ibid., 13.

10 Alex P. Schmid, *Al-Qaeda's "Single Narrative" and Attempts to Develop Counter-Narratives: The State of Knowledge* (The Hague: International Centre for Counter Terrorism, 2014): 5.

11 Ibid., 7.

12 Ibid., 6.

13 Al Raffie, "Whose Hearts and Minds?" 14–5.

14 Frazer Egerton, *Jihad in the West: The Rise of Militant Salafism* (Cambridge: Cambridge University Press, 2011); Melissa Finn, *Al Qaeda and Sacrifice: Martyrdom, War and Politics* (London: Pluto Press, 2012).

15 John C. Amble and Alexander Meleagrou-Hitchens, "Jihadist Radicalization in East Africa: Two Case Studies," *Studies in Conflict & Terrorism* 37, no. 6 (2014): 523–40. https://doi.org/10.1080/1057610X.2014.893406

16 Catarina Kinnvall, "Globalization and Religious Nationalism: Self, Identity, and the Search for Ontological Security," *Political Psychology* 25, no. 5 (2004): 741–67, 746. https://doi.org/10.1111/j.1467-9221.2004.00396.x

17 Anthony D. Smith, "The Sacred Dimension of Nationalism," *Millennium: Journal of International Studies* 29, no. 3 (2000): 71–81. https://doi.org/10.1177/03058298000290030301

18 Audrey Kurth Cronin, "Behind the Curve: Globalization and International Terrorism," *International Security* 27, no. 3 (2003): 30–58. https://doi.org/10.1162/01622880260553624

19 Cesare Merlini, "A Post-Secular World?" *Survival* 53, no. 2 (2011): 117–30. https://doi.org/10.1080/00396338.2011.571015

20 David Cook, *Understanding Jihad* (Berkeley, CA: University of California Press, 2015).

21 Ibid., 14.

22 Suleiman A. Mourad and James E. Lindsay, *Intensification and Reorientation of Sunni Jihad Ideology in the Crusader Period* (Leiden: Brill, 2013).

23 Niall Christie, *The Book of the Jihad of 'Ali Ibn Tahir al-Sulami* (Farnham, England: Ashgate, 2015).

24 Halim Rane, "Narratives and Counter-Narratives of Islamist Extremism," in *Violent Extremism Online: New Perspectives on Terrorism and the Internet*, edited by Anne Aly, Stuart Macdonald, Lee Jarvis, and Thomas Chen, 167–85. New York: Routledge, 2016, 168–71.

25 Angel Rabasa and Cheryl Benard, *Eurojihad: Patterns of Islamist Radicalisation and Terrorism in Europe* (Cambridge: Cambridge University Press, 2015).

26 Jonathan Matusitz, "Gender Communal Terrorism or War Rape: Ten Symbolic Reasons," *Sexuality & Culture* 21, no. 3 (2017): 830–44. https://doi.org/10.1007/s12119-017-9424-z; Demi Simi and Jonathan Matusitz, "War Rape Survivors of the Second Congo War: A Perspective from Symbolic Convergence Theory," *Africa Review* 6, no. 2 (2014): 81–93. https://doi.org/10.1080/09744053.2014.914636

27 Christian Leuprecht, Todd Hataley, Sophia Moskalenko, and Clark Mccauley, "Containing the Narrative: Strategy and Tactics in Countering the Storyline of Global Jihad," *Journal of Policing, Intelligence and Counter Terrorism* 5, no. 1 (2010): 42–57. https://doi.org/10.1080/18335300.2010.9686940

28 Jean-Pierre Filiu, *Apocalypse in Islam* (Berkeley, CA: University of California Press, 2011).

29 Justin O'Shea, "ISIS: The Role of Ideology and Eschatology in the Islamic State," *The Pardee Periodical Journal of Global Affairs* 1, no. 2 (2016): 51–65.

30 Kaya Şahin, "Constantinople and the End Time: The Ottoman Conquest as a Portent of the Last Hour," *Journal of Early Modern History* 14, no. 4 (2010): 317–54. https://doi.org/10.1163/157006510X512223

31 David Cook, *Contemporary Muslim Apocalyptic Literature* (Syracuse, NY: Syracuse University Press, 2005).

32 Cited in Christian Leuprecht, Todd Hataley, Sophia Moskalenko, and Clark McCauley, "Winning the Battle but Losing the War? Narrative and Counter-Narratives Strategy," *Perspectives on Terrorism* 3, no. 2 (2009): 25–35.

33 Thomas X. Hammes, "War Evolves into the Fourth Generation," *Contemporary Security Policy* 26, no. 2 (2005): 189–221, 206. https://doi.org/10.1080/13523260500190500

34 Loretta Napoleoni, *Insurgent Iraq: Al Zarqawi and the New Generation* (New York: Seven Stories Press, 2005).

35 O'Shea, "ISIS," 61.

36 William McCants, *The ISIS Apocalypse: The History, Strategy, and Doomsday Vision of the Islamic State* (New York: St. Martin's Press, 2015).

37 Jonathan Matusitz, Andrea Madrazo, and Catalina Udani, *Online Jihadist Magazines to Promote the Caliphate: Communicative Perspectives* (New York: Peter Lang, 2019).

38 *Dabiq,* "Dabiq: The Return of the Khilafah," *Dabiq* 1 (2014): 3–4.

39 Ibid.

40 "The Prophecies Regarding the Roman Crusaders," *Dabiq* 4 (2014): 35.

41 John Turner, "The Impact of Islamic State's Ideological Correction Initiative on Al Qaeda's Bid for Relevance," *Small Wars & Insurgencies* 30, no. 3 (2019): 563–89. https://doi.org/10.1080/09592318.2019.1601843

42 Celine Marie I. Novenario, "Differentiating Al Qaeda and the Islamic State through Strategies Publicized in Jihadist Magazines," *Studies in Conflict & Terrorism* 39, no. 11 (2016): 953–67. https://doi.org/10.1080/10576 10X.2016.1151679

43 Martin Chulov, "ISIS Releases Video of Fighters in Baghuz as Kurdish Forces Advance," *The Guardian* (2019, March 12): A1.

44 Kirsen E. Schultze, and Joseph Chinyong Liow, "Making Jihadis, Waging Jihad: Transnational and Local Dimensions of the ISIS Phenomenon in Indonesia and Malaysia," *Asian Security* 15, no. 2 (2019): 122–39. https://doi.org/10.1080/14799855.2018.1424710

45 Matusitz, Madrazo, and Udani, *Online Jihadist Magazines to Promote the Caliphate*, 133.

46 Mario Mikulincer and Phillip R. Shaver, "Attachment Theory and Emotions in Close Relationships: Exploring the Attachment-Related Dynamics of Emotional Reactions to Relational Events," *Personal Relationships* 12, no. 2 (2005): 149–68. https://doi.org/10.1111/j.1350-4126.2005.00108.x; Thomas J. Scheff and Suzanne M. Retzinger, *Emotions and Violence: Shame and Rage in Destructive Conflicts* (Bloomington, IN: iUniverse, 2001).

47 Jytte Klausen, Eliane Tschaen Barbieri, Aaron Reichlin-Melnick, and Aaron Y. Zelin, "The YouTube Jihadists: A Social Network Analysis of Al-Muhajiroun's Propaganda Campaign," *Perspectives on Terrorism* 6, no. 1 (2012): 10–21.

48 Edward E. Royzman, Clark McCauley and Paul Rozin, "From Plato to Putnam: Four Ways of Thinking about Hate," in *The Psychology of Hate*, ed. Robert Sternberg (Washington, D.C.: American Psychological Association, 2004): 3–35.

49 Umbreen Javaid and Nighat Noureen, "An Insight into the Philosophical Dynamics of Al-Qaeda," *Journal of Political Studies* 20, no. 2 (2013): 10–21; James A. Sheppard, "Charlemagne's Tactic: Using Theology as a Weapon in the Fight against Al-Qa'ida," *American Intelligence Journal* 29, no. 1 (2011): 102–10.

50 Robert J. Sternberg, "A Duplex Theory of Hate: Development and Application to Terrorism, Massacres, and Genocide," *Review of General Psychology* 7, no. 3 (2003): 299–328. https://doi.org/10.1037/1089-2680.7.3.299

51 Ibid., 303.

52 Ibid., 300–6.

53 Ibid., 300–6.

54 Daveed Gartenstein-Ross and Laura Grossman, *Homegrown Terrorism in the U.S. and U.K.: An Empirical Examination of the Radicalization Process* (Washington, D.C.: Foundation for the Defense of Democracies, 2009).

55 Guido Steinberg and Isabelle Werenfels, "Between the 'Near' and the 'Far' Enemy: Al-Qaeda in the Islamic Maghreb," *Mediterranean Politics* 12, no. 3 (2007): 407–13. https://doi.org/10.1080/13629390701622473

56 Akil N. Awan, *Spurning This Worldly Life: Martyrdom amongst British Jihadists* (London: University of London Press, 2014).

57   Cited in Akil N. Awan, "Antecedents of Islamic Political Radicalism among Muslim Communities in Europe," *PS: Political Science & Politics* 41, no. 1 (2008): 13–7. https://doi.org/10.1017/S1049096508080013
58   *The Guardian*, "Extracts of Tanweer's Speech," *The Guardian* (2006, October 14): A1. Retrieved on September 28, 2019 from www.theguardian.com/uk/2006/oct/15/terrorism.alqaida1
59   *BBC News*, "London Bomber: Text in Full," *BBC News* (2005, September 1). Retrieved on September 28th, 2019 from http://news.bbc.co.uk/2/hi/uk/4206800.stm
60   Awan, *Spurning This Worldly Life*, 10–3.
61   Quintan Wiktorowicz, "A Genealogy of Radical Islam," *Studies in Conflict & Terrorism* 28, no. 2 (2005): 75–97. https://doi.org/10.1080/10576100590905057
62   Andrew McGregor, "'Jihad and the Rifle Alone:' 'Abdullah 'Azzam and the Islamist Revolution," *The Journal of Conflict Studies* 23, no. 2 (2003): 10–21.
63   Johannes J. G. Jansen, *The Neglected Duty: The Creed of Sadat's Assassins and Islamic Resurgence in the Middle East* (New York: Macmillan, 1986): 199.
64   Ibid.
65   Nelly Lahoud, "The Neglected Sex: The Jihadis' Exclusion of Women from Jihad," *Terrorism and Political Violence* 26, no. 5 (2014): 780–802, 783. https://doi.org/10.1080/09546553.2013.772511
66   Nanshan Chen, Min Zhou, Xuan Dong, Jieming Qu, Fengyun Gong, Yang Han, Yang Qiu, Jingli Wang, Ying Liu, Yuan Wei, Jia'an Xia, Ting Yu, Xinxin Zhang, and Li Zhang, "Epidemiological and Clinical Characteristics of 99 Cases of 2019 Novel Coronavirus Pneumonia in Wuhan, China: A Descriptive Study," *Lancet* 395, no. 10223 (2020): 507–13. https://doi.org/10.1016/S0140-6736(20)30211-7
67   The entire Al-Qaeda narrative regarding the so-called deserved coronavirus can be found on   www.memri.org/reports/al-qaeda-central-covid-19-divine-punishment-sins-mankind-muslims-must-repent-west-must
68   Ibid.
69   More information on ISIS's narrative on the coronavirus can be found on https://economictimes.indiatimes.com/news/defence/isis-travel-advisory-warns-terrorists-off-coronavirus-hit-europe/articleshow/74638096.cms?from=mdr
70   Jason Burke, "Opportunity or Threat? How Islamic Extremists Are Reacting to Coronavirus," *The Guardian* (2020, April 16): A1.
71   James E. Mitchell and Bill Harlow, *Enhanced Interrogation: Inside the Minds and Motives of the Islamic Terrorists Trying to Destroy America* (New York: Crown Forum, 2016).
72   Robert Spencer, *Stealth Jihad: How Radical Islam Is Subverting America without Guns or Bombs* (Washington, D.C.: Regnery, 2008).
73   Cited in Open Source Center, *Detained al-Qa'ida Leader Sayf al-Adl Chronicles al-Zarqawi's Rise in Organization* (Reston, VA: Open Source Center, 2005). Retrieved on February 13, 2019 from www.opensource.gov/portal/server.pt/gateway/PTARGS_0_0_200_989_51_43/http%3B/apps.opensource.gov%3B7011/opensource.gov/content/Display/PRINCE/GMP20050606371001?action=advancedSearch
74   Laith Saud, "The Islamic roots of the Egyptian Revolution," *Journal of Islamic Law and Culture* 12, no. 3 (2010): 187–96. https://doi.org/10.1080/1528817X.2010.618024; Patrick Sookhdeo, *Global Jihad: The Future in the Face of Militant Islam* (McLean, VA: Isaac Publishing, 2007).
75   See Shandon Harris-Hogan, "Understanding the Logic: An Analysis of Jihadist Targeting and Tactics in Western Countries from 2000 to Mid-2012," *Security Challenges* 11, no. 1 (2015): 73–89.
76   Sarfaroz Niyozov and Nadeem Memon, "Islamic Education and Islamization: Evolution of Themes, Continuities and New Directions," *Journal of Muslim Minority Affairs* 31, no. 1 (2011): 5–30. https://doi.org/10.1080/13602004.2011.556886
77   Assaf Moghadam, "Mayhem, Myths, and Martyrdom: The Shi'a Conception of Jihad," *Terrorism and Political Violence* 19, no. 1 (2007): 125–43; 129. https://doi.org/10.1080/09546550601079656

78 Cited in Michael Scheuer, *Imperial Hubris: Why the West Is Losing the War on Terror* (Washington, D.C.: Potomac Books, 2007): 17.
79 Ibid., 17.

References

Al Raffie, Dina, "Whose Hearts and Minds? Narratives and Counter-Narratives of Salafi Jihadism," *Journal of Terrorism Research* 3, no. 2 (2012): 13–31.

Amble, John C., and Alexander Meleagrou-Hitchens, "Jihadist Radicalization in East Africa: Two Case Studies," *Studies in Conflict & Terrorism* 37, no. 6 (2014): 523–540. https://doi.org/10.1080/1057610X.2014.893406.

Awan, Akil N., "Antecedents of Islamic Political Radicalism among Muslim Communities in Europe," *PS: Political Science & Politics* 41, no. 1 (2008): 13–17. https://doi.org/10.1017/S1049096508080013.

Awan, Akil N., *Spurning This Worldly Life: Martyrdom amongst British Jihadists*. London: University of London Press, 2014.

Burke, Jason, "Opportunity or Threat? How Islamic Extremists Are Reacting to Coronavirus," *The Guardian* (2020, April 16): A1.

Chen, Nanshan, Min Zhou, Xuan Dong, Jieming Qu, Fengyun Gong, Yang Han, Yang Qiu, Jingli Wang, Ying Liu, Yuan Wei, Jia'an Xia, Ting Yu, Xinxin Zhang, and Li Zhang, "Epidemiological and Clinical Characteristics of 99 Cases of 2019 Novel Coronavirus Pneumonia in Wuhan, China: A Descriptive Study," *Lancet* 395, no. 10223 (2020): 507–513. https://doi.org/10.1016/S0140-6736(20)30211-30217.

Christie, Niall, *The Book of the Jihad of 'Ali Ibn Tahir al-Sulami*. Farnham: Ashgate, 2015.

Chulov, Martin, "ISIS Releases Video of Fighters in Baghuz as Kurdish Forces Advance," *The Guardian* (2019, March 12): A1.

Cook, David, *Contemporary Muslim Apocalyptic Literature*. Syracuse, NY: Syracuse University Press, 2005.

Cook, David, *Understanding Jihad*. Berkeley, CA: University of California Press, 2015.

Cronin, Audrey Kurth, "Behind the Curve: Globalization and International Terrorism," *International Security* 27, no. 3 (2003): 30–58. https://doi.org/10.1162/01622880260553624.

Egerton, Frazer, *Jihad in the West: The Rise of Militant Salafism*. Cambridge: Cambridge University Press, 2011.

Filiu, Jean-Pierre, *Apocalypse in Islam*. Berkeley, CA: University of California Press, 2011.

Finn, Melissa, *Al Qaeda and Sacrifice: Martyrdom, War and Politics*. London: Pluto Press, 2012.

Freedman, Lawrence, *The Transformation of Strategic Affairs*. London: International Institute for Strategic Studies, 2006.

Gartenstein-Ross, Daveed, and Laura Grossman, *Homegrown Terrorists in the U.S. and U.K.: An Empirical Examination of the Radicalization Process*. Washington, D.C.: Foundation for Defense of Democracies, 2009.

Geist-Martin, Patricia, Eileen B. Ray, and Barbara Sharf, *Communicating Health: Personal, Cultural, and Political Complexities*. Belmont, CA: Wadsworth Press, 2003.

Guerrero, Laura K., Peter A. Andersen, and Walid Afifi, *Close Encounters* (5th ed.). Thousand Oaks, CA: Sage, 2017.

Halverson, Jeffry, H. Loyd Goodall, Jr., and Steven R. Corman, *Master Narratives of Islamist Extremism*. New York: Palgrave Macmillan, 2011.

Hammes, Thomas X., "War Evolves into the Fourth Generation," *Contemporary Security Policy* 26, no. 2 (2005): 189–221. https://doi.org/10.1080/13523260500190500.

Harris-Hogan, Shandon, "Understanding the Logic: An Analysis of Jihadist Targeting and Tactics in Western Countries from 2000 to Mid-2012," *Security Challenges* 11, no. 1 (2015): 73–89.

Holstein, James A., and Jaber F. Gubrium, *The Self We Live By: Narrative Identity in a Postmodern World*. New York: Oxford University Press, 2000.

Jackson, Richard, "Language, Policy and the Construction of a Torture Culture in the War on Terrorism," *Review of International Studies* 33, no. 3 (2007): 353–371. https://doi.org/10.1017/S0260210507007553.

Jansen, Johannes J. G., *The Neglected Duty: The Creed of Sadat's Assassins and Islamic Resurgence in the Middle East*. New York: Macmillan, 1986.

Javaid, Umbreen, and Nighat Noureen, "An Insight into the Philosophical Dynamics of Al-Qaeda," *Journal of Political Studies* 20, no. 2 (2013): 10–21.

Kinnvall, Catarina, "Globalization and Religious Nationalism: Self, Identity, and the Search for Ontological Security," *Political Psychology* 25, no. 5 (2004): 741–767. https://doi.org/10.1111/j.1467-9221.2004.00396.x.

Klausen, Jytte, Eliane Tschaen Barbieri, Aaron Reichlin-Melnick, and Aaron Y. Zelin, "The YouTube Jihadists: A Social Network Analysis of Al-Muhajiroun's Propaganda Campaign," *Perspectives on Terrorism* 6, no. 1 (2012): 10–21.

Lahoud, Nelly, "The Neglected Sex: The Jihadis' Exclusion of Women from Jihad," *Terrorism and Political Violence* 26, no. 5 (2014): 780–802. https://doi.org/10.1080/09546553.2013.772511.

Leuprecht, Christian, Todd Hataley, Sophia Moskalenko, and Clark McCauley, "Winning the Battle but Losing the War? Narrative and Counter-Narratives Strategy," *Perspectives on Terrorism* 3, no. 2 (2009): 25–35.

Leuprecht, Christian, Todd Hataley, Sophia Moskalenko, and Clark McCauley, "Containing the Narrative: Strategy and Tactics in Countering the Storyline of Global Jihad," *Journal of Policing, Intelligence and Counter Terrorism* 5, no. 1 (2010): 42–57. https://doi.org/10.1080/18335300.2010.9686940.

Matusitz, Jonathan, "Gender Communal Terrorism or War Rape: Ten Symbolic Reasons," *Sexuality & Culture* 21, no. 3 (2017): 830–844. https://doi.org/10.1007/s12119-017-9424-z.

Matusitz, Jonathan, Andrea Madrazo, and Catalina Udani, *Online Jihadist Magazines to Promote the Caliphate: Communicative Perspectives*. New York: Peter Lang, 2019.

McCants, William, *The ISIS Apocalypse: The History, Strategy, and Doomsday Vision of the Islamic State*. New York: St. Martin's Press, 2015.

McGregor, Andrew, "'Jihad and the Rifle Alone:' 'Abdullah 'Azzam and the Islamist Revolution," *The Journal of Conflict Studies* 23, no. 2 (2003): 10–21.

Merlini, Cesare, "A Post-Secular World?" *Survival* 53, no. 2 (2011): 117–130. https://doi.org/10.1080/00396338.2011.571015.

Mikulincer, Mario, and Phillip R. Shaver, "Attachment Theory and Emotions in Close Relationships: Exploring the Attachment-Related Dynamics of Emotional Reactions to Relational Events," *Personal Relationships* 12, no. 2 (2005): 149–168. https://doi.org/10.1111/j.1350-4126.2005.00108.x.

Mitchell, James E., and Bill Harlow, *Enhanced Interrogation: Inside the Minds and Motives of the Islamic Terrorists Trying to Destroy America*. New York: Crown Forum, 2016.

Moghadam, Assaf, "Mayhem, Myths, and Martyrdom: The Shi'a Conception of Jihad," *Terrorism and Political Violence* 19, no. 1 (2007): 125–143. https://doi.org/10.1080/09546550601079656

Mourad, Suleiman A., and James E. Lindsay, *Intensification and Reorientation of Sunni Jihad Ideology in the Crusader Period*. Leiden: Brill, 2013.

Napoleoni, Loretta, *Insurgent Iraq: Al Zarqawi and the New Generation*. New York: Seven Stories Press, 2005.

Niyozov, Sarfaroz, and Nadeem Memon, "Islamic Education and Islamization: Evolution of Themes, Continuities and New Directions," *Journal of Muslim Minority Affairs* 31, no. 1 (2011): 5–30. https://doi.org/10.1080/13602004.2011.556886.

Novenario, Celine Marie I., "Differentiating Al Qaeda and the Islamic State through Strategies Publicized in Jihadist Magazines," *Studies in Conflict & Terrorism* 39, no. 11 (2016): 953–967. https://doi.org/10.1080/1057610X.2016.1151679

Open Source Center, *Detained al-Qa'ida Leader Sayf al-Adl Chronicles al-Zarqawi's Rise in Organization*. Reston, VA: Open Source Center, 2005.

O'Shea, Justin, "ISIS: The Role of Ideology and Eschatology in the Islamic State," *The Pardee Periodical Journal of Global Affairs* 1, no. 2 (2016): 51–65.

Rabasa, Angel, and Cheryl Benard, *Eurojihad: Patterns of Islamist Radicalisation and Terrorism in Europe*. Cambridge: Cambridge University Press, 2015.

Rane, Halim, "Narratives and Counter-Narratives of Islamist Extremism," in *Violent Extremism Online: New Perspectives on Terrorism and the Internet*, edited by Anne Aly, Stuart Macdonald, Lee Jarvis, and Thomas Chen, 167–185. New York: Routledge, 2016.

Royzman, Edward E., Clark McCauley and Paul Rozin, "From Plato to Putnam: Four Ways of Thinking about Hate," in *The Psychology of Hate*, edited by Robert Sternberg, 3–35. Washington, D.C.: American Psychological Association, 2004.

Şahin, Kaya, "Constantinople and the End Time: The Ottoman Conquest as a Portent of the Last Hour," *Journal of Early Modern History* 14, no. 4 (2010): 317–354. https://doi.org/10.1163/157006510X512223.

Saud, Laith, "The Islamic roots of the Egyptian Revolution," *Journal of Islamic Law and Culture* 12, no. 3 (2010): 187–196. https://doi.org/10.1080/1528817X.2010.618024.

Scheff, Thomas J., and Suzanne M. Retzinger, *Emotions and Violence: Shame and Rage in Destructive Conflicts*. Bloomington, IN: iUniverse, 2001.

Scheuer, Michael, *Imperial Hubris: Why the West Is Losing the War on Terror*. Washington, D. C.: Potomac Books, 2007.

Schmid, Alex P., *Al-Qaeda's "Single Narrative" and Attempts to Develop Counter-Narratives: The State of Knowledge*. The Hague: International Centre for Counter Terrorism, 2014.

Schultze, Kirsen E., and Joseph Chinyong Liow, "Making Jihadis, Waging Jihad: Transnational and Local Dimensions of the ISIS Phenomenon in Indonesia and Malaysia," *Asian Security* 15, no. 2 (2019): 122–139. https://doi.org/10.1080/14799855.2018.1424710.

Sheppard, James A., "Charlemagne's Tactic: Using Theology as a Weapon in the Fight against Al-Qa'ida," *American Intelligence Journal* 29, no. 1 (2011): 102–110.

Simi, Demi, and Jonathan Matusitz, "War Rape Survivors of the Second Congo War: A Perspective from Symbolic Convergence Theory," *Africa Review* 6, no. 2 (2014): 81–93. https://doi.org/10.1080/09744053.2014.914636.

Smith, Anthony D., "The Sacred Dimension of Nationalism," *Millennium: Journal of International Studies* 29, no. 3 (2000): 71–81. https://doi.org/10.1177/03058298000290030301.

Sookhdeo, Patrick, *Global Jihad: The Future in the Face of Militant Islam*. McLean, VA: Isaac Publishing, 2007.

Spencer, Robert, *Stealth Jihad: How Radical Islam Is Subverting America without Guns or Bombs*. Washington, D.C.: Regnery, 2008.

Steinberg, Guido, and Isabelle Werenfels, "Between the 'Near' and the 'Far' Enemy: Al-Qaeda in the Islamic Maghreb," *Mediterranean Politics* 12, no. 3 (2007): 407–413. https://doi.org/10.1080/13629390701622473.

Sternberg, Robert J., "A Duplex Theory of Hate: Development and Application to Terrorism, Massacres, and Genocide," *Review of General Psychology* 7, no. 3 (2003): 299–328. https://doi.org/10.1037/1089-2680.7.3.299.

Turner, John, "The Impact of Islamic State's Ideological Correction Initiative on Al Qaeda's Bid for Relevance," *Small Wars & Insurgencies* 30, no. 3 (2019): 563–589. https://doi.org/10.1080/09592318.2019.1601843.

Vlahos, Michael, "The Long War: A Self-defeating Prophecy," *Asia Times* (2006, September 9): A1.

Wiktorowicz, Quintan, "A Genealogy of Radical Islam," *Studies in Conflict & Terrorism* 28, no. 2 (2005): 75–97. https://doi.org/10.1080/10576100590905057.

8

THE FATWA

One of the most dangerous communicative conduits of hatred in global jihad is the fatwa. A fatwa is a legal decree issued by an established authority on matters of Islamic legislation.[1] A legal expert who emits fatwas is called a mufti. Muftis are jurists who interpret, defend, and alter Islamic laws. They are authorized to produce authoritative legal opinions like fatwas. Traditionally, muftis were associated with the ulama.[2] The act of emitting a fatwa is called ifta.[3] A fatwa must be rooted in fiqh, which includes the Quran and the Sunna.[4] As sharia is not the same everywhere in the world and Islam is highly non-hierarchical in structure,[5] fatwas do not bear the same degree of influence as secular common-law opinions. Some interpretations of Islamic norms are the antithesis of secular laws. Thanks to globalization, most of these interpretations are growing similar and easily available—due to all sorts of electronic fatwas.[6] Daily, thousands of fatwas are disseminated on various issues, ranging from mundane topics (such as laws about fixing one's hair or cutting one's nails) to how to wage jihad.[7]

The advent of social media and increasing access to education has altered the traditional institution of ifta in multiple ways. In contrast to the concise or technical fatwas of the past, fatwas disseminated through social media attempt to be broader and more accessible to the public.[8] In the present day, fatwas are adapting to economic, social, and political conditions, and tackle issues involving the ummah. The emergence of codified state laws and Westernized legal education in the Muslim world replaces the traditional role played by muftis; their role is to clarify and expand the sharia doctrine implemented in courts. Hence, contemporary fatwas are used to advise the public on additional aspects of sharia, such as questions about religious rituals and social life.[9] Nevertheless, the extent to which fatwas influence the beliefs or conduct of Muslim audiences is unclear. Instead of mirroring the actual behavior or opinions of Muslims, some fatwas merely reflect a collection of views on how Muslims should think or behave.

Fatwa shopping

Fatwa shopping is the quest of opinions and edicts by authority figures on matters that are ambiguous. The purpose is to determine whether a certain concept, action, or product conforms to sharia or not.[10] Although the word "fatwa" is not mentioned in the Quran, people commonly seek fatwas to guide them in daily life. Owing to the absence of a central hierarchy in Islam, different muftis and religious clerics may provide different answers to the same question. A problem of credibility can erode the impact of a legal interpretation or argument by making the audience doubt the motives of the source and whether the message is a genuine representation of Islam and Allah's will. Accordingly, this opens the door for the contested practice of fatwa shopping, in which a person raises the same question of different legal experts until he or she is given a satisfactory answer.[11]

Fatwa shopping also entails searching Muslim websites for appropriate religious opinions. To the degree that fatwas are debatable, displeased questioners may search for another scholar to have a second (or even a third or fourth) opinion until they find what they want. Some authority figures, too, engage in fatwa shopping to maintain or defend their own opinions. In theory, this provides opportunities for all kinds of new and alternative opinions on Islam (in addition to the more traditional ones).[12] In like fashion, a Muslim can shop around until he or she finds an imam who can answer his or her wishes, a phenomenon dubbed "imam shopping,"[13] which involves looking for suitable theological opinions[14] or unconventional voices either inside or outside the conventional Muslim faith.[15]

When a fatwa benefits from a universal scholarly agreement (*ijma*), then it becomes legally binding.[16] Though individual fatwas cannot be universally binding, institutional fatwas carry more weight and can reach some type of universal consensus. They can only be overturned or altered by another institutional fatwa.[17] Since the late twentieth century, a new system has developed for the release of fatwas: the introduction of collective opinions through special institutions established for this purpose (instead of opinions by single authority figures that monopolized the Islamic jurisprudence for a long time). In those legal circles called "juristic councils," numerous *fiqh* jurists and experts from various disciplines—particularly the juristic, cultural, scientific, and economic disciplines—convene to examine new issues related to contemporary life and work on integral solutions grounded in Muslim heritage and Islamic thought.[18]

Jihadist fatwas

Jihadist fatwas only account for a small percentage of fatwas in general. However, they have been known to result in the killing of enemies. According to the classic Islamic doctrine, attacking *dar al-harb* in the form of an offensive jihad for reasons of conquest and conversion necessitates a fatwa from an authentic Muslim scholar (or ruler) and for a precise purpose (or act).[19] During the Caliphate era, only the Caliph (despite being anything but a Muslim scholar) could release jihadist fatwas, generally after consultation with his learned scholars.[20] Furthermore, by tradition, the caliph would engage in offensive operations into *dar al-harb* once or twice a year both to gather booty and deter potential attacks on Muslim communities within *dar al-Islam* territories.[21]

Since the late twentieth century, a great number of fatwas have been issued by jihadists who do not have the qualifications required of muftis. The best example discussed in this chapter is the fatwa issued in 1998 by Osama bin Laden and four of his close friends, declaring "jihad against Jews and Crusaders" and urging the ummah to kill American civilians. Besides criticizing its content, many Islamic jurists emphasized the fact that bin Laden did not have the qualifications to either emit a fatwa or proclaim jihad.[22] To instigate jihad against the *kuffar* (unbelievers), one must seek advice from a "learned Muslim scholar." Only this type of scholar (and/or Islamic ruler) can emit a fatwa on whether or not jihad is to be waged, how it can be validated (as enshrined in the Quran and hadith), and how it must be carried out.[23] Weimann (2011)[24] adds the following in regards to the legitimacy of jihadist fatwas:

> The authors of jihadist fatwas come from diverse backgrounds. Some are scholars, some are religious authoritative figures, and others are political leaders of radical movements who are not seen in the wider Islamic world as having authority to provide fatwas, but are accepted as authorities by their followers.

Enter Abdullah Azzam (who was discussed in ample detail in Chapter 3). Azzam contributed tremendously in the acceptance, within the ummah, of the legal principle of defensive jihad to galvanize Muslims against the Soviet invaders of Afghanistan. The passage from his fatwa makes it clear that defensive jihad is obligatory for all Muslims, including women and adolescents, to wage jihad. In that very fatwa, Azzam brings up key questions that Muslims might ask about the importance of implementing the principle of defensive jihad today.[25] Among these is the question on the applicability of a widespread call to arms (*nafir 'amm*). Some individuals, he affirmed, might say that "a general call to arms as required in Islam [stipulates that] a woman should go out to fight without her husband's permission, a boy without his father's permission."[26]

Burki (2011)[27] refers to this phenomenon as "anarchical jihad," whereby any famous Joe or Jane in the Muslim world can publish his or her own fatwa and decide on how to proceed with jihad, regardless of any moral or ethical constraints. This explains, in part, the current state of affairs in regards to global jihadism today. This situation also leads to a "fatwa war" with legitimate Islamic authorities who have the power to emit fatwas. Global "fatwa wars" have mirrored polemics in the Muslim world, from anti-colonial battles to the First Gulf War. Whereas muftis in some nations published fatwas asking for cooperation with Coalition Forces, muftis from other nations supported the Iraqi call for jihad against these Coalition Forces.[28]

Fatwa as violence against free speech

One of the hallmarks of democracy is free speech, a convention that supports the freedom of a person or a community to express viewpoints and ideas—without too much concern about retaliation, censorship, punishment, or legal actions—on an array of topics like religion (and their respective prophets, forefathers, and philosophers). Jihadism has produced multifaceted political movements whose goal is, among many things, to violently suppress free speech. Commentators, caricaturists, and cartoonists are fair game because they are inclined to ridicule the ravages of theocracy and Islam's threats of depicting the Prophet Muhammad. Not surprisingly, commentators, caricaturists, and cartoonists have been cowed by fear.[29]

The Danish filmmaker Finn Norgaard was murdered about a decade after another moviemaker, Theo van Gogh, was killed in plain sight in Amsterdam in 2004. The latter released a movie that was disapproving of Islam's treatment of women. The jihadists' war is against everything that democracy stands for: freedom of expression, of conscience, of the press, of blasphemy, and of sexual relations with anyone. The mainstay of democracy is perceived by pro-Caliphate fighters as a symptom of human debasement.[30] As will be described in detail in this chapter, the publication of 12 Muhammad cartoons by *Jyllands-Posten*, the Danish newspaper, in September 2005 not only landed the cartoonists a jihadist fatwa against them; it also sparked much controversy about self-censorship, freedom of expression, and accusations of religious hatred. Muslim activists staged protests and hundreds of people were killed or injured as a result of violent reactions to the cartoons. A small proportion of those activists even called for global jihad against the West.[31]

Likewise, in 1989, Ayatollah Khomeini emitted his fatwa against Salman Rushdie. The Satanic Verses ridiculed Quranic verses that sanction intercessory prayers to be addressed toward three Pagan Meccan goddesses: Allāt, Uzza, and Manāt.[32] In January 2015, two Al-Qaeda-inspired jihadists killed 12 civilians associated with the *Charlie Hebdo* satirical magazine in Paris. After the tragedy, Richard Dawkins, the retired English ethologist and atheist from the University of Oxford, who wrote *The God Delusion* (a bestseller in 2006), posted the following tweets about the Paris attackers, "They shouted 'We have avenged the Prophet Muhammad.' Some useful idiot will claim it had nothing to do with religion." And, subsequently, "No, all religions are NOT equally violent. Some have never been violent, some gave it up centuries ago. One religion conspicuously didn't."[33]

Case study I: fatwa against Salman Rushdie

Sir Salman Rushdie (b. 1947) is a British author of Indian origin. He has often entertained controversies through his works like *Midnight's Children* and *The Satanic Verses*. The latter elicited dangerous and intensely passionate responses from

Muslim religious orders, giving rise to a fatwa from Ayatollah Ruhollah Khomeini in Iran.[34] Calling the book "blasphemous against Islam" and proclaiming Salman Rushdie to be an apostate,[35] Khomeini released a fatwa in 1989 as a legal pronouncement of a death sentence on the British novelist for his disrespectful portrayal of the Prophet Muhammad. In fact, the title *Satanic Verses* alludes to a controversial Muslim tradition described in the book.[36] Chase (1996)[37] states that "for some, the fatwa is a case study of Islam's fierce intolerance. For others, the fatwa is a response to the United States and Europe's cultural aggression, which holds nothing above ironic scorn and base insults."

Article 57 and Ayatollah Khomeini

According to Article 57 of the Iranian constitution, the Supreme Leader (i.e., Ayatollah) has a decisive authority over the three branches of government and his orders are final. Based on the four schools of jurisprudence in Sunni Islam, fatwas are non-binding and, therefore, not mandatory decrees. On the contrary, they remain optional or consultative in nature. There is no compulsion to them. On the other hand, in Shia Islam, fatwas are generally binding and required to be followed—depending on the status of the scholar who releases it. In this manner, if an Ayatollah publishes a fatwa, it becomes binding in the eyes of Shia Muslims who care about the issue.[38]

The robust unity between religion and politics in the Islamic Republic signifies that the Supreme Leader's fatwas are binding—both legislatively and religiously. This also includes the position of a fatwa on matters related to weapons of mass destruction. Moreover, his authority guarantees that his fatwas cannot be questioned or invalidated by politicians and religious clerics. Today, Ali Khamenei is the current Ayatollah. His fatwa acts as a *hokme hokumati*, or State Decree. It is a type of legislation passed by a religious leader who also runs the entire nation (*velayat-e faqih*). Such a decree is not only absolute at the executive level; it is also endorsed by other religious leaders.[39]

Ayatollah Khomeini's fatwa against Salman Rushdie was a defining moment in international relations. The reactions to it, particularly by European leaders, suggested that such unrestrained decisions were an easy way to attract the world's attention (and to get anything he wanted). Many have continued to comply with the intensely passionate extremist minority in Iran.[40] Unlike popular Western belief, most fatwas do not act as "contracts" set up by mullahs to eliminate apostates, like Khomeini's fatwa giving permission to any Muslim to kill Salman Rushdie. This was a textbook case of extremist decision-making, which today still causes misunderstandings about the very meaning of "fatwa."[41] The Iranian régime supported the fatwa against Rushdie until 1998, when the following administration of Iranian President Mohammad Khatami said it did not support the murder of Rushdie any longer. To alleviate tensions with the West, Iran changed the fatwa into a "religious fatwa," thereby making a decree that was not part of the government's agenda. Nevertheless, the fatwa remains valid.[42]

Global reverberations

The publication of *The Satanic Verses* and the subsequent fatwa also generated physical violence around the world, with bookstores set aflame. Muslim groups in the West organized public rallies, burning copies of Rushdie's book.[43] Several people who translated or published the book were assaulted, seriously wounded, and even murdered. For instance, a Saudi Arabian imam and his Tunisian aide were killed in Brussels for claiming, on TV, that Rushdie should not be murdered. Many people died during demonstrations in other countries.[44] In August 1989, while Mustafa Mahmoud Mazeh was working on a book bomb laden with explosives in a hotel in Central London, the bomb was detonated too early, damaging two floors and killing Mazeh in the process.[45] A minor Lebanese terrorist group, the Organization of the Mujahidin of Islam, said that Mazeh was preparing an attack "on the apostate Rushdie." There is a tomb in Behesht-e Zahra cemetery (in Iran) for Mazeh that has an inscription with the following words: "Martyred in London, 3 August 1989. The first martyr to die on a mission to kill Salman Rushdie."[46]

Case study II: Osama bin Laden's fatwas

Osama bin Laden authored two fatwas in the late 1990s. The first was published in August 1996 and the second in February 1998. In 1996, a few months after going back to Afghanistan to live with the Taliban, Osama bin Laden published a 30-page fatwa titled "Declaration of War against the Americans Occupying the Land of the Two Holy Places." It was published in a London-based newspaper, *Al-Quds Al-Arabi*, and faxed to sympathizers around the world. It was bin Laden's first open call for global jihad against America.[47] His text, which often starts with "Praise be to Allah Who said …," harangues the victimization of the ummah. The following two excerpts condense his rationalization for jihad against "the Jewish–Crusader alliance of aggression:" "The people of Islam have suffered from aggression, iniquity and injustice imposed on them by the Jewish–Christian alliance" and "Their collaborators to the extent that the Muslims' blood became the cheapest and their wealth and assets looted by the hands of the enemies. Their blood was spilled in Palestine and Iraq."

Glorifying attacks against U.S. forces

The objective of this fatwa was twofold: (1) To justify Al-Qaeda's agenda of waging jihadist attacks on soft targets in *dar al-harb* and (2) to muster widespread support, within the ummah, toward a "just war" in order to free Muslim soil from the oppression exerted by the Crusaders and Jews.[48] In his text, Osama bin Laden glorified attacks against U.S. forces in Lebanon and Somalia. In 1990, Saudi Arabia conceded to U.S. forces crossing the holy Muslim land to fight in the First Gulf War. Six years later, U.S. troops were still deployed in Saudi Arabia in an attempt to contain Saddam Hussein. Osama bin Laden believed that America was making decisions for the Saudi royals; America was the "far enemy" that bolstered apostate governments in the Middle East. Muslims, he thought, should give up local hostilities and join forces to kick the Americans out of Saudi Arabia: "Destroying, fighting and killing the enemy until, by the Grace of Allah, it is completely defeated."[49]

Osama bin Laden's second fatwa in February 1998, *Al Quds Al Arabi*, was also distributed by fax. It was signed by five Islamists: (1) Osama bin Laden himself, (2) Ayman al-Zawahiri (who, today, is the current Al-Qaeda leader), (3) Ahmed Refai Taha (of al-Gama'a al-Islamiyya in Egypt), (4) Mir Hamzah (a Pakistani jihadist), and (5) Fazul Rahman (the "emir of the Jihad Movement in Bangladesh"). The signatories became known as the "World Islamic Front for Jihad against Jews and Crusaders."[50] Articulated in rhyming Arabic prose—which earned the praises of many would-be jihadists—this 1998 fatwa blamed the U.S. for invading and polluting the "sacred lands of Islam." It included the following: "It is an individual obligation for every Muslim who is able to do so in any country to kill and fight Americans and their allies, whether civilians or military."[51]

In August 1998, exactly six months after the second bin Laden fatwa came out, the U.S. embassy bombings occurred. Al-Qaeda and the Egyptian Islamic Jihad were the perpetrators. In the terrorist attack, a truck with hundreds of pounds of TNT and aluminum nitrate was detonated in the automobile park of the U.S. embassy in central Nairobi. More than 200 Kenyans and 12 Americans lost their lives. Nine minutes later, a second bomb was detonated at the embassy in Dar es Salaam in Tanzania, killing 11 Tanzanians, most of whom were Muslim.[52] The bombings took place on August 7, the eighth anniversary of the arrival of U.S. troops in Saudi Arabia (at the beginning of the First Gulf War)—certainly a tactful choice by Osama bin Laden.[53]

The "Zionist–Crusader alliance"

Osama bin Laden was the one who issued threats against the "Zionist–Crusader alliance" in the mid–1990s. In this narrative, jihadists believed that this alliance was launching a historically global assault on Islam. Today, they continue trying to convince Muslims to regard present-day conflicts through this lens.[54] They do so by broadcasting narratives of brutality and violence that can be heard from spellbinding sermons or other forms of communiqués: "They are decisively trying to maintain a nation brand based on extremism through beheading under the umbrella of the right Islam and the right religion."[55] Another method is the cherry-picking of excerpts from the Quran and prophetic traditions, often without context. This method serves to challenge modern interpretations of the scriptures, or to come up with more extreme interpretations to justify jihadist violence.[56]

An additional perspective has been articulated by Halverson, Goodall, and Corman (2011).[57] For them, the main message of jihadist narratives consists of convincing recruits to (1) resist foreign invaders like the Zionist–Crusader alliance and others who seek to destabilize Islam both externally and internally;

(2) repudiate apostate leaders who are in collusion with the perceived enemies of Islam (who have adopted non-Islamic policies and actions); and (3) encourage movement of Islamic revival so as to re-establish the Caliphate and apply sharia across space and time.

Textual manipulation

Upon examining Osama bin Laden's fatwa, it can be easily deduced that a meticulous method of textual manipulation was employed. For example, the late Al-Qaeda leader cherry-picked a verse that says "but when the forbidden months are past, then fight and slay the pagans wherever ye find them, seize them, beleaguer them and lie in wait for them in every stratagem (of war)."[58] The fatwa also quoted a hadith that read, "I have been sent with the sword between my hands to ensure that no one but God is worshipped. God who put my livelihood under the shadow of my spear, and, who inflicts humiliation and scorn on those who disobey my orders."[59]

Osama bin Laden (and his co-authors) ended their fatwa as follows: "We—with God's help—call on every Muslim who believes in God and wishes to be rewarded to comply with God's order to kill the Americans and plunder their money wherever and whenever they find it." A study by Lentini and Bakashmar (2007)[60] identified several issues, including (1) cherry-picking of religious texts, (2) radical interpretation of Quranic texts and hadith (i.e., taking quotes out of context), (3) the refusal to offer a comprehensive view of sharia under the pretext of a "just war," and (4) complete dismissal of the rigid limitations imposed on the legitimate conduct of war (jihad). Osama bin Laden argued that one should not refer to any religious scriptures that urge compromise or negotiation in times of conflict. As such, jihadists rarely make use of the following Quranic verses:

1. **Quran 16:125**: "Invite [all] to the way of your Lord with wisdom and beautiful preaching; and argue with them in ways that are best and most gracious: for thy Lord Knoweth best who have strayed from His Path, and who receive guidance."[61]
2. **Quran 16:126**: "And if you do catch the mout, catch the mout no worse than they catch you out: But if you show patience, that is indeed the best (course) for those who are patient."[62]
3. **Quran 16:127**: "And do thou be patient, for thy patience is but from Allah; nor grieve over them: and distress not thyself because of their plots. For Allah is with those who restrain themselves, and those who do good."[63]
4. **Quran 2:190**: "Fight in the path of God those who fight you but do not transgress limits; for God does not love transgressors."[64]

These verses reflect a sense of justice in the conduct of jihad and the value of embracing a conciliatory approach in times of conflict. Verse 16:126, for instance, mentions that a mujahedin should not afflict his or her enemy with harm (not more than what has been done to him or her). Killing unarmed civilians would happen at much lower frequencies if these verses were observed by jihadists.[65]

Case study III: fatwa against the Danish cartoonists

The *Jyllands-Posten* Muhammad cartoons were a controversy whereby 12 editorial cartoons were published by *Jyllands-Posten*, one of the largest-selling newspapers in Denmark, on September 30, 2005. Most of these cartoons depicted Muhammad. The newspaper said that this was political iconography in an effort to participate in the debate about disapproval of Islam and self-censorship. The Muhammad cartoon crisis led to demonstrations around the world in early 2006, including fierce riots in Muslim countries. This Danish cartoon controversy was possibly the second most important event, after the September 11, 2001 terrorist attacks, that united Muslims as political players in international politics.[66]

The cultural editor of *Jyllands-Posten*, Flemming Rose, initially supported the idea of drawing and printing those cartoons and contacted about 40 members of the Danish Illustrators' Trade Association (ITA) on this matter. Twelve artists accepted the challenge and created 12 different illustrations. One of these cartoons portrayed the Prophet with a bomb in his turban. It was authored by Kurt Westergaard, who became famous for this.[67] While the first reactions to the controversy were observed in a small country in northern Europe, these reactions reverberated worldwide, ranging from peaceful demonstrations to diplomatic injunctions to consumer boycotts, and eventually to physical violence against any symbol of the West. Infuriated Muslims from nations as remote as Lebanon, the Sudan, and Indonesia assaulted or looted Danish embassies, and threatened any tourist or professional coming from a European Union nation.[68] Hundreds of people lost their lives and thousands of others were injured due to the violence elicited by the cartoons.[69]

Condemnations of Denmark and its interests reached the internet through online attacks, as more than 600 Danish websites were either vandalized or hacked.[70] In fact, a website was created. It was called No4denmark.com and received over 67,280,389 visits by February 2009; it carried many banners like "Boycott their Products" and "No Denmark."[71] In a National Opinion Poll (NOP) conducted in Great Britain in the summer of 2006,[72] when inquired about attitudes towards free speech, there was little support for it in the event that it violates religious sensibilities. In fact, 78% of Muslims thought that the publishers of the Danish cartoons should be prosecuted, whereas 68% thought those who insult Islam should be indicted as well.

The levels of political action were perplexed; responsibilities and what sorts of actions to take were still confusing. Confusion for would-be jihadists stopped in 2010 when Anwar al-Awlaki issued an official fatwa in the form of an Al-Qaeda hit list in his *Inspire* magazine. The hit list included Rushdie and important people accused to have insulted Islam, such as Ayaan Hirsi Ali (a Somali-born Dutch-American activist against Islam), Lars Vilks (a Danish cartoonist), and three *Jyllands-*

Posten editorial members: Flemming Rose, Kurt Westergaard, and Carsten Juste (the editor-in-chief of the newspaper).[73] The list became heavier when it later included Stéphane "Charb" Charbonnier, who was killed in a terrorist operation on *Charlie Hebdo* in Paris, along with 11 other people. After the attack, Al-Qaeda pushed for even more killings.[74]

Notes

1 Wael B. Hallaq, *Authority, Continuity and Change in Islamic Law* (Cambridge: Cambridge University Press, 2004).
2 Jakob Skovgaard-Petersen, *Defining Islam for the Egyptian State: Muftis and Fatwas of the Dâr al-Iftâ, Social, Economic, and Political Studies of the Middle East and Asia* (Leiden: Brill, 1997).
3 Alexandre Caeiro, "The Shifting Moral Universes of the Islamic Tradition of Ifta': A Diachronic Study of Four Adab al-Fatwa Manuals," *The Muslim World* 96 (2006): 661–85.
4 Shmuel Bar, *Warrant for Terror: The Fatwas of Radical Islam and the Duty to Jihad* (Lanham, MD: Rowman & Littlefield, 2008): 8.
5 Carolyn M. Warner and Manfred W. Wenner, "Religion and the Political Organization of Muslims in Europe," *Perspectives on Politics* 4, no. 3 (2006): 457–79, 461. https://doi.org/10.1017/S1537592706060300; Corinne N. Ortega, "Issues in Multicultural Correctional Assessment and Treatment," in *Correctional Mental Health: From Theory to Best Practice*, ed. Thomas J. Fagan and Robert K. Ax (Thousand Oaks, CA: Sage, 2011): 125–44.
6 Jocelyne Cesari, *Why the West Fear Islam: An Exploration of Muslims in Liberal Democracies* (New York: Palgrave Macmillan, 2013): 119.
7 Rudolph Peters, *Jihad in Classical and Modern Islam: A Reader* (Princeton, NJ: Markus Wiener Publishers, 1996).
8 Moustafa Kassem, "Fatwa in the Era of Globalization," in *Ifta' and Fatwa in the Muslim World and the West*, ed. Zulfiqar Ali Shah (Washington, D.C.: The International Institute of Islamic Thought, 2014): 89–104.
9 Carool Kersten, *The Fatwa as an Islamic Legal Instrument: Concept, Historical Role, Contemporary Relevance* (New Orleans: Gerlach Press, 2018).
10 Muhammad Shaukat Malik, Ali Malik, and Waqas Mustafa, "Controversies that Make Islamic Banking Controversial: An Analysis of Issues and Challenges," *American Journal of Social and Management Sciences* 2, no. 1 (2011): 41–6.
11 Andrew C. Miller, "Opinions on the Legitimacy of Brain Death among Sunni and Shi'a Scholars," *Journal of Religion and Health* 55, no. 2 (2016): 394–402. https://doi.org/10.1007/s10943-015-0157-8
12 Nardisiyah Hosen, "Online Fatwa in Indonesia: From Fatwa Shopping to Googling a Kiai," in *Expressing Islam: Religious Life and Politics in Indonesia*, ed. Greg Fealy and Sally White (Singapore: Institute of Southeast Asian Studies, 2008): 159–73.
13 Cited in Nadia Sonneveld, "Review of Anna C. Korteweg and Jennifer A. Selby (eds.), *Debating Sharia: Islam, Gender Politics, and Family Law Arbitration*, Toronto: University of Toronto Press 2012, 397 pp., ISBN 978-1-4426-4262-1," *Religion & Gender* 4, no. 1 (2014): 80–2.
14 Jonathan Schanzer and Steven Miller, *Facebook Fatwa: Saudi Clerics, Wahhabi Islam and Social Media* (Washington, D.C.: Foundation for Defense of Democracies, 2012).
15 Malcolm Voyce and Adam Possamai, "Legal Pluralism, Family Personal Laws, and the Rejection of Shari'a in Australia: A Case of Multiple or 'Clashing' Modernities?," *Democracy and Security* 7, no. 4 (2011): 338–53. https://doi.org/10.1080/17419166.2011.617603
16 Frank Vogel, *Islamic Law and Legal System: Studies of Saudi Arabia* (Leiden: Brill, 2000).

17 Ghiath Alahmad and Kris Dierickx, "What Do Islamic Institutional Fatwas Say about Medical and Research Confidentiality and Breach of Confidentiality?," *Developing World Bioethics* 12, no. 2 (2012): 104–12. https://doi.org/10.1111/j.1471-8847.2012.00329.x

18 Ibid., 105.

19 Shireen K. Burki, "Jihad or Qatal? Examining Al Qaeda's *Modus Operandi*," *Defense & Security Analysis* 29, no. 3 (2013): 234–52. https://doi.org/10.1080/14751798.2013.820965

20 Awad Halabi, "Liminal Loyalties: Ottomanism and Palestinian Responses to the Turkish War of Independence, 1919–22," *Journal of Palestine Studies* 41, no. 3 (2012): 19–37. https://doi.org/10.1525/jps.2012.XLI.3.19

21 George Joffé, "Global Jihad and Foreign Fighters," *Small Wars & Insurgencies* 27, no. 5 (2016): 800–16. https://doi.org/10.1080/09592318.2016.1208284

22 Ahmad S. Dallal and Jocelyn Hendrickson, "Fatwā: Modern Usage," in *The Oxford Encyclopedia of the Islamic World*, ed. John L. Esposito (Oxford: Oxford University Press, 2009).

23 Burki, "Jihad or Qatal?," 240.

24 Gabriel Weimann, "Cyber-Fatwas and Terrorism," *Studies in Conflict & Terrorism* 34, no. 10 (2011): 765–81, 768. https://doi.org/10.1080/1057610X.2011.604831

25 Nelly Lahoud, "The Neglected Sex: The Jihadis' Exclusion of Women from Jihad," *Terrorism and Political Violence* 26, no. 5 (2014): 780–802. https://doi.org/10.1080/09546553.2013.772511

26 Ibid., 784.

27 Shireen K. Burki, "Haram or Halal? Islamists' Use of Suicide Attacks as 'Jihad'," *Terrorism and Political Violence* 23, no. 4 (2011): 582–601. https://doi.org/10.1080/09546553.2011.578185

28 Bettina Gräf, "Fatwā, Modern Media," in *Encyclopaedia of Islam* (3rd Ed.), ed. Kate Fleet, Gudrun Krämer, Denis Matringe, John Nawas, and Everett Rowson (Boston: Brill Publishers, 2017).

29 Geoffrey Brahm Levey and Tariq Modood, "The Muhammad Cartoons and Multicultural Democracies," *Ethnicities* 9, no. 3 (2009): 427–47. https://doi.org/10.1177/1468796809337427

30 Roger Cohen, "Islam and the West at War," *The New York Times* (2015, February 16): A23.

31 Ahmed Al-Rawi, "Online Reactions to the Muhammad Cartoons: YouTube and the Virtual Ummah," *Journal for the Scientific Study of Religion* 54, no. 2 (2015): 261–76. https://doi.org/10.1111/jssr.12191

32 John D. Erickson, *Islam and Postcolonial Narrative* (Cambridge: Cambridge University Press, 1998).

33 Cited in Cavan Sieczkowski, "Richard Dawkins Says 'Religions Are NOT Equally Violent' After Charlie Hebdo Attack," *Huffington Post* (2015, January 8): A1.

34 Kenan Malik, *From Fatwa to Jihad: The Rushdie Affair and Its Aftermath* (New York: Melville House, 2010).

35 Mohamed Arkoun, "Islam, the West, and Human Rights," *Index on Censorship* 18, no. 5 (1989): 13–6. https://doi.org/10.1080/03064228908534637

36 Amin Malak, *Muslim Narratives and the Discourse of English* (Albany, NY: SUNY Press, 2005).

37 Anthony Chase, "Legal Guardians: Islamic Law, International Law, Human Rights Law, and the Salman Rushdie Affair," *American University International Law Review* 11, no. 3 (1996): 375–435, 375.

38 Burki, "Jihad or Qatal," 247.

39 Seyed Hossein Mousavian, "Globalising Iran's Fatwa Against Nuclear Weapons," *Survival* 55, no. 2 (2013): 147–62. https://doi.org/10.1080/00396338.2013.784471

40 Weimann, "Cyber-Fatwas and Terrorism," 767–70.

41 Manzar Zaidi, "A Taxonomy of Jihad," *Arab Studies Quarterly* 31, no. 3 (2009): 21–34.

42 Mehdi Khalaji, "Great Expectations: Iran after the Deal," *The Washington Quarterly* 38, no. 3 (2015): 61–77. https://doi.org/10.1080/0163660X.2015.1099025

43 Michael M. J. Fischer and Mehdi Abedi, "Bombay Talkies, the Word and the World: Salman Rushdie's Satanic Verses," *Cultural Anthropology* 5, no. 2 (1990): 107–59. https://doi.org/10.1525/can.1990.5.2.02a00010
44 Michael M. J. Fischer and Mehdi Abedi, *Debating Muslims: Cultural Dialogues in Postmodernity and Tradition* (Madison: University of Wisconsin Press, 1990).
45 Matthew Levitt, "Iran's Deadly Diplomats," *CTC Sentinel* 16 (2018): 10–5.
46 Anthony Lloyd, "First Rushdie 'Martyr'—Untold Assassination Plot Revealed," *Telegraph India* (2005, June 8): A1.
47 Dominic Tierney, "The Twenty Years' War," *The Atlantic* (2016, August 23). Retrieved on February 11, 2019 from www.theatlantic.com/international/archive/2016/08/twenty-years-war/496736/
48 Burki, "Jihad or Qatal," 240.
49 Tierney, "The Twenty Years' War."
50 Weimann, "Cyber-Fatwas and Terrorism," 768.
51 James Buchan, "Osama bin Laden: Terrorist Leader Who Waged Jihad against 'Jews and Crusaders' and Ordered the Attacks of 11 September 2001," *The Independent* (2011, May 3): A1.
52 Michele Malvesti, "Explaining the United States' Decision to Strike Back at Terrorists," *Terrorism and Political Violence* 13, no. 2 (2001): 85–106. https://doi.org/10.1080/09546550109609682
53 Rohan Gunaratna, *Inside Al Qaeda* (New York: Columbia University Press, 2002).
54 Akil N. Awan, "Success of the Meta-Narrative: How Jihadists Maintain Legitimacy," *CTC Sentinel* 2, no. 11 (2009): 6–8.
55 Luna Shamieh and Zoltán Szenes, "The Propaganda of ISIS/DAESH through the Virtual Space," *DATR* 7, no. 1 (2015): 7–31, 28.
56 Awan, "Success of the Meta-Narrative," 6–8.
57 Jeffry Halverson, H. Loyd Goodall, Jr., and Steven R. Corman, *Master Narratives of Islamist Extremism* (New York: Palgrave Macmillan, 2011).
58 The fatwa of Osama bin Laden, Ayman al-Zawahiri, Ahmed Refai Taha, Mir Hamzah, and Fazul Rahman appears as "The World Islamic Front," in *Messages to the World: The Statements of Osama bin Laden*, ed. Bruce Lawrence (trans. James Howarth) (London: Verso, 2005): 58–62.
59 Ibid., 59–60.
60 Pete Lentini and Muhammad Bakashmar, "Jihadist Beheading: A Convergence of Technology, Theology, and Teleology?," *Studies in Conflict & Terrorism* 30, no. 4 (2017): 303–25. https://doi.org/10.1080/10576100701200140
61 Available at http://corpus.quran.com/translation.jsp?chapter=16&verse=125
62 Available at www.quranproject.org/Patience-and-Gratitude-563-d
63 Available at http://corpus.quran.com/translation.jsp?chapter=16&verse=128
64 Available at http://corpus.quran.com/translation.jsp?chapter=2&verse=190
65 Ibid., 306.
66 Marion G. Müller and Esra Özcan, "The Political Iconography of Muhammad Cartoons: Understanding Cultural Conflict and Political Action," *PS: Political Science & Politics* 40, no. 2 (2007): 287–91. https://doi.org/10.1017/S104909650707045X
67 John Lykkegaard, *Kurt Westergaard: The Man behind the Mohammed Cartoon* (Stavnsvej, Denmark: Forlaget Mine Erindringer, 2012).
68 Müller and Özcan, "The Political Iconography of Muhammad Cartoons," 287.
69 Al-Rawi, "Online Reactions to the Muhammad Cartoons," 265–8.
70 Jeffrey Carr, *Inside Cyber Warfare: Mapping the Cyber Underworld* (Sebastopol, CA: O'Reilly Media, 2010).
71 Al-Rawi, "Online Reactions to the Muhammad Cartoons," 262.
72 NOP Poll of British Muslims (2006, August 8). Retrieved on February 11, 2019 from http://ukpollingreport.co.uk/blog/archives/291

73 Dashiell Bennett, "Look Who's on Al Qaeda's Most-Wanted List," *The Atlantic* (2013, March 1). Retrieved on February 11, 2019 from www.theatlantic.com/international/archive/2013/03/al-qaeda-most-wanted-list/317829/

74 Lucy Cormack, "Charlie Hebdo Editor Stephane Charbonnier Crossed off Chilling Al-Qaeda Hit List," *The Age* (2015, January 8). Retrieved on February 11, 2019 from www.theage.com.au/world/charlie-hebdo-editor-stephane-charbonnier-crossed-off-chilling-alqaeda-hitlist-20150108-12k97z.html

References

Alahmad, Ghiath, and Kris Dierickx, "What Do Islamic Institutional Fatwas Say about Medical and Research Confidentiality and Breach of Confidentiality?," *Developing World Bioethics* 12, no. 2 (2012): 104–112. https://doi.org/10.1111/j.1471-8847.2012.00329.x.

Al-Rawi, Ahmed, "Online Reactions to the Muhammad Cartoons: YouTube and the Virtual Ummah," *Journal for the Scientific Study of Religion* 54, no. 2 (2015): 261–276. https://doi.org/10.1111/jssr.12191.

Arkoun, Mohamed, "Islam, the West, and Human Rights," *Index on Censorship* 18, no. 5 (1989): 13–16. https://doi.org/10.1080/03064228908534637.

Awan, Akil N., "Success of the Meta-Narrative: How Jihadists Maintain Legitimacy," *CTC Sentinel* 2, no. 11 (2009): 6–8.

Bar, Shmuel, *Warrant for Terror: The Fatwas of Radical Islam and the Duty to Jihad*. Lanham, MD: Rowman & Littlefield, 2008.

Bennett, Dashiell, "Look Who's on Al Qaeda's Most-Wanted List," *The Atlantic* (2013, March 1). Retrieved on February 11, 2019 from www.theatlantic.com/international/archive/2013/03/al-qaeda-most-wanted-list/317829/.

Buchan, James, "Osama bin Laden: Terrorist Leader Who Waged Jihad against 'Jews and Crusaders' and Ordered the Attacks of 11 September 2001," *The Independent* (2011, May 3): A1.

Burki, Shireen K., "Haram or Halal? Islamists' Use of Suicide Attacks as 'Jihad'," *Terrorism and Political Violence* 23, no. 4 (2011): 582–601. https://doi.org/10.1080/09546553.2011.578185.

Burki, Shireen K., "Jihad or Qatal? Examining Al Qaeda's Modus Operandi," *Defense & Security Analysis* 29, no. 3 (2013): 234–252. https://doi.org/10.1080/14751798.2013.820965.

Caeiro, Alexander, "The Shifting Moral Universes of the Islamic Tradition of Ifta': A Diachronic Study of Four Adab al-Fatwa Manuals," *The Muslim World* 96 (2006): 661–685.

Carr, Jeffrey, *Inside Cyber Warfare: Mapping the Cyber Underworld*. Sebastopol, CA: O'Reilly Media, 2010.

Cesari, Jocelyne, *Why the West Fear Islam: An Exploration of Muslims in Liberal Democracies*. New York: Palgrave Macmillan, 2013.

Chase, Anthony, "Legal Guardians: Islamic Law, International Law, Human Rights Law, and the Salman Rushdie Affair," *American University International Law Review* 11, no. 3 (1996): 375–435.

Cohen, Roger, "Islam and the West at War," *The New York Times* (2015, February 16): A23.

Cormack, Lucy, "Charlie Hebdo Editor Stephane Charbonnier Crossed off Chilling Al-Qaeda Hit List," *The Age* (2015, January 8). Retrieved on February 11, 2019 from www.theage.com.au/world/charlie-hebdo-editor-stephane-charbonnier-crossed-off-chilling-alqaeda-hitlist-20150108-12k97z.html.

Dallal, Ahmad S., and Jocelyn Hendrickson, "Fatwā: Modern Usage," in *The Oxford Encyclopedia of the Islamic World*, edited by John L. Esposito. Oxford: Oxford University Press, 2009.

Erickson, John D., *Islam and Postcolonial Narrative*. Cambridge: Cambridge University Press, 1998.

Fischer, Michael M. J., and Mehdi Abedi, "Bombay Talkies, the Word and the World: Salman Rushdie's Satanic Verses," *Cultural Anthropology* 5, no. 2 (1990): 107–159. https://doi.org/10.1525/can.1990.5.2.02a00010.

Fischer, Michael M. J., and Mehdi Abedi, *Debating Muslims: Cultural Dialogues in Postmodernity and Tradition*. Madison, WI: University of Wisconsin Press, 1990.

Gräf, Bettina, "Fatwā, Modern Media," in *Encyclopaedia of Islam* (3rd ed.), edited by Kate Fleet, Gudrun Krämer, Denis Matringe, John Nawas, and Everett Rowson. Boston, MA: Brill Publishers, 2017.

Gunaratna, Rohan, *Inside Al Qaeda*. New York: Columbia University Press, 2002.

Halabi, Awad, "Liminal Loyalties: Ottomanism and Palestinian Responses to the Turkish War of Independence, 1919–22," *Journal of Palestine Studies* 41, no. 3 (2012): 19–37. https://doi.org/10.1525/jps.2012.XLI.3.19.

Hallaq, Wael B., *Authority, Continuity and Change in Islamic Law*. Cambridge: Cambridge University Press, 2004.

Halverson, Jeffry, H. Loyd Goodall, Jr., and Steven R. Corman, *Master Narratives of Islamist Extremism*. New York: Palgrave Macmillan, 2011.

Hosen, Nardisiyah, "Online Fatwa in Indonesia: From Fatwa Shopping to Googling a Kiai," in *Expressing Islam: Religious Life and Politics in Indonesia*, edited by Greg Fealy and Sally White, 159–173. Singapore: Institute of Southeast Asian Studies, 2008.

Joffé, George, "Global Jihad and Foreign Fighters," *Small Wars & Insurgencies* 27, no. 5 (2016): 800–816. https://doi.org/10.1080/09592318.2016.1208284.

Kassem, Moustafa, "Fatwa in the Era of Globalization," in *Ifta' and Fatwa in the Muslim World and the West*, edited by Zulfiqar Ali Shah, 89–104. Washington, D.C.: The International Institute of Islamic Thought, 2014.

Kersten, Carool, *The Fatwa as an Islamic Legal Instrument: Concept, Historical Role, Contemporary Relevance*. New Orleans, LA: Gerlach Press, 2018.

Khalaji, Mehdi, "Great Expectations: Iran after the Deal," *The Washington Quarterly* 38, no. 3 (2015): 61–77. https://doi.org/10.1080/0163660X.2015.1099025.

Lahoud, Nelly, "The Neglected Sex: The Jihadis' Exclusion of Women from Jihad," *Terrorism and Political Violence* 26, no. 5 (2014): 780–802. http://dx.doi.org/10.1080/09546553.2013.772511.

Lentini, Pete, and Muhammad Bakashmar, "Jihadist Beheading: A Convergence of Technology, Theology, and Teleology?," *Studies in Conflict & Terrorism* 30, no. 4 (2017): 303–325. https://doi.org/10.1080/10576100701200140.

Levey, Geoffrey Brahm, and Tariq Modood, "The Muhammad Cartoons and Multicultural Democracies," *Ethnicities* 9, no. 3 (2009): 427–447. https://doi.org/10.1177/1468796809337427.

Levitt, Matthew, "Iran's Deadly Diplomats," *CTC Sentinel* 16 (2018): 10–15.

Lloyd, Anthony, "First Rushdie 'Martyr'—Untold Assassination Plot Revealed," *Telegraph India* (2005, June 8): A1.

Lykkegaard, John, *Kurt Westergaard: The Man behind the Mohammed Cartoon*. Stavnsvej, Denmark: Forlaget Mine Erindringer, 2012.

Malak, Amin, *Muslim Narratives and the Discourse of English*. Albany, NY: SUNY Press, 2005.

Malik, Kenan, *From Fatwa to Jihad: The Rushdie Affair and Its Aftermath*. New York: Melville House, 2010.

Malik, Muhammad Shaukat, Ali Malik, and Waqas Mustafa, "Controversies that Make Islamic Banking Controversial: An Analysis of Issues and Challenges," *American Journal of Social and Management Sciences* 2, no. 1 (2011): 41–46.

Malvesti, Michele, "Explaining the United States' Decision to Strike Back at Terrorists," *Terrorism and Political Violence* 13, no. 2 (2001): 85–106. https://doi.org/10.1080/09546550109609682.

Miller, Andrew C., "Opinions on the Legitimacy of Brain Death among Sunni and Shi'a Scholars," *Journal of Religion and Health* 55, no. 2 (2016): 394–402. https://doi.org/10.1007/s10943-015-0157-8.

Mousavian, Seyed Hossein, "Globalising Iran's Fatwa Against Nuclear Weapons," *Survival* 55, no. 2 (2013): 147–162. https://doi.org/10.1080/00396338.2013.784471.

Müller, Marion G., and Esra Özcan, "The Political Iconography of Muhammad Cartoons: Understanding Cultural Conflict and Political Action," *PS: Political Science & Politics* 40, no. 2 (2007): 287–291. https://doi.org/10.1017/S104909650707045X.

Ortega, Corinne N., "Issues in Multicultural Correctional Assessment and Treatment," in *Correctional Mental Health: From Theory to Best Practice*, edited by Thomas J. Fagan and Robert K. Ax, 125–144. Thousand Oaks, CA: Sage, 2011.

Peters, Rudolph, *Jihad in Classical and Modern Islam: A Reader*. Princeton, NJ: Markus Wiener Publishers, 1996.

Schanzer, Jonathan, and Steven Miller, *Facebook Fatwa: Saudi Clerics, Wahhabi Islam and Social Media*. Washington, D.C.: Foundation for Defense of Democracies, 2012.

Shamieh, Luna, and Zoltán Szenes, "The Propaganda of ISIS/DAESH through the Virtual Space," *DATR* 7, no. 1 (2015): 7–31.

Sieczkowski, Cavan, "Richard Dawkins Says 'Religions Are NOT Equally Violent' After Charlie Hebdo Attack," *Huffington Post* (2015, January 8): A1.

Skovgaard-Petersen, Jakob, *Defining Islam for the Egyptian State: Muftis and Fatwas of the Dâr al-Iftâ, Social, Economic, and Political Studies of the Middle East and Asia*. Leiden: Brill, 1997.

Sonneveld, Nadia, "Review of Anna C. Korteweg and Jennifer A. Selby (eds.), *Debating Sharia: Islam, Gender Politics, and Family Law Arbitration*, Toronto: University of Toronto Press 2012, 397 pp., ISBN 978-1-4426-4262-1," *Religion & Gender* 4, no. 1 (2014): 80–82.

Tierney, Dominic, "The Twenty Years' War," *The Atlantic* (2016, August 23). Retrieved on February 11, 2019 from www.theatlantic.com/international/archive/2016/08/twenty-years-war/496736/.

Vogel, Frank, *Islamic Law and Legal System: Studies of Saudi Arabia*. Leiden: Brill, 2000.

Voyce, Malcolm, and Adam Possamai, "Legal Pluralism, Family Personal Laws, and the Rejection of Shari'a in Australia: A Case of Multiple or 'Clashing' Modernities?," *Democracy and Security* 7, no. 4 (2011): 338–353. https://doi.org/10.1080/17419166.2011.617603.

Warner, Carolyn M., and Manfred W. Wenner, "Religion and the Political Organization of Muslims in Europe," *Perspectives on Politics* 4, no. 3 (2006): 457–479. https://doi.org/10.1017/S1537592706060300.

Weimann, Gabriel, "Cyber-Fatwas and Terrorism," *Studies in Conflict & Terrorism* 34, no. 10 (2011): 765–781. https://doi.org/10.1080/1057610X.2011.604831.

Zaidi, Manzar, "A Taxonomy of Jihad," *Arab Studies Quarterly* 31, no. 3 (2009): 21–34.

9

ISLAMIC REVIVAL

Religious reforms happen when a religious community concludes that it has veered too much from the foundational principles of the faith. The majority of religious reforms are initiated by members of the religious élite and encounter resistance by other members of the same religious community.[1] The general description of Islamic reform covers three main themes: (1) Reformism within the Muslim faith or tradition; (2) Islamic modernism; a historical movement that arose in the nineteenth century to reconcile the Muslim religion with modernity; and (3) liberalism and progressivism in Islam; a wide-ranging philosophy and movement that seek to merge Islam with liberalism or progressivism.[2] For reform-minded leaders in moderate Islam, modernizations are a necessary adaptation to the politico-cultural challenge of the West. The burden of Western colonization has also impelled some Muslim reformers to request that the possibility of religious interpretation (*ijtihad*) be offered. "New Muslim intellectuals" with a secular education are contesting the monopoly of religious power that was shared earlier by the *ulama* (the classically trained Muslim scholars).[3]

Two opposite directions

Moderate reform-minded leaders and activists work for a broad audience instead of a few religious disciples. Rather than having esoteric legal debates, champions of the modernization of Islam frame their faith as a source of practical knowledge that can be distinguished from others and consciously reinterpreted. They mingle verses from the Quran with discussions of modern affairs, contemporary moral dilemmas, and even Western political theory. They challenge the wisdom of a monolithic Islam, but want democracy, individual will, and a balance of powers in a state and society.[4] Liberalism and progressivism are professed by Muslims who have a significant record of expertise and thoughts on the reinterpretation and reform of Islam's understanding and practice.[5]

However, Islamic "reform" differs from Islamic "revival." Islamic revival goes in the opposite direction. In this context, Islamic revival covers two main themes: (1) The Salafist conjecture that the Quran is the perfect, straightforward word of Allah and should be taken literally and (2) the corresponding support of jihad to attain such radical aims (which have been embraced by Salafist and jihadist movements across the world). Besides advocating ultra-violence against both non-Muslims and Muslim apostates, this brand of Islamic revival goes back to the fundamentals of Islam that outright reject fundamental human rights and democracy by all means.[6] In *Islam and Modernity: Transformation of an Intellectual Tradition*, Rahman (1982)[7] states that "to insist on absolute uniformity of interpretation is therefore neither possible nor desirable." The ideal climate of the free marketplace of ideas, typified by intellectual rigor and vigor, is virtually non-existent in countries like Afghanistan, Pakistan, Somalia, the Sudan, and Yemen—among many others. The byproduct of such revivalism is worsening intellectual poverty. *Apropos* the substance of Salafists' views, there is generally a reference to "freedom of interpretation," but they do not meet their own criterion. Rather, they are determined to uphold the fundamentalist tradition in an uncritical manner, notwithstanding appearances to the contrary.[8]

The concept of *tajdid*

Islamic revival is called *tajdid* in Arabic (i.e., "regeneration" or "renewal"). It refers to a revival of the Muslim religion through a global social movement. In the Islamic tradition, *tajdid* has a been a significant religious phase that has surfaced sporadically throughout Islamic history—particularly after calls for a refreshed commitment to the basic principles of Islam or calls for a restoration of society in line with the Quran and the traditions of the Prophet Muhammad. *Tajdid* plays a large part in contemporary Islamic revival.[9] In the early twentieth century, the Muslim Brotherhood movement was born in hopes of reviving pure, traditional Islam. In the second half of the twentieth century, particularly the 1970s, a global Islamic revival re-emerged, mostly because of widespread dissatisfaction with the secular Arab states and Westernized ruling élites. The latter had dominated the Muslim world for several decades and were more and more regarded as authoritarian, incompetent, and devoid of religious authenticity.[10]

Islamic revival has also been a response to Western influences such as individualism, consumerism, the emancipation of women, and sexual freedom, which are allegedly perverting Muslim values and identities.[11] Islamic revival has stressed the "re-Islamization" of society from above and below. Manifestations of this range from sharia-compliant laws to rampant adherence to Islamic traditions (e.g., increased attendance at the annual pilgrimage to Mecca or *hajj*) by Muslims.[12] Since the 1970s, more veiled and scarfed women have been seen on the streets of both Western and non-Western countries. The attendance at the annual pilgrimage to Mecca grew from 90,000 in 1926 to 2,000,000 in 1979.[13] In 2017, there were over 2,300,000 Muslim pilgrims to Mecca.[14] In 1979, the return of the Ayatollah

Khomeini in Iran signaled an Islamic revival in the entire Muslim world and the establishment of a fundamentalist Islamic republic in Iran. The subsequent Iranian revolution heartened Muslim fundamentalists everywhere.[15]

Salafist/Wahhabi influences

Islamic revival has coincided with a rise in reformist-political movements in Islam. Among Muslim immigrants in Western countries, there is a growing sentiment of a universal Islamic identity vehicle through digital communication technologies, globalization, and travel. The revival has also coincided with the heightened influence of puritanical Islamic preachers and terrorist attacks by jihadist groups on a transnational level.[16] Salafism appeared during Muhammad's apostolate in the seventh century. His teachings pulled men and women together, the most famous of whom were the four Righteous Caliphs (i.e., Aboubakr, Omar, Othman, and Ali). Later, they became, among others, the Prophet's "companions." They created what Islamic theologians called the *Salaf*, the devout, virtuous predecessors (i.e., a new generation that symbolized the Golden Age of Islam).[17]

Salafist jihadism

"Salafist jihadism" was invented by Gilles Kepel, a French political scientist specializing in the Middle East and Western Muslims.[18] Salafist jihadism is the most noticeable—and aggressive—contemporary movement that supports the violent interpretation of jihad. Present-day Salafists exalt the virtues of jihad to the same degree as the five daily "pillars of Islam," namely prayer (*salah*), the pilgrimage to Mecca (*hajj*), alms-giving (*zakat*), the profession of faith (*shahadah*), and fasting/Ramadan (*sawm*).[19] Renowned Arabists such as Muhammad Abed al-Jabir and Fahmi Jedaan believe that every jihadist is a Salafist. Because all jihadists are deeply committed to the Quran and the Prophet's Sunna, then it is only logical to deduce that all jihadist organizations are Salafist.[20]

As Moghadam (2007)[21] explains, while the historical, reform-oriented Salafists did not promote the use of violence as a vehicle toward Muslim reform, contemporary Salafist jihadists do. This distinction is obvious in several ways, the most visible of which concerns the issue of jihad. In general, mainstream Salafists believe that dawah—the proselytization to Islam—should have precedence over jihad, whereas Salafist jihadists consider jihad an imperative holy war. Salafist jihadists admit that external jihad takes two forms: offensive and defensive jihad. They agree that offensive jihad can only be undertaken under the authority of a Caliph. They also concede that defensive jihad requires that holy war must take place if an external force violates a Muslim territory. They interpreted the Soviet invasion of Afghanistan in 1979 as a direct affront against Muslims, which justified defensive jihad.

Another topic that sets Salafist jihadists apart from mainstream Salafists is the topic of *takfir*, or disbelief (for the Infidels), thereby warranting jihad against them. A third topic that sets them apart is the rationalization for targeting unarmed civilians. Most Muslims, including nonviolent Salafists, quote a number of Quranic verses (and hadith texts) against the slaying of civilians, though mainstream Salafists understand that innocent civilians may lose their lives in times of war, which should be seen as "normal" if this is a just war.[22] As a violent doctrine, Salafist jihadism shares many similarities with radical leftist philosophies in twentieth-century Europe. Like the radical left, Salafist jihadism is predicated upon a feeling against injustice and a rejection of bourgeois values, Western interventionism, and materialism. The objective of both radical leftism and Salafist jihadism is, at their core, a utopian quest to establish a more egalitarian society. Hence, violence is regarded as a justifiable means to an end. Both Salafist jihadists and leftist radicals see the extent of their activities and the significance of their actions as universal in nature.[23] As Stephen Holmes remarked, for Salafist jihadists, the Caliphate "is the religious equivalent of Marx's Communist utopia."[24]

Of equal importance is the fact that many Salafist jihadists—and many Islamists for that matter—believe that the decadence of ungodly youth heralds the end times. Muslim society and Muslim minorities in the West are in a phase of religious anomie (i.e., indifference toward divine law and values). Therefore, such Muslims are unable to see and combat the enemies of Islam. The Salafist jihadists' political mythology also highlights an apocalyptic millenarian dimension; the final days are approaching and there are manifold signs of the prophetic tradition announcing their proximity. The end times will be heralded by a holy war between Muslims and non-Muslims, but Islam will defeat evil as embodied by the West.[25]

Wahhabism

Before the September 11, 2001 terrorist attacks, few Westerners had been exposed to the concept of Wahhabism. Today, it is a household word. Often associated with the likes of Osama bin Laden, Wahhabism is depicted by the media and public spokespersons as an intolerant, ultra-conservative, militant interpretation of Islam. Salafism has been used interchangeably with Wahhabism, the Saudi Arabian variation of the movement that has characterized the Saudi régime for a very long time. Both Wahhabism and Salafism share intellectual sources and theological emphases, but they also diverge in the way they address Islamic jurisprudence. On the one hand, Wahhabis adhere to one of the main Sunni traditional schools of law; on the other hand, Salafists tend to contemplate legal matters independently. So, equating the two is fair in many respects (but not in *all* respects).[26] Just like Salafism, Wahhabism stresses the importance of the holy scriptures and the hadith as the only valid sources of Islam. Scripture should be interpreted literally and without criticism; it should be adopted as the only guide for proper religious conduct.[27]

This philosophy of the return to the pious forefathers as a response to Muslim decadence was shored up by Muhammad Ibn Abdel Wahhab (1720–1792), who was enthused by the works of Ibn Hanbal and Ibn Taymiyya. Wahhab aspired to clearly explain the causes of the Ottoman Empire's declining strength as rooted in European hegemony. The origin of the Ottoman Empire's weakening was not attributable to political or economic issues, but to the Muslim rulers' betrayal of the fundamental Quranic message centered on the concept of *tawhid* (the oneness of Allah)—in the way the *Salafs* interpreted and applied it.[28] Wahhab grounded his new doctrine in a literal interpretation of the Quran and the unity of Allah. He strongly rejected idolatry in all shapes and forms and resisted anything that could possibly stand in the way of Allah. Hence, he undertook iconoclastic measures like the destruction of sacred tombs and shrines.[29] Lastly, he not only permitted but also urged holy war against the Infidels and Apostates who had fallen back in *jahiliyyah* (i.e., the state of divine ignorance that was prevalent in the Arabian peninsula before the Prophet Muhammad arose).[30]

Moderate reformers threatened by Salafists

The Muslim world has witnessed moderate Muslims attempting to reform Islam and denouncing the radical practices of Salafism or Wahhabism. Such Muslim reformers are few and far between. Examples include Maajid Nawaz (through his Quilliam Foundation in England), Zuhdi Jasser (president and founder of American Islamic Forum for Democracy in the United States), Tarek Fatah (a non-religious progressive and liberal activist in Canada), and Irshad Manji (a feminist writer, educator, and champion of a reformist interpretation of Islam [also based in Canada], and nicknamed "Osama bin Laden's worst nightmare"[31]). Among the few brave ones who openly supported secularism and Western-style human rights in the Greater Middle East was Farag Foda, a renowned Muslim reformer, human rights campaigner, professor, and author based in Egypt.[32]

Farag Foda rose to fame after publishing his seminal articles and satires about Islamic fundamentalism in Egypt. In his numerous newspaper articles, he identified the weaknesses of Islamist ideology and its obsession with sharia—by asking, for example, how it would tackle modern problems like the housing shortage.[33] He also condemned prominent Islamist figures. He pointed out that Anwar al-Jundi—an Egyptian journalist and literary critic—supported the secularist, anti-Muslim Brotherhood administration of Abdul-Nasser in a 1965 book, or that Muhammad al-Hayyawan—a Muslim Brotherhood spearhead who said that the 1988 Armenian earthquake was Allah's punishment of the "atheist" Soviet Union—remained silent when an earthquake devastated Iran in 1990 (which killed 50,000 people).[34] Farag Foda was murdered on June 9, 1992 by al-Jama'a al-Islamiyya, an Egyptian Sunni jihadist group, after being charged with blasphemy by a group of clerics (*ulama*) at Al-Azhar University. Farag Foda was one of 202 people killed in politically motivated attacks in Egypt between March 1992 and September 1993. In December 1992, his entire publications were removed from public circulation.[35]

Abu Bakr Naji

Born Mohammad Hasan Khalil al-Hakim, and sometimes using the *nom-de-guerre* Abu Jihad al-Masri, Abu Bakr Naji was a chief propaganda strategist for Al-Qaeda until his death in 2008. In his book titled *Management of Savagery: The Most Critical Stage Through Which the Islamic Nation Will Pass*,[36] published on the internet in 2004, Naji laid out his plan for a successful Islamic revival by offering guidelines on how to erode Western superpowers and Muslim apostate states (i.e., by waging an ongoing war of attrition on them). In particular, he recommended that mujahedin focus their attacks on tourist sites and financial centers. Jihadist missions would instigate the development of a network of Islamic revival in "regions of savagery." By the same token, network links would reproduce and proliferate when the forces of Evil gradually disappear and cause people to subjugate their souls to the invading Caliphate forces. Taken as a whole, Abu Bakr Naji vehemently thought that a widespread civil war within the ummah would pave the way for a triumphant Sunni caliphate.[37]

Social movement theory

A theoretical model that can shed light on the radicalization process and violent extremism inherent to the Islamic revival movement is social movement theory (SMT). Zald and McCarthy (1987)[38] define a social movement as "a set of opinions and beliefs in a population, which represents preferences for changing some elements of the social structure and/or reward distribution of a society." SMT describes how movements and social collectives create and communicative meaning. In the past, when people only communicated through print media, social movements were scarcer. When people wanted to air their grievances or opinions as to how society should be organized, they ran into many hurdles when attempting to create connections and obtain popular support for their ideas. Contentious politics mostly relied on word-of-mouth communication. The rapid expansion of social media has changed all that. Today, social movements enable disaffected people to access knowledge of other people's hardships and injustices. There is heightened group consciousness among those who previously internalized their struggles or did not have the ideal way to express them to unfamiliar individuals.[39] As Tarrow (1998)[40] explains, modern media "did not themselves produce new grievances and conflicts but diffused ways of mounting claims that helped ordinary people to think of themselves as part of broader collectives and on the same plane as their betters."

Jihadist recruitment

Examining global jihad through the lens of SMT presents several possible explanations for understanding the radicalization process.[41] To begin, it introduces the framework of "mobilization potential" to explain how a movement's human resources are formed and to fathom how different individuals with the same beliefs may undertake different roles and actions. Second, it introduces the concept of "recruitment networks" by helping people navigate the processes by which those networks are developed. Third, it introduces the process of "frame alignment" to explain how a movement affects members' beliefs and feelings to best meet the objectives of the movement. Fourth, it emphasizes radicalization in terms of how groups identify and eliminate barriers to participation in non-Islamic matters.[42]

As SMT theorists claim, when members of a global social movement attempt to attract recruits, they act as "rational prospectors." They want to be successful in their endeavors, so they will work with those who are the most likely to further the jihadist cause effectively. Generally, in the recruitment process, they follow two stages: (1) They gather as much information as possible to find the best recruits; and (2) after identifying them, they employ manipulative tactics to get recruits to say "yes." During the recruitment process, the value of socials bonds and relationships is of utmost importance. Hence, excelling at interpersonal communication with prospective jihadists is critical.[43]

According to Ayman al-Zawahiri, the current Al-Qaeda leader, "the victory of Islam and the establishment of a caliphate in the manner of the Prophet will not be accomplished by the mujahid movement while it is cut off from public support."[44] Recruitment for global jihad can be successful when the movement's architects frame messages that best resonate with the objectives, attitudes, and beliefs of its constituents. As the latter agree with the movement's frames of reference, they identify with the collective movement and then join it.[45] Dalgaard-Nielsen (2008)[46] concludes that,

> Movements diagnose problems and attribute responsibility, offer solutions, strategies, and tactics (prognostic framing), and provide motivational frames to convince potential participants to become active. Key to mobilization, according to this perspective, is whether the movement's version of the "reality" resonates or can be brought to resonate with the movement's potential constituency. Some scholars have referred to this process as "frame alignment" the emergence of congruence between an individual's and an organization's interests, values, and beliefs.

The Arab Spring

At the end of the first decade of the twenty-first century, Salafism was growing more dangerous in the Arab world, particularly in Egypt and Tunisia, increasing both the number of its disciples and its formal scope, which now comprised charity, relief, and community organizations. They stopped short of formal political groups, largely because of the autocratic régimes under which they lived, but they quietly developed the infrastructure for such groups. It was under these circumstances that the Salafists found themselves at the beginning of the Arab Spring.[47]

The Arab Spring was a sequence of anti-régime demonstrations, uprisings, and armed insurgencies that proliferated across the Middle East. It started as a reaction to oppressive leadership and a miserable standard of living.[48] The first one occurred in December 2010 in Tunisia and soon spread to Libya, Egypt, Yemen, Syria, and Bahrain. It lasted for exactly two years.[49] The initial social movement of rebellions and protests dwindled by mid-2012, as many Arab Spring protesters encountered armed forces from authorities. In addition to its innovative types of organization, grassroots deployment, networked activism, and widespread revolts—all allegedly fighting for democratic transformation and social justice[50]—the Arab Spring was also a social movement of Islamic revival that sought a violent revolution to establish a new Islamic world order, like the one promulgated by the Muslim Brotherhood (and its dream of the global Caliphate).[51]

The Arab Spring has dramatically redefined the Salafist landscape in the Middle East. After years of oppression and exclusion, Salafist parties seized power in Egypt, Tunisia, and Morocco. The impressive rise of Salafism remains the most noticeable aspect of the new Islamist landscape in the region today. After staying out of politics for theological and political motivations, Salafist movements and organizations have effectively engaged in electoral politics. They are enthusiastic to create political parties, challenge elections, and compete for power. In Egypt, Salafist parties made big strides in the post-Arab Spring parliamentary elections and were a key contributor to Egypt's new constitution.[52]

One of the most threatening foreign policy occurrences during the Arab Spring was the escalation of violence in North Africa, particularly by a high number of violent non-state actors (VNSAs) like insurgent units, terrorist groups, and foreign fighters. This state of affairs is puzzling; most critics anticipated that the Arab Spring would lead to better socioeconomic and political-military conditions in North Africa, thereby leading to a reduction in violence. The opposite happened, even in Tunisia where the government evolved from dictatorship to democracy.[53] North Africa's only democratic government continues to wrestle with terrorist attacks and insurrections in the southeastern and southwestern parts of the country. Tunisia is also one of the largest global sources of foreign fighters who have migrated to Syria and Iraq to join ISIS.[54]

The "jihad cool" phenomenon

The precipitous rise of ISIS in 2014 made it the most successful jihadist group in the twenty-first century. Its image of unstoppable growth made it highly appealing to potential volunteers. The portrayals (real or exaggerated) used in the Western news and in political debates stressed the everlasting threat that ISIS was said to pose to the West, thereby inadvertently encouraging Western youths to join a movement of winners. Winners attract winners. This image transformed ISIS into a pull force for young foreign fighters. The power of ISIS lies in its success in persuading youths that "jihad is cool" and that they could join the coolest trend in multiple ways, a phenomenon also dubbed "jihad cool."[55]

Jihad cool has been used by U.S. security experts to refer to the reframing of jihadism into something hip, or "cool," thanks to conduits like social media platforms, magazines, propaganda videos, pop-jihad videos, style of dress, toys, and so forth. For instance, jihadist rap videos make participants look more like the MTV generation than mosque-goers. It is efficient because a certain number of these youths form a subculture of individuals who eventually migrate to conflict zones plagued by jihad.[56] In jihad cool, the pro-jihad attitude is transformed into something fashionable and trendy among online audiences. Frequently, the jihadist rebranding into a hip subculture is a form of propaganda aimed at disaffected youth.[57]

Hippest and sexiest jihad

In June 2014, ISIS became the "hottest" phenomenon in the history of jihad, drawing the majority of Western foreign fighters, to such an extent that these recruits desired an exhilarating experience and adventure and looked up to ISIS as the "hippest"[58] and "sexiest jihadi group on the block."[59] Bennhold (2015)[60] remarked that some ISIS youths came "from a world in which Islam is punk rock. The headscarf is liberating. Beards are sexy." Other accounts on "pop jihadists" in Europe also match this category, and they can be best described as "Muslim youngsters who flirt with terrorist symbols" through social media platforms.[61] Popular culture can exploit the media establishment as a type of discourse for power to be implemented and preserved. Those media manipulators will seize any opportunity to engage mass audiences.[62]

The efforts of the "jihad cool" fervor bore their fruit. ISIS successfully recruited many Western youths into its ranks. Based on reports by U.S. intelligence experts, by 2014, about 1,000 foreign fighters were become ISIS members every month.[63] Some recruits came from Western nations. According to a source in the FBI, more than 150 Americans are supposedly in Syria to fight for ISIS, while the Canadian Intelligence believes that approximately 130 Canadians had already joined ISIS in 2014.[64] According to the Canadian Standing Senate Committee on National Security and Defence (2015),[65] "eighty radicalized Canadians have been identified as participating with terrorists overseas and have returned to Canada and approximately 145 Canadians are believed to be abroad providing support to terrorist groups."

Jihad selfie

"Jihad selfies"[66] are a frequent occurrence in the "jihad cool" fanaticism. Consider Yassin Salhi, then a 35-year-old delivery man on June 26, 2015. On that day, Yassin Salhi beheaded his boss, Herve Cornara, in Saint-Quentin-Fallavier (France) and took a selfie with his boss's head hung on a chain-link fence next to two black standards imprinted with the *shahada* (the Islamic profession of faith). His subsequent action was to crash his delivery van into an industrial storeroom full of gas canisters, triggering an explosion. Before his arrest, Salhi sent his infamous selfie to Yunes-Sebastien V.-Z., a friend and Muslim convert (also from France) who joined ISIS in Syria.[67]

In like fashion, upon arrival in Syria and Iraq, young Muslim recruits' aspiration to put themselves at the heart of events is demonstrated through a multitude of selfies and social media posts. This mirrors a certain level of narcissism that was rarely observed among their older predecessors. Many Syria-based fighters appeared to be self-centered and well aware of the image they want to convey. The decision to migrate to Syria is just the outcome of the jihadization process as it is a proud response to daily challenges in their immediate environment. Again, this is more the case among jihadists today than in the past.[68] Kardaş and Özdemir (2018)[69] concur that foreign fighters leaving for the Syrian Civil War are "narcissists" brandishing their AK-47s through selfies or posting photos of their dead enemies.

Nevertheless, it is important to remark that jihadists' extensive use of social media can sometimes help intelligence agencies identify who they are or where they are, especially if the uploaded photo is available to the world at large. In summer 2015, intelligence agencies eventually tracked ISIS terrorists after one of their selfies was posted on a Twitter account. Less than one day afterwards, that selfie was forwarded to the U.S. Air Force, which launched a successful surgical airstrike on the ISIS location. The U.S. Air Force looked into the ISIS fighter's online activities further and discovered more posts about his bragging statements concerning control and command capabilities (which gave the U.S. Air Force even more information).[70]

A new direction in life

Islamic revival should be understood within the framework of a global identity-seeking and -enhancing trend. Some scholars[71] have observed that jihadist organizations offer youths a new direction in life: besides eternal life in *Jannah* (the Heavenly Garden), jihad presents a new perspective of belonging, brotherhood and sisterhood, honor and social status (through martyrdom), heroism, and thrill. It is a much better option than drugs and petty crime, and an alternative lifestyle with clear and upfront rules (moral absolutes are an element of jihad's magnetism). It also comes with material wealth: financial remuneration and sometimes a villa with a pool. It grants special power over others and, for those who would not always admit it, even carnage in support of a higher goal.

The Salafist version of Islam is espoused by many youths thanks to, in part, the reward of a better life. Silber and Bhatt (2007)[72] mention that "the catalyst for this religious seeking is often a cognitive event, or crisis, which challenges one's certitude in previously held beliefs, opening the individual's mind to a new perception or view of the world." The decision to follow a new direction in life can be sparked by various socioeconomic, political or social conflicts. At the individual level, the concept of "social relative deprivation"—defined as unmet expectations of being totally accepted as a member of society, with the same rights—can be an important factor in motivating Muslim youths to join the GJM. Many case studies point to the problems that Muslim migrants had with respect to fitting into Western society. Jihadist organizations give so-called alienated Muslim youths many social benefits in terms of identity, socialization, and goals.[73]

Phenomenological perspectives

When an individual believes that he or she has new direction in life, that individual may combat his or her perception of failure in other domains of life too. In such circumstances, success is not always based on competition, but on one's interpretations of experience and consciousness.[74] Phenomenology is a philosophical approach that analyzes the interpretations of experience and consciousness. A person views him- or herself through his or her life history, beliefs, and worldviews.[75] This process can be so crucial to one's life experience that, upon navigating through difficult times, one can more easily deal with one's own needs. This is how people can develop both their own selves and personal objectives in order to conquer their adversities.[76]

Phenomenology investigates our constructions of experience and consciousness. We become who we are is through our life experiences, judgments, and outlooks of the world. Consequently, the phenomenological perspective predicates that life is interpreted as a phenomenon that we experience. This involves focusing on our own experience in situations of vulnerability. It also focuses on our relationship with self and others. Thus, the phenomenological method enhances our understanding of the "fields" of actions and identity of humans when they are subjected to vulnerability.[77]

Jihadist suicide terrorism

Within the framework of jihadist suicide terrorism, expanding our field of vision can signify "going elsewhere," often to a better place. This objective can be accomplished if the individual rises above the actual situation of vulnerability. When a jihadist organization gives that individual a new project in life, he or she will feel more powerful/less vulnerable. For instance, for Palestinian would-be martyrs, the new project is the attainment of everlasting life in *Jannah*.[78] So, to experience eternal life in the Heavenly Garden, would-be martyrs have to fully trust jihad propagandists that, by using their own bodies as weapons (and the Infidels' in the process), the highest place in *Jannah* will be the next and final step. The Hamas jihadist group likes to quote certain Quranic verses, such as Quran 4:74: "He who fights in the cause of Allah and is killed or achieves victory, we will bestow upon him the greatest reward."[79] Now, it is the Palestinian martyr's belief that a true Muslim will sacrifices him- or herself for Allah. Only then will he or she be granted a *bona fide*, dignified life.[80]

When people entertain lofty aspirations about the future that are actually achievable, they will work on developing problem-solving skills and will be more motivated to control their own lives. At the same time, they will feel less vulnerable to their own adversity.[81] For future suicide bombers, their highest satisfaction is arguably their conviction that they will earn the best reward that Allah bestows his favorite people: eternal life in Paradise. Mentioned on many occasions in the Quran, *Jannah* is for righteous Muslims—i.e., pious disciples who have attained martyrdom.[82] In Islamist discourse, it is a paradisiacal place of luxurious greenery, gorgeous waterfalls, and *huris* (black-eyed virgins).[83]

Notes

1 See Elie Elhadj, *The Islamic Shield: Arab Resistance to Democratic and Religious Reforms* (Irvine, CA: Brown Walker Press, 2007); Thomas A. Fudge, *Jan Hus: Religious Reform and Social Revolution in Bohemia* (New York: I.B. Tauris, 2017).
2 Samira Haj, *Reconfiguring Islamic Tradition: Reform, Rationality, and Modernity* (Stanford, CA: Stanford University Press, 2009).
3 Robert W. Hefner, *Civil Islam: Muslims and Democratization in Indonesia* (Princeton, NJ: Princeton University Press, 2000).
4 Ibid., 3–6.
5 Nabeel Qureshi, *Answering Jihad: A Better Way Forward* (Grand Rapids, MI: Zondervan, 2016).
6 David L. Johnston, "Review of Shadi Hamid: Temptations of Power: Islamists and Illiberal Democracy in a New Middle East," *Sociology of Islam* 4, no. 3 (2016): 303–22. https://doi.org/10.1163/22131418-00403007
7 Fazlur Rahman, *Islam and Modernity: Transformation of an Intellectual Tradition* (Chicago: University of Chicago Press, 1982): 144.
8 Wilna A. J. Meijer, "Fanaticism, Fundamentalism and the Promotion of Reflexivity in Religious Education," in *International Handbook of Inter-Religious Education*, ed. Kath Engebretson, Marian de Souza, Gloria Durka, and Liam Gearon (New York: Springer, 2010): 729–41.
9 Yvonne Yazbeck Haddad, John Obert Voll, and John L. Esposito, *The Contemporary Islamic Revival: A Critical Survey and Bibliography* (Westport, CT: Greenwood Publishing, 1991).
10 Ira M. Lapidus, *A History of Islamic Societies* (Cambridge: Cambridge University Press, 2014).
11 Vali Nasr, *The Shia Revival: How Conflicts within Islam will Shape the Future* (New York: W.W. Norton & Company, 2006).
12 Ira M. Lapidus, "Islamic Revival and Modernity: The Contemporary Movements and the Historical Paradigms," *Journal of the Economic and Social History of the Orient* 40, no. 4 (1997): 444–60. https://doi.org/10.1163/1568520972601486
13 Gilles Kepel, *Jihad: The Trail of Political Islam* (Cambridge, MA: Harvard University Press, 2002).
14 Retrieved on June 15, 2019 from https://web.archive.org/web/20180620024237/https://www.stats.gov.sa/en/28
15 Robin Wright, *Dreams and Shadows: The Future of the Middle East* (New York: Penguin Press, 2008).
16 Arolda Elbasani and Olivier Roy, "Islam in the Post-Communist Balkans: Alternative Pathways to God," *Southeast European and Black Sea Studies* 15, no. 4 (2015): 457–71. https://doi.org/10.1080/14683857.2015.1050273
17 Margaret Gonzalez-Perez, "The False Islamization of Female Suicide Bombers," *Gender Issues* 28, no. 1 (2011): 50–65. https://doi.org/10.1007/s12147-011-9097-0
18 Gilles Kepel, "The Origins and Development of the Jihadist Movement: From Anti-Communism to Terrorism," *Asian Affairs* 34, no. 2 (2003): 91–108. https://doi.org/10.1080/0306837032000118198
19 Assaf Moghadam, "Mayhem, Myths, and Martyrdom: The Shi'a Conception of Jihad," *Terrorism and Political Violence* 19, no. 1 (2007): 125–43. https://doi.org/10.1080/09546550601079656
20 Omayma Abdel-Latif, "Trends in Salafism," in *Islamist Radicalisation: The Challenge for Euro-Mediterranean Relations*, ed. Michael Emerson, Kristina Kausch, and Richard Youngs (Brussels: Center for European Policy Studies, 2009): 69–86.

21 Moghadam, "Mayhem, Myths, and Martyrdom," 128.
22 Ibid., 129.
23 Assaf Moghadam, "The Salafi-Jihad as a Religious Ideology," *CTC Sentinel* 1, no. 3 (2008): 1–3.
24 Stephen Holmes, *The Matador's Cape: America's Reckless Response to Terror* (Cambridge: Cambridge University Press, 2007): 63.
25 Chetan Bhatt, "The Virtues of Violence: The Salafi-Jihadi Political Universe," *Theory, Culture & Society* 31, no. 1 (2014): 25–48. https://doi.org/10.1177/0263276413500079; Bassam Tibi, *Islam's Predicament with Modernity: Religious Reform and Cultural Change* (New York: Routledge, 2009).
26 Daniel Ungureanu, "Wahhabism, Salafism and the Expansion of Islamic Fundamentalist Ideology," *Argumentum* 9, no. 2 (2011): 140–7.
27 Michael Cook, "On the Origin of Wahhabism," *Journal of the Royal Asiatic Society of Great Britain and Ireland* 2, no. 2 (1992): 191–202.
28 Samir Amghar, "Salafism and Radicalisation of Young European Muslims," in *European Islam: Challenges for Public Policy and Society*, ed. Samir Amghar, Amel Boubekeur, and Michael Emerson (Brussels: Centre for European Policy Studies, 2007): 38–51, 40.
29 Marc Sageman, *Understanding Terror Networks* (Philadelphia: University of Pennsylvania Press, 2004).
30 John L. Esposito, *Unholy War: Terror in the Name of Islam* (New York: Oxford University Press, 2003).
31 Clifford Krauss, "An Unlikely Promoter of an Islamic Reformation," *The New York Times* (2003, October 4): A1.
32 Shmuel Bar, *Warrant for Terror: The Fatwas of Radical Islam and the Duty to Jihad* (Lanham, MD: Rowman & Littlefield, 2008).
33 Nathan J. Brown, *The Rule of Law in the Arab World: Courts in Egypt and the Gulf* (Cambridge: Cambridge University Press, 1997).
34 Ana Belén Soage, "Faraj Fawda, or the Cost of Freedom of Expression," *Middle East Review of International Affairs* 11, no. 2 (2007): 26–33.
35 Antoon de Baets, *Censorship of Historical Thought: A World Guide, 1945–2000* (Westport, CT: Greenwood Publishing, 2001).
36 Available at www.booktopia.com.au/the-management-of-savagery-abu-bakr-naji/book/9781643542454.html
37 Lawrence Wright, "ISIS's Savage Strategy in Iraq," *The New Yorker* (2014, June 16): 10–8.
38 Mayer Zald and John David McCarthy, *Social Movements in an Organizational Society* (New Brunswick, NJ: Transaction Books, 1987): 2.
39 Sydney G. Tarrow, *Power in Movement: Social Movements and Contentious Politics* (2nd ed.) (Cambridge: Cambridge University Press, 1998).
40 Ibid., 43.
41 Jeroen Gunning, "Social Movement Theory and the Study of Terrorism," in *Critical Terrorism Studies: A New Research Agenda*, ed. Richard Jackson, Marie Breen Smyth, and Jeroen Gunning (New York: Routledge, 2009): 156–77.
42 Randy Borum, "Radicalization into Violent Extremism I: A Review of Social Science Theories," *Journal of Strategic Security* 4, no. 4 (2011): 7–36. https://doi.org/10.5038/1944-0472.4.4.1
43 Henry Brady, Kay Schlozman, and Sydney Verba, "Prospecting for Participants: Rational Expectations and the Recruitment of Political Activists," *American Political Science Review* 93, no. 1 (1999): 153–68. https://doi.org/10.2307/2585767
44 Cited in Akil N. Awan, "Success of the Meta-Narrative: How Jihadists Maintain Legitimacy," *CTC Sentinel* 2, no. 11 (2009): 6–8, 6.
45 Michael Marcusa, "Radicalism on the Periphery: History, Collective Memory, and the Cultural Resonance of Jihadist Ideology in Tunisia," *Comparative Politics* 51, no. 2 (2017): 177–97. https://doi.org/10.5129/001041519825256632

46 Anja Dalgaard-Nielsen, *Studying Violent Radicalization in Europe I: The Potential Contribution of Social Movement Theory* (Copenhagen: Danish Institute for International Studies, 2008): 40.

47 Kamran Bokhari, "Salafism and Arab Democratization," *Geopolitical Weekly* 12 (2012): 10–21, 13.

48 Habibul Haque Khondker, "Role of the New Media in the Arab Spring," *Globalizations* 8, no. 5 (2011): 675–9. https://doi.org/10.1080/14747731.2011.621287

49 William C. Taylor, *Military Responses to the Arab Uprisings and the Future of Civil-Military Relations in the Middle East: Analysis from Egypt, Tunisia, Libya, and Syria* (New York: Palgrave Macmillan, 2014).

50 Nezar AlSayyad and Mejgan Massoumi, "Religious Fundamentalisms in the City: Reflections on the Arab Spring," *Journal of International Affairs* 65, no. 2 (2012): 31–42.

51 Olivier Roy, "The Transformation of the Arab World," *Journal of Democracy* 23, no. 3 (2012): 5–18. https://doi.org/10.1353/jod.2012.0056

52 Khalil al-Anani and Maszlee Malik, "Pious Way to Politics: The Rise of Political Salafism in Post-Mubarak Egypt," *DOMES: Digest of Middle East Studies* 22, no. 1 (2013): 57–73, 57.

53 Michael J. Schumacher and Peter J. Schraeder, "The Evolving Impact of Violent Non-State Actors on North African Foreign Policies during the Arab Spring: Insurgent Groups, Terrorists and Foreign Fighters," *The Journal of North African Studies* 24, no. 4 (2019): 682–703. https://doi.org/10.1080/13629387.2018.1525014

54 Geoffrey Macdonald and Luke Waggoner, "Dashed Hopes and Extremism in Tunisia," *Journal of Democracy* 29, no. 1 (2018): 126–40.

55 See Caroline Joan S. Picart, "'Jihad Cool/Jihad Chic:' The Roles of the Internet and Imagined Relations in the Self-Radicalization of Colleen LaRose (Jihad Jane)," *Societies* 5, no. 2 (2015): 354–83. https://doi.org/10.3390/soc5020354

56 Laura Italiano, "American Muslims Flocking to Jihadist Group," *New York Post* (2014, June 20): p. A1; Jytte Klausen, Eliane Tschaen Barbieri, Aaron Reichlin-Melnick, and Aaron Y. Zelin, "The YouTube Jihadists: A Social Network Analysis of Al-Muhajiroun's Propaganda Campaign," *Perspectives on Terrorism* 6, no. 1 (2012): 10–21.

57 Laura Huey, "This Is Not Your Mother's Terrorism: Social Media, Online Radicalization and the Practice of Political Jamming," *Journal of Terrorism Research* 6, no. 2 (2015): 1–16. http://doi.org/10.15664/jtr.1159

58 Paul Tassi, "ISIS Uses 'GTA 5' in New Teen Recruitment Video," *Forbes* (2014, September 20): A1.

59 Francesca Trianni and Andrew Katz, "Why Westerners Are Fighting for ISIS," *Time* (2014, September 5).

60 Katrin Bennhold, "Jihad and Girl Power: How ISIS Lured 3 London Girls," *The New York Times* (2015, August 17): A1.

61 Cited in Ahmed Al-Rawi, "Video Games, Terrorism, and ISIS's Jihad 3.0," *Terrorism and Political Violence* 30, no. 4 (2018): 740–60, 744. https://doi.org/10.1080/09546553.2016.1207633

62 Audrey Pafford and Jonathan Matusitz, "ABC's Quantico: A Critical Discourse Analysis of Female Superiority and Racial Stereotypes," *Critical Studies in Television* 12, no. 3 (2017): 273–88. https://doi.org/10.1177/1749602017717167

63 Cited in Eric Schmitt, "In Battle to Defang ISIS, U.S. Targets Its Psychology," *The New York Times* (2014, December 28): A1.

64 Cited in Al-Rawi, "Video Games, Terrorism, and ISIS's Jihad 3.0," 144–7.

65 Standing Senate Committee on National Security and Defence, *Countering the Terrorist Threat in Canada: An Interim Report* (Ottawa: Senate of Canada, 2015).

66 Elis Zuliati Anis, "Countering Terrorist Narratives: Winning the Hearts and Minds of Indonesian Millennials," *The International Conference on South East Asia Studies* 1 (2018): 189–210.

67 John Rosenthal, "Merah: The 'Untold Story' of a French Jihadist Icon," *World Affairs* 178, no. 4 (2016): 50–60.

68 Rik Coolsaet, *What Drives Europeans to Syria, and to IS? Insights from the Belgian Case* (Brussels: Royal Institute for International Relations, 2015).

69 Tuncay Kardaş and Ömer Behram Özdemir, "The Making of European Foreign Fighters: Identity, Social Media and Virtual Radicalization," in *Non-State Armed Actors in the Middle East*, ed. Murat Yeşiltaş and Tuncay Kardaş (New York: Palgrave Macmillan, 2018): 213–35.

70 James Dunn, "US Air Force Reveal They Destroyed ISIS Base within Hours of a 'Moron' Militant Posting Pictures on Social Media and Giving Its Location Away," *Daily Mail* (2015, June 4): A1.

71 See Laila Bokhari, "Jihad in a Globalized World, Local Arenas for Global Violent Extremism: Local and Global Contexts, Causes and Motivations," in *Suicide as a Weapon* (Ankara: Centre of Excellence Defence against Terrorism, 2007): 22–7; Coolsaet, *What Drives Europeans to Syria, and to IS?*, 19.

72 Mitchell D. Silber and Arvin Bhatt, *Radicalization in the West: The Home-Grown Threat* (New York: New York City Police Department, 2007): 32.

73 Petter Nesser, "Jihadism in Western Europe after the Invasion of Iraq: Tracing Motivational Influences from the Iraq War on Jihadist Terrorism in Western Europe," *Studies in Conflict & Terrorism* 29, no. 4 (2006): 323–42. https://doi.org/10.1080/10576100600641899

74 Michael Rutter, "Psychosocial Resilience and Protective Mechanisms," *American Journal of Orthopsychiatry* 57, no. 3 (1987): 316–31. https://doi.org/10.1111/j.1939-0025.1987.tb03541.x

75 Dan Zahavi, *Husserl's Phenomenology* (Stanford, CA: Stanford University Press, 2003).

76 David M. Clarke and David W. Kissane, "Demoralization: Its Phenomenology and Importance," *Australian and New Zealand Journal of Psychiatry* 36, no. 6 (2002): 733–42. https://doi.org/10.1046/j.1440-1614.2002.01086.x

77 Carl Lacharité, "From Risk to Psychosocial Resilience: Conceptual Models and Avenues for Family Intervention," *Texto Contexto Enferm* 14 (2005): 71–7. https://doi.org/10.1590/S0104-07072005000500009

78 Jonathan Matusitz, "Martyrdom as a Result of Psychosocial Resilience: The Case of Palestinian Suicide Terrorists," in *The Routledge International Handbook of Psychosocial Resilience*, ed. Updesh Kumar (New York: Routledge, 2016): 285–95.

79 Available at http://corpus.quran.com/translation.jsp?chapter=4&verse=74

80 Ibid., 288–92.

81 Raija-Leena Punamaki, "Content of and Factors Affecting Coping Modes among Palestinian Children," *Scandinavian Journal of Development Alternatives* 6, no. 1 (1987): 86–98.

82 Philipp Holtmann, *Martyrdom, Not Suicide: The Legality of Hamas' Bombings in the Mid-1990s in Modern Islamic Jurisprudence* (Munich: GRIN Publishing, 2009); David Zeidan, "The Islamic Fundamentalist View of Life as a Perennial Battle," *Middle East Review of International Affairs* 5, no. 4 (2001): 26–53.

83 Assaf Moghadam, "Palestinian Suicide Terrorism in the Second Intifada: Motivations and Organizational Aspects," *Studies in Conflict & Terrorism* 26, no. 2 (2003): 65–92. https://doi.org/10.1080/10576100390145215

References

Abdel-Latif, Omayma, "Trends in Salafism," in *Islamist Radicalisation: The Challenge for Euro-Mediterranean Relations*, edited by Michael Emerson, Kristina Kausch, and Richard Youngs, 69–86. Brussels: Center for European Policy Studies, 2009.

al-Anani, Khalil, and Maszlee Malik, "Pious Way to Politics: The Rise of Political Salafism in Post-Mubarak Egypt," *DOMES: Digest of Middle East Studies* 22, no. 1 (2013): 57–73.

Al-Rawi, Ahmed, "Video Games, Terrorism, and ISIS's Jihad 3.0," *Terrorism and Political Violence* 30, no. 4 (2018): 740–760. https://doi.org/10.1080/09546553.2016.1207633

AlSayyad, Nezar, and Mejgan Massoumi, "Religious Fundamentalisms in the City: Reflections on the Arab Spring," *Journal of International Affairs* 65, no. 2 (2012): 31–42.

Amghar, Samir, "Salafism and Radicalisation of Young European Muslims," in *European Islam: Challenges for Public Policy and Society*, edited by Samir Amghar, Amel Boubekeur, and Michael Emerson, 38–51. Brussels: Centre for European Policy Studies, 2007.

Anis, Elis Zuliati, "Countering Terrorist Narratives: Winning the Hearts and Minds of Indonesian Millennials," *The International Conference on South East Asia Studies* 1 (2018): 189–210.

Awan, Akil N., "Success of the Meta-Narrative: How Jihadists Maintain Legitimacy," *CTC Sentinel* 2, no. 11 (2009): 6–8.

Bar, Shmuel, *Warrant for Terror: The Fatwas of Radical Islam and the Duty to Jihad*. Lanham, MD: Rowman & Littlefield, 2008.

Bennhold, Katrin, "Jihad and Girl Power: How ISIS Lured 3 London Girls," *The New York Times* (2015, August 17): A1.

Bhatt, Chetan, "The Virtues of Violence: The Salafi-Jihadi Political Universe," *Theory, Culture & Society* 31, no. 1 (2014): 25–48. https://doi.org/10.1177/0263276413500079

Bokhari, Kamran, "Salafism and Arab Democratization," *Geopolitical Weekly* 12 (2012): 10–21.

Bokhari, Laila, "Jihad in a Globalized World, Local Arenas for Global Violent Extremism: Local and Global Contexts, Causes and Motivations," in *Suicide as a Weapon*, edited by Centre of Excellence Defence against Terrorism, 22–27. Ankara: Centre of Excellence Defence against Terrorism, 2007.

Borum, Randy, "Radicalization into Violent Extremism I: A Review of Social Science Theories," *Journal of Strategic Security* 4, no. 4 (2011): 7–36. https://doi.org/10.5038/1944-0472.4.4.1

Brady, Henry, Kay Schlozman, and Sydney Verba, "Prospecting for Participants: Rational Expectations and the Recruitment of Political Activists," *American Political Science Review* 93, no. 1 (1999): 153–168. https://doi.org/10.2307/2585767

Brown, Nathan J., *The Rule of Law in the Arab World: Courts in Egypt and the Gulf*. Cambridge: Cambridge University Press, 1997.

Clarke, David M., and David W. Kissane, "Demoralization: Its Phenomenology and Importance," *Australian and New Zealand Journal of Psychiatry* 36, no. 6 (2002): 733–742. https://doi.org/10.1046/j.1440-1614.2002.01086.x

Cook, Michael, "On the Origin of Wahhabism," *Journal of the Royal Asiatic Society of Great Britain and Ireland* 2, no. 2 (1992): 191–202.

Coolsaet, Rik, *What Drives Europeans to Syria, and to IS? Insights from the Belgian Case*. Brussels: Royal Institute for International Relations, 2015.

Dalgaard-Nielsen, Anja, *Studying Violent Radicalization in Europe I: The Potential Contribution of Social Movement Theory*. Copenhagen: Danish Institute for International Studies, 2008.

de Baets, Antoon, *Censorship of Historical Thought: A World Guide, 1945–2000*. Westport, CT: Greenwood Publishing, 2001.

Dunn, James, "US Air Force Reveal They Destroyed ISIS Base within Hours of a 'Moron' Militant Posting Pictures on Social Media and Giving Its Location Away," *Daily Mail* (2015, June 4): A1.

Elbasani, Arolda, and Olivier Roy, "Islam in the Post-Communist Balkans: Alternative Pathways to God," *Southeast European and Black Sea Studies* 15, no. 4 (2015): 457–471. https://doi.org/10.1080/14683857.2015.1050273

Elhadj, Elie, *The Islamic Shield: Arab Resistance to Democratic and Religious Reforms*. Irvine, CA: Brown Walker Press, 2007.

Esposito, John L., *Unholy War: Terror in the Name of Islam*. New York: Oxford University Press, 2003.

Fudge, Thomas A., *Jan Hus: Religious Reform and Social Revolution in Bohemia*. New York: I. B. Tauris, 2017.

Gonzalez-Perez, Margaret, "The False Islamization of Female Suicide Bombers," *Gender Issues* 28, no. 1 (2011): 50–65. https://doi.org/10.1007/s12147-011-9097-0

Gunning, Jeroen, "Social Movement Theory and the Study of Terrorism," in *Critical Terrorism Studies: A New Research Agenda*, edited by Richard Jackson, Marie Breen Smyth, and Jeroen Gunning, 156–177. New York: Routledge, 2009.

Haddad, Yvonne Yazbeck, John Obert Voll, and John L. Esposito, *The Contemporary Islamic Revival: A Critical Survey and Bibliography*. Westport, CT: Greenwood Publishing, 1991.

Haj, Samira, *Reconfiguring Islamic Tradition: Reform, Rationality, and Modernity*. Stanford, CA: Stanford University Press, 2009.

Hefner, Robert W., *Civil Islam: Muslims and Democratization in Indonesia*. Princeton, NJ: Princeton University Press, 2000.

Holmes, Stephen, *The Matador's Cape: America's Reckless Response to Terror*. Cambridge: Cambridge University Press, 2007.

Holtmann, Philipp, *Martyrdom, Not Suicide: The Legality of Hamas' Bombings in the Mid-1990s in Modern Islamic Jurisprudence*. Munich: GRIN Publishing, 2009.

Huey, Laura, "This Is Not Your Mother's Terrorism: Social Media, Online Radicalization and the Practice of Political Jamming," *Journal of Terrorism Research* 6, no. 2 (2015): 1–16. http://doi.org/10.15664/jtr.1159

Italiano, Laura, "American Muslims Flocking to Jihadist Group," *New York Post* (2014, June 20): A1.

Johnston, David L., "Review of Shadi Hamid: Temptations of Power: Islamists and Illiberal Democracy in a New Middle East," *Sociology of Islam* 4, no. 3 (2016): 303–322. https://doi.org/10.1163/22131418-00403007

Kardaş, Tuncay, and Ömer Behram Özdemir, "The Making of European Foreign Fighters: Identity, Social Media and Virtual Radicalization," in *Non-State Armed Actors in the Middle East*, edited by Murat Yeşiltaş and Tuncay Kardaş, 213–235. New York: Palgrave Macmillan, 2018.

Kepel, Gilles, *Jihad: The Trail of Political Islam*. Cambridge, MA: Harvard University Press, 2002.

Kepel, Gilles, "The Origins and Development of the Jihadist Movement: From Anti-Communism to Terrorism," *Asian Affairs* 34, no. 2 (2003): 91–108. https://doi.org/10.1080/0306837032000118198

Khondker, Habibul Haque, "Role of the New Media in the Arab Spring," *Globalizations* 8, no. 5 (2011): 675–679. https://doi.org/10.1080/14747731.2011.621287

Klausen, Jytte, Eliane Tschaen Barbieri, Aaron Reichlin-Melnick, and Aaron Y. Zelin, "The YouTube Jihadists: A Social Network Analysis of Al-Muhajiroun's Propaganda Campaign," *Perspectives on Terrorism* 6, no. 1 (2012): 10–21.

Krauss, Clifford, "An Unlikely Promoter of an Islamic Reformation," *The New York Times* (2003, October 4): A1.

Lacharité, Carl, "From Risk to Psychosocial Resilience: Conceptual Models and Avenues for Family Intervention," *Texto Contexto Enferm* 14 (2005): 71–77. https://doi.org/10.1590/S0104-07072005000500009

Lapidus, Ira M., "Islamic Revival and Modernity: The Contemporary Movements and the Historical Paradigms," *Journal of the Economic and Social History of the Orient* 40, no. 4 (1997): 444–460. https://doi.org/10.1163/1568520972601486

Lapidus, Ira M., *A History of Islamic Societies*. Cambridge: Cambridge University Press, 2014.

Macdonald, Geoffrey, and Luke Waggoner, "Dashed Hopes and Extremism in Tunisia," *Journal of Democracy* 29, no. 1 (2018): 126–140.

Marcusa, Michael, "Radicalism on the Periphery: History, Collective Memory, and the Cultural Resonance of Jihadist Ideology in Tunisia," *Comparative Politics* 51, no. 2 (2017): 177–197. https://doi.org/10.5129/001041519825256632

Matusitz, Jonathan, "Martyrdom as a Result of Psychosocial Resilience: The Case of Palestinian Suicide Terrorists," in *The Routledge International Handbook of Psychosocial Resilience*, edited by Updesh Kumar, 285–295. New York: Routledge, 2016.

Meijer, Wilna A. J., "Fanaticism, Fundamentalism and the Promotion of Reflexivity in Religious Education," in *International Handbook of Inter-Religious Education*, edited by Kath Engebretson, Marian de Souza, Gloria Durka, and Liam Gearon, 729–741. New York: Springer, 2010.

Moghadam, Assaf, "Mayhem, Myths, and Martyrdom: The Shi'a Conception of Jihad," *Terrorism and Political Violence* 19, no. 1 (2007): 125–143. https://doi.org/10.1080/09546550601079656

Moghadam, Assaf, "Palestinian Suicide Terrorism in the Second Intifada: Motivations and Organizational Aspects," *Studies in Conflict & Terrorism* 26, no. 2 (2003): 65–92. https://doi.org/10.1080/10576100390145215

Moghadam, Assaf, "The Salafi-Jihad as a Religious Ideology," *CTC Sentinel* 1, no. 3 (2008): 1–3.

Nasr, Vali, *The Shia Revival: How Conflicts within Islam will Shape the Future.* New York: W. W. Norton & Company, 2006.

Nesser, Petter, "Jihadism in Western Europe after the Invasion of Iraq: Tracing Motivational Influences from the Iraq War on Jihadist Terrorism in Western Europe," *Studies in Conflict & Terrorism* 29, no. 4 (2006): 323–342. https://doi.org/10.1080/10576100600641899

Pafford, Audrey, and Jonathan Matusitz, "ABC's Quantico: A Critical Discourse Analysis of Female Superiority and Racial Stereotypes," *Critical Studies in Television* 12, no. 3 (2017): 273–288. https://doi.org/10.1177/1749602017717167

Picart, Caroline Joan S., "'Jihad Cool/Jihad Chic:' The Roles of the Internet and Imagined Relations in the Self-Radicalization of Colleen LaRose (Jihad Jane)," *Societies* 5, no. 2 (2015): 354–383. https://doi.org/10.3390/soc5020354

Punamaki, Raija-Leena, "Content of and Factors Affecting Coping Modes among Palestinian Children," *Scandinavian Journal of Development Alternatives* 6, no. 1 (1987): 86–98.

Qureshi, Nabeel, *Answering Jihad: A Better Way Forward.* Grand Rapids, MI: Zondervan, 2016.

Rahman, Fazlur, *Islam and Modernity: Transformation of an Intellectual Tradition.* Chicago, IL: University of Chicago Press, 1982.

Rosenthal, John, "Merah: The 'Untold Story' of a French Jihadist Icon," *World Affairs* 178, no. 4 (2016): 50–60.

Roy, Olivier, "The Transformation of the Arab World," *Journal of Democracy* 23, no. 3 (2012): 5–18. https://doi.org/10.1353/jod.2012.0056

Rutter, Michael, "Psychosocial Resilience and Protective Mechanisms," *American Journal of Orthopsychiatry* 57, no. 3 (1987): 316–331. https://doi.org/10.1111/j.1939-0025.1987.tb03541.x

Sageman, Marc, *Understanding Terror Networks.* Philadelphia, PA: University of Pennsylvania Press, 2004.

Schmitt, Eric, "In Battle to Defang ISIS, U.S. Targets Its Psychology," *The New York Times* (2014, December 28): A1.

Schumacher, Michael J., and Peter J. Schraeder, "The Evolving Impact of Violent Non-State Actors on North African Foreign Policies during the Arab Spring: Insurgent Groups,

Terrorists and Foreign Fighters," *The Journal of North African Studies* (2019). https://doi.org/10.1080/13629387.2018.1525014

Silber, Mitchell D., and Arvin Bhatt, *Radicalization in the West: The Home-Grown Threat.* New York: New York City Police Department, 2007.

Soage, Ana Belén, "Faraj Fawda, or the Cost of Freedom of Expression," *Middle East Review of International Affairs* 11, no. 2 (2007): 26–33.

Standing Senate Committee on National Security and Defence, *Countering the Terrorist Threat in Canada: An Interim Report.* Ottawa: Senate of Canada, 2015.

Tarrow, Sydney G., *Power in Movement: Social Movements and Contentious Politics* (2nd ed.). Cambridge: Cambridge University Press, 1998.

Tassi, Paul, "ISIS Uses 'GTA 5' in New Teen Recruitment Video," *Forbes* (2014, September 20): A1.

Taylor, William C., *Military Responses to the Arab Uprisings and the Future of Civil-Military Relations in the Middle East: Analysis from Egypt, Tunisia, Libya, and Syria.* New York: Palgrave Macmillan, 2014.

Tibi, Bassam, *Islam's Predicament with Modernity: Religious Reform and Cultural Change.* New York: Routledge, 2009.

Trianni, Francesca, and Andrew Katz, "Why Westerners Are Fighting for ISIS," *Time* (2014, September 5).

Ungureanu, Daniel, "Wahhabism, Salafism and the Expansion of Islamic Fundamentalist Ideology," *Argumentum* 9, no. 2 (2011): 140–147.

Wright, Lawrence, "ISIS's Savage Strategy in Iraq," *The New Yorker* (2014, June 16): 10–18.

Wright, Robin, *Dreams and Shadows: The Future of the Middle East.* New York: Penguin Press, 2008.

Zahavi, Dan, *Husserl's Phenomenology.* Stanford, CA: Stanford University Press, 2003.

Zald, Mayer, and John David McCarthy, *Social Movements in an Organizational Society.* New Brunswick, NJ: Transaction Books, 1987.

Zeidan, David, "The Islamic Fundamentalist View of Life as a Perennial Battle," *Middle East Review of International Affairs* 5, no. 4 (2001): 26–53.

10

THE JIHADISPHERE

The jihadisphere is the internet-based community of jihadists and their supporters who are connected through their shared devotion to the global Salafist/jihadist ideology. Not only do jihadist organizations dedicate much time and effort to forging bonds with global audiences, but jihad sympathizers from all corners of the globe are also working hard to expand the diffusion of online jihadist content through digital media technologies. The growing usage of non-Arabic languages such as English, French, German, Russian, and Dutch by jihadists is an important consideration.[1] The jihadisphere is a perfect world for jihadists-as-communicators: it is a decentralized world that is subjected to little control or restriction. It receives little censorship (which could be easily circumvented in any case) and it gives access to anyone who is curious. Websites are a major internet service so valuable to modern terrorists. There exist many other possibilities in cyberspace—email, chat rooms, news groups, forums, online bulletin boards—that evade detection by law enforcement.[2]

The internet

The internet has grown into a global platform through which users can effortlessly proliferate and exchange ideas. According to Internet World Stats, as of March 2019, the internet was used by close to 4.4 billion people worldwide.[3] The internet can become instrumental in galvanizing or radicalizing the public *vis-à-vis* political and social issues. Western academics emphasize that the World Wide Web has become a knowledge resource of exceptional depth and wealth, not just for news correspondents, but also for the public at large. News items have become much more available.[4]

Social media sites

Social media is a consolidation of websites, services, and routines that foster cooperation, community building, and participation through social network sites (e.g., Facebook and Twitter).[5] The social media environment is mostly impervious to policing. Regulation practices that were efficient in the older vertical structure of the internet environment can hardly be applied in the new sphere of social networking and micro-blogging. The prevalent use of lateral integration across manifold file-sharing platforms creates redundancy through the many postings of the same document. It also creates resilience against disruption and censorship by the state and internet service providers.[6] Social media sites have altered the way people engage in social activism, making it a lot more convenient and, in large part, anonymous. When activism through social media becomes viral, we can simply call it "viral activism."[7] Viral activism has considerably reduced the time in which boycott messages diffuse to mass audiences.

Social media sites such as Facebook, Instagram, Twitter, and YouTube represent a powerful propaganda conduit for the jihadist cause as they function as recruitment platforms, interactive forums, and psychological warfare. Many Islamic youths are now using social networks as new battlefields for jihad. On top of social media sites, jihadists take advantage of other internet services like blogs, webpages, forums, and email. Consequently, social media allows vulnerable people to get in contact with radicalized people (or even people with the same gripes). The jihadisphere, then, can nurture one other's radical ideas, which buttresses the radicalization process. Additionally, these networks foster global communications among disparate or unrelated people through a transnational movement.[8]

Jihadists have successfully exploited the popularity of social media and similar tools to reach different audiences. They use social media sites for a multitude of reasons. The first reason is to diffuse their messages to a large audience. The second is to recruit potential fighters. The third is to indoctrinate would-be jihadists who have already been recruited. In this manner, social media sites operate as a platform of radicalization. Lastly, jihadists use such online tools for engaging in mundane conversations among equals across time and distance.[9] Social media networks can operate as a substitute media channel. The role of social media channels in contemporary society is rising so quickly that they have reached a level of protest action where they have become part of virtually every social and political activist program—including activism that involves religious causes.[10] The internet allows users to create an abstract (i.e., virtual) community of adherents that lies outside the limits of a specific city, nation, or region.[11] Besides following a local religious leader—as was the tradition in previous generations—today's youths can log on the internet and follow or believe whomever they want.

Case study: ISIS and Twitter

ISIS has gained much experience in using and praising the jihadisphere and knows how to exploit its foreign fighters in the most optimal way: before cameras instead of just using them as mere recorders in the front lines. Foreign fighters do appear as frequently in videos posted on social media. When they do, they like to communicate their individual and personal motivation as to why they are espousing the cause, describing in their own words to potential recruits in their home nation what Islam really is, while also tackling legitimate and real issues and injustices experienced by Sunni noncombatants in Syria or other places.[12] ISIS has spearheaded the practice of producing mostly Arabic videos to incite the Arabic-speaking ummah. ISIS does this by presenting its soldiers, ideologues, and preachers as definite role models, modern-day mujahedin, or defenders of Sunni communities in times of tribulations. ISIS portrays itself as an Arab movement that fights for independence, but that also welcomes non-Arab jihadist fighters into their ranks (who are strategically placed on a tactical level for jihadist media), where they can be valuable to state-building initiatives. Non-Arab media activists acting on behalf of the "Caliphate" can justify attacks in their home countries (in their respective native tongues or dialects) and become guides luring potential recruits on social media applications such as Twitter.[13]

By mid-2015, the organization has already diffused its entire official propaganda through Twitter.[14] Twitter is a gargantuan domain for terroristic propaganda. Terrorist groups, extremist groups, hate groups, and White supremacist groups are using it to promulgate their ideology, simplify internal communications, target their enemies, and engage in all sorts of criminal activities.[15] Twitter-based jihad is an example of the jihadisphere as the Global Village, a space for interaction between users from a multitude of cultural backgrounds. It can unify individuals or divide them for motives grounded in creed, politics, history, race, or religion. It can smooth the progress for the formation of a second order of culture, which varies from the synchronous sharing of symbols and sounds between earthlings in three-dimensional space.[16]

Twitter plays an essential part in ISIS's operational strategy beyond Syria and Iraq. It has been manipulated to move communications over other social media platforms. Twitter streams from ISIS give the group an aura of authenticity, taking the form of a spontaneous activity of a generation clinging to smartphones for self-publication. In her study of Western ISIS fighters in Syria, Klausen (2015)[17] collected data from the Twitter accounts of about 60 of such individuals over the course of three months in 2014. Her social network analysis on the information obtained from those Twitter accounts indicates the highly important role played by jihadist groups' feeder accounts. In a more recent study, Huey, Inch, and Peladeau (2019)[18] analyzed Twitter accounts to understand the levels of engagement by pro-ISIS women online and how the latter regard the roles that they should perform as jihadist women on social media platforms. The study revealed that pro-ISIS women generally seek to maintain traditional gendered roles of support in the jihadisphere.

Habermas's public sphere

Twitter, of course, is only one node in the wider jihadisphere.[19] When ordinary citizens have more difficulties communicating through or even reaching traditional media channels, they can turn to social media as alternative media outlets. These allow them to express their views or grievances. Internet and social media are sometimes referred to as the "public sphere." The public sphere was described by Habermas (1989)[20] as "a sphere between civil society and the state, in which critical public discussion of matters of general interest" took place. One key feature of social media is the ability to carry a debate anonymously in the public sphere in order to attain an agreement, which is what Habermas refers to as "communicative action." Communicative action is a process through which actors share ideas by using language to arrive at a mutual understanding and arrange their actions. In this process, the actor tries to rationally (not coercively) persuade the hearer to embrace what Habermas called "validity claims." These are claims made rationally by the speaker to legitimate particular issues by linking them with truth, correctness, and honesty.[21]

Jihadists' freedom in the public sphere

In this new era of globalization and the jihadisphere, social access to content in the media environment is decentralized. Anyone can play a part. Distribution of content is decentralized thanks to "hubs." Contributors share mainstream interactive and interconnected platforms, forums, and file-sharing programs. Posting on other sites and re-tweeting capabilities by any user are a cost-free method of diffusion to wide audiences. The internet and social media have liberated jihadist organizations like ISIS and Al-Qaeda from the reliance on mainstream media. Such jihadist groups and individuals have evolved to mainstream social media platforms and created thousands of accounts on Facebook and Twitter. Although most jihadist groups' media outlets continue to control jihadist forums, they simultaneously post content on sponsored Facebook and Twitter accounts to publish new statements and videos.[22]

Zahran Hashim, the mastermind of the Sri Lanka Easter suicide attacks in April 2019, relied on social media to make his public calls for the death of non-Muslims. In the process, he used private chatrooms for months to convince six young men to sacrifice their lives for the cause.[23] Schmid and de Graaf (1982)[24] emphasized that "an act of terrorism is in reality an act of communication. For the terrorist, the message matters, not the victim." Numerous other scholars[25] accurately state that communication and terrorism should be used in the same sentence because communication is the heart of terrorist attacks. In similar fashion, Freedman and Thussu (2012)[26] believe that the internet and social media are the oxygen of terrorism because they are "increasingly seen as active agents in the actual conceptualization of terrorist events."

The internet has been central to terrorism for a long time, but what astonishes experts is the rampant expansion of jihadist sites. Their fast rise indicates that recruitment for a holy war against the rest of the world is relentless, using any means possible (despite the fact that key leaders are constantly captured). Jihadist groups across the board publish a string of propaganda materials, backing each other's local causes and sharing injustices and tribulations. Images, symbols, and emblems depicting oppression of the ummah worldwide are used to whip the mujahedin into a frenzy. The internet has become a powerful conduit to share ideological material to stir up sentiments of hatred among dispersed individuals. Media efforts are also concentrating more and more on independent, user-generated content, frequently without official jihadist approval. Sophisticated audio-visual editing of jihadist video clips, supported by emotionally evocative songs, can strike a chord within listeners and make issues of theological validation less relevant and even obsolete. What all this boils down to saying is that, to be convinced of jihad through the internet or social media, one does not need to be a web-savvy youth. Put simply, the global jihadisphere is easy to access and easy to use. Cyberspace-mediated propaganda is for both Arabic-speaking and non-Arabic speaking Muslim diaspora audiences, both of whom contribute tremendously to the popularity of jihadist culture.[27]

The jihadisphere of fatwas

The jihadisphere has become a space for releasing fatwas or reinterpreting them. The heavy consequence is the influence of militant Islamist activism on users, particularly when fatwas are integral to jihad campaigns. Although a certain number of online fatwas do not pertain to violence, radicalism, or jihad, recently extremist groups have used the internet to post jihad-driven fatwas. A sharp rise in the number of radical fatwas has been noticed as they urge the ummah to undertake jihad as a religious obligation. Most of these online fatwas offer moral and religious validation for the use of terrorist violence. They even provide guidelines (1) as to how the battle space of attacks has to be used, (2) on the identity of the targets, (3) what appropriate means of actions should be taken, and (4) the legitimacy of martyrdom operations.[28] The jihadisphere of fatwas plays a critical part in the social and political justification of terrorism and in the motivation of its constituents.[29]

Postmodern perspectives

Postmodernism represents a deviation from spatialization; it ignores the space-time aspect of human relations.[30] The main characteristic of the jihadisphere is post-modernism, where anonymity and open access provide users with unconstrained liberty of expression. Postmodernism also involves a new form of social order of morality. To be more precise, postmodern morality is predicated on the notion that every individual can do or disregard anything that he or she wants, because every online user is free to (1) communicate his or her faith and agenda, (2) come up with his or her own truth, and (3) follow his or her own moral guidelines.[31]

Online jihadist users as postmodern terrorists

Postmodern terrorists are exploiting the manifold benefits of globalization and modern communication technologies—particularly the most advanced ones—to interact, captivate, plot, and organize their deadly campaigns. The reliance on the internet as social space has unquestionably altered the dynamics of jihadism in the sense that it has widened the communicative action repertoire for everyone. We know that the internet has played a crucial role in the postmodern terrorists' operations in Iraq and Syria. ISIS uses Twitter to drive communications across all social media platforms. Twitter streams from the civil wars in the Middle East may provide the illusion of authenticity, because many people spontaneously use their smartphones for self-publication. The jihadist rebels in Syria and Iraq apply all kinds of social media apps and file-sharing platforms, such as Facebook, Instagram, WhatsApp, Ask.fm, PalTalk, Kik, Viper, JustPaste.it, and Tumblr.[32] When one wants to use the internet and remain anonymous, one can use encryption software like TOR, which can obscure communications with reporters—particularly local information. TOR works by creating connections through countless relays, thereby making it hard to detect your location.[33]

Going back to Twitter, circumstances have made this platform the most popular application in the world today. Initially engineered for cellphones, it is a stress-free and cost-effective method. Tweets are posts that may include photos or texts. Links to other platforms can be used and a new tweet can easily be forwarded to every user in an address list. While some types of social media necessitate either 3G or Wi-Fi access, Twitter does not need either one.[34] Website coordinators in back offices can incorporate the Twitter feeds of active jihadists with YouTube uploads and propagate them to various audiences. These back-office coordinators have purportedly been the wives and young female sympathizers of those active jihadists. It does not matter if they are operating from Raqqa or Nice. In the event that the quality of their smartphones and internet access declines on the ground, the terrorists can use disseminators outside the war zone to communicate their messages.[35]

The postmodern lone-wolf jihadist

The postmodern lone-wolf jihadist heavily relies on the internet to gain information or join a virtual community.[36] It is not the passive use, but the active use of social media platforms, chat rooms, emails, list-servs, texting, and tweeting that contributes the most to radicalization. Anonymity allows people to self-disclose at much higher levels. This, in turn, leads to higher degrees of intimacy among individuals in a virtual group.[37] Online feelings have been reported to be as intense as—if not more intense than—offline feelings. As Bargh and McKenna (2004)[38] explain,

> Research has found that the relative anonymity aspect encourages self-expression, and the relative absence of physical and nonverbal interaction cues (e.g., attractiveness) facilitates the formation of relationships on other, deeper bases such as shared values and beliefs. At the same time, however, these "limited bandwidth" features of Internet communication also tend to leave a lot unsaid and unspecified, and open to inference and interpretation.

Like radical milieus in the three-dimensional space, online radical milieus are groupings within which (ostensible) terrorists form a sub-community. Terrorist organizations and their attacks can emerge from their online variants. As Wald-mann (2008)[39] explains, "what distinguishes the milieu from simple sympathizers is that within the former, there exists a form of social structure responsible for the observed in-group cohesion. It is not merely a sum of individuals holding similar political/cultural attitudes." A giant online jihadist environment is what the jiha-disphere truly represents. It absorbs a large cross-section of producers and con-sumers, from ISIS to Al-Shabaab, from Al-Qaeda Central to the myriad offshoots of the Al-Qaeda franchise. There is a wide globally dispersed range of jihobbyists with no recorded connections to any jihadist organization. Yet, they all contribute to violent jihadist narratives on a daily basis.[40]

Case study I: Anwar al-Awlaki

Sometimes known as "the bin Laden of the internet," Anwar al-Awlaki was a Yemeni-American jihadist ideologue and preacher who acted as an online recruiter and motivator for jihad. He was a central planner of terrorist operations for Al-Qaeda until he was killed by a predator drone in 2011.[41] An elegant rhetor fluent in both English and Arabic, al-Awlaki was a fervent Muslim preacher who liked to condemn the West for the victimization of the ummah. He had a distinct ability to influence would-be jihadists around the globe through his online sermons. His profound knowledge of English, his ardent support of jihadist organizations, and his ability to communicate via a plethora of online platforms made him one of the most effective recruiters of lone-wolf ter-rorists.[42] Notorious lone-wolf jihadists such as Abdul Farouk Abdulmutallab (aka, the Underwear Bomber), Faisal Shahzad (aka, the Times Square bomber), and Major Nidal Hasan (who carried out the 2009 massacre at Fort Hood, killing 13 people) were all inspired by al-Awlaki.[43]

Case study II: Abu Musab al-Zarqawi

Sometimes known as "Sheikh of the slaughterers," Abu Musab al-Zarqawi was a Jordanian jihadist who led a terrorist training camp in Afghanistan and perpetrated a string of bombings, decapitations, and attacks during the Iraq War until he was killed in a targeted strike in 2006.[44] In a little more than a month between April and May 2004, Abu Musab al-Zarqawi became infamous worldwide for his stra-tegic blend of extreme violence and internet know-how. In early April 2004, al-Zarqawi posted a 30-minute audio recording online to describe who he was, why he was engaged in jihad, and how exactly the attacks were conducted by him and his group.[45]Eedle (2005)[46] described the latter as "a comprehensive branding statement." The internet allowed al-Zarqawi to construct a brand very quickly: "Suddenly this mystery man had a voice, if not a face, and a clear ideology to explain his violence."

Al-Zarqawi's utilization of the internet was not the only reason for grave concern *apropos* violent online radicalization. The rise of the jihadisphere was also motivated by changes in cyberspace—particularly regarding access and technologies—that were happening at about the same time al-Zarqawi's publicity strategy captured the world's attention. A great many people acquired cheap and easy access to the internet. Today, 24/7 mobile internet access is the norm, especially among youth who log on through their smartphones and other mobile devices. Online social networking, when becoming a fundamental part of Web 2.0, emerged in the mid-2000s.[47]

The ISIS online communication strategy

ISIS has abundantly exploited the benefits of online platforms to disseminate its propaganda, generate widespread impact on its audiences, and recruit sympathizers. The jihadist organization uses a communication method based on emphasizing certain appeals. Ingram (2014)[48] identified three methods followed by ISIS:

> The use of a multidimensional, multi-platform approach that simultaneously targets "friends and foes" to enhance the reach, relevance and resonance of its messaging; the synchronization of narrative and action to maximize operational and strategic "effects" in the field; and the centrality of the Islamic State "brand" to its entire campaign.

In this respect, the high volume of ISIS recruits points to the fact that ISIS remains up-and-coming not only because of its online reach, but also because of its accent on a conservative version of Islam (i.e., purist Salafism). The *salaf* brand is ISIS's key marketing tool and the group insists on displaying the Black Standard (the banner originally used during the first Islamic conquests in the seventh century). There is an ongoing flow of communication from ISIS's online platforms to tens of thousands of mujahedin in cities on most continents. This demonstrates that the group wants to rule supreme, in a manner reminiscent of the Golden Age of Islam.[49]

ISIS uses a "jihadist cloud," which allows it to keep "its virtual spaces and niches on the internet."[50] With the jihadist cloud, ISIS can spread propaganda and misinformation by disseminating its ideology to as many individuals as possible and in multiple languages. In a speech delivered in February 2015, President Obama detailed some of ISIS's strategies: "The high-quality videos, the online magazines, the use of social media, terrorist Twitter accounts—it's all designed to target today's young people online, in cyberspace."[51] In addition to the various tools that bypass internet censorship, ISIS and its affiliates use the services of the Al-Hayat, Al-Furqan, and Al-Ethar media centers, which together comprise their centralized Information Ministry. These three media centers find social media platforms like YouTube, Twitter, and Facebook useful. Other media tools include the "Clanging of the Swords" promotional videos and its *Dabiq* magazine—among other online jihadist magazines—to diffuse its ideology.[52]

Jihad 3.0

ISIS media strategy can be called "Jihad 3.0." This label denotes a state-of-the-art media campaign based on "multidimensional propaganda," advanced filming, and neat editing equipment.[53] The term is an analogy to Web 3.0 (an improvement from Web 2.0).[54] According to Manuel Castells (2011),[55] this new trend refers to "the cluster of technologies, devices, and applications that support the proliferation of social spaces on the Internet thanks to increased broadband capacity, open source software, and enhanced computer graphics and interface, including avatar interaction in threedimensional virtual spaces."

Jihadist organizations have been known for planting the seeds of their violent ideology in the minds of youths with video games, which can be downloaded on the internet. These video games focus on defending the ummah against the Infidels.[56] To be sure, ISIS is taking advantage of highly sophisticated technologies beyond social media. Examples include the latest versions of video games, cyberterrorism thanks to its Cyber Caliphate Army, new apps, and the Dark Web.[57] The Dark Web refers to internet content that can be found on darknets and overlay networks that require special routing software, configurations, or authorization.[58] The Dark Web is essentially the reverse side of the Web used by extremists, who can now gain and exchange more information to elude law enforcement detection. Obstacles caused by information overload and the trouble to obtain a full picture of jihadist activities prevent effective and efficient understanding of jihadist information on other online platforms as well.[59]

ISIS's mix of visual propaganda

ISIS uses both negative and positive images to diffuse its propaganda online. At one end of the spectrum, ISIS ill-uses the internet by posting deadly and gory images to communicative the unequivocal message that, until the world submits to ISIS's interpretation of sharia and the Caliphate, global jihad will never stop. Remember the shocking beheading videos of Steven Sotloff, David Haines, and James Foley that were transmitted online by ISIS in 2014.[60] In regards to the latter, James Foley, an American video journalist, his beheading video was a prototypical case of ultra-violence disseminated via the web. First broadcast online, this video soon traveled to social networks and online magazines for quite a few months.[61] Such use of videos is a jihadist communication method that is quick and successful for conveying messages, particularly the distribution of disturbing footage of ISIS's arbitrary executions.[62]

Visual literacy theory examines "image viewing" as an acquired skill, much like reading. A viewer can learn the required skills to decipher an image for its visual accuracy. A visually literate individual can then interpret and verbalize the visual meanings ascribed to images and symbols, and gain a sharper awareness of them.[63] The deadly and gory executions were designed to create awareness about ISIS, which is akin to the shock advertising techniques used by PETA and other organizations to generate shock value and, by the same token, attract people's attention.[64] Creating shock value is a persuasive strategy by ISIS to brand itself as a medieval-like barbaric group that is protecting Islam against the Infidels. In this respect, social network platforms not only attract attention, but they also lure possible victims, after which other media technologies are employed—examples include mobile services like Viber, Surespot, WhatsApp, FaceTime, Kik, Skype, and Telegram.[65] Regarding the latter, Telegram soon became one of ISIS's favorite vehicles for media releases. Telegram allows users to publish material over public channels to an unlimited number of viewers/readers. After the November 13, 2015 attacks in Paris, ISIS's use of Telegram was countered or occasionally suspended. Nevertheless, the jihadist group still managed to expose tens of thousands of messages to its various audiences by using other social network platforms.[66]

At the other end of the spectrum, ISIS transmits positive images by playing up its charitable side, such as assisting seniors or organizing events in the cities (at least the ones that they used to control until losing all its territories). Some images featured soldiers resting, swimming, eating, and even toying with pets.[67] In a study conducted by Tarabay, Shiloach, Weiss, and Gilat (2015),[68] which examined ISIS's promotional materials during a one-month period, it was reported that 45% of the materials published online are focused "on its efforts to build and sustain the caliphate." The study also revealed that only 2% of the materials posted were against the West, in comparison to 4% on Libya (a country witnessing a growing ISIS presence). Farwell (2014)[69] asserts that these "warmer images aim to communicate the message that, while strictly Islamic, ISIS stands for promoting the welfare of people, not murdering them."

The virtual ummah

Technology is changing the face of Islam by introducing a virtual version of the ummah. Also known as "online ummah" and "cyber ummah,"[70] the virtual ummah refers to online networks of the global Muslim community. It comprises all sorts of media forums for education, propaganda, or simple discussions of religious matters. The virtual ummah is no longer limited to a community of élites imparted with cultural capital and technological knowledge. Rather, this gigantic online community living in diaspora is made up of Muslims from all walks of life, transcending all 200 nations and cultures.[71] It symbolizes what Benkler (2006)[72] calls the "networked public sphere," or what Castells (2008)[73] terms the "global network society" or the "global public sphere built around the media communication system and internet networks, particularly in the social spaces of the Web 2.0, as exemplified by YouTube, MySpace, Facebook, and the growing blogosphere."

Without a doubt, the internet has united many Muslims worldwide by relaying their messages as well as consuming and generating Muslim materials.[74] There is data confirming that traditional imams and religious clerics consider social networking sites useful in communicating their messages and bonding with online audiences.[75] Worship and religious services are now deterritorialized and disseminated with the assistance of transnational figures or online resources. The rise of internet forums, online discussion boards, and "ask-a-mufti" types of question-

and-answer sessions is unprecedented. Any member of the ummah has a much larger venue for "shopping" when making legal or religious choices.[76] A mufti is a traditional religious leader who is regarded as an "expert" on religious issues.

Normalization theory

Normalization refers to social processes whereby ideas and actions become "normal," "natural," or taken-for-granted in daily life.[77] Put simply, patterns of normalization become more ingrained as time goes by. According to Resnick's (1998)[78] normalization theory, traditional activists in the real world are switching online to diffuse their messages and organize events. Overall, the normalization model proposes that the openness granted by cyberspace functions to support already entrenched political players.[79] Both the online and offline spheres are of equal importance; they balance each other as a new brand of religious culture emerges: the "networked religion."[80] The virtual ummah would not exist without the religious and the network components. A certain number of scholars[81] stress the relationship between online and offline religious practices. One should simply look at the rise of cyber churches or congregations that have a large online following.[82] Based on the tenets of normalization theory, the possibilities of the internet do not necessarily replace or reverse traditional power structures, but they develop at faster rates and can still operate along the traditional lines of the offline world.[83]

Offline jihadist organizations apply digital communication technologies as the main method to direct the ummah. As Seib and Janbek (2010)[84] explain, "for the terrorists themselves, new media are, collectively, a transformative tool that offers endless possibilities for communication and expansion." In this respect, there are multiple psychological motivations that normalize the actions and attitudes of extremists who can be classified as "revenge seekers [who] need an outlet for their frustration, status seekers [who] need recognition, identity seekers [who] need a group to join, and thrill seekers [who] need adventure."[85]

Normalization theory also stresses that participants with the most influence will likely enjoy new online methods the most.[86] Owing to this reason of influence, normalization theory rests on additional tenets: (1) the dependence on mainstream media to publicize and draw citizens to their websites and (2) the advantage of wealthy or powerful people to build a more cutting-edge website and offer technical services.[87] Given these circumstances, normalization creates situations in which risk behavior has or is in the phase of moving into mainstream Muslim culture in cyberspace—attracting regular and well-adjusted Muslims youths (unlike deviant ones only). According to normalization theory, it can be deduced that frequency and level of specific risk behaviors has a cultural foundation.

Online Islamic forums: a double-edged sword

The reframing of the virtual ummah can be observed through the Muslims' interactions and deliberations on the discussion boards of multiple Islamic websites, like

Islamonline.net and Islamway.com—this is a way to strengthen their collective identity. These online discussion forums exemplify Habermas's public sphere, through Islamic concepts such as *shura* (consultation), *ijtihad* (interpretation), and *ijma* (consensus).[88] The main language used in these forums is the national language (e.g., Arabic, Urdu, or Farsi), or the lingua franca of English for an international audience. However, participation in present-day Muslim discussion boards is a double-edged sword. Although it helps advocate the notion of religious communalism and collectivism (which enables members of the ummah to redefine their identities as members of the global Muslim faith), it also advocates jihadist violence.[89] Islamonline.net was founded by Yusuf Al-Qaradawi (born in 1926), an Egyptian Islamic theologian who became known for his online fatwas to validate jihadism. On several occasions, online Islamic forums on Islamonline.net have urged Muslims to wage holy war in Iraq.[90]

The online public sphere does not imply that the virtual ummah has an overwhelming presence there. Instead, it is divided among different online communities, through public sphericules.[91] The concept of "public sphericule" indicates that no single public sphere exists (not the way Habermas imagined it). The reality is that there are many public spheres.[92] In fact, there are so many public sphericules that they represent the mouthpiece for extreme opinions from both sides of the ideological spectrum. Public sphericules show that opinions online, most of which are anonymous, can facilitate the rise of extremism, resentment, and partisanship.[93] Indeed, the internet is an enabler of radicalization by heightening particular fears and threats.[94]

The open university of global jihad

The "open university of global jihad" is a platform for open source jihad on the internet; a public sphere to share new ideas or tricks on jihad. It is also an alternative venue for other voices; a venue that welcomes new interpretations of warfare or religious issues. The "open university of global jihad" is gradually superseding the influence of political and religious figures not only in Western societies, but also in countries under dictatorial régimes. The popularity of social media has magnified the exchange of thoughts, discourses, and practices within Muslim communities in diaspora Muslims and homeland Muslims. The "open university" model offers an extensive range of discourses about Islam, from fundamentalist to reformist.[95]

The online sphere includes innumerable chat groups, websites, blogs, and discussion forums on Islam that are visited primarily by Muslims. Militant Muslims who promote global jihad exploit these online environments. They use these venues for recruiting, plotting, and fundraising purposes. Individuals who are identified as potential recruits in chat rooms are sent surveys and tests to determine whether they can become new members of jihadist organizations. The jihadisphere has detailed instruction manuals on kidnapping, guerilla tactics in urban areas, and military battle procedures for jihadists. This online sphere even has a video tutorial to explain, step by step, how to detonate bombs through smartphones, which is exactly how the commuter train bombings were executed in Madrid in March 2004. When the jihadisphere is used for religious education, it often includes the participation of so-called religious experts. For instance, mullahs from Saudi Arabia have made recommendations to Dutch radical Muslims.[96]

Through the "open university of global jihad," groups like Al-Qaeda have effectively inspired millions of Muslim youths to fashion a new sense of identity as brothers and sisters within the ummah. One of the results of the virtual ummah, since the dawn of the twenty-first century, is the dangerous vision and dream for the apocalypse. Such a vision, based on radical interpretations of Islamic texts, stems from the hopeless desire, promulgated by purist Salafists, for radical change. The belief is that jihadist groups will lead the fight for the new Islamic world order.[97]

Salafist influences

Because the virtual ummah exists within a virtually unlimited space, it will inevitably encounter the public sphere of Salafist Muslims. The latter dream of states founded on purist principles. Because very few restraints exist, a quasi-infinite number of sites also exist. Linked through mutual references, quoting and recycling the same group of ideas, Salafist influences are an unescapable part of the virtual ummah. In this context, creativity is difficult. Rather than having unique thoughts and original ideas, we encounter that old-fashioned copy-and-paste technique, which the online sphere facilitates. It is a new trend; spreading hatred can be done fast, easy, and superficially. It is devoid of critical thinking and accountability.[98]

The pure, traditional Islam of Salafism, which the revived Islamic youth encounter in cyberspace, challenges important intellectual dogmas of Islam. The Salafist doctrine wants to rest directly on the Quran and the Sunna. The virtual ummah will never be totally fundamentalist at the heart. There are many Muslims who do not even care about the main canons of their own religion, a phenomenon observed in other religions too. However, the danger here is the Salafist influence that is deeply entrenched within the texts of the Quran and the tradition of the Prophet.[99] The Salafists' "supreme" truth, which comes with an "absolute" context-free validity, contributes a great deal to that "open university of global jihad." Any user online can look "for a norm that can be applied to strongly diverging contexts, or rather, a norm that can ignore context: this explains why the 'Salafi' doctrine is the most suitable to inform the virtual ummah."[100] Within Salafism lies the concept of *salaf*, denoting the Golden Age during which the Prophet's companions and devout followers of the first generations of Islam were conquering large territories and nations.[101]

Notes

1 Benjamin Ducol, "Uncovering the French-Speaking Jihadisphere: An Exploratory Analysis," *Media, War & Conflict* 5, no. 1 (2012): 51–70. https://doi.org/10.1177/1750635211434366

2   Ramaswami Harindranath, "Malign Images, Malevolent Networks: Social Media, Extremist Violence, and Public Anxieties," in *Cybercrime and Its Victims*, ed. Elena Martellozzo and Emma A Jane (New York: Routledge, 2017): 148–64.
3   See www.internetworldstats.com/stats.htm
4   Kiran Hassan, "Social Media, Media Freedom and Pakistan's War on Terror," *The Round Table* 107, no. 2 (2018): 189–202. https://doi.org/10.1080/00358533.2018. 1448339
5   Reynol Junco, Greg Heibergert, and Eric Loken, "The Effect of Twitter on College Student Engagement and Grades," *Journal of Computer Assisted Learning* 27, no. 2 (2011): 119–32. https://doi.org/10.1111/j.1365-2729.2010.00387.x
6   Jytte Klausen, "Tweeting the Jihad: Social Media Networks of Western Foreign Fighters in Syria and Iraq," *Studies in Conflict & Terrorism* 38, no. 1 (2015): 1–22. http s://doi.org/10.1080/1057610X.2014.974948
7   Jen Birks and John Downey, "'Pay Your Tax!' How Tax Avoidance Became a Prominent Issue in the Public Sphere in the UK," in *Media, Margins and Civic Agency*, ed. Einar Thorsen, Daniel Jackson, Heather Savigny, and Jenny Alexander (New York: Springer, 2015): 166–81.
8   Raúl Lara-Cabrera, Antonio González Pardo, Karim Benouaret, Noura Faci, Djamal Benslimane, and David Camacho, "Measuring the Radicalisation Risk in Social Networks," *IEEE Access* 5 (2017): 10892–900. https://doi.org/10.1109/ACCESS.2017. 2706018
9   Shaun Wright, David Denney, Alasdair Pinkerton, Vincent A. A. Jansen, and John Bryden, "Resurgent Insurgents: Quantitative Research into Jihadists Who Get Suspended but Return on Twitter," *Contemporary Voices: St Andrews Journal of International Relations* 7, no. 2 (2016): 1–13. http://doi.org/10.15664/jtr.1213
10 W. Lance Bennett and Alexandra Segerberg, "Digital Media and the Personalization of Collective Action: Social Technology and the Organization of Protests against the Global Economic Crisis," *Information, Communication & Society* 14, no. 6 (2011): 770–99. https://doi.org/10.1080/1369118X.2011.579141
11 Howard Rheingold, *The Virtual Community: Homesteading on the Electronic Frontier* (Boston: MIT Press, 1993); Howard Rheingold, *Smart Mobs: The Next Social Revolution* (New York: Basic Books, 2002).
12 Nico Prucha, "IS and the Jihadist Information Highway—Projecting Influence and Religious Identity via Telegram," *Perspectives on Terrorism* 10, no. 6 (2016): 48–58.
13 Ibid., 50.
14 Charlie Winter, "Apocalypse, Later: A Longitudinal Study of the Islamic State Brand," *Critical Studies in Media Communication* 35, no. 1 (2018): 103–21. https://doi.org/10. 1080/15295036.2017.1393094
15 Elizabeth Minei and Jonathan Matusitz, "Cyberspace as a New Arena for Terroristic Propaganda: An Updated Examination," *Poiesis & Praxis* 9, no. 1 (2012): 163–76. http s://doi.org/10.1007/s10202-012-0108-3
16 Jonathan Matusitz, "Intercultural Perspectives on Cyberspace: An Updated Examination," *Journal of Human Behavior in the Social Environment* 24, no. 7 (2014): 713–24. http s://doi.org/10.1080/10911359.2013.849223
17 Klausen, "Tweeting the Jihad," 1.
18 Laura Huey, Rachel Inch, and Hillary Peladeau, "'@ Me If You Need Shoutout': Exploring Women's Roles in Islamic State Twitter Networks," *Studies in Conflict & Terrorism* 42, no. 5 (2019): 445–63. https://doi.org/10.1080/1057610X.2017.1393897
19 Maura Conway and Stuart Macdonald, "Introduction to the Special Issue: Islamic State's Online Activity and Responses, 2014–2017," *Studies in Conflict & Terrorism* 42, no. 1 (2018): 1–4. https://doi.org/10.1080/1057610X.2018.1513684
20 Jürgen Habermas, *The Structural Transformation of the Public Sphere* (Cambridge, MA: MIT Press, 1989): ix.
21 Jürgen Habermas, *Moral Consciousness and Communicative Action* (Cambridge, MA: MIT Press, 1990).

22   Klausen, "Tweeting the Jihad," 3.
23   *The Times of India*, "Sri Lanka Attack Mastermind Used Chatrooms to Sway Suicide Bombers," *The Times of India* (2019, May 3): A1.
24   Alex P. Schmid and Janny De Graaf, *Violence as Communication: Insurgent Terrorism and the Western News Media* (London: Sage, 1982): 14.
25   See Cristina Archetti, *Understanding Terrorism in the Age of Global Media: A Communication Approach* (New York: Palgrave Macmillan, 2013); Brigitte Nacos, *Mass-Mediated Terrorism: The Central Role of the Media in Terrorism and Counterterrorism* (Lanham, MD: Rowman & Littlefield, 2002); Susan Currie Sivek, "Packaging Inspiration: Al Qaeda's Digital Magazine *Inspire* in the Self-Radicalization Process," *International Journal of Communication* 7, n. 1 (2013): 584–606.
26   Des Freedman and Daya Thussu, "Introduction: Dynamics of Media and Terrorism," in *Media and Terrorism: Global Perspectives*, ed. Des Freedman and Daya Thussu (Thousand Oaks, CA: Sage, 2012): 1–20, 10.
27   Jonathan Matusitz, *Symbolism in Terrorism: Motivation, Communication, and Behavior* (Lanham, MD: Rowman & Littlefield, 2015).
28   Gabriel Weimann, "Cyber-Fatwas and Terrorism," *Studies in Conflict & Terrorism* 34, no. 10 (2011): 765–81. https://doi.org/10.1080/1057610X.2011.604831
29   Shmuel Bar, *Warrant for Terror: The Fatwas of Radical Islam and the Duty to Jihad* (Lanham, MD: Rowman & Littlefield, 2008).
30   Jonathan Matusitz, "Cyberterrorism: Postmodern State of Chaos," *Information Security Journal: A Global Perspective* 17, no. 4 (2008): 179–87. https://doi.org/10.1080/19393550802397033
31   Tomáš Kozík, Henryk Noga, and Jana Depešová, "The Symptoms of Postmodernism in Media and Multimedia," *European Journal of Science and Theology* 11, no. 6 (2015): 119–25.
32   Maxime Bérubé and Benoit Dupont, "Mujahideen Mobilization: Examining the Evolution of the Global Jihadist Movement's Communicative Action Repertoire," *Studies in Conflict & Terrorism* 42, no. 1 (2019): 5–24. https://doi.org/10.1080/1057610X.2018.1513689
33   Siddharth Arora, Anupama Pankaj, and Prasenjit Banerjee, "Anonymity and Anonymous Connections Using TOR," *International Journal of Advanced Studies of Scientific Research* 3, no. 10 (2018): 10–4.
34   Klausen, "Tweeting the Jihad," 4–5.
35   Ibid., 10–2.
36   Jeffrey D. Simon, "Lone Wolf Terrorism: Understanding a Growing Threat," in *Lone Actors—An Emerging Security Threat*, ed. Aaron Richman and Yair Sharan (Amsterdam: IOS Press, 2015): 3–10.
37   Marc Sageman, *Leaderless Jihad: Terror Networks in the Twenty-First Century* (Philadelphia: University of Pennsylvania Press, 2008).
38   John A. Bargh and Katelyn Y. A. McKenna, "The Internet and Social Life," *Annual Review of Psychology* 55 (2004): 573–90, 586. https://doi.org/10.1146/annurev.psych.55.090902.141922
39   Peter Waldmann, "The Radical Milieu: The Under-Investigated Relationship between Terrorists and Sympathetic Communities," *Perspectives on Terrorism* 2, no. 9 (2008): 25–7.
40   Maura Conway, "From al-Zarqawi to al-Awlaki: The Emergence of the Internet as a New Form of Violent Radical Milieu," *Combating Terrorism Exchange* 2, no. 4 (2012): 12–22.
41   Riyad Hosain Rahimullah, Stephen Larmar, and Mohamad Abdalla, "Understanding Violent Radicalization amongst Muslims: A Review of the Literature," *Journal of Psychology and Behavioral Science* 1, no. 1 (2013): 19–35.
42   Denis MacEoin, "Anwar al-Awlaki: 'I Pray that Allah Destroys America'," *Middle East Quarterly* 17, no. 2 (2010): 13–9.
43   Jerrold M. Post, Cody McGinnis, and Kristen Moody, "The Changing Face of Terrorism in the 21st Century: The Communications Revolution and the Virtual

Community of Hatred," *Behavioral Sciences & the Law* 32, no. 3 (2014): 306–34. http s://doi.org/10.1002/bsl.2123

44 Jeffrey Gettleman, "Abu Musab al-Zarqawi Lived a Brief, Shadowy Life Replete with Contradictions," *The New York Times* (2006, June 9): A10; Michael Weiss and Hassan Hassan, *ISIS: Inside the Army of Terror* (New York: Simon & Schuster, 2016).

45 Conway, "From al-Zarqawi to al-Awlaki," 13.

46 Paul Eedle, "Al Qaeda's Media Strategy," in *Al Qaeda Now*, ed. Karen G. Greenberg (Cambridge: Cambridge University Press, 2005): 124–5, 124.

47 Conway, "From al-Zarqawi to al-Awlaki," 14–7.

48 Haroro J. Ingram, "Three Traits of the Islamic State's Information Warfare," *The RUSI Journal* 159, no. 6 (2014): 4–11, 4. https://doi.org/10.1080/03071847.2014. 990810

49 Cited in Ahmed Al-Rawi, "Video Games, Terrorism, and ISIS's Jihad 3.0," *Terrorism and Political Violence* 30, no. 4 (2018): 740–60, 744. https://doi.org/10.1080/09546553.2016.1207633

50 Ibid., 741.

51 Cited in Kathy Gilsinan, "Is ISIS's Social-Media Power Exaggerated?," *The Atlantic* (2015, February 23): A1.

52 Steve Rose, "The ISIS Propaganda War: A Hi-Tech Media Jihad," *The Guardian* (2014, October 7): A1.

53 Scott Shane and Ben Hubbard, "ISIS Displaying a Deft Command of Varied Media," *The New York Times* (2014, August 30): A1.

54 Claudia Carvalho, "'Kids in the Green Lands of the Khilafat'—A Tumblr Case Study of Imagery within the Jihad 3.0 Narrative," in *European Muslims and New Media*, ed. Merve Kayıkcı and Leen d'Haenens (Leuven, Belgium: Leuven University Press, 2017): 91–112.

55 Manuel Castells, *The Rise of the Network Society: The Information Age: Economy, Society, and Culture* (Oxford: John Wiley & Sons, 2011), xxvii.

56 Gary Adkins, "Red Teaming the Red Team: Utilizing Cyber Espionage to Combat Terrorism," *Journal of Strategic Security* 6, no. 3 (2013): 1–9. https://doi.org/10.5038/1944-0472.6.3S.1

57 Al-Rawi, "Video Games, Terrorism, and ISIS's Jihad 3.0," 745.

58 Sion Retzkin, *Hands-On Dark Web Analysis: Learn What Goes on in the Dark Web, and How to Work with It* (Birmingham, England: Packt Publishing, 2018).

59 Robert W. Gehl, *Weaving the Dark Web: Legitimacy on Freenet, Tor, and I2P* (Cambridge: The MIT Press, 2018).

60 Simone Molin Friis, "'Beyond Anything We Have Ever Seen': Beheading Videos and the Visibility of Violence in the War against ISIS," *International Affairs* 91, no. 4 (2015): 725–46. https://doi.org/10.1111/1468-2346.12341

61 Matteo Vergani and Dennis Zuev, "Neojihadist Visual Politics: Comparing Youtube Videos of North Caucasus and Uyghur Militants," *Asian Studies Review* 39, no. 1 (2015): 1–22. https://doi.org/10.1080/10357823.2014.976171

62 Elizabeth Minei and Jonathan Matusitz, "Cyberterrorist Messages and Their Effects on Targets: A Qualitative Analysis," *Journal of Human Behavior in the Social Environment* 21, no. 8 (2011): 995–1019. https://doi.org/10.1080/10911359.2011.588569

63 April Raneri and Jonathan Matusitz, "Source Representation in the Communication of Childhood Immunisation," *Child Care in Practice* 21, no. 2 (2015): 114–27. https://doi.org/10.1080/13575279.2014.966651

64 Darren W. Dahl, Kristina D. Frankenberger, and Rajesh V. Manchanda, "Does It Pay to Shock? Reactions to Shocking and Nonshocking Advertising Content among University Students," *Journal of Advertising Research* 43, no. 3 (2003): 268–80. https://doi.org/10.1017/S0021849903030332; Nathalie Dens, Patrick De Pelsmacker, and Wim Janssens, "Exploring Consumer Reactions to Incongruent Mild Disgust Appeals," *Journal of Marketing Communications* 14, no. 4 (2008): 249–69. https://doi.org/10.1080/13527260802141231

65 Rukmini Callimachi, "ISIS and the Lonely Young American," *The New York Times* (2015, June 27): A1; Nabeelah Jaffer, "The Secret World of ISIS Brides: 'U dnt hav 2 pay 4 ANYTHING if u r wife of a martyr,'" *The Guardian* (2015, June 24): A1.

66 Laura Wakeford and Laura Smith, "IS' Propaganda and the Social Media: Dissemination, Support, and Resilience," in *ISIS Propaganda: A Full-Spectrum Extremist Message*, ed. Stephane J. Baele, Katharine A. Boyd, and Travis G. Coan (New York: Oxford University Press, 2019): 155–87.

67 Al-Rawi, "Video Games, Terrorism, and ISIS's Jihad 3.0," 744.

68 Jamie Tarabay, Gilad Shiloach, Amit Weiss, and Matan Gilat, "To Its Citizens, ISIS also Shows a Softer Side," *Vocativ* (2015, March 20): A1.

69 James P. Farwell, "The Media Strategy of ISIS," *Survival* 56, no. 6 (2014): 49–55, 50. https://doi.org/10.1080/00396338.2014.985436

70 Sahar Khamis, "'Cyber *Ummah*:' The Internet and Muslim Communities," in *Handbook of Contemporary Islam and Muslim Lives*, ed. Mark Woodward and Ronald Lukens-Bull (New York: Springer, 2018): 1–22.

71 Peter Mandaville, *Transnational Muslim Politics: Reimagining the Umma* (New York: Routledge, 2001); Peter Mandaville, "Communication and Diasporic Islam: A Virtual Ummah?," in *The Media of Diaspora*, ed. Karim H. Karim (New York: Routledge, 2003): 135–47.

72 Yochai Benkler, *The Wealth of Networks: How Social Production Transforms Markets and Freedoms* (New Haven, CT: Yale University Press, 2006).

73 Manuel Castells, "The New Public Sphere: Global Civil Society, Communication Networks and Global Governance," *Annals of the American Academy of Political and Social Science* 616, no. 1 (2008): 78–93, 90. https://doi.org/10.1177/0002716207311877

74 Ahmed Al-Rawi, "Online Reactions to the Muhammad Cartoons: YouTube and the Virtual Ummah," *Journal for the Scientific Study of Religion* 54, no. 2 (2015): 261–76. https://doi.org/10.1111/jssr.12191

75 Randolph Kluver and Pauline Hope Cheong, "Technological Modernization, the Internet, and Religion in Singapore," *Journal of Computer-Mediated Communication* 12, no. 3 (2007): 1122–242. https://doi.org/10.1111/j.1083-6101.2007.00366.x

76 Saminaz Zaman, "From Imam to Cyber-Mufti: Consuming Identity in Muslim America," *The Muslim World* 98, no. 4 (2008): 465–74. https://doi.org/10.1111/j.1478-1913.2008.00240.x

77 Michel Foucault, *The History of Sexuality, Volume I: An Introduction* (New York: Vintage, 1990).

78 David Resnick, "The Normalisation of Cyberspace," in *The Politics of Cyberspace*, ed. Chris Toulouse and Timothy W. Luke (London: Routledge, 1998): 48–68.

79 Joshua D. Potter and Johanna L. Dunaway, "Reinforcing or Breaking Party Systems? Internet Communication Technologies and Party Competition in Comparative Context," *Political Communication* 33, no. 3 (2016): 392–413. https://doi.org/10.1080/10584609.2015.1069767

80 Heidi Campbell, *When Religion Meets New Media* (London: Routledge, 2010): 193.

81 See Debbie Herring, "Virtual as Contextual: A Net News Theology," in *Religion and Cyberspace*, ed. Morten Højsgaard and Margit Warburg (New York: Routledge, 2005): 149–65; Glenn Young, "Reading and Praying Online: The Continuity of Religion Online and Online Religion in Internet Christianity," in *Religion Online: Finding Faith on the Internet*, ed. Lorne L. Dawson and Douglas E. Cowan (New York: Routledge, 2004): 93–106.

82 Heidi Campbell, "Understanding the Relationship between Religion Online and Offline in a Networked Society," *Journal of the American Academy of Religion* 80, no. 1 (2012): 64–93. https://doi.org/10.1093/jaarel/lfr074; Heidi Campbell, "Religion and the Internet: A Microcosm for Studying Internet Trends and Implications," *New Media and Society* 15, no. 5 (2013): 680–94. https://doi.org/10.1177/1461444812462848

83   Rachel Gibson and Ian McAllister, "Normalising or Equalising Party Competition? Assessing the Impact of the Web on Election Campaigning," *Political Studies* 63, no. 3 (2015): 529–47. https://doi.org/10.1111/1467-9248.12107

84   Philip Seib and Dana M. Janbek, *Global Terrorism and New Media: The Post-Al Qaeda Generation* (Abingdon, UK: Routledge, 2010): ix.

85   Cited in Al-Rawi, "Video Games, Terrorism, and ISIS's Jihad 3.0," 741.

86   Rosalynd Southern, "Is Web 2.0 Providing a Voice for Outsiders? A Comparison of Personal Web Site and Social Media Use by Candidates at the 2010 UK General Election," *Journal of Information Technology & Politics* 12, no. 1 (2015): 1–17. https://doi.org/10.1080/19331681.2014.972603

87   Tom Carlson and Göran Djupsund, "Old Wine in New Bottles? The 1999 Finnish Election Campaign on the Internet," *Harvard International Journal of Press/Politics* 6, no. 1 (2001): 68–87. https://doi.org/10.1177/1081180X01006001005; Rachel Gibson, Stephen Ward, and Wainer Lusoli, "The Internet and Political Campaigning: The New Medium Comes of Age?," *Representation* 39, no. 3 (2003): 166–80. https://doi.org/10.1080/00344890308523221; Michael Margolis, David Resnick, and Jonathan Levy, "Major Parties Dominate, Minor Parties Struggle US Elections and the Internet," in *Political Parties and the Internet: Net Gain?*, ed. Rachel Kay Gibson, Payl Nixon, and Stephen Ward (London: Routledge, 2003): 53–69.

88   Mohammed el-Nawawy and Sahar Khamis, "Collective Identity in the Virtual Islamic Public Sphere: Contemporary Discourses in Two Islamic Websites," *International Communication Gazette* 72, no. 3 (2010): 229–50. https://doi.org/10.1177/1748048509356949

89   Mohammed el-Nawawy and Sahar Khamis, "Divergent Identities in the Virtual Islamic Public Sphere: A Case Study of the English Discussion Forum 'Islamonline'," *Journal of Arab & Muslim Media Research* 5, no. 1 (2012): 31–48. https://doi.org/10.1386/jammr.5.1.31_1

90   See www.investigativeproject.org/profile/167/yusuf-al-qaradawi

91   Ahmed Al-Rawi, "Facebook as a Virtual Mosque: The Online Protest against *Innocence of Muslims*," *Culture and Religion* 17, no. 1 (2016): 19–34. https://doi.org/10.1080/14755610.2016.1159591

92   Stuart Cunningham, Gay Hawkins, Audrey Yue, Tina Nguyen, and John Sinclair, "Multicultural Broadcasting and Diasporic Video as Public Sphericules," *American Behavioral Scientist* 43, no. 9 (2000): 1533–47. https://doi.org/10.1177/00027640021955919

93   Jennifer Brundidge, "Encountering 'Difference' in the Contemporary Public Sphere: The Contribution of the Internet to the Heterogeneity of Political Discussion Networks," *Journal of Communication* 60, no. 4 (2010): 680–700. https://doi.org/10.1111/j.1460-2466.2010.01509.x; Magdalena Wojcieszak, "'Don't Talk to Me': Effects of Ideologically Homogeneous Online Groups and Politically Dissimilar Offline Ties on Extremism," *New Media & Society* 12, no. 4 (2010): 637–55. https://doi.org/10.1177/1461444809342775

94   Lincoln Dahlberg, "The Internet, Deliberative Democracy, and Power: Radicalizing the Public Sphere," *International Journal of Media and Cultural Politics* 3, no. 1 (2007): 47–64. https://doi.org/10.1386/macp.3.1.47_1

95   Reuven Paz, *Global Jihad and WMD: Between Martyrdom and Mass Destruction* (Washington, D.C.: Hudson Institute, 2005).

96   Peter Mascini, "Can the Violent Jihad Do without Sympathizers?," *Studies in Conflict & Terrorism* 29, no. 4 (2006): 343–57. https://doi.org/10.1080/10576100600641832

97   Paz, *Global Jihad and WMD*, 75.

98   Olivier Roy, *Globalized Islam: The Search for a New Ummah* (New York: Columbia University Press, 2006): 154–5.

99   Angela Gendron, "The Call to Jihad: Charismatic Preachers and the Internet," in *Violent Extremism Online: New Perspectives on Terrorism and the Internet*, ed. Anne Aly,

Stuart Macdonald, Lee Jarvis, and Thomas Chen (New York: Routledge, 2016): 25–44.
100 Roy, *Globalized Islam*, 162.
101 Alexander Thurston, *Salafism in Nigeria: Islam, Preaching, and Politics* (Cambridge: Cambridge University Press, 2018).

References

Adkins, Gary, "Red Teaming the Red Team: Utilizing Cyber Espionage to Combat Terrorism," *Journal of Strategic Security* 6, no. 3 (2013): 1–9. https://doi.org/10.5038/1944-0472.6.3S.1

Al-Rawi, Ahmed, "Online Reactions to the Muhammad Cartoons: YouTube and the Virtual Ummah," *Journal for the Scientific Study of Religion* 54, no. 2 (2015): 261–276. https://doi.org/10.1111/jssr.12191.

Al-Rawi, Ahmed, "Facebook as a Virtual Mosque: The Online Protest against Innocence of Muslims," *Culture and Religion*   17, no. 1 (2016): 19–34. https://doi.org/10.1080/14755610.2016.1159591.

Al-Rawi, Ahmed, "Video Games, Terrorism, and ISIS's Jihad 3.0," *Terrorism and Political Violence* 30, no. 4 (2018): 740–760. https://doi.org/10.1080/09546553.2016.1207633.

Archetti, Cristina, *Understanding Terrorism in the Age of Global Media: A Communication Approach*. New York: Palgrave Macmillan, 2013.

Arora, Siddharth, Anupama Pankaj, and Prasenjit Banerjee, "Anonymity and Anonymous Connections Using TOR," *International Journal of Advanced Studies of Scientific Research* 3, no. 10 (2018): 10–14.

Bar, Shmuel, *Warrant for Terror: The Fatwas of Radical Islam and the Duty to Jihad*. Lanham, MD: Rowman & Littlefield, 2008.

Bargh, John A., and Katelyn Y. A. McKenna, "The Internet and Social Life," *Annual Review of Psychology* 55 (2004): 573–590. https://doi.org/10.1146/annurev.psych.55.090902.141922.

Benkler, Yochai, *The Wealth of Networks: How Social Production Transforms Markets and Freedoms*. New Haven, CT: Yale University Press, 2006.

Bennett, W. Lance, and Alexandra Segerberg, "Digital Media and the Personalization of Collective Action: Social Technology and the Organization of Protests against the Global Economic Crisis," *Information, Communication & Society* 14, no. 6 (2011): 770–799. https://doi.org/10.1080/1369118X.2011.579141.

Bérubé, Maxime, and Benoit Dupont, "Mujahideen Mobilization: Examining the Evolution of the Global Jihadist Movement's Communicative Action Repertoire," *Studies in Conflict & Terrorism* 42, no. 1 (2019): 5–24. https://doi.org/10.1080/1057610X.2018.1513689.

Birks, Jen, and John Downey, "'Pay Your Tax!' How Tax Avoidance Became a Prominent Issue in the Public Sphere in the UK," in *Media, Margins and Civic Agency*, edited by Einar Thorsen, Daniel Jackson, Heather Savigny, and Jenny Alexander, 166–181. New York: Springer, 2015.

Brundidge, Jennifer, "Encountering 'Difference' in the Contemporary Public Sphere: The Contribution of the Internet to the Heterogeneity of Political Discussion Networks," *Journal of Communication* 60, no. 4 (2010): 680–700. https://doi.org/10.1111/j.1460-2466.2010.01509.x.

Callimachi, Rukmini, "ISIS and the Lonely Young American," *The New York Times* (2015, June 27): A1.

Campbell, Heidi, *When Religion Meets New Media*. London: Routledge, 2010.

Campbell, Heidi, "Understanding the Relationship between Religion Online and Offline in a Networked Society," *Journal of the American Academy of Religion* 80, no. 1 (2012): 64–93. https://doi.org/10.1093/jaarel/lfr074.

Campbell, Heidi, "Religion and the Internet: A Microcosm for Studying Internet Trends and Implications," *New Media and Society* 15, no. 5 (2013): 680–694. https://doi.org/10.1177/1461444812462848.

Carlson, Tom, and Göran Djupsund, "Old Wine in New Bottles? The 1999 Finnish Election Campaign on the Internet," *Harvard International Journal of Press/Politics* 6, no. 1 (2001): 68–87. https://doi.org/10.1177/1081180X01006001005.

Carvalho, Claudia, "'Kids in the Green Lands of the Khilafat'—A Tumblr Case Study of Imagery within the Jihad 3.0 Narrative," in *European Muslims and New Media*, edited by Merve Kayıkcı and Leen d'Haenens, 91–112. Leuven, Belgium: Leuven University Press, 2017.

Castells, Manuel, "The New Public Sphere: Global Civil Society, Communication Networks and Global Governance," *Annals of the American Academy of Political and Social Science* 616, no. 1 (2008): 78–93. https://doi.org/10.1177/0002716207311877.

Castells, Manuel, *The Rise of the Network Society: The Information Age: Economy, Society, and Culture*. Oxford: John Wiley & Sons, 2011.

Conway, Maura, "From al-Zarqawi to al-Awlaki: The Emergence of the Internet as a New Form of Violent Radical Milieu," *Combating Terrorism Exchange* 2, no. 4 (2012): 12–22.

Conway, Maura, and Stuart Macdonald, "Introduction to the Special Issue: Islamic State's Online Activity and Responses, 2014–2017," *Studies in Conflict & Terrorism* 42, no. 1 (2018): 1–4. https://doi.org/10.1080/1057610X.2018.1513684.

Cunningham, Stuart, Gay Hawkins, Audrey Yue, Tina Nguyen, and John Sinclair, "Multicultural Broadcasting and Diasporic Video as Public Sphericules," *American Behavioral Scientist* 43, no. 9 (2000): 1533–1547. https://doi.org/10.1177/00027640021955919.

Dahl, Darren W., Kristina D. Frankenberger, and Rajesh V. Manchanda, "Does It Pay to Shock? Reactions to Shocking and Nonshocking Advertising Content among University Students," *Journal of Advertising Research* 43, no. 3 (2003): 268–280. https://doi.org/10.1017/S0021849903030332.

Dahlberg, Lincoln, "The Internet, Deliberative Democracy, and Power: Radicalizing the Public Sphere," *International Journal of Media and Cultural Politics* 3, no. 1 (2007): 47–64. https://doi.org/10.1386/macp.3.1.47_1.

Dens, Nathalie, Patrick De Pelsmacker, and Wim Janssens, "Exploring Consumer Reactions to Incongruent Mild Disgust Appeals," *Journal of Marketing Communications* 14, no. 4 (2008): 249–269. https://doi.org/10.1080/13527260802141231.

Ducol, Benjamin, "Uncovering the French-Speaking Jihadisphere: An Exploratory Analysis," *Media, War & Conflict* 5, no. 1 (2012): 51–70. https://doi.org/10.1177/1750635211434366.

Eedle, Paul, "Al Qaeda's Media Strategy," in *Al Qaeda Now*, edited by Karen G. Greenberg, 124–125. Cambridge: Cambridge University Press, 2005.

el-Nawawy, Mohammed, and Sahar Khamis, "Collective Identity in the Virtual Islamic Public Sphere: Contemporary Discourses in Two Islamic Websites," *International Communication Gazette* 72, no. 3 (2010): 229–250. https://doi.org/10.1177/1748048509356949.

el-Nawawy, Mohammed, and Sahar Khamis, "Divergent Identities in the Virtual Islamic Public Sphere: A Case Study of the English Discussion Forum 'Islamonline'," *Journal of Arab & Muslim Media Research* 5, no. 1 (2012): 31–48. https://doi.org/10.1386/jammr.5.1.31_1.

Farwell, James P., "The Media Strategy of ISIS," *Survival* 56, no. 6 (2014): 49–55. https://doi.org/10.1080/00396338.2014.985436.

Foucault, Michel, *The History of Sexuality, Volume I: An Introduction*. New York: Vintage, 1990.

Freedman, Des, and Daya Thussu, "Introduction: Dynamics of Media and Terrorism," in *Media and Terrorism: Global Perspectives*, edited by Des Freedman and Daya Thussu, 1–20. Thousand Oaks, CA: Sage, 2012.

Friis, Simone Molin, "'Beyond Anything We Have Ever Seen': Beheading Videos and the Visibility of Violence in the War against ISIS," *International Affairs* 91, no. 4 (2015): 725–746. https://doi.org/10.1111/1468-2346.12341.

Gehl, Robert W., *Weaving the Dark Web: Legitimacy on Freenet, Tor, and I2P*. Cambridge, MA: The MIT Press, 2018.

Gendron, Angela, "The Call to Jihad: Charismatic Preachers and the Internet," in *Violent Extremism Online: New Perspectives on Terrorism and the Internet*, edited by Anne Aly, Stuart Macdonald, Lee Jarvis, and Thomas Chen, 25–44. New York: Routledge, 2016.

Gettleman, Jeffrey, "Abu Musab al-Zarqawi Lived a Brief, Shadowy Life Replete with Contradictions," *The New York Times* (2006, June 9): A10.

Gibson, Rachel, Stephen Ward, and Wainer Lusoli, "The Internet and Political Campaigning: The New Medium Comes of Age?," *Representation* 39, no. 3 (2003): 166–180. https://doi.org/10.1080/00344890308523221.

Gibson, Rachel, and Ian McAllister, "Normalising or Equalising Party Competition? Assessing the Impact of the Web on Election Campaigning," *Political Studies* 63, no. 3 (2015): 529–547. https://doi.org/10.1111/1467-9248.12107.

Gilsinan, Kathy, "Is ISIS's Social-Media Power Exaggerated?," *The Atlantic* (2015, February 23): A1.

Habermas, Jürgen, *The Structural Transformation of the Public Sphere*. Cambridge, MA: MIT Press, 1989.

Habermas, Jürgen, *Moral Consciousness and Communicative Action*. Cambridge, MA: MIT Press, 1990.

Harindranath, Ramaswami, "Malign Images, Malevolent Networks: Social Media, Extremist Violence, and Public Anxieties," in *Cybercrime and Its Victims*, edited by Elena Martellozzo and Emma A. Jane, 148–164. New York: Routledge, 2017.

Hassan, Kiran, "Social Media, Media Freedom and Pakistan's War on Terror," *The Round Table* 107, no. 2 (2018): 189–202. https://doi.org/10.1080/00358533.2018.1448339.

Herring, Debbie, "Virtual as Contextual: A Net News Theology," in *Religion and Cyberspace*, edited by Morten Højsgaard and Margit Warburg, 149–155. New York: Routledge, 2005.

Huey, Laura, Rachel Inch, and Hillary Peladeau, "'@ Me If You Need Shoutout': Exploring Women's Roles in Islamic State Twitter Networks," *Studies in Conflict & Terrorism* 42, no. 5 (2019): 445–463. https://doi.org/10.1080/1057610X.2017.1393897.

Ingram, Haroro J., "Three Traits of the Islamic State's Information Warfare," *The RUSI Journal* 159, no. 6 (2014): 4–11. https://doi.org/10.1080/03071847.2014.990810.

Jaffer, Nabeelah, "The Secret World of ISIS Brides: 'U dnt hav 2 pay 4 ANYTHING if u r wife of a martyr,'" *The Guardian* (2015, June 24): A1.

Junco, Reynol, Greg Heibergert, and Eric Loken, "The Effect of Twitter on College Student Engagement and Grades," *Journal of Computer Assisted Learning* 27, no. 2 (2011): 119–132. https://doi.org/10.1111/j.1365-2729.2010.00387.x.

Khamis, Sahar, "'*CyberHandbook of Contemporary Islam and Muslim Lives*, edited by Mark Woodward and Ronald Lukens-Bull, 1–22. New York: Springer, 2018.

Klausen, Jytte, "Tweeting the Jihad: Social Media Networks of Western Foreign Fighters in Syria and Iraq," *Studies in Conflict & Terrorism* 38, no. 1 (2015): 1–22. https://doi.org/10.1080/1057610X.2014.974948.

Kluver, Randolph, and Pauline Hope Cheong, "Technological Modernization, the Internet, and Religion in Singapore," *Journal of Computer-Mediated Communication* 12, no. 3 (2007): 1122–1242. https://doi.org/10.1111/j.1083-6101.2007.00366.x.

Kozík, Tomáš, Henryk Noga, and Jana Depešová, "The Symptoms of Postmodernism in Media and Multimedia," *European Journal of Science and Theology* 11, no. 6 (2015): 119–125.

Lara-Cabrera, Raúl, Antonio González Pardo, Karim Benouaret, Noura Faci, Djamal Benslimane, and David Camacho, "Measuring the Radicalisation Risk in Social Networks," *IEEE Access* 5 (2017): 10892–10900. https://doi.org/10.1109/ACCESS.2017.2706018.

MacEoin, Denis, "Anwar al-Awlaki: 'I Pray that Allah Destroys America'," *Middle East Quarterly* 17, no. 2 (2010): 13–19.

Mandaville, Peter, *Transnational Muslim Politics: Reimagining the Umma*. New York: Routledge, 2001.

Mandaville, Peter, "Communication and Diasporic Islam: A Virtual Ummah?," in *The Media of Diaspora*, edited by Karim H. Karim, 135–147. New York: Routledge, 2003.

Margolis, Michael, David Resnick, and Jonathan Levy, "Major Parties Dominate, Minor Parties Struggle US Elections and the Internet," in *Political Parties and the Internet: Net Gain?*, edited by Rachel Kay Gibson, Payl Nixon, and Stephen Ward, 53–69. London: Routledge, 2003.

Mascini, Peter, "Can the Violent Jihad Do without Sympathizers?," *Studies in Conflict & Terrorism* 29, no. 4 (2006): 343–357. https://doi.org/10.1080/10576100600641832.

Matusitz, Jonathan, "Cyberterrorism: Postmodern State of Chaos," *Information Security Journal: A Global Perspective* 17, no. 4 (2008): 179–187. https://doi.org/10.1080/19393550802397033.

Matusitz, Jonathan, "Intercultural Perspectives on Cyberspace: An Updated Examination," *Journal of Human Behavior in the Social Environment* 24, no. 7 (2014): 713–724. https://doi.org/10.1080/10911359.2013.849223.

Matusitz, Jonathan, *Symbolism in Terrorism: Motivation, Communication, and Behavior*. Lanham, MD: Rowman & Littlefield, 2015.

Minei, Elizabeth, and Jonathan Matusitz, "Cyberterrorist Messages and Their Effects on Targets: A Qualitative Analysis," *Journal of Human Behavior in the Social Environment* 21, no. 8 (2011): 995–1019. https://doi.org/10.1080/10911359.2011.588569.

Minei, Elizabeth, and Jonathan Matusitz, "Cyberspace as a New Arena for Terroristic Propaganda: An Updated Examination," *Poiesis & Praxis* 9, no. 1 (2012): 163–176. https://doi.org/10.1007/s10202-012-0108-3.

Nacos, Brigitte, *Mass-Mediated Terrorism: The Central Role of the Media in Terrorism and Counterterrorism*. Lanham, MD: Rowman & Littlefield, 2002.

Paz, Reuven, *Global Jihad and WMD: Between Martyrdom and Mass Destruction*. Washington, D.C.: Hudson Institute, 2005.

Post, Jerrold M., Cody McGinnis, and Kristen Moody, "The Changing Face of Terrorism in the 21st Century: The Communications Revolution and the Virtual Community of Hatred," *Behavioral Sciences & the Law* 32, no. 3 (2014): 306–334. https://doi.org/10.1002/bsl.2123.

Potter, Joshua D., and Johanna L. Dunaway, "Reinforcing or Breaking Party Systems? Internet Communication Technologies and Party Competition in Comparative Context," *Political Communication* 33, no. 3 (2016): 392–413. https://doi.org/10.1080/10584609.2015.1069767.

Prucha, Nico, "IS and the Jihadist Information Highway—Projecting Influence and Religious Identity via Telegram," *Perspectives on Terrorism* 10, no. 6 (2016): 48–58.

Rahimullah, Riyad Hosain, Stephen Larmar, and Mohamad Abdalla, "Understanding Violent Radicalization amongst Muslims: A Review of the Literature," *Journal of Psychology and Behavioral Science* 1, no. 1 (2013): 19–35.

Raneri, April, and Jonathan Matusitz, "Source Representation in the Communication of Childhood Immunisation," *Child Care in Practice* 21, no. 2 (2015): 114–127. https://doi.org/10.1080/13575279.2014.966651.

Resnick, David, "The Normalisation of Cyberspace," in *The Politics of Cyberspace*, edited by Chris Toulouse and Timothy W. Luke, 48–68. London: Routledge, 1998.

Retzkin, Sion, *Hands-On Dark Web Analysis: Learn What Goes on in the Dark Web, and How to Work with It*. Birmingham, England: Packt Publishing, 2018.

Rheingold, Howard, *The Virtual Community: Homesteading on the Electronic Frontier*. Boston: MIT Press, 1993.

Rheingold, Howard, *Smart Mobs: The Next Social Revolution*. New York: Basic Books, 2002.

Rose, Steve, "The ISIS Propaganda War: A Hi-Tech Media Jihad," *The Guardian* (2014, October 7): A1.

Roy, Olivier, *Globalized Islam: The Search for a New Ummah*. New York: Columbia University Press, 2006.

Sageman, Marc, *Leaderless Jihad: Terror Networks in the Twenty-First Century*. Philadelphia, PA: University of Pennsylvania Press, 2008.

Schmid, Alex P., and Janny De Graaf, *Violence as Communication: Insurgent Terrorism and the Western News Media*. London: Sage, 1982.

Seib, Philip, and Dana M. Janbek, *Global Terrorism and New Media: The Post-Al Qaeda Generation*. Abingdon, UK: Routledge, 2010.

Shane, Scott, and Ben Hubbard, "ISIS Displaying a Deft Command of Varied Media," *The New York Times* (2014, August 30): A1.

Simon, Jeffrey D., "Lone Wolf Terrorism: Understanding a Growing Threat," in *Lone Actors—An Emerging Security Threat*, edited by Aaron Richman and Yair Sharan, 3–10. Amsterdam: IOS Press, 2015.

Sivek, Susan Currie, "Packaging Inspiration: Al Qaeda's Digital Magazine *Inspire* in the Self-Radicalization Process," *International Journal of Communication* 7, no. 1 (2013): 584–606.

Southern, Rosalynd, "Is Web 2.0 Providing a Voice for Outsiders? A Comparison of Personal Web Site and Social Media Use by Candidates at the 2010 UK General Election," *Journal of Information Technology & Politics* 12, no. 1 (2015): 1–17. https://doi.org/10.1080/19331681.2014.972603.

Tarabay, Jamie, Gilad Shiloach, Amit Weiss, and Matan Gilat, "To Its Citizens, ISIS also Shows a Softer Side," *Vocativ* (2015, March 20): A1.

Thurston, Alexander, *Salafism in Nigeria: Islam, Preaching, and Politics*. Cambridge: Cambridge University Press, 2018.

The Times of India, "Sri Lanka Attack Mastermind Used Chatrooms to Sway Suicide Bombers," *The Times of India* (2019, May 3): A1.

Vergani, Matteo, and Dennis Zuev, "Neojihadist Visual Politics: Comparing Youtube Videos of North Caucasus and Uyghur Militants," *Asian Studies Review* 39, no. 1 (2015): 1–22. https://doi.org/10.1080/10357823.2014.976171.

Wakeford, Laura, and Laura Smith, "IS' Propaganda and the Social Media: Dissemination, Support, and Resilience," in *ISIS Propaganda: A Full-Spectrum Extremist Message*, edited by Stephane J. Baele, Katharine A. Boyd, and Travis G. Coan, 155–187. New York: Oxford University Press, 2019.

Waldmann, Peter, "The Radical Milieu: The Under-Investigated Relationship between Terrorists and Sympathetic Communities," *Perspectives on Terrorism* 2, no. 9 (2008): 25–27.

Weimann, Gabriel, "Cyber-Fatwas and Terrorism," *Studies in Conflict & Terrorism* 34, no. 10 (2011): 765–781. https://doi.org/10.1080/1057610X.2011.604831.

Weiss, Michael, and Hassan Hassan, *ISIS: Inside the Army of Terror.* New York: Simon & Schuster, 2016.

Winter, Charlie, "Apocalypse, Later: A Longitudinal Study of the Islamic State Brand," *Critical Studies in Media Communication* 35, no. 1 (2018): 103–121. https://doi.org/10.1080/15295036.2017.1393094.

Wojcieszak, Magdalena, "'Don't Talk to Me': Effects of Ideologically Homogeneous Online Groups and Politically Dissimilar Offline Ties on Extremism," *New Media & Society* 12, no. 4 (2010): 637–655. https://doi.org/10.1177/1461444809342775.

Wright, Shaun, David Denney, Alasdair Pinkerton, Vincent A. A. Jansen, and John Bryden, "Resurgent Insurgents: Quantitative Research into Jihadists Who Get Suspended but Return on Twitter," *Contemporary Voices: St Andrews Journal of International Relations* 7, no. 2 (2016): 1–13. http://doi.org/10.15664/jtr.1213.

Young, Glenn, "Reading and Praying Online: The Continuity of Religion Online and Online Religion in Internet Christianity," in *Religion Online: Finding Faith on the Internet*, edited by Lorne L. Dawson and Douglas E. Cowan, 93–106. New York: Routledge, 2004.

Zaman, Saminaz, "From Imam to Cyber-Mufti: Consuming Identity in Muslim America," *The Muslim World* 98, no. 4 (2008): 465–474. https://doi.org/10.1111/j.1478-1913.2008.00240.x.

11

JIHAD THROUGH POPULAR CULTURE

Popular music is a cultural commodity, a domain in which consumer-citizen identities are shaped, and a way for listeners to come to grips with the meanings of citizenship and dissent on a daily basis. Youths, in particular, interpret notions of the citizen through popular music, instead of the more traditional avenues of citizenship (like formal institutions or political organizations). When youths feel excluded from traditional, public venues of political participation, they may find popular music to be a type of remedy.[1] It is important to observe that the creation of cultural citizenship through a cultural commodity cannot be totally separated from relationships with the state and market, both of which play an important role in the meanings ascribed to citizenship by youths. Rebellious or unorthodox citizenship, too, can be commodified and consumed, as has been witnessed with progressive hip-hop or anti-war music (in addition to commodities like T-shirts and buttons).[2]

Within the current globalization of entertainment, popular music can be used as a universal influence to realize an agenda.[3] Social movements on the fringes of society use music (and accompanying videos) to expose people to new perspectives in socially acceptable and engaging manners.[4] Popular music is often the mouthpiece for lower- and middle-class opinions and dissatisfactions directed toward higher classes and those who exercise authority over the masses.[5] While many jihadists regard hip-hop through a negative lens (owing to its Western origins), there have also been recorded cases of hip-hop songs with pro-jihad texts or, in a reverse direction, cases whereby jihadists appropriated hip-hop or gangsta songs to lure Westerners into joining their organizations.[6]

Culture: definition

Let us begin by discussing the notion of culture. Clifford Geertz (1973)[7] defines culture as "a historically transmitted pattern of meanings embodied in symbols by means of which men communicate, perpetuate, and develop their knowledge about and attitudes toward life." Culture is a system of shared philosophies, morals, beliefs, principles, norms, rules, and expectations for human behavior. Culture also includes the symbols—both physical and nonphysical—that embody, evoke, and activate these philosophies, morals, and the like.[8] Not only is culture fluid, but it also varies from individual to individual or from group to group. "Structure" is sometimes used as a substitute for culture. Structure uses both systems (of rules and expectations for group action) and resources (to solidify power or reach objectives) in an interactive framework. Just like the fluid character of culture, structures are dynamic entities; they assume different shapes based on how systems and resources interact over time—again, among individuals or among groups.[9]

Through popular music, self-organizing jihadist groups can be framed as a type of gang, and their activities in support of global jihad and the Caliphate as a type of delinquent behavior. Jihadist organizations create structures that operate as radical milieus. In these milieus, culture, narratives, and symbols are designed to produce new individuals and groups through networks and relationships.[10] Waldmann (2005)[11] ascribes distinct and independent traits to these radical social environments; they are social units in their own right—i.e., groups of people with common perspectives and a unified identity: a culture or community. This does not imply that conflict is nonexistent between any radical milieu and the extremist or terrorist minds produced from within it. Milieus have their own agendas that can lead them to criticize and sometimes even combat their now-violent creations.[12]

Subcultures of angry people

A subculture is a group of people within a culture that separates itself from the predominant culture, sometimes preserving some of its original principles. Over time, subcultures develop their own rules and standards regarding cultural, religious, political, or ideological matters. Subcultures remain in society while attempting to protect their particular characteristics.[13] From a cultural standpoint, subcultures are both homogeneous (in terms of similarities among group members) and heterogeneous (in terms of their relationships with the outside world). Such collectivities work hard at creating constant uniqueness, identity, commitment, and independence.[14] The notion of belonging to a subculture is a crucial characteristic in the recruitment of youths within jihadist organizations. The latter could be understood as criminal subcultural groups.[15] Visual styles and manifestations of subcultural identity are a hallmark of jihadists.[16]

In many ways, subcultures are like countercultures. A counterculture is a group whose values and rules of behavior differ from those of the dominant society, but a counterculture *always* fights mainstream cultural mores in order to improve society as a whole.[17] A subculture does not necessarily fight the larger society, but in the context of this book, "subculture" is to be seen as a form of resistance. Subcultures often arise out of the existence of interests and affiliations around which cultural models develop. Confronting a waning class identity, subcultures offer new opportunities for collective identification, for the expression of symbolic resistance against the dominant culture, and for the creation of potential solutions to existential problems.[18] When subcultures sense that they are under threat from external forces, their levels of strength, unity, and interdependence increase, which also inflames their passion and commitment to resist mainstream society.

As one can see, these are the reasons for the appearance of subcultures of angry individuals: insecurity and confusion over identity. As Kinnvall (2004)[19] argues, "as individuals feel vulnerable and experience existential anxiety, is not uncommon for them to wish to reaffirm a threatened self-identity." Explained differently, individuals and collectivities that are not capable of identifying with their host or native country are relegated to the "unassimilated" category. Sooner or later, they look for like-minded people with whom they can identify. In this manner, they build a close-knit social network with different identities and objectives in life, making up a clique-like model of subculture. This pathway is often formed through feelings of revenge for real or imaginary harm inflicted upon those individuals—again, by an external threat (generally, perceived as the dominant society). This pathway comes with other psychodynamic processes, such as groupthink, an "in-group vs. out-group" attitude, and a higher inclination toward violence.[20]

Martyrdom culture

Though personal temperaments and mindsets play an important role in groupthink and group polarization, mental illness is hardly ever a cause of jihadism or ideological radicalization. Even when it comes to martyrdom operations, psychological problems—i.e., sociopathy and schizophrenia to cite a few—are virtually non-existent.[21] Rather, martyrdom culture, with its glorification of heroism and respect, is a massive motivator for suicide missions in the name of Allah. The martyr sacrifices him- or herself for the cause and carries symbols of power. Identifying a Muslim as a martyr elevates his or her death to a grand level.[22] For the *shahid*, martyrdom is saluted as the noblest of all acts, which upraises his or her status symbol in society.[23] Within the Palestinian territories like Gaza, an entire cultural structure composed of friends, kinsfolks, educators, clerics, reporters, and politicians share a deep-seated belief in the status symbol of such self-sacrifice.[24]

In *Manufacturing Human Bombs*, Mohammad Hafez (2006)[25] stresses the themes of salvation and concern for the Palestinian people; themes that often appear in the martyrs' wills, tributes, or interviews conducted before their last mission. As he argues, "suicide bombing is not only an opportunity to punish an enemy and fulfill God's command to fight injustice but also a privilege and a reward to those most committed to their faith and their values." To be selected for the ultimate sacrifice (i.e., the martyrdom operation) is "akin to receiving a stamp of approval or a certificate of accomplishment from one's peers. It is a form of endorsement of one's moral character and dedication." According to a Palestinian martyr wannabe, "I did this because of the suffering of the Palestinian people. The falling of *shuhada* [those martyred by Israeli forces] and the destruction everywhere in Palestine. I did this for God and the Palestinian people." Another said, "I believe the operation would hurt the enemy. Also [a] successful mission greatly influences society. It raises the morale of the people; they are happy, they feel strong."[26]

Acts of killing, whereby attackers are certain of their demise, defy our Western logic of human rationality to the core. Understanding martyrdom culture helps identify the particular recruiting strategies used by jihadist groups that seek to gain followers for their cause.[27] Within a jihadist group, highly dangerous behavior is a quasi-guaranteed route to status in the sense that it becomes framed as bravery and unrelenting commitment to the cause. As McCauley and Moskalenko (2009)[28] explain,

> Disproportionate involvement in risk taking and status seeking is particularly true of those young men who come from disadvantaged family backgrounds, have lower IQ levels, are of lower socioeconomic status, and who therefore have less opportunity to succeed in society along a traditional career path. These young men are more likely to be involved in gang activity, violent crime, and other high-risk behavior.

From this vantage point, martyrdom violence provides a conduit to success, social acceptance, and financial rewards that might otherwise not be available.

Jihadist videos

Solid evidence indicates that active jihadists are driven to wage global jihad through jihadist videos.[29] Music in jihadist videos gets extreme or socially unacceptable perspectives to be heard by young people especially.[30] Enter Wafa Idris, the first female suicide bomber of the Israeli–Palestinian clashes. The Palestinian Authority made Idris an instant heroine, organizing a parade in her honor with young women holding placards showing her picture and praising her with "great pride." Jihadist videos morphed images of a singing heroine into a uniformed female warrior expressing her enthusiasm to sacrifice her life as a martyr. A concert in honor of Idris was transmitted repeatedly and all-female summer camps were named after Idris (along with other female suicide terrorists).[31]

Jihadist videos are a potent tool, especially when coming from within territory deemed "Islamic." This definition is reflected in ISIS videos which, for instance, pretended to document the observation of sharia and the implementation of a lifestyle in the Caliphate under its control. Such lifestyle is regularly romanticized in salafist and salafi-jihadist literature. The widespread production and publication of videos on Twitter during 2013–2015 became a game changer, as acknowledged by a sympathizer of Ahrar al-Sham (another ISIS-like group) on Twitter: "#dangers on the path of jihad; my knowledge on jihad is based on professionally produced jihadist videos affecting the youth more than a thousand books or [religious] sermons."[32]

Although radical online content is not necessarily a sufficient source of radicalization, it contributes greatly to the complex mechanism by which ordinary web users become radicalized toward extremism.[33] At times, jihadist videos contain rich symbolism within the overlaid graphics, and inspirational music can be heard in the background.[34] Jihadist videos include scenes of what the successful ummah ought to look like: Muslim companionship and triumphant attacks, loud chants and songs, and an unequivocal invitation to "join" the GJM because it consists of brave soldiers who defend the entire ummah. Jihadist videos explain what to do and how to do it. They are motivational and communicate hope; the Infidels and Apostates can be targeted and killed notwithstanding their superior material strength. The men in jihadist videos are role models: because they can do it, any motivated Muslim can do it. Inaction, then, is shameful and should be rebuked. Is the average Muslim less a man than those role models? The Muslim companionship with a small group in holy war is clearly felt through the videos: any man can join a band of brothers. The social status of fighter is obvious: he can become a person that women admire and other men fear to confront, a man with battlefield experience and brothers with him.[35]

Case study I: jihadist videos by al-Hayat

Macnair and Frank (2017)[36] analyzed videos published by the al-Hayat Media Center, an organ of ISIS's larger media campaign directed specifically at a Western public. It was reported that al-Hayat videos are made to attract potential Western jihadists and partisans by depicting life within ISIS as religiously and existentially rewarding, while simultaneously disparaging the West as materialistic, depraved, and felonious. By using well-crafted propaganda videos that exploit the discontents of Western Muslims, al-Hayat has managed to carry a sophisticated and legitimate message that may contribute to the broader radicalization process. Three music videos, titled *Hijrah, Blood for Blood,* and *My Revenge,* were produced in a genre reflecting modern music videos. They are accompanied by rapid cuts, fast edits, and symbolism that corresponds to the lyrics of the songs. The songs in these three videos are sung in French and dubbed with English subtitles. These videos include no narration; rather, all information is communicated through lyrics and images. Lasting for four minutes on average, these videos are probably designed to be effortlessly appealing to a younger public.

For instance, with regard to the second video, *Blood for Blood,* the entire piece is a music video sung in French, dedicated to emphasizing the evil deeds that the West has committed against ISIS. During the entire video, a young boy meditatively walks through the rubble of demolished buildings as both other images and the English subtitles of the song are superimposed over the screen. The allusion is that this young boy's milieu was totally damaged by Western forces. As the boy miserably looks into the exploded buildings, finding no person alive, flashes of "enemy" rulers such as President Obama, Vladimir Putin, and Manuel Valls turn up, supplemented by the song's lyrics: "Your soldiers kill our children and you call them heroes, you show no remorse for the thousands you killed" and "You are liars and manipulators."[37]

Case study II: martyrdom videos by Hezbollah

Hezbollah is a Shia Islamist political party and terrorist organization headquartered in Lebanon. Hezbollah was launched by Muslim clerics and financed by the Islamic Republic of Iran with the chief purpose of combating the State of Israel. Its frontrunners were admirers of Ayatollah Khomeini, and its soldiers were trained by no fewer than 1,500 Revolutionary Guards.[38] Hezbollah is considered a foreign terrorist group by the United States, Israel, and the United Kingdom, among numerous other countries. On October 23, 1983, during the First Lebanon War, two of its suicide terrorists exploded truck bombs at U.S. Marine barracks in Beirut, an attack that claimed the lives of 241 U.S. and 58 French servicemen.[39]

A martyrdom video is a video production (usually from jihad activists) that extolls the virtues of participating in suicide missions and subsequently experiencing an "honorable" death. The videos are of lower standard, though they have been known to include text, music, and sentimental/emotional segments. The average martyrdom video opens with a prerecorded "farewell" testament delivered by the martyr-to-be (with a black Islamic flag behind him or her).[40] Hezbollah is notoriously prolific in its creation of martyrdom videos to enhance more local support.[41] In this fashion, a martyrdom video becomes a visual medium located within many media-soaked cultural, social, and political contexts.[42] This approach to suicide missions is not new at all; nor are claims of the jihadists' obligation to defend the ummah overall. Nevertheless, Hezbollah's approach is distinct in its widespread use of video clips that circulate on the internet and the online pressure placed on jihadists to embark on the global jihad bandwagon. The jihadist media establishment is well aware of this.[43]

Hezbollah's martyrdom culture has helped maintain the organization's dreams of supremacy since the organization's founding. In the fall of 2016, Arabipress, Hezbollah's online media branch, published a music video in which a male youth serenaded, "For you, my mother," overly dramatizing their close-knit connection and her response to his ultimate martyrdom. Often, Hezbollah's media branch quotes a song by Marcel Khalife (a famous Lebanese performer) to honor the group's martyrs' mothers. An example is "ajmal al omahat" (i.e., the most beautiful mother). These excerpts are not merely rhetorical schemes; they also fulfill a strategic aim. Thanks to martyrdom videos, Hezbollah exploits the persona of a fallen soldier's mother to uphold a culture of martyrdom that encourages and invigorates the idea of fighting the holy war. This has been noticeable throughout the group's history and even today.[44]

Hezbollah's martyrdom videos are a frequent reminder of the triumphs of the party's military faction and of the power that they like to flaunt to their constituents in Lebanon and the Arab world. An important target audience is the Israeli audience. In fact, the Al-Manar channel, Hezbollah's sponsored satellite television channel, began broadcasting via satellite in 2000.[45] Al-Manar broadcasts from Beirut.[46] The propelling of Al-Manar via satellite decisively corresponded to the date of Liberation Day—i.e., the liberation of the South of Lebanon on May 25, 2000 (when the IDF withdrew from the territory). Al-Manar broadcasted a program focusing on a special coverage of the liberation.[47]

Death is unsurprisingly the biggest anathema in war propaganda. Yet, it is amazing to realize how explicitly death is extolled in jihadist media. The martyr cult turns the taboo into a domain where the liminal space that separates life and death can be discovered. As the martyr is not dead but, rather, living with Allah (see Quran 3:169), the bodies and even their images are searched for indicators or symbols of this ethereal life. The images of martyrs embody concepts of both death and eternal life.[48] Pictures of obviously dead heroes are not only proof of the wounding and death of a mujahedin; they also impart a narrative rooted in the Salafist tradition surrounding martyrdom. Here, the blood spilled in the beginning of the martyrdom operation signifies the redemption of one's sins which, based on a hadith, occurs "with the first spurt of his blood." At the same time, the set of wounds and cut limbs symbolize one's readiness to make sacrifices.[49]

Pop-jihad

Pop-jihad is a musical genre that glorifies jihad by including intentionally con-troversial lyrics. Heavily inspired by everyday situations and individual experiences, pop-jihad is politicized and included Islamic issues to relay doctrinal messages to the audience. Pop-jihadists seek to convert their listeners and give an aura of authenticity through their alleged life experiences and biographies.[50] Pop-jihad claims to offer a remedy to perceived unproductive and pointless life and lays out clear differences between good and evil. Such violent form of pop music provides "solutions" to disillusionment or exclusion from mainstream society (whether in the educational, social, or political environment). With pop-jihad songs, individual recruits get acquainted with an élite which challenges humiliation and degradation, and instructs to "fight back" to defend justice. When listeners become involved in pop-jihad on a daily basis, they may come to believe that, now, they have higher self-esteem, an explanation as to why they are willing to join global jihad so they can be part of that élite group. Pop-jihad will use marketing and merchandizing techniques catered to youth culture, such as outfits, T-shirts, and other cultural materials. Pop-jihad not only indulges in Salafist paranoia; it is also anti-American in spirit and content. Taken as a whole, it is useful vehicle to gain sympathy and recruits for the global Caliphate.[51]

In 2006, a member of the group Fun-Da-Mental, Aki Nawaz, released an album with lyrics that likened Osama bin Laden to Che Guevara and that portrayed the Statue of Liberty as an Abu Ghraib detainee.[52] Related posts on social media refer to Tupac Shakur, the renowned gangsta rapper killed in 1996, as one of "them." To this point, several Belgian foreign fighters for ISIS identify with Tupac Shakur's life and his rap lyrics, which bears striking resemblance with the world outlook of pop-jihadists.[53] Another rap group that falls into the same camp is Mujahideen Team, made up of Puerto Rican Muslims from Brooklyn and Boston. Mujahideen Team quickly gained notoriety in some Muslim circles. In 2006–2007, they were featured at a conference co-hosted by the Islamic Circle of North America and the Muslim American Society. They have given music performances in Atlanta, Cleveland, and San Diego, among other cities.[54] Nicknamed Jihadi John, British-based Abdel-Majed Abdel Bary was a rapper under the assumed name L Jinny. Son of Egyptian militant Adel Abdel Bari, he allegedly recorded the beheading of journalists James Foley and Steven Sotloff on video. L Jinny even tweeted a picture of himself holding a person's severed head aloft, with the inscription "Chillin' with my homie or what's left of him." This type of rapper's behavior has inspired certain jihadist atrocities.[55]

Deso Dogg

Also known as Abu-Maleeq, Deso Dogg was a German rapper who actively participated in jihad before losing his life to a U.S. airstrike in Syria in January 2018.[56] Abandoning his music career for a career in militant Islam, Deso Dogg (born Denis Cuspert) traveled to Syria in 2012 and pledged allegiance to ISIS in 2014. The U. S. State Department soon designated Cuspert as an international terrorist: "Cuspert is 'emblematic of the type of foreign recruit' ISIS seeks, has been a 'willing pitchman' for the organization's 'atrocities' and as such been officially designated as a 'foreign terrorist fighter and operative'."[57] A 21-year-old man from Kosovo was inspired by Deso Dogg's lyrics to open fire on a U.S. military bus in Frankfurt, killing two servicemen in the process.[58]

The role of communication in terrorism examines new meanings within traditional cultures or subcultures. Deso Dogg's YouTube videos embody visual jihadism by way of repetition of semantic elements. In some videos, he turns up as gangsta rapper. His videos bear titles such as *Gangsta Inferno, Willkommen in meiner Welt* (meaning "Welcome to my world"). In other videos, Deso Dogg is dressed like an archetypical jihadist, wearing camouflage or black clothes, and brandishing the black standard of ISIS. The camouflage suit is an attire frequently worn by rappers and the ISIS uniform is purposely oversized to look like a rapper's outfit. Deso Dogg liked to include traditional clothing elements such as the *keffiyeh*. The *keffiyeh* is reminiscent of the PLO from the 1970s to 1990s. Many of his videos were propaganda visuals with state-of-the-art colored graphics that promulgated ISIS's global dream.[59]

There is a clear connection between visuality and extremist propaganda. As Volosinov (1973)[60] explains, "the domain of ideology coincides with the domain of signs (semiology) as they equate with one another. Whenever a sign is present, ideology is present too. Everything ideological possesses a semiotic value." Jihadist videos are produced in a professional, up-to-date fashion. The targeted audience is mostly the Western youth of Muslim origin. The purposes are proselytization, brainwashing, recruitment, and self-recruitment. Many videos feature the head or body of the enemy, who is to be totally annihilated. The enemy is portrayed in non-human or subhuman terms. It often consists of Occidental politicians and citizens, anyone whom ISIS believes should be a target.[61]

"Dirty Kuffar"

Pop-jihad reached a pinnacle in 2004 when the song "Dirty Kuffar" was released. Created and performed by Sheikh Terra and the Soul Salah Crew, "Dirty Kuffar" is a controversial pop-jihad video. The video begins with a CNN clip displaying an image of U.S. troops getting exhilarated at the shooting down of an unarmed Iraqi man, afterwards bragging: "Hell, yeah, it was awesome. Let's do it again." The words "Dirty Kuffar murder innocent Iraqi civilian" also turn up against a black backdrop.[62] Subsequently in the clip, a logo appears, "Digihad," a port-manteau of Digital and Jihad.[63] Owing to the success of "Dirty Kuffar," an unquestionable trend toward pop-jihad followed. As opposed to any other con-troversial rap or hip-hop song, "Dirty Kuffar" immediately made the mainstream media news upon its release in 2004 (even internationally). Since its release, "Dirty Kuffar" has been downloaded onto several millions of computers and remixed by a great many pro-jihadists. The video can still be found on video-sharing sites such as YouTube.[64]

Heuston (2005)[65] noted that "Dirty Kuffar" drew the attention of the global media establishment soon after becoming available for free download on the internet. The video also mixes music with elements of martyrdom videos produced by Islamist suicide bombers before blowing themselves up. "Dirty Kuffar" perso-nalized a new trend of jihadist activism that edits and manipulates videos of the 9/11 attacks, videos of terrorist training, and even videos of Daniel Pearl's execu-tion—all of which is done for recruiting purposes. Jihadist videos even teach ter-rorism skills (including bomb-making instructions, assassination recommendations, and hostage-taking techniques); they encourage their viewers to plot new attacks.

Jihadist nasheeds

A long-established musical genre, a nasheed is a spiritual hymn devoted to worship Allah, express authentic religious sentiments, or invite others to worship Islam.[66] In practical terms, a nasheed is a type of vocal music sung *a cappella* or supplemented with percussion instruments like the *daf*, a hefty Middle Eastern frame drum common in popular and classical music.[67] Islamic nasheeds do not include lamel-laphone music, string instruments, or wind and brass instruments, though digital remastering to imitate percussion instruments or produce overtones is allowed.[68]

Jihadist nasheeds are radical Islamist hymns as an expression of jihadist culture.[69] The jihadist nasheed surfaced in the late 1970s and early 1980s during an epoch of Islamic revival in the Middle East. Afterwards, Salafism's stringent views on music determined the spirit and substance of jihadi nasheeds, which explains why their *a cappella* structure consists of one or several men's voices.[70] Four main categories are found within jihadist nasheeds: "battle hymns" (focusing on holy war); "martyr hymns" (emphasizing martyrdom); "mourning hymns" (lamenting the death of a brother or sister); and "praising hymns" (honoring high-standing people). Other types exist too, the most widespread being nasheeds focused on particular fighters, wars, prisoners, and martyrs' widows or mothers.[71]

A conduit of jihadism

Nasheeds are an efficient communicative conduit of jihadism as they concentrate on a specific number of themes with broad appeal to the ummah.[72] They have been utilized as a blueprint for social revolution through extreme violence. They are frequently heard at social events like weddings and gatherings before a battle (to boost morale). They are often downloaded as audio files on jihadist websites. More importantly, however, they are widely accessible on video-sharing sites like You-Tube. Unlike more violent jihadist content, nasheeds are less often taken down from these sites. This, in part, explains why they are among the most popular jihadist content in the jihadisphere.[73]

ISIS's media productivity is unrivaled by any other jihadist organization. This productivity is central to ISIS's strategy because it diffuses the group's political messaging designed to strike fear within the hearts of its enemies and gain new followers. ISIS's jihadist nasheeds are downloaded by individual fighters and supporters as well as the Ajnad Media Foundation, ISIS's foundation for Arabic language media, especially audio materials in several Arabic dialects. Established in 2013, its purpose is to create and disseminate audio recordings such as nasheeds. The audiences of ISIS's propaganda can be classified into enemies, the population that needs to be converted, and supporters (including active members, possible recruits, propagandists, proselytizers, and recruiters).[74] According to Winter (2015),[75] ISIS's messaging consists of six related themes: cruelty, victimhood, compassion, war, social membership, and apocalyptic millennialism.

In the most visited jihadist forums, there are special segments for *sautiyat* (audios), where virtually all types of nasheeds are available, sometimes even whole sections with over 400 tracks. The website of the "Islamic Emirate of Afghanistan" (Taliban) features extremist songs, which they call *tarana* ("ballad" in Pastho and Dari). In addition to forums and websites, jihadist nasheeds are distributed via ringtones for smartphones. In many cases, jihadist nasheeds are produced in Arabic, but one can occasionally listen to them in other languages too—including Pashto, Urdu, Turkish, and Bosnian, as well as English, German, and Dutch. What this demonstrates is that jihadist groups will use any means to reach out to the ummah in order become the paragon of global jihadism.[76]

A bricolage

Developed by Hall and Jefferson (1976),[77] the notion of *bricolage* explains how groups restructure their style to convey new meanings. Different subcultural forms allow youth to become more prominent and distinguish themselves from their peers. "Object and meaning," Hall and Jefferson continue, "constitute a sign, and, within any one culture, such signs are assembled, repeatedly, into characteristic forms of discourse."[78] *Bricolage* entails practices and ideas like cultural appropriation, hybridity, mélange, and plagiarism. Many scholars[79] in media and cultural studies employ *bricolage* when depicting the mixture, re-organization, and reusing of different objects, actions, concepts, signs, symbols, and genres in order to produce novel insights or meanings.

From a semantic perspective, jihadist videos that feature nasheeds are a type of *bricolage*. They amalgamate traditional cultural aspects with pop-jihad lyrics that resonate with Western youths, such as European Muslims.[80] The semantic parts of jihadist nasheeds, like dresses and outfit, are combined to form new elements, like a jihadist uniform. Hence, *bricolage* emerges out of a union between a conventional subculture and a new subculture. *Bricolage* can be looked at as a discourse between normative codes and individual characters, which makes jihadism more accessible to the youth.[81] Numerous jihadist subcultures amply use *bricolage* through nasheeds in that the meaning of conventional artifacts and symbols (or those regarding other subcultures) is coopted and united with the respective "Islamic" or "national" ideological positions.[82] Dantschke (2013)[83] found that,

> a central role within "pop-jihad" is played by "battle-nasheeds" with highly militant lyrics. These nasheeds are traditional chants focusing on the lyrics and thus providing the possibility to connect with the youth rap and hip-hop cultures of the 1990s and early 2000s.

In a certain number of jihadist nasheeds, music themes are a mélange of the classic historical Muslim themes with Straight Edge, Animal Rights, or Anti Capitalism. Other examples include symbols like the Antifa flag and English-speaking slogans such as "We will rock you" and "Fuck the law!"[84] Classic historical Muslim themes include the message of the Prophet Muhammad (e.g., the "word of the sword") and the accompanying necessity of bloodshed until the ummah can fulfill its dream of justice and prosperity.[85]

Notes

1 Nestor García Canclini, *Consumers and Citizens: Globalization and Multicultural Conflicts* (Minneapolis, MN: University of Minnesota Press, 2001).
2 Sunaina Maira, "Citizenship and Dissent: South Asian Muslim Youth in the US after 9/11," *South Asian Popular Culture* 8, no. 1 (2010): 31–45. https://doi.org/10.1080/14746681003633135
3 Jonathan Matusitz and Pam Payano, "Globalisation of Popular Culture: From Hollywood to Bollywood," *South Asia Research* 32, no. 2 (2012): 123–38. https://doi.org/10.1177/0262728012453977
4 Marjie T. Britz, "Terrorism and Technology: Operationalizing Cyberterrorism and Identifying Concepts," in *Crime Online: Correlates, Causes, and Context*, ed. Tom Holt (Raleigh, NC: Caroline Academic Press, 2010): 193–220.

5 Michael T. Putnam, "Music as a Weapon: Reactions and Responses to RAF Terrorism in the Music of Ton Steine Scherben and Their Successors in Post-9/11 Music," *Popular Music and Society* 32, no. 5 (2009): 595–606. https://doi.org/10.1080/03007760903251417

6 Tuncay Kardaş, and Ömer Behram Özdemir, "The Making of European Foreign Fighters: Identity, *Social Media and Virtual Radicalization,*" in *Non-State Armed Actors in the Middle East*, ed. Murat Yeşiltaş and Tuncay Kardaş (New York: Palgrave Macmillan, 2018): 213–35.

7 Clifford Geertz, "Religion as a Cultural System," in *The Interpretation of Cultures: Selected Essays*, ed. Clifford Geertz (New York: Basic, 1973): 87–125, 89.

8 Wendy Griswold, *Cultures and Societies in a Changing World* (Thousand Oaks, CA: Pine Forge Press, 1994).

9 William H. Sewell, "A Theory of Structure: Duality, Agency, and Transformation," *American Journal of Sociology* 98, no. 1 (1992): 1–29. https://doi.org/10.1086/229967

10 Peter Waldmann, "The Radical Milieu: The Under-Investigated Relationship between Terrorists and Sympathetic Communities," *Perspectives on Terrorism* 2, no. 9 (2008): 25–7.

11 Peter Waldmann, "The Radical Community: A Comparative Analysis of the Social Background of ETA, IRA, and Hezbollah," *Sociologus* 55, no. 2 (2005): 239–57.

12 Maura Conway, "From al-Zarqawi to al-Awlaki: The Emergence of the Internet as a New Form of Violent Radical Milieu," *Combating Terrorism Exchange* 2, no. 4 (2012): 12–22.

13 Ken Gelder, *Subcultures: Cultural Histories and Social Practice* (New York: Routledge, 2007); Michel Maffesoli, *The Time of the Tribes: The Decline of Individualism in Mass Society* (London: Sage, 1996).

14 Ethan Watters, *Urban Tribes: A Generation Redefines Friendship, Family, and Commitment* (London: Bloomsbury, 2003).

15 Uliano Conti, "Between Rap and Jihad: Spectacular Subcutlures, Terrorism and Visuality," *Contemporary Social Science* 12, no. 3 (2017): 272–84. https://doi.org/10.1080/21582041.2017.1385828

16 Ibid., 281.

17 Ken Goffman, *Counterculture through the Ages* (New York: Villard Books, 2004).

18 Stuart Hall and Tony Jefferson, *Resistance through Rituals: Youth Subcultures in Post-War Britain* (New York: Routledge, 1976).

19 Catarina Kinnvall, "Globalization and Religious Nationalism: Self, Identity, and the Search for Ontological Security," *Political Psychology* 25, no. 5 (2004): 741–67, 742. https://doi.org/10.1111/j.1467-9221.2004.00396.x

20 Marc Sageman, *Understanding Terror Networks* (Philadelphia: University of Pennsylvania Press, 2004).

21 Robert Pape, *Dying to Win: The Strategic Logic of Suicide Terrorism* (New York: Random House, 2005).

22 Michael Barkun, "Appropriated Martyrs: The Branch Davidians and the Radical Right," *Terrorism and Political Violence* 19, no. 1 (2007): 117–24. https://doi.org/10.1080/09546550601054956

23 Jonathan Matusitz, *Symbolism in Terrorism: Motivation, Communication, and Behavior* (Lanham, MD: Rowman & Littlefield, 2015).

24 Giovanni Caracci, "Cultural and Contextual Aspects of Terrorism," in *The Psychology of Terrorism: Theoretical Underpinnings and Perspectives*, ed. Chris Stout (London: Praeger, 2002): 57–83.

25 Mohammed Hafez, *Manufacturing Human Bombs: The Making of Palestinian Suicide Bombers* (Washington, D.C.: United States Institute of Peace Press, 2006): 44.

26 Cited in Hafez, ibid., 50.

27 Taylor Armstrong and Jonathan Matusitz, "Hezbollah as a Group Phenomenon: Differential Association Theory," *Journal of Human Behavior in the Social Environment* 23, no. 4 (2013): 475–84. https://doi.org/10.1080/10911359.2013.772425; Kari Olechowicz and Jonathan Matusitz, "The Motivations of Islamic Martyrs: Applying the Collective Effort Model," *Current Psychology* 32, no. 4 (2013): 338–47. https://doi.org/10.1007/s12144-013-9187-0

28 Clark McCauley and Sophia Moskalenko, *Friction: How Radicalization Happens to Them and Us* (New York: Oxford University Press, 2009): 62.
29 For example, see Thomas Hegghammer, *Jihadi Culture: The Art and Social Practices of Militant Islamists* (Cambridge: Cambridge University Press, 2017).
30 Tom Holt, Joshua D. Freilich, Steven Chermak, and Clark McCauley, "Political Radicalization on the Internet: Extremist Content, Government Control, and the Power of Victim and Jihad Videos," *Dynamics of Asymmetric Conflict* 8, no. 2 (2015): 107–20. https://doi.org/10.1080/17467586.2015.1065101
31 Cited in Terri Toles Patkin, "Explosive Baggage: Female Palestinian Suicide Bombers and the Rhetoric of Emotion," *Women and Language* 27, no. 2 (2004): 79–88.
32 Cited in Nico Prucha, "IS and the Jihadist Information Highway—Projecting Influence and Religious Identity via Telegram," *Perspectives on Terrorism* 10, no. 6 (2016): 48–58, 49.
33 Alexander Meleagrou-Hitchens, Audrey Alexander, and Nick Kaderbhai, "Literature Review: The Impact of Digital Communications Technology on Radicalization and Recruitment," *International Affairs* 93, no. 5 (2017): 1233–49. https://doi.org/10.1093/ia/iix103
34 Tom Quiggin, "Contemporary Jihadist Narratives: The Case of Momin Khawaja," in *Countering Violent Extremist Narratives*, ed. Eelco J. A. M. Kessels (Breda, Netherlands: National Coordinator for Counter Terrorism, 2010): 84–93.
35 Holt, Freilich, Chermak, and McCauley, "Political Radicalization on the Internet," 115.
36 Logan Macnair and Richard Frank, "'To My Brothers in the West…': A Thematic Analysis of Videos Produced by the Islamic State's al-Hayat Media Center," *Journal of Contemporary Criminal Justice* 33, no. 3 (2017): 234–53. https://doi.org/10.1177/1043986217699313
37 Ibid., 245.
38 Matthew Levitt, *Hezbollah: The Global Footprint of Lebanon's Party of God* (Washington, D.C.: Georgetown University Press).
39 Jonathan Matusitz, "Brand Management in Terrorism: The Case of Hezbollah," *Journal of Policing, Intelligence and Counter Terrorism* 13, no. 1 (2018): 1–16. https://doi.org/10.1080/18335330.2017.1412489
40 Jonathan Matusitz, "Communication of Terrorism: Social Noise, the Signature Method, and the Conduit Metaphor," *Journal of Applied Security Research* 13, no. 4 (2018): 455–72. https://doi.org/10.1080/19361610.2018.1498258
41 Pape, *Dying to Win*, 10–5.
42 Johanna Sumiala and Lilly Korpiola, "Mediated Muslim Martyrdom: Rethinking Digital Solidarity in the 'Arab Spring'," *New Media & Society* 19, no. 1 (2017): 52–66. https://doi.org/10.1177/1461444816649918
43 Mina Al-Lami, Andrew Hoskins, and Ben O'Loughlin, "Mobilisation and Violence in the New Media Ecology: The Dua Khalil Aswad and Camilia Shehata Cases," *Critical Studies on Terrorism* 5, no. 2 (2012): 237–56. https://doi.org/10.1080/17539153.2012.692509
44 Kendall Bianchi, "Letters from Home: Hezbollah Mothers and the Culture of Martyrdom," *CTC Sentinel* 11, no. 2 (2018): 20–4.
45 Walid el Houri and Dima Saber, "Filming Resistance: A Hezbollah Strategy," *Radical History Review* 106 (2010): 70–85. https://doi.org/10.1215/01636545-2009-021
46 Avi Jorisch, "Al-Manar: Hizbullah TV, 24/7," *Middle East Quarterly* 11, no. 1 (2004): 17–31.
47 el Houri and Saber, "Filming Resistance," 84.
48 Silvia Horsch, "Making Salvation Visible. Rhetorical and Visual Representations of Martyrs in Salafi Jihadist Media," in *Martyrdom in the Modern Middle East*, ed. Sasha Dehghani and Silvia Horsch (Baden-Baden, Germany: Nomos Verlagsgesellschaft, 2014): 141–66.
49 Ibid., 159.
50 Claudia Dantschke, *"Pop-Jihad:" History and Structure of Salafism and Jihadism in Germany* (Berlin: Institute for the Study of Radical Movements, 2013).

51 Nina Wiedl, *The Making of a German Salafiyya. The Emergence, Development and Missionary Work of Salafi Movements in Germany* (Aarhus, Denmark: Centre for Studies in Islamism and Radicalization, 2012).
52 Ted Swedenburg, "Fun^Da^Mental's 'Jihad Rap'," in *Being Young and Muslim: New Cultural Politics in the Global South and North*, ed. Linda Herrera and Asef Bayat (New York: Oxford University Press, 2010): 291–307.
53 Coolsaet, *What Drives Europeans to Syria, and to IS?*, 19.
54 Putnam, "Music as a Weapon," 605.
55 Richard Spencer, "A Journey into the Mind of 'Jihadi John'," *The Telegraph* (2014, September 4): A1.
56 Rick Noack and Souad Mekhennet, "German Officials Believe Rapper-Turned-Militant Denis Cuspert Has Been Killed," *The Washington Post* (2015, January 19): A1.
57 Cited in Lisa Blaker, "The Islamic State's Use of Online Social Media," *Military Cyber Affairs* 1, no. 1 (2015): Article 4.
58 Jack Ewing and Elisabeth Bumiller, "Shooting at Germany Airport Kills 2 U.S. Airmen," *The New York Times* (2011, March 3): A4.
59 Conti, "Between Rap and Jihad," 275–9.
60 Ladislav Matejka Volosinov, *Marxism and the Philosophy of Language* (New York: Seminar Press, 1973): 79.
61 Conti, "Between Rap and Jihad," 277.
62 Mehrak Golestan, "Dirty Kuffar," *Index on Censorship* 33, no. 3 (2004): 8–10. https://doi.org/10.1080/03064220408537364?journalCode=rioc20
63 Gary R. Bunt, *IMuslims: Rewiring the House of Islam* (Chapel Hill: University of North Carolina Press, 2009).
64 Travis Morris, *Dark Ideas: How Neo-Nazi and Violent Jihadi Ideologues Shaped Modern Terrorism* (Lanham, MD: Lexington Books, 2017).
65 Sean Heuston, "Weapons of Mass Instruction: Terrorism, Propaganda Film, Politics, and Us: New Media, New Meanings," *Studies in Popular Culture* 27, no. 3 (2005): 59–73.
66 Michael Frishkopf, "Inshad Dini and Aghani Diniyya in Twentieth Century Egypt: A Review of Styles, Genres, and Available Recordings," *Middle East Studies Association Bulletin* 34, no. 2 (2000): 167–83. https://doi.org/10.1017/S0026318400040396
67 Veronica Doubleday, "The Frame Drum in the Middle East: Women, Musical Instruments and Power," *Ethnomusicology* 43, no. 1 (1999): 101–34. https://doi.org/10.2307/852696
68 Sharon Yin Zi Chong, I-Wei Foo, James Lai Hock Yeow, Geraldine Ming Ming Law, and Johnson Stanslas, "The Birth of the Malaysian Society for Music in Medicine: A Concerted Move to Promote the Use of Music for Therapeutic Purposes," *Music and Medicine: An Interdisciplinary Journal* 6, no. 1 (2014): 10–21.
69 Behnam Said, "Hymns (Nasheeds): A Contribution to the Study of the Jihadist Culture," *Studies in Conflict & Terrorism* 35, no. 12 (2012): 863–79. https://doi.org/10.1080/1057610X.2012.720242
70 Gilbert Ramsay, *Jihadi Culture on the World Wide Web* (London: Bloomsbury Publishing, 2013).
71 Said, "Hymns (Nasheeds)," 871.
72 Henrik Gråtrud, "Islamic State Nasheeds as Messaging Tools," *Studies in Conflict & Terrorism* 39, no. 12 (2016): 1050–70. https://doi.org/10.1080/1057610X.2016.1159429
73 Jonas Otterbeck, "Wahhabi Ideology of Social Control versus a New Publicness in Saudi Arabia," *Contemporary Islam* 6, no. 3 (2012): 341–53. https://doi.org/10.1007/s11562-012-0223-x
74 Daniel Milton, "The Islamic State: An Adaptive Organization Facing Increasing Challenges," in *The Group That Calls Itself a State: Understanding the Evolution and Challenges of the Islamic State*, ed. Bryan Price, Daniel Milton, Muhammad al-'Ubaydi, and Nelly Lahoud (West Point, NY: Combating Terrorism Center, 2014).
75 Charlie Winter, *The Virtual "Caliphate:" Understanding Islamic State's Propaganda Strategy* (London: Quilliam Foundation, 2015): 32.

76 Said, "Hymns (Nasheeds)," 864.
77 Hall and Jefferson, *Resistance through Rituals*, 175–7.
78 Ibid., 177.
79 See Mark Deuze, "Participation, Remediation, Bricolage: Considering Principal Components of a Digital Culture," *The Information Society* 22, no. 2 (2006): 63–75. https://doi.org/10.1080/01972240600567170; John Hartley, *Communication, Cultural and Media Studies: The Key Concepts* (3rd Ed.) (London: Routledge, 2002).
80 Conti, "Between Rap and Jihad," 278.
81 Ibid., 280.
82 Daniela Pisoiu, "Subcultural Theory Applied to Jihadi and Right-Wing Radicalization in Germany," *Terrorism and Political Violence* 27, no. 1 (2015): 9–28. https://doi.org/10.1080/09546553.2014.959406
83 Dantschke, *"Pop-Jihad"*, 14.
84 Pisoiu, "Subcultural Theory Applied to Jihadi," 18.
85 Chase Laurelle Knowles, "Towards a New Web Genre: Islamist Neorealism," *Journal of War & Culture Studies* 1, no. 3 (2008): 357–80. https://doi.org/10.1386/jwcs.1.3.357_1

References

Al-Lami, Mina, Andrew Hoskins, and Ben O'Loughlin, "Mobilisation and Violence in the New Media Ecology: The Dua Khalil Aswad and Camilia Shehata Cases," *Critical Studies on Terrorism* 5, no. 2 (2012): 237–256. https://doi.org/10.1080/17539153.2012.692509.

Armstrong, Taylor, and Jonathan Matusitz, "Hezbollah as a Group Phenomenon: Differential Association Theory," *Journal of Human Behavior in the Social Environment* 23, no. 4 (2013): 475–484. https://doi.org/10.1080/10911359.2013.772425.

Barkun, Michael, "Appropriated Martyrs: The Branch Davidians and the Radical Right," *Terrorism and Political Violence* 19, no. 1 (2007): 117–124. https://doi.org/10.1080/09546550601054956.

Bianchi, Kendall, "Letters from Home: Hezbollah Mothers and the Culture of Martyrdom," *CTC Sentinel* 11, no. 2 (2018): 20–24.

Blaker, Lisa, "The Islamic State's Use of Online Social Media," *Military Cyber Affairs* 1, no. 1 (2015): article 4.

Britz, Marjie T., "Terrorism and Technology: Operationalizing Cyberterrorism and Identifying Concepts," in *Crime Online: Correlates, Causes, and Context*, edited by Tom Holt, 193–220. Raleigh, NC: Caroline Academic Press, 2010.

Bunt, Gary R., *IMuslims: Rewiring the House of Islam*. Chapel Hill, NC: University of North Carolina Press, 2009.

Canclini, Nestor García, *Consumers and Citizens: Globalization and Multicultural Conflicts*. Minneapolis, MN: University of Minnesota Press, 2001.

Caracci, Giovanni, "Cultural and Contextual Aspects of Terrorism," in *The Psychology of Terrorism: Theoretical Underpinnings and Perspectives*, edited by Chris Stout, 57–83. London: Praeger, 2002.

Chong, Sharon Yin Zi, I-Wei Foo, James Lai Hock Yeow, Geraldine Ming Ming Law, and Johnson Stanslas, "The Birth of the Malaysian Society for Music in Medicine: A Concerted Move to Promote the Use of Music for Therapeutic Purposes," *Music and Medicine: An Interdisciplinary Journal* 6, no. 1 (2014): 10–21.

Conti, Uliano, "Between Rap and Jihad: Spectacular Subcutlures, Terrorism and Visuality," *Contemporary Social Science* 12, no. 3 (2017): 272–284. https://doi.org/10.1080/21582041.2017.1385828.

Conway, Maura, "From al-Zarqawi to al-Awlaki: The Emergence of the Internet as a New Form of Violent Radical Milieu," *Combating Terrorism Exchange* 2, no. 4 (2012): 12–22.

Dantschke, Claudia, *"Pop-Jihad:" History and Structure of Salafism and Jihadism in Germany*. Berlin: Institute for the Study of Radical Movements, 2013.

Deuze, Mark, "Participation, Remediation, Bricolage: Considering Principal Components of a Digital Culture," *The Information Society* 22, no. 2 (2006): 63–75. https://doi.org/10. 1080/01972240600567170.

Doubleday, Veronica, "The Frame Drum in the Middle East: Women, Musical Instruments and Power," *Ethnomusicology* 43, no. 1 (1999): 101–134. https://doi.org/10.2307/852696.

el Houri, Walid, and Dima Saber, "Filming Resistance: A Hezbollah Strategy," *Radical History Review* 106 (2010): 70–85. https://doi.org/10.1215/01636545-2009-021.

Ewing, Jack, and Elisabeth Bumiller, "Shooting at Germany Airport Kills 2 U.S. Airmen," *The New York Times* (2011, March 3): A4.

Frishkopf, Michael, "Inshad Dini and Aghani Diniyya in Twentieth Century Egypt: A Review of Styles, Genres, and Available Recordings," *Middle East Studies Association Bulletin* 34, no. 2 (2000): 167–183. https://doi.org/10.1017/S0026318400040396.

Geertz, Clifford, "Religion as a Cultural System," in *The Interpretation of Cultures: Selected Essays*, edited by Clifford Geertz, 87–125. New York: Basic, 1973.

Gelder, Ken, *Subcultures: Cultural Histories and Social Practice*. New York: Routledge, 2007.

Goffman, Ken, *Counterculture through the Ages*. New York: Villard Books, 2004.

Golestan, Mehrak, "Dirty Kuffar," *Index on Censorship* 33, no. 3 (2004): 8–10. https://doi. org/10.1080/03064220408537364?journalCode=rioc20.

Gråtrud, Henrik, "Islamic State Nasheeds as Messaging Tools," *Studies in Conflict & Terrorism* 39, no. 12 (2016): 1050–1070. https://doi.org/10.1080/1057610X.2016.1159429.

Griswold, Wendy, *Cultures and Societies in a Changing World*. Thousand Oaks, CA: Pine Forge Press, 1994.

Hafez, Mohammed, *Manufacturing Human Bombs: The Making of Palestinian Suicide Bombers*. Washington, D.C.: United States Institute of Peace Press, 2006.

Hall, Stuart, and Tony Jefferson, *Resistance through Rituals: Youth Subcultures in Post-War Britain*. New York: Routledge, 1976.

Hartley, John, *Communication, Cultural and Media Studies: The Key Concepts* (3rd ed.). London: Routledge, 2002.

Hegghammer, Thomas, *Jihadi Culture: The Art and Social Practices of Militant Islamists*. Cambridge: Cambridge University Press, 2017.

Heuston, Sean, "Weapons of Mass Instruction: Terrorism, Propaganda Film, Politics, and Us: New Media, New Meanings," *Studies in Popular Culture* 27, no. 3 (2005): 59–73.

Holt, Tom, Joshua D.Freilich, StevenChermak, and Clark McCauley, "Political Radicalization on the Internet: Extremist Content, Government Control, and the Power of Victim and Jihad Videos," *Dynamics of Asymmetric Conflict* 8, no. 2 (2015): 107–120. https://doi. org/10.1080/17467586.2015.1065101.

Horsch, Silvia, "Making Salvation Visible. Rhetorical and Visual Representations of Martyrs in Salafi Jihadist Media," in *Martyrdom in the Modern Middle East*, edited by Sasha Dehghani and Silvia Horsch, 141–166. Baden-Baden, Germany: Nomos Verlagsgesellschaft, 2014.

Jorisch, Avi, "Al-Manar: Hizbullah TV, 24/7," *Middle East Quarterly* 11, no. 1 (2004): 17–31.

Kardaş, Tuncay, and Ömer Behram Özdemir, "The Making of European Foreign Fighters: Identity, Social Media and Virtual Radicalization," in *Non-State Armed Actors in the Middle East*, edited by Murat Yeşiltaş and Tuncay Kardaş, 213–235. New York: Palgrave Macmillan, 2018.

Kinnvall, Catarina, "Globalization and Religious Nationalism: Self, Identity, and the Search for Ontological Security," *Political Psychology* 25, no. 5 (2004): 741–767. https://doi.org/ 10.1111/j.1467-9221.2004.00396.x.

Knowles, Chase Laurelle, "Towards a New Web Genre: Islamist Neorealism," *Journal of War & Culture Studies* 1, no. 3 (2008): 357–380. https://doi.org/10.1386/jwcs.1.3.357_1.

Levitt, Matthew, *Hezbollah: The Global Footprint of Lebanon's Party of God*. Washington, D.C.: Georgetown University Press.

Macnair, Logan, and Richard Frank, "'To My Brothers in the West…': A Thematic Analysis of Videos Produced by the Islamic State's al-Hayat Media Center," *Journal of Contemporary Criminal Justice* 33, no. 3 (2017): 234–253. https://doi.org/10.1177/1043986217699313.

Maira, Sunaina, "Citizenship and Dissent: South Asian Muslim Youth in the US after 9/11," *South Asian Popular Culture* 8, no. 1 (2010): 31–45. https://doi.org/10.1080/14746681003633135.

Matusitz, Jonathan, and Pam Payano, "Globalisation of Popular Culture: From Hollywood to Bollywood," *South Asia Research* 32, no. 2 (2012): 123–138. https://doi.org/10.1177/0262728012453977.

Matusitz, Jonathan, *Symbolism in Terrorism: Motivation, Communication, and Behavior*. Lanham, MD: Rowman & Littlefield, 2015.

Matusitz, Jonathan, "Brand Management in Terrorism: The Case of Hezbollah," *Journal of Policing, Intelligence and Counter Terrorism* 13, no. 1 (2018): 1–16. https://doi.org/10.1080/18335330.2017.1412489.

Matusitz, Jonathan, "Communication of Terrorism: Social Noise, the Signature Method, and the Conduit Metaphor," *Journal of Applied Security Research* 13, no. 4 (2018): 455–472. https://doi.org/10.1080/19361610.2018.1498258.

McCauley, Clark, and Sophia Moskalenko, *Friction: How Radicalization Happens to Them and Us*. New York: Oxford University Press, 2009.

Meleagrou-Hitchens, Alexander, Audrey Alexander, and Nick Kaderbhai, "Literature Review: The Impact of Digital Communications Technology on Radicalization and Recruitment," *International Affairs* 93, no. 5 (2017): 1233–1249. https://doi.org/10.1093/ia/iix103.

Milton, Daniel, "The Islamic State: An Adaptive Organization Facing Increasing Challenges," in *The Group That Calls Itself a State: Understanding the Evolution and Challenges of the Islamic State*, edited by Bryan Price, Daniel Milton, Muhammad al-'Ubaydi, and Nelly Lahoud. West Point, NY: Combating Terrorism Center, 2014.

Morris, Travis, *Dark Ideas: How Neo-Nazi and Violent Jihadi Ideologues Shaped Modern Terrorism*. Lanham, MD: Lexington Books, 2017.

Noack, Rick, and Souad Mekhennet, "German Officials Believe Rapper-Turned-Militant Denis Cuspert Has Been Killed," *The Washington Post* (2015, January 19): A1.

Olechowicz, Kari, and Jonathan Matusitz, "The Motivations of Islamic Martyrs: Applying the Collective Effort Model," *Current Psychology* 32, no. 4 (2013): 338–347. https://doi.org/10.1007/s12144-013-9187-0.

Otterbeck, Jonas, "Wahhabi Ideology of Social Control versus a New Publicness in Saudi Arabia," *Contemporary Islam* 6, no. 3 (2012): 341–353. https://doi.org/10.1007/s11562-012-0223-x.

Pape, Robert, *Dying to Win: The Strategic Logic of Suicide Terrorism*. New York: Random House, 2005.

Patkin, Terri Toles, "Explosive Baggage: Female Palestinian Suicide Bombers and the Rhetoric of Emotion," *Women and Language* 27, no. 2 (2004): 79–88.

Pisoiu, Daniela, "Subcultural Theory Applied to Jihadi and Right-Wing Radicalization in Germany," *Terrorism and Political Violence* 27, no. 1 (2015): 9–28. https://doi.org/10.1080/09546553.2014.959406.

Prucha, Nico, "IS and the Jihadist Information Highway—Projecting Influence and Religious Identity via Telegram," *Perspectives on Terrorism* 10, no. 6 (2016): 48–58.

Putnam, Michael T., "Music as a Weapon: Reactions and Responses to RAF Terrorism in the Music of Ton Steine Scherben and Their Successors in Post-9/11 Music," *Popular Music and Society* 32, no. 5 (2009): 595–606. https://doi.org/10.1080/03007760903251417.

Quiggin, Tom, "Contemporary Jihadist Narratives: The Case of Momin Khawaja," in *Countering Violent Extremist Narratives*, edited by Eelco J. A. M. Kessels, 84–93. Breda, Netherlands: National Coordinator for Counter Terrorism, 2010.

Ramsay, Gilbert, *Jihadi Culture on the World Wide Web*. London: Bloomsbury Publishing, 2013.

Sageman, Marc, *Understanding Terror Networks*. Philadelphia, PA: University of Pennsylvania Press, 2004.

Said, Behnam, "Hymns (Nasheeds): A Contribution to the Study of the Jihadist Culture," *Studies in Conflict & Terrorism* 35, no. 12 (2012): 863–879. https://doi.org/10.1080/1057610X.2012.720242.

Sewell, William H., "A Theory of Structure: Duality, Agency, and Transformation," *American Journal of Sociology* 98, no. 1 (1992): 1–29. https://doi.org/10.1086/229967.

Spencer, Richard, "A Journey into the Mind of 'Jihadi John'," *The Telegraph* (2014, September 4): A1.

Sumiala, Johanna, and Lilly Korpiola, "Mediated Muslim Martyrdom: Rethinking Digital Solidarity in the 'Arab Spring'," *New Media & Society* 19, no. 1 (2017): 52–66. https://doi.org/10.1177/1461444816649918.

Swedenburg, Ted, "Fun^Da^Mental's 'Jihad Rap'," in *Being Young and Muslim: New Cultural Politics in the Global South and North*, edited by Linda Herrera and Asef Bayat, 291–307. New York: Oxford University Press, 2010.

Volosinov, Ladislav Matejka, *Marxism and the Philosophy of Language*. New York: Seminar Press, 1973.

Waldmann, Peter, "The Radical Community: A Comparative Analysis of the Social Background of ETA, IRA, and Hezbollah," *Sociologus* 55, no. 2 (2005): 239–257.

Waldmann, Peter, "The Radical Milieu: The Under-Investigated Relationship between Terrorists and Sympathetic Communities," *Perspectives on Terrorism* 2, no. 9 (2008): 25–27.

Watters, Ethan, *Urban Tribes: A Generation Redefines Friendship, Family, and Commitment*. London: Bloomsbury, 2003.

Wiedl, Nina, *The Making of a German Salafiyya. The Emergence, Development and Missionary Work of Salafi Movements in Germany*. Aarhus, Denmark: Centre for Studies in Islamism and Radicalization, 2012.

Winter, Charlie, *The Virtual "Caliphate:" Understanding Islamic State's Propaganda Strategy*. London: Quilliam Foundation, 2015.

12

CONCLUSIONS AND SOLUTIONS

The rise of global jihadism presents an immense international crisis and one of the worst geopolitical challenges to the global order. The grand vision of the Caliphate in the twenty-first century is a long-term dream within the GJM. Concerns for global jihadist terrorism have occasioned increased measures that impact national security. Most of the 193 nations feel compelled to secure economic and military power. Improvements in information and communication technology benefit global jihadist groups. Four major conclusions were drawn from the conceptual analysis conducted across the 11 previous chapters: (1) The more global communication, the more jihadism, (2) a dangerous shrinking world, (3) an emancipating communication environment, and (4) parallel globalization of terror.

The more global communication, the more jihadism

Enhanced global communication is also enhancing risks that transcend national boundaries. It is like a contagion effect. Research has found that global communication increases civil wars which, in turn, create a contagion effect; the eruption of one civil war increases the chances that civil war will explode in neighboring territories.[1] This has been demonstrated by the rapid diffusion of jihadism. Present-day terrorism is inseparably associated with the modern media. A network of jihadist activism has, in fact, been empowered by the globalization of media. With the rise of international communication, so too individuals are no longer segregated in their ideological commitments. In the context of jihadism, globalization is not only a tool for extremists to spread their violent Caliphate ideology; it is also a new paradigm for reasoning and framing actions in order to achieve the best results for their cause. Hence, the more globalization, the more jihadism. Part of the reason is that, today, the dissemination of jihadist information does not happen in a top-down manner (as was experienced in the past, when mass communications were distributed in a sequential, predictable manner, often under strong regulations). In the present day, highly flexible networks such as all-channel networks (see Chapter 5) allow any user to participate in the public sphere by giving or receiving information with just a few mouse clicks away.

When we live in a universe where media images are conveyed throughout the world, this alters who we are and how we behave. Recent attacks by ISIS on Western targets, cultural heritage sites, and even their own people are viewed over and over again through global communication channels. ISIS's crimes against civilization not only demonstrate their open barbarity and absolute evil; they can also be easily emulated by any user who supports such terrorist methods. In a sense, global communication technologies facilitate copycat behavior. This was explained through the beheading videos in Chapter 10, particularly the disturbing beheading videos of Steven Sotloff, David Haines, and James Foley that were widely disseminated by ISIS in 2014. This was also explained through the martyrdom videos in Chapter 11, when terrorist organizations like Hezbollah, for example, extoll the virtues of participating in suicide missions and the social status earned by the martyrs who die as heroes in holy war.

A dangerous shrinking world

The second conclusion of today's global jihad is that we live in a dangerous shrinking world. The global jihad threat that came to the forefront of the media on September 11, 2001 offered a spectacular testimony of globalization in the sense of a shrinking world.[2] Globalization has smoothed the development of identity politics that is connecting and mutually reinforcing unrelated people (both across geographical boundaries and across ethnic and religious lines)—even though some groups want to reinforce these boundaries to their own benefit.[3] The international movement of jihad has expanded its influence as a promoter of religious, political, and ideological legitimacy for tens of millions of Muslims, bestowing it a new meaning or rekindling old meanings.

The growth of global jihad is not a one-way street, moving in one direction from a center. Rather, it is moving by defying geometry from all possible angles. It transcends the more commonplace relationships among jihadists and would-be jihadists in the three-dimensional world. With globalization processes, jihadism is simplified through a mechanism of integration that unites people from different countries. In this manner, it nullifies national differences and makes them less consequential. Much technological and cultural progress in various parts of the world—for good or ill purposes—will probably have a bearing on individuals living elsewhere, sometimes at a staggering speed.

The success of global jihad can be attributed, in part, to the fact that, in the twenty-first century, online communications significantly reduce barriers among users. As Beyer (1994)[4] suggests, we now live in "a globalizing social reality, one in which previously effective barriers to communication no longer exist." Communication is the cornerstone of globalization; globalization is the transnational sharing of ideas, values, resources, and humans through communication.[5] The long-established organizational models of terrorist organizations still have much relevance today. However, the expansion of the international community of jihadists has considerably improved through ease of online communications, thereby helping disseminate messages and connecting with like-minded individuals across state boundaries.

Access to online social media and reduction of communication barriers through the World Wide Web, cable TV, and mobile telephone systems are enablers of global jihad—wittingly and unwittingly. The jihadists' popularity in cyberspace (aka, the jihadisphere) can be ascribed by what Wesch (2009)[6] calls "context collapse." This denotes the unique features of cyberspace, where both jihadists and inquisitive users exchange dangerous information without fear of being identified or arrested. Individuals who are timid, reserved, or hesitant to participate in face-to-face communication consider the internet the ideal tool for defeating geographical and psychological barriers in order to communicate with others.[7] Suler (2005)[8] refers to this occurrence as the "online disinhibition effect." We also discussed the fact that digital communication tools can turn any person with no record of criminal behavior or deviance into a killing machine. As we have seen, online jihadist magazines like *Inspire, Dabiq, Rumiyah*, and *Gaidi Mtaani* allow jihadist organizations to publish terrorist manuals and weapon-assembling guidelines (e.g., "How to Build a Bomb in the Kitchen of Your Mom") in virtual space. These magazines frame a fanatic interpretation of Islam determined to fight the rest of the world.

Now that digital communication technologies escalate the speed and accessibility of jihad propaganda, the ensuing improvements in networking and communication have fostered virtual micro-communities of mujahedin and even spaces for lone-wolf jihadists. As explained through social movement theory (SMT), cyberspace has facilitated Islamic revival and unprecedented movements of radical Islamist ideas. An example of Islamic revival is pop-jihad, or popular music glorifying jihad. In many regards, popular music presents a reflection of lower- and middle-class views and dissatisfactions with the current state of affairs and the leaders who wield power over the masses.[9] Although many Salafists or jihadists look at hip-hop through a negative sense (owing to its Western origins), there exist today many examples of hip-hop songs with pro-jihadist lyrics and jihadist nasheeds extolling the virtues of ritualistic beheadings of infidels and apostates. This all reflects the syndrome of jihad cool, which includes music, videos, and other types of entertainment.

An emancipating communication environment

Communicating ideology on the internet is highly convenient for terrorist organizations, as the content of the message is difficult to supervise, filter, or expurgate. The diffusion of ideology can be achieved in any place, at any time, and at a low cost.[10] As mentioned in Chapter 6, the media has a symbiotic relationship with terrorism, the profundities of which challenge simple description. This symbiotic relationship makes the media both an enabler of terrorism[11] and a tool for countering it.[12] This concept has mostly been attributed to mass media reporting on terrorism news. With the massive expansion of the internet, however, the global communication space for jihadists is even more rapid and grows exponentially. Jihadists have exploited the jihadisphere as their emancipating communication environment. It is a globalized public sphere differentiated by unparalleled turmoil and volatility in the communication space.[13] It is a digitized, internationally networked system[14] that has engendered a frenzied communication environment, innovative in terms of "structure" and informational capacity. Overall, the jihadisphere negates geometry because it defies the three-dimensional, analogue era.[15]

The new information environment will probably help individual citizens (especially those in totalitarian countries) more than political élites in these totalitarian countries. Dictators and absolute rulers are running more and more hurdles in restraining the flow of information and ideology that their citizens exchange. The result could fuel violent demonstrations and grassroots organizing like the Arab Spring in the early 2010s. Studies on tweets posted by demonstrators in Egypt, for example, revealed that social media allowed them to better coordinate their actions and eschew government crackdowns. The internet is benefiting jihadist organizations that have global objectives, because they can reach wider audience from which to generate financial proceeds and recruits. In short, information technologies have transformed the advantage from homegrown groups with local seats of support to groups with international networks and connections.[16]

As discussed in Chapter 5, internet media campaigns smooth the progress of jihad propagandists, particularly those with weak local backing, to harvest international attention and solicit recruits and financing required to initiate a holy war. Expected outcomes include higher external involvement in civil wars, in various ways, and a higher proportion of warring factions. On a similar note, the decentralized aspect of the internet means that insurgent groups no longer need to depend on a single supply of income or a single financial sponsor. If they lose one source of income (e.g., oil) or one sponsor (e.g., Iran), they can cultivate millions of other potential donors.[17] Taken as a whole, insurgent groups that receive significant financial support from external sponsors will often use more violence toward unarmed combatants.[18]

Parallel globalization of terror

Global communication today is as much a benefit as it is a problem. Though communication has become so decentralized, diversified, and democratized, social progress is not always a guarantee. As McNair (2018)[19] explains, "the same digital tools as were employed by the Umbrella Revolution in Hong Kong can be utilized by reactionary social movements violently opposed to democracy and human rights, notably ISIS." The consequences of global communication are clashing. At least two contradictions exist. On the one hand, it expands the horizons for the betterment of civil society. On the other hand, it expands horizons for malicious deeds. Within the context of this monograph, malicious deeds through global communication were plentiful. Put simply, jihadists take advantage of globalization to expand their ideologies and recruitment methods.

With the rapid expansion of the internet, many optimistic scholars believe that the long-established, normative, pro-democratic roles of journalism as an objective scrutineer, Fourth Estate, and source of solid knowledge for the public sphere would become even stronger. Today, however, online platforms are being exploited, with a tremendous impact, by the adversaries of liberal democracy.[20] The new information environment has become an arena for global communication that is available at one's fingertips in just a few seconds. As we have seen in multiple chapters in this book, a great percentage of jihadist recruitment is done online.[21] Social media remains central to the communication strategies of organizations like ISIS. Cyberspace offers unprecedented opportunities to draw public attention for dangerous reasons which, in turn, boost the influence of extremist actions.[22] Social media networks can effortlessly reach millions of individuals, some of whom are susceptible to ISIS's recruitment approaches. These groups consist of Muslims (by birth or by faith) across the globe and Muslims living in the West. Some of them come from well-off families, whereas others feel marginalized in their own societies.[23] The internet is also more and more appealing to Muslim converts.

To begin as a solution: know thy enemy

Why law enforcement agencies in certain countries do not act aggressively on memos before terrorist attacks occur is always a big question. What comes next are a few recommendations or thoughts as to what governments and law enforcement agencies can do to prevent—or, at least, be better prepared for—potential jihadist attacks in the future. Sun Tzu famously said, "Know the enemy and know yourself; in a hundred battles you will never be in peril."[24] Our triumph in the war on terror is contingent upon our knowledge of the enemy and our understanding of his or her ideology.

Consider jihadist immigration influxes to Europe. Europe is experiencing the world's largest refugee crisis since World War II. The recent jihadist attacks on the Old Continent have brought to light the correlation between migrants and terrorists. The escalating numbers of refugees and asylum seekers escaping chaos in Africa and the Middle East present multipart challenges for European leaders. Evidence shows that Muslim immigration has heightened the risk of jihadism in Europe. A case in point is the Berlin Christmas market attack on December 19, 2016. Anis Amri, a Tunisian migrant who moved to Germany in July 2015, intentionally plowed a truck into the Christmas market, killing 12 people and injured 50 others. Six month prior, in June 2016, Anis Amri was ordered to be removed from Germany, but could not be flown back to Tunisia because the country refused to recognize him as a citizen (as he was not in possession of a valid passport).[25]

To cite other examples, on July 14, 2016, Mohamed Lahouaiej Bouhlel plowed a 19-tonne cargo truck into thousands of revelers on Bastille Day in Nice, France, killing 86 people and hurting another 400. He was a Tunisian immigrant.[26] Likewise, Italian mobsters declined to sell Kalashnikovs and ammo to Mohamed Khemiri, also a Tunisian immigrant, who was later arrested in San Marcellino, Italy, in August 2016. He was sentenced to eight years in prison on terrorism-related charges and for assisting in illegal immigration.[27] The Stockholm truck attack in April 2017, which killed five pedestrians, was committed by Rakhmat Akilov, a 39-year-old asylum seeker from Uzbekistan. More distressingly, Akilov had already been listed as a suspect by the Swedish police and had published ISIS jihad propaganda on social media.[28] Lastly, some of the perpetrators of the vehicle-ramming attacks in Barcelona (August 2017) were Moroccan immigrants living in Spain.[29] It would be beneficial to meditate on the number of European-born Muslims who migrate to Syria and come back as potential would-be killers. This was the case for some of the terrorists on November 13, 2015 in Paris, who killed 130 people.[30]

Huntington (1993)[31] said it clearly: the West needs "to develop a more profound understanding of the basic religious and philosophical assumptions underlying other civilizations and the ways in which people in those civilizations see their interests." With regard to issues of terrorism, law enforcement and policymakers must be attentive to the types of Muslim groups with which they cooperate. Numerous self-identified civil rights organizations—like CAIR (the Council on American–Islamic Relations) and ISNA (the Islamic Society of North America)—adhere to more radical versions of Islam. Organizations such as the American Islamic Congress and the American Islamic Forum for Democracy champion gender equality and human rights, but because countries like Saudi Arabia do not agree with their efforts against radicalism, they often lack resources or funding. If provided alternative funding, they might be more likely to assist in an attempt to instruct Muslims against extremism.[32] CAIR and ISNA, however, are "peaceful revolutionaries." They are organizations that reject any model of government that does allow some forms of sharia. Yet, they do not—at least openly—use direct violent methods to further their agenda.[33]

Case study: the mistake of the Sri Lankan authorities

In the aftermath of the 2019 Easter bombings in Sri Lanka, the country's government was castigated for not honoring the warnings from Indian intelligence services—at least three in April alone—that a large-scale attack was imminent. On April 9, 2019, a top security memo, labeled "Top Secret (Eyes Only)," stated that the National Thawheedh Jamaath (NTJ), a lesser known jihadist organization, was "planning to target some important churches."[34] The memo gave ample details, such as the names, addresses, phone numbers, and the times at night during which one suspect would visit his wife. Sri Lanka's security agencies had been carefully surveilling a clandestine cell of NTJ. Security officials in Sri Lanka are now certain that NTJ was responsible for the attacks and may have benefited from assistance abroad. They were clearly made aware that the organization was dangerous.[35]

The history of acrimonious hidden conflicts among Sri Lanka's leaders may have led to a colossal security breakdown that facilitated one of the world's deadliest jihadist operations. Because of Sri Lanka's president and prime minister wrangling with each other for months, a political breakdown erupted in 2018. As a result, the president removed the prime minister from top security meetings, and the latter's office had no clue about the possibility of pending suicide attacks.[36] These missteps have questioned the ability of Sri Lanka to react properly to such attacks and prevent future ones. The president was also blaming his subordinates for not having informed him about the warnings, whereas the prime minister apologized and took the blame.[37] This phenomenon is reminiscent of the longstanding feud between the CIA and the FBI. By the time George W. Bush began his first term as president of the United States, the Al-Qaeda hijackers who would slaughter 3,000 people on September 11, 2001 were already inside the country. The CIA was aware of this, but never told the FBI.[38]

Euphemisms for "Islamic terrorism" are dangerous

Ascribing labels to an enemy is purposeful if the labels are defined clearly; otherwise, vague characterizations obfuscate our aptitude to truly understand the enemy. While "jihadism" or "Islamic terrorism" is labeled as such in numerous non-Western nations, there is a tendency among advocacy groups in North America and Europe to evade, ignore, or reject the term "jihadism" or "Islamic terrorism." One argument is that these terms are confusing and imbued with racism, xenophobia, and/or risks of harming Muslims. Another argument by those advocacy groups is that such terms are inappropriate because they symbolize an overreaction to a nonexistent threat that will further marginalize Muslims. The problem is that terrorist activities that are transnational in nature need to be understood and countered through international cooperation. If a clear definition is not reached, it may complicate things. It is a well-known fact that international cooperation can be problematic when politically sensitive issues are in the way.

A euphemism occurs when an unpleasant or offensive concept or phrase is replaced by a friendly or less offensive one. The word "euphemism" originates from Greek and signifies "good speech."[39] Fighting against a religious ideology such as global jihadism is a daunting task that necessitates commitment and imagination. Emphasizing a few simple, yet important aspects about the damage caused by jihadists can make us move in the right direction. Do euphemisms for jihadism help the global community? A chief conclusion is that euphemisms are dangerous because they act as language manipulators and remove the meaning out of the message. By referring to jihadists as "radicals," "insurgents," or "rebels," the Western establishment falls back on semantic deviance and distracts our attention from reality. This could make populations lower their guard when they should actually feel in danger.[40]

A case in point is the "2018 Public Report on the Terrorism Threat to Canada," published by the Government of Canada in April 2019.[41] The public report eliminated all references to Islam, but did not hesitate to warn of the danger posed by Islamophobia. The introduction includes the following statement: "A review of the language used to describe extremism has been undertaken and is ongoing. The government's communication of threats must be clear, concise, and cannot be perceived as maligning any groups." As the report continues, "it is apparent that in outlining a threat, it must be clearly linked to an ideology rather than a community. The government will carefully select terminology that focuses on the intent or ideology." This brief case study reveals that dangerous euphemisms represent obstacles in the fight against jihad. Unless we identify and name the enemy, we cannot vanquish that enemy. Western authorities continue to fail us on this issue.[42]

What ordinary citizens can do

Ordinary citizens must be equipped with every means that can win the war of ideas against political correctness, like semantic shifts created by the media establishment. The latter insufficiently confronts the true nature of global jihad. Although a certain number of imams have been ousted from various countries in the United States and Europe, rarely have citizens been able to reach their objective of banning radical centers. In Western civilization, such programs would be difficult to implement because they would infringe on constitutional rights of freedom of religion and fair treatment of all, which is one of the hallmarks of Western democracy.[43] In like fashion, several attempts have been made to stop the construction of questionable mosques across the United States since the Ground Zero mosque controversy in 2010. Peter King, Member of the U.S. House of Representatives in New York, was spearheading that movement, stating that the Ground Zero mosque project was a violation of our moral values.[44]

Western-style multiculturalism?

On April 28, 2019, Hizb ut-Tahrir, a global Islamist political party, held a four-hour conference in Sydney, in which they dissuaded the audience from singing the Australian national anthem. Fanatics of sharia and supporters of ISIS, the group rented a community hall at Campsie, in the southwestern part of Sydney, for their conference. Yellow-taped dividers were glued on the carpet to separate men from women. During the event, Wassim Doureihi of Hizb ut-Tahrir denounced multiculturalism as an impracticable philosophy that does not genuinely believe in tolerating Muslims, particularly the sharia-compliant ones. For him, "tolerance, diversity, and multiculturalism" are "a lie."[45]

Multiculturalism is the philosophy that moral or ethical principles, which differ from culture to culture, should be treated equally and that no cultural system is superior to any other. This is predicated on the notion that there is no steadfast criterion of good or evil. Judgments about right or wrong, then, are a creation of society.[46] Western efforts to welcome Islam with open arms are plentiful, even though it is clear that a certain number of Muslim leaders (e.g., imams) aspire to end not only Western civilization, but also Western criticism of Islam. In November 2008, at the request of Muslim leaders, the United Nations General Assembly expressed disapproval of "defamation" of religions, stating that "Islam is frequently and wrongly associated with human rights violations and terrorism." All nations in the world were charged with the mission of taking "all possible measures to promote tolerance and respect for all religions and beliefs."[47]

The theory of dialogue among civilizations, a counterbalance to Huntington's clash of civilizations, has become the heart of global attention. The theory was originally developed by Austrian philosopher Hans Köchler (1973)[48] in a treatise on cultural identity. Similarly, in his book titled *Terror and Liberalism*, Paul Berman (2003)[49] contends that divergent cultural boundaries do not exist today. He maintains there is no "Islamic civilization" nor a "Western civilization." In fact, the existence of a clash of civilizations has not been proven, especially when evaluating relationships between countries such as the United States and Saudi Arabia. To corroborate his argument, he mentioned the fact that many Islamists spend a good amount of time residing and/or pursuing their studies in the Western world. For Berman, conflict emerges because of philosophical doctrines that different groups share (or do not share), irrespective of cultural or religious character.

Western-style human rights policies?

To trounce the various forms of human rights appropriation or violations, what has also been recommended is to undertake a self-critical examination of one's own culture. As Westerners, it has been suggested that we distance ourselves from the notion that these rights are merely individualistic claims that are harmful to communitarian solidarity. In other words, we are told to abstain from developing human rights into a philosophy of general progress patterned on Western civilization and to focus on human rights monitoring (rather than requesting to impose or apply a Western-style market economy). In any event, a self-critical examination of one's own human rights package is deemed necessary before engaging in any profound intercultural dialogue on human rights.

What this set of arguments also implies is that, to avoid ramping up conflict between civilizations, we should reject universalism. In this epoch of globalization, we need to make certain that imagined boundaries, like exclusion and discrimination, do not lead disaffected youths to violence. Embracing a multicultural worldview at the local, regional, and global levels would be stepping in the right direction, though this would mean that every culture involved engages in critical adaptation. It is now a self-evident truth, in foreign policy committees, that genuine reformation of the Muslim world cannot happen by way of Western-style human rights policies. It is essential to understand why this is the case. It is the case because the Muslim world is utterly disturbed by both its religious fanaticism and the significant percentage of jihadists (and an equally dangerous minority of Islamic fundamentalists).[50]

Spreading democracy to the Muslim world?

Friedman depicts a "fast world" in which virtually all humans on earth are affected to some level. It is a fast world with high-speed internet, global telecommunications, interlocked financial markets, and omnipresent fast-food restaurants. One simply needs to hear the ring of a smartphone or the automatic diction produced by voice simulation software to remind the plentiful (or painful) examples of this globalized world. It is exactly this "fast world" of novelty and avant-gardism that terrifies Salafists because they see it as the biggest threat they have ever encountered; it is threatening their religious and cultural identities. Under these circumstances, spreading democracy in the Muslim world will probably not reduce this perceived threat to Islam. Although many scholars[51] have ascertained this issue of threatened identities as a reason of violence, there are very few arguments supporting the idea that democracy in the Muslim world would improve identity formation.

The more probable consequence of spreading democracy would be that it would escalate the perceived threat to Islam, at least for those who espouse Salafist ideology because of the aforementioned threat. They see Islam as incompatible with democracy. This topic of the compatibility of Islam and democracy has drawn a lot of attention since the September 11, 2001 attacks.[52] Cheryl Benard (2003)[53] has categorized Muslims into four "essential positions" that sum up differences in views clearly. The fundamentalists are unambiguously hostile to the West and democracy. The traditionalists are doubtful of democracy and modernity. Modernists and secularists are more accepting of democracy, with the former being more willing to reform Islam, whereas the latter focus more on the separation between religion and politics. No one knows for sure what the percentage of Muslims is for each of the four categories.[54]

Reintegrating those negatively influenced by global jihad

By increasing our awareness of the mental and physical phases that global jihadists undergo to become killing machines, and the consequences that they sometimes suffer within their own communities (which is often witnessed after they return from years of violent missions), what ordinary citizens can also do is reintegrate those negatively influenced by the GJM into society, especially those who may have become actively involved with jihadist groups. By the same token, it could inspire scholars and practitioners alike to become positive agents of change in the fight against terrorism. This can be achieved by ensuring that all men and women involved in the GJM return to society and restore their confidence as members of their communities by developing adequate interpersonal communication skills. More importantly, former jihadists can be channeled as a vital resource for building international communication networks to reach objectives of global peace and meet various development goals in territories plagued by years of internal conflicts.

What moderate Muslims can do

For several decades, the main voice for youths in the Muslim world has been the voice of radicalism, which has extolled the virtues of jihad. The fact that the aggressive advocacy for holy war and martyrdom has largely been unopposed has brought about insidious effects. The monopoly of the faith by moderate Muslims is not likely. If it does occur, it will be a very slow process. The more opportunities are available to moderate Muslims, the more likely the hatred will be decreased, with a corresponding decrease in recruitment into jihadism. So long as sacrificing one's life to kill the enemy and please Allah is the best way to attain significance, martyrdom will continue to motivate youths; for every mujahedin killed or arrested, new ones will emerge to take their place.[55] Only Muslims could ever resolve this crisis. On a global level, there are certain measures that can diminish the temptations of militant Islam. Giving peaceful Muslims a stronger voice on the international stage would be a step in the right direction.

Supporting pro-democracy politicians in the Muslim world

Although democracy may not create more economic or social benefits, the democratic route might alleviate some of the criticisms or injustices felt by citizens; it can achieve this by providing a more wide-ranging and lawful government that cares more for procedural justice (or even distributive justice).[56] Procedural justice applies the principle of fairness in the methods that settle disputes and allocate resources.[57] Some commentators believe that democracies are more able to provide procedural justice. For example, fair elections operate through peaceful mechanisms thanks to which citizens can transform the régime. Likewise, freedom of speech and of assembly enable peaceful opposition against the government and enable citizens to change the views of the government between elections. To this point, Windsor (2003)[58] asserts that democracies decrease the occurrence of terrorism through the following characteristics: opportunities for pacific change of government, avenues for disagreement and political discussion, the rule of law, civil liberties, and the free movement of information.

Moderate Muslims do not hesitate to dismiss Salafists and pro-jihadist policy-makers as counterproductive and contributing to the advance of Islamism. During elections in France, Salafists were afraid of moderate Muslims planning to vote. Disputes flared up in mosques between older Muslim generations (who urged the youths to vote) and Salafists (who claimed that it was illegal to participate in non-Islamic institutions). An old man reportedly quoted Yusuf Al-Qaradawi to support his belief that youths be allowed to take part in politics. After this event, a Salafist replied that Al-Qaradawi was a deviant scholar.[59]

Rejecting other people's political opportunities is one of the easiest forms of control, and it benefits international terrorism. A large part of terrorism is facilitated by a political environment amicable to the terrorist cause or movement. In some cases, political environments are not overtly supportive, but they indirectly make resources and recruits available for terrorists. Denying terrorists a platform for their actions is a powerful strategy of control.[60] As Paul Wilkinson (1977)[61] explains, "mainstream mass parties engaged in constitutional opposition have both the opportunity and the resources to at least respond sensitively and rapidly to deeply felt discontents and feelings of injustice voiced by citizens." Likewise, Mohammed Hafez (2003)[62] argues that jihadist movements are a reaction to repressive régimes and, therefore, "if the democratic process grants Islamists substantive access to state institutions, the opposition will be channeled toward conventional political participation and shun violence."

Supporting citizenship education

These issues elicit new considerations for citizenship education in schools. In spite of new globalization trends, citizenship education in schools has been under-represented in the media. A robust democracy will be highly effective when everybody participates fully (including the youths). Schools should not ignore educating young minds for active citizenship. However, the demographic changes that are happening mean that citizenship education cannot be bolstered without tackling the flawed models that govern current educational approaches. Examples are frameworks that keep stressing loyalty to the nation-state as the foundation for citizenship and social membership.[63] The experiences of Muslim youths from the ummah indicate a necessity for new educational strategies to help motivated, active young citizens accomplish a more equitable and peaceful future for nations around the world. Developing these new strategies requires a better understanding of how youths are creating "glocal" lives.[64] Glocalization is the adaptation of globalizing practices and values to the tastes and mores of local cultures and societies.

Supporting religious education

Muslim children immersed in narratives of extremism and jihadism by Salafist teachers are already programmed for martyrdom, but various dissenting factions within Islam can provide opportunities for deradicalization.[65] In the contemporary Muslim world, a sharp division exists between those who are committed to orthodox religious dogmas and those who are discarding traditional orthodoxy in support of more modern views. These religious tensions have escalated into a widespread ideological battle in which religious conservatives wrangle with religious liberals (and secularists) to promote new religious and cultural norms.[66] This battle is waged over profoundly varying interpretations of current affairs, moral authority, or the universe overall.[67] In a nutshell, it is a war that its "orthodox" or "theistic" individuals with "progressive" or "enlightened" ones.[68]

Religious education is a possible remedy. By striving to keep the balance between tradition and modernity, it can be used to challenge the fundamentalist, Salafistic type of religious education that is found both in traditional classrooms and on the internet. Religious education should encourage critical reinterpretation and redefinition of Islamic tradition and its holy texts for the present day—Western-influenced life bringing a new historical context for Islam and the ummah. For the Muslim theist, the position of authority is external and transcendent (Allah). Truth and values rest on absolute tenets imparted through revelation in sacred scriptures; the duty of every one of us is to serve God. For the Muslim modernist, the position of authority is still external, but today it resides in the secular world.[69]

For moderate Muslims, to interpret the world in black and white is to not acknowledge the true nature of reality. Although Islam did not embark on the Reformation and the Enlightenment (an argument regularly made by its detractors), it is not represented by a monolithic religious group at all. A significant percentage of ordinary Muslims are fighting against jihadists, and sometimes to the detriment of their own lives. In Iraq, the Iraqi, Kurdish, and Iranian soldiers combating ISIS are predominantly Muslims. In Pakistan and Afghanistan, the government forces against jihadists also consist of virtually all Muslims.

Supporting counter-fatwas

To every fatwa, there should be an equally credible counter-fatwa.[70] It can be done by pinpointing the fatwas and creating counter-narratives to challenge Islamist verdicts generally issued by ultra-conservative clerics.[71] Although democratic participation can pit Muslim activists and scholars with one another, counter-fatwas can be crafted from afar (through the internet) and be diffused rapidly through the jihadisphere.[72] The objective here is to expose would-be jihadists online to new information to change their minds. This can work through blogs, social network platforms like Facebook, and online newspapers and magazines (whose significance should not be undervalued). A peaceful Muslim cyberspace allows users to post their own comments, thereby confronting the radicalism of ultra-traditional authorities and providing some sort of renegotiation of Islamic norms.[73] Norms are abstract principles for behavior, "a standard embodying a judgment about what should be the case."[74]

The justification of suicide bombings by fatwas has been already challenged by counter-fatwas. For example, in August 2005, Abu-Basir al-Tartusi, a Syrian cleric against jihadism who lives in London, published an online fatwa that was titled "A Word of Warning about Suicide Operations." These suicide operations were guided by fatwas issued by clerics a few months prior. As al-Tartusi argued, "I have received 1,000 questions about these operations, which are for me closer to suicide than martyrdom. They are *haram* (forbidden) and impermissible, for several reasons." He quoted in the fatwa some of the Prophet's sayings, among them: "Anyone who harms a believer has no jihad." Islamic fundamentalists around the world staged bitter attacks against Al-Tartusi's counter-fatwa on their websites and accused him of deliberately targeting Al-Qaeda's supporters. One of them wrote, "What do you expect from him when he lives in London?" As another posting mentioned, nobody should "get attached to these people because they did not fight before. The rules on jihad are taken from the mujahidin. I never thought of learning about jihad from those sitting who are used to issuing fatwas from London."[75]

Consider the Amman Message. Largely praised by the political élite in the Arab world as proof of the tolerant and peaceful nature of Islam, and by lawmakers and religious leaders across the world who aspire to expand the volume of moderate Muslims, the Amman Message has become akin to an international reference document. The Amman Message was a declaration signed in 2005 in Jordan by close to 200 prominent Muslim jurists. It functioned as a counter-fatwa against the growing use of *takfir* (excommunication) by jihadist organizations that legitimize jihad against Muslim rulers. The Amman Message recognized eight official schools of sharia and forbade pronouncements of apostasy against them. The declaration also stipulated that fatwas can only be published by appropriately trained muftis, in an attempt to delegitimize fatwas issued by extremists who are devoid of the requisite qualifications.[76]

Hermeneutics: general perspectives

Another solution to overcome global jihad is to counter extremist ideologies that occasion, motivate, and justify it. Because one of the mechanisms through which jihadist ideologues recruit members is the manipulation of madrassas, it is imperative to introduce measures that deter the diffusion of extremism through educational institutions. More importantly, moderate Muslims must unmask the aberrant teachings of jihadists and assume leadership for the future sake of Islam and its constituents.[77] Discussions as to who is allowed to interpret Islam and who speaks on behalf of Muslim communities are among the most vivacious both within and outside Muslim communities. What these debates tend to ignore is the junction of conventional standards of authority with modern ones, where novel forms of religious authority clash with old ones. What is also lacking is a balanced discussion of manifold types of authorities and representations that avoids the straightforward use of these concepts and even creates problems for them when needed.[78]

What Muslims need against jihad is a more profound intellectual philosophy to reform age-old doctrines like Salafism. Fundamental assumptions reside in hermeneutics; this can apply to the types of education that are inherent to such intellectual philosophy. Hermeneutics is a methodological approach to interpretation, particularly the interpretation of biblical scriptures, holy texts, works of wisdom, and philosophical manuscripts.[79] The hermeneutic method nurtures a questioning and critical mindset; it attaches importance to the quest for truth. This carries unequivocal educational implications. Based on the hermeneutic approach, "good religious education" is reflexive in nature and fosters understanding of religion, unlike the promotion of faith as a type of fixed and immutable "religious belief." It is the absolute opposite of the categorical rejection of doubt that, at the same time, removes the possibility of self-criticism.[80]

Exegesis

Hermeneutics was originally employed when interpreting scriptures, a practice known as exegesis. Later, the field of hermeneutics was extended to issues of general interpretation. The concepts of hermeneutics and exegesis are occasionally used interchangeably. Hermeneutics is a broader discipline that consists of written, verbal, and nonverbal communication.[81] Exegesis mostly emphasizes the word and grammar of texts.[82] It is a critical account or interpretation of a text, often a religious text. Traditionally, the term was employed when interpreting the Bible. Today, "biblical exegesis" is used more specifically to differentiate it from any other larger explanation of a critical text.[83]

Literal analysis implies that a text is to be decoded based on the "plain meaning" articulated by its linguistic creation and historical context. The authors' intention is said to signify the literal meaning. Literal hermeneutics is generally likened to the verbal inspiration.[84] Conversely, allegorical interpretation of biblical narratives often determines that there is a second level of reference that transcends the people and their stories (i.e., those that are described explicitly). One category of allegorical interpretation is called "typological," where the central people, stories, and establishments of a holy text like the Old Testament are regarded as "types" (patterns). In the New Testament, this can also consist of making predictions about figures and events.[85]

This historical-grammatical approach is a hermeneutic approach that seeks to interpret the authors' intended meaning in a holy scripture.[86] The purpose is to understand the meaning of the excerpt as the original author had intended and how the original audience would have interpreted it. The original extract is perceived as having only meaning or sense. As Terry (1974)[87] said, "a fundamental principle in grammatico-historical exposition is that the words and sentences can have but one significance in one and the same connection. The moment we neglect this principle we drift out upon a sea of uncertainty and conjecture." Once the meaning is derived by way of interpretation, one last step involves establishing both the theoretical and practical significance of the excerpt (or even the whole text) and applying it to the present-day context.[88]

Hermeneutic circle

Some texts, and those who created them, cannot be examined by the same scientific methods common in the natural sciences. Part of the reason is that such texts are traditionalized reflections of the experience of the authors. Therefore, interpreting such texts is crucial and will uncover elements about the context in which they emerged. More importantly, they will give the reader a way to share the experiences of the authors. The reciprocity between text and context is what Martin Heidegger (1962)[89] referred to as the hermeneutic circle. Among other intellectuals who developed this idea was Max Weber, a German sociologist and philosopher. The hermeneutic circle reflects the idea that a person's understanding of the text in its entirety is established by connecting its individual parts to the context in which it was formed. No text is created in a vacuum. Neither the entire text nor any individual part will be understood without association with one another; this is why it is a circle. Nevertheless, it is important to note that this "circle" aspect is insufficient to generate the interpretation of a text; rather, it emphasizes that the meaning of a text resides within its social, historical, and literary context.[90] Understanding the meaning of a text is not only contingent upon decoding the author's intentions. It also depends on developing profound relationships between reader, text, and context.[91]

Hermeneutics as applied to Quranic interpretation

Human knowledge is, *inter alia*, an interpretive explanation of the world, not a phenomenon happening in a vacuum. This is why hermeneutics is a theory that is fundamental to critical reading.[92] Culture is transferred from generation to generation. Unavoidably, during the entire process, questions surface in regards to meaningfulness and meaning, which often corresponds to swift cultural change and cultural diversity. Interpretation is the practice of uncovering the meaning of a text by way of critical reading. Critical reading is a type of linguistic analysis that does not absorb a text at face value, but examines the claims presented and the supporting points and/or counterarguments. The task of redefining for improved clarity and readability is also part of critical reading. Identifying possible uncertainties and flaws in the author's reasoning, and addressing them systematically and painstakingly, are key to this process. Critical reading is analogous to academic writing; it requires associating evidential themes to corresponding arguments.[93] As the "hermeneutic circle" explains, the understanding of single themes, sentences, or series of words depends on the understanding of the text in its entirety. It also depends on the context in which the text was created. The reverse is also true: One cannot understand a text without understanding the words in it.[94]

Tafsir

Arabic for "interpretation," *tafsir* refers to exegesis or commentary of the Quran. A *tafsir* scholar is a *mufassir*. *Tafsir* excludes esoteric or mystical interpretations.[95] This concept was developed by disciples of Sufism and Ilm al-Kalam.[96] They operated on the principle that the Prophet Muhammad believed that the Quran possesses an inner meaning, and that this inner meaning, in turn, has even more profound inner meaning.[97] *Tafsir* seeks to offer clarification, explanation, interpretation, context, or annotation for better understanding and persuasion of Allah's will. First and foremost, *tafsir* is popular in the disciplines of linguistics, jurisprudence, and theology. In regards to perspective and approach, *tafsir* can be divided into two general categories: (1) Literal *tafsirs*, which are concepts and directives communicated during the infancy of Islam by the Prophet and his companions, and (2) opinion-based *tafsirs*, which are achieved by way of personal reflection or independent critical thinking.[98]

Particularly important is how one acquires the meaning of each word. To this effect, it should be acknowledged that Classical Arabic must be grasped entirely because one word may possess multiple meanings. A scholar may only know two or three meanings for a word, without being aware of the fact that such a word may mean something different in the Quran. Other disciplines of the Arabic language include philology of Arabic. This is crucial because any alteration of the diacritical marks impacts the meaning, and understanding the diacritical marks is contingent upon the science of Arabic philology.[99] Morphology of the Arabic language also matters because variations in the structure of verb and noun forms alter the meaning.[100] Literary components of the Arabic language—such as morphology, eloquence, and syntax—are an essential part of *tafsir* because they are the source of understanding and interpretation. Arabic has a methodical way of molding words so that people can know the meaning by looking at the root and the form the word from which it was developed. If any word can be ascribed a meaning that corresponds with the rules of grammar, Quranic scriptures can be understood in this manner. With regard to historical resources, scholars may opt to interpret verses based on external factors, such as their historical background and their point of revelation.[101]

Historical and socio-cultural contexts

Historical context is also an important factor when interpreting verses in accordance with (1) how the Quran was brought to light, (2) when and under what conditions, and (3) how much commentary was devoted to history.[102] This is where the hermeneutic circle comes into play: the socio-cultural context for Quranic reading is of utmost significance because it entails understanding and interpreting verses while considering the cultural and social environment in which it came into existence—or even in relation to the scholars' own time. Generally, the distinction can be drawn between the *'amm* (general) verses created for universal conditions for Muslims and *khass* (specific) verses created for specific purposes, time, or need.[103]

The category of the place of revelation, whether it was in Mecca or Medina, is of great consequence as well. This is a throwback to the Principle of Abrogation described in Chapter 6 on the religious motivations of jihad. By and large, Meccan verses often have an *iman* (translated as "faith") nature that includes having faith in Allah, the Prophet Muhammad, and the Day of Reckoning—and whether it be theological bases or fundamental faith principles. Conversely, Medinan verses deal with legal issues, administrative affairs, social obligations, and establishment of a state.[104] This is why the concept of *maqasid* (objective or purpose) is something to behold. Verses may be interpreted to uphold the overall objectives of sharia, which may simply consist of making people happy in this life and *Jannah*. In this respect, any interpretation that endangers the protection of religion, life, family lines, or possessions may be dismissed or replaced in order to guarantee these goals.[105]

Ijtihad

Hermeneutics scholars of the Quran favor a methodical approach that enables a revitalized, liberated reading and interpretation of the holy text. If Islam is to be seen as a living tradition, and inscribed within the new context of Western influences, then a re-reading and reinterpretation of primary sources must be applied. The most difficult part is dealing with differences of interpretation. It is evident that the role of education is important here. The search for meaning and understanding is accompanied by differences of interpretation, all of which require critical reflection. Nevertheless, this constitutes a perfect climate for education. The process of critical thinking *vis-à-vis* the Quran and the expertise of the *mujtahid* (an individual regarded as an original authority in Islamic law), producing a judgment for a new case of jurisprudence, is called *ijtihad*. Within conventional Sunni Islam, *ijtihad* only arises in case new questions do not have answers in the first three sources of Islam (i.e., Quran, hadith, and Sunna). It is in this context that one can work hard to come up with new interpretations and call for Muslim modernists to go back to the ultimate source of Islam, the Quran.[106]

Definitions

Ijtihad is a concept in Muslim law that refers to independent reasoning or the full application of a jurist's mental faculty in finding a remedy to a legal issue.[107] *Ijtihad* is a significant undertaking in the development of sharia or personal judgment in juridical cases.[108] It is the method and the mechanism by which the revealed rulings, as in the Quran and Sunna, may be construed, established, and maintained so long as they are in accordance with the intellectual, socioeconomic, legal, political, and moral aspects of society. Since the laws and guidelines enshrined in the Quran and Sunna are quite limited, and Muslims encounter new situations and problems as life goes by, the revealed law cannot always offer specific answers. This eventually gives rise to the necessity for *ijtihad* and makes it an ideal tool for the advance of Islamic law.[109] *Ijtihad* can be employed as an approach to Islamic law that examines the holy scriptures of Islam (the Quran and Sunna). The purpose is to achieve an adequate resolution to a legal issue that has not yet been made clear in the writings of Sunni scholars in legal schools (*madhhab*). The ultimate goal is to deconstruct patriarchal jurisprudence in sharia.[110]

Ijtihad offers a challenge to literal interpretations of Islam and provides a separation between age-old cultural and religious practices and new understandings of Islam that mirror today's cultural contexts and the interests of the ummah.[111] Honoring individual rights in Islam is a crucial element inherent to this hermeneutic technique. This technique promotes the intent of Islam as universally beneficial—an intent that increases flexibility and diversity of Quranic interpretations. Because Islam has no central authority that imposes strict interpretations of how the Quran is to be read and how the religion is to be practiced, Muslims' right to participate in *ijtihad* would allow them to confront injustices and persecutions through alternative interpretations of holy texts.[112]

Ijtihad has become the hermeneutic approach for any mufti facing what he believes is a novel or unresolved legal problem. The opposite approach is *taqlid* (i.e., "following" or "imitation"), which consists of following the statements of previous scholars without questioning them. While *taqlid* maintains the tradition, *ijtihad* expands it further by tweaking it or overstepping traditional boundaries of a given Sunni school. A mufti who, by *ijtihad*, arrives at new solutions that are in discord with the academic consensus of the respective school can be charged with apostasy as he would be introducing "unlawful innovations" that disobey existing rules.[113]

Context-based ijtihad

Context-based *ijtihad* is a newer technique, though it already existed to some degree and in clandestine forms in early Islam. Context-based *ijtihad* seeks to address a problem by looking at both its historical and modern contexts. If a problem needs an Islamic interpretation, the *mujtahid* first examines the problem carefully by detecting its characteristics, reasons, outward-inward aspects, and place in today's society. A great deal confusion emerges as to what should be the best method of *ijtihad* in the present day. To this point, there is considerable diversity and it would be erroneous to assume that the views of Muslim scholars across the world are similar.[114]

The local context has a significant influence. Examples include inside and outside threats, demographics, degrees of development, external contact, contact with different cultures, educational avenues, and so forth. They can all be different. Scholars' views vary with regard to the socioeconomic, political, and legal issues that their respective communities are facing. Consequently, diverse scholars stress diverse issues and champion different things. The spectrum of *ijtihad* can go from the least to the most liberal. The meaning of a Quranic passage is a "revelation" with multiple interpretations; its expression in words is perceived as the work of the Prophet in his corresponding time and context. The corollary is that liberal/progressive Muslims will interpret Quranic passages metaphorically or ignore them altogether.[115]

Context-based *ijtihad* involves a reader-response method. In this method, the emphasis is on the way the Quran is interpreted by the reader, not on the intent of the book's creator. Individuals who see the text as divinely inspired will believe every intention of the divine author; thus, they will stay away from any hermeneutic approach because of the many possible interpretations. They see them as contradicting scripture and devoid of any official foundation of the text.[116] On the other hand, the reader-response method sees the reader as an active participant who applies "real existence" to the text and derives meaning through interpretation.[117]

Collective ijtihad

The category of scholar considered the most qualified to derive conclusions from the Quran based on *ijtihad* is the *mujtahid*. If *ijtihad* would no longer be used as a method of interpretation, it would eliminate alternative channels of interpretations of sharia's opinions and issues that Muslim communities face on a daily basis. This type of situation could cause many problems, such as the demise of sharia, which is inconceivable at this point.[118] Collective *ijtihad* should also be regarded as an appropriate solution for the current crisis in the Muslim world. The reason is that it provides opportunities to resolve contemporary difficult problems and assuage the fundamentalism of many Sunni schools of Islamic law. How would collective *ijtihad* happen? A number of *mujtahids* from various schools and scholarly backgrounds could convene and apply *ijtihad* collectively. This procedure occurs occasionally because *mujtahids* recognize that problems in today's era are much more complex than those that emerged 1,400 years ago when the Prophet Muhammad was ruling supreme. Therefore, modern Muslim communities expect *mujtahids* to come up with general solutions to their problems—not only from the perspective of Islamic law, but also from additional perspectives.[119]

Notes

1 See Jacob D. Kathman, "Civil War Contagion and Neighboring Interventions," *International Studies Quarterly* 54, no. 4 (2010): 989–1012; Nils B. Weidmann, "Communication Networks and the Transnational Spread of Ethnic Conflict," *Journal of Peace Research* 52, no. 3 (2015): 285–96. https://doi.org/10.1177/0022343314554670

2 Marc F. Plattner, "Globalization and Self-Government," *Journal of Democracy* 13, no. 3 (2002): 54–67. https://doi.org//doi/10.1353/jod.2002.0054

3 Cassandra Balchin, "The Network 'Women Living under Muslim Laws:' Strengthening Local Struggles through Cross-Boundary Networking," *Society for International Development* 45, no. 1 (2002): 126–31.

4 Peter F. Beyer, *Religion and Globalization* (London: Sage, 1994): 1.

5 Claudio Baraldi, "New Forms of Intercultural Communication in a Globalized World," *International Communication Gazette* 68, no. 1 (2006): 53–69. https://doi.org/10.1177/1748048506060115

6 Michael Wesch, "YouTube and You: Experiences of Self-Awareness in the Context Collapse of the Recording Webcam," *Explorations in Media Ecology* 8, no. 2 (2009): 19–34.

7 Jonathan Matusitz, "The Implications of the Internet for Human Communication," *Journal of Information Technology Impact* 7, no. 1 (2007): 21–34. https://doi.org/10.1.1.99.5597&rep=rep1&type=pdf

8 John Suler, "The Online Disinhibition Effect," *International Journal of Applied Psychoanalytic Studies* 2, no. 2 (2005): 184–8. https://doi.org/10.1002/aps.42

9 Michael T. Putnam, "Music as a Weapon: Reactions and Responses to RAF Terrorism in the Music of Ton Steine Scherben and Their Successors in Post-9/11 Music," *Popular Music and Society* 32, no. 5 (2009): 595–606. https://doi.org/10.1080/03007760903251417

10 Moran Yarchi, "ISIS's Media Strategy as Image Warfare: Strategic Messaging over Time and across Platforms," *Communication and the Public* 4, no. 1 (2019): 53–67. https://doi.org/10.1177/2057047319829587

11 Brigitte Nacos, *Mass-Mediated Terrorism: The Central Role of the Media in Terrorism and Counterterrorism* (New York: Rowman & Littlefield, 2002).

12 Rafał Zgryziewicz, *Violent Extremism and Communications* (Riga, Latvia: NATO Strategic Communications Centre of Excellence, 2018).

13 Brian McNair, "From Control to Chaos, and Back Again," *Journalism Studies* 19, no. 4 (2018): 499–511. https://doi.org/10.1080/1461670X.2017.1389297

14 Ingrid Volkmer, *The Global Public Sphere, Public Communication in the Age of Reflective Interdependence* (Cambridge: Polity Press, 2014).
15 McNair, "From Control to Chaos, and Back Again," 499.
16 Barbara F. Walter, "The New New Civil Wars," *Annual Review of Political Science* 20 (2017): 469–86. https://doi.org/10.1146/annurev-polisci-060415-093921
17 Ibid., 479.
18 Ibid., 481.
19 McNair, "From Control to Chaos, and Back Again," 507.
20 Ibid., 499.
21 Abraham David Benavides, Laura M. Keyes, and Brittany Pulley, "Understanding the Recruitment Methods and Socialization Techniques of Terror Networks by Comparing Them to Youth Gangs: Similarities and Divergences," in *Countering Terrorist Recruitment in the Context of Armed Counter-Terrorism Operations*, ed. Siddik Ekici, Hüseyin Akdoğan, Eman Ragab, Ahmet Ekici, and Richard Warnes (Washington, D. C.: IOS Press, 2016): 40–54.
22 Claire Smith, Rosslyn von der Borch, Benjamin Isakhan, Sukendar Sukendar, Priyambudi Sulistiyanto, Ian Ravenscroft, Ida Widianingsih, and Cherrie de Leiuen, "The Manipulation of Social, Cultural and Religious Values in Socially Mediated Terrorism," *Religions* 9 (168): 1–19. https://doi.org/10.3390/rel9050168
23 Ibid., 2.
24 Sun Tzu, *The Art of War* (London: Oxford University Press, 1963): 84.
25 Alison Smale, Gaia Pianigiani, and Carlotta Gall, "Anis Amri, Suspect in the Berlin Truck Attack: What We Know," *The New York Times* (2016, December 22): A1.
26 Anthony Bergin, "Local Government and Australian Counter-Terrorism Strategy," *Journal of Policing, Intelligence and Counter Terrorism* 12, no. 1 (2017): 74–7. https://doi.org/10.1080/18335330.2017.1295510
27 Sam Mullins, *Jihadist Infiltration of Migrant Flows to Europe: Perpetrators, Modus Operandi and Policy Implications* (New York: Palgrave Macmillan, 2019).
28 Ely Karmon, "Central Asian Jihadists in the Front Line," *Perspectives on Terrorism* 11, no. 4 (2017): 78–86.
29 Stephen Burgen and Ian Cobain, "Barcelona Attack: Four Suspects Face Court after Van Driver Is Shot Dead," *The Guardian* (2017, August 22): A1.
30 Patrick J. McDonnell and Alexandra Zavis, "Slain Paris Plotter's Europe Ties Facilitated Travel from Syria," *Los Angeles Times* (2015, November 29): A1.
31 Samuel P. Huntington, "The Clash of Civilizations?" *Foreign Affairs* 72, no. 3 (1993): 22–49, 49.
32 Phyllis Chesler, "Are Honor Killings Simply Domestic Violence?" *Middle East Quarterly* 16, no. 2 (2009): 61–9.
33 Lorenzo Vidino, "Islamism and the West: Europe as a Battlefield," *Totalitarian Movements and Political Religions* 10, no. 2 (2009): 165–76. https://doi.org/10.1080/14690760903192081
34 Jeffrey Gettleman and Dharisha Bastians, "Sri Lanka Authorities Were Warned, in Detail, 12 Days before Attack," *The New York Times* (2019, April 29): A1.
35 Jeffrey Gettleman, Mujib Mashal, and Dharisha Bastians, "Sri Lanka Was Warned of Possible Attacks. Why Didn't It Stop Them?" *The New York Times* (2019, April 22): A1.
36 Ibid., A1.
37 Mujib Mashal, Dharisha Bastians, and Jeffrey Gettleman, "Errors Raise Questions About Sri Lankan Response to Bombing," *The New York Times* (2019, April 26): A1.
38 Mark Ensalaco, *Middle Eastern Terrorism: From Black September to September 11* (Philadelphia: University of Pennsylvania Press, 2008).
39 Jonathan Matusitz, *Terrorism & Communication: A Critical Introduction* (Thousand Oaks, CA: Sage, 2013).
40 Jonathan Matusitz, "Euphemisms for Terrorism: How Dangerous Are They?" *Empedocles: European Journal for the Philosophy of Communication* 7, no. 2 (2016): 225–37. https://doi.org/10.1386/ejpc.7.2.225_1

41 Government of Canada, *2018 Public Report on the Terrorism Threat to Canada* (Ottawa: Government of Canada, 2019). Retrieved on May 3, 2019 from https://www.pub licsafety.gc.ca/cnt/rsrcs/pblctns/pblc-rprt-trrrsm-thrt-cnd-2018/index-en.aspx

42 Vidino, "Islamism and the West," 167–9.

43 Jocelyne Cesari, *Why the West Fear Islam: An Exploration of Muslims in Liberal Democracies* (New York: Palgrave Macmillan, 2013): 94–7.

44 Ibid., 97.

45 Stephen Johnson, "'We've Bought into the Lie That Is Tolerance and Diversity': Inside Radical Muslim Group Hizb Ut-Tahrir's Sydney Conference—Where Gender Segregated Members Heard Children Should Not Sing the National Anthem," *Daily Mail* (2019, April 28): A1.

46 Viviane Teitelbaum, "The European Veil Debate," *Israel Journal of Foreign Affairs* 5, no. 1 (2011): 89–99.

47 Doug Bandow, "Obama's Interfaith Dialogue: Let's Talk Persecution," *Lebanon Daily Star* (2009, June 1): A1.

48 Hans Köchler, "Kulturelles Selbstverständnis und Koexistenz: Voraussetzungen für einen fundamentalen Dialog" [Cultural Identity and Co-existence: Preconditions for a Fundamental Dialogue], in *Philosophie und Politik. Dokumentation eines interdisziplinären Seminars* (Innsbruck, Austria: Arbeitsgemeinschaft für Wissenschaft und Politik, 1973): 75–8.

49 Paul Berman, *Terror and Liberalism* (New York: W. W. Norton & Company, 2003).

50 Sam Harris, *Letter to a Christian Nation* (New York: Vintage, 2006).

51 For example, see Gordon Allport, *The Nature of Prejudice* (Reading, MA: Addison-Wesley Publishing, 1954); Amir Lupovici, "Ontological Dissonance, Clashing Identities, and Israel's Unilateral Steps towards the Palestinians," *Review of International Studies* 38, no. 4 (2012): 809–33. https://doi.org/10.1017/S0260210511000222

52 Michael Freeman, "Democracy, Al Qaeda, and the Causes of Terrorism: A Strategic Analysis of U.S. Policy," *Studies in Conflict & Terrorism* 31, no. 1 (2008): 40–59, 48–50. https://doi.org/10.1080/10576100701759996

53 Cheryl Benard, *Civil Democratic Islam: Partners, Resources, Strategies* (Santa Monica: RAND Corporation, 2003).

54 Hugh Goddard, "Islam and Democracy," *The Political Quarterly* 73, no. 1 (2002): 3–9. https://doi.org/10.1111/1467-923X.00435

55 Jerrold M. Post, "Reframing of Martyrdom and Jihad and the Socialization of Suicide Terrorists," *Political Psychology* 30, no. 3 (2009): 381–5. https://doi.org/10.1111/j.1467-9221.2009.00702.x

56 Fathali M. Moghaddam, "The Staircase to Terrorism: A Psychological Explanation," *American Psychologist* 60, no. 2 (2005): 161–9. http://dx.doi.org/10.1037/0003-066X.60.2.161

57 Tom Tyler and Steven Blader, "The Group Engagement Model: Procedural Justice, Social Identity, and Cooperative Behavior," *Personality and Social Psychology Review* 7, no. 4 (2003): 349–61. https://doi.org/10.1207/s15327957pspr0704_07

58 Jennifer L. Windsor, "Promoting Democratization Can Combat Terrorism," *The Washington Quarterly* 26, no. 3 (2003): 43–58. https://doi.org/10.1162/016366003765609561

59 Mohamed Ali Adraoui, "Purist Salafism in France," *ISIM Review* 21, no. 1 (2008): 12–3.

60 Anthony Oberschall, "Explaining Terrorism: The Contribution of Collective Action Theory," *Sociological Theory* 22, no. 1 (2004): 26–37, 36. https://doi.org/10.1111/j.1467-9558.2004.00202.x

61 Paul Wilkinson, *Terrorism and the Liberal State* (London: MacMillan Press, 1977): 46.

62 Mohammed Hafez, *Why Muslims Rebel: Repression and Resistance in the Islamic World* (Boulder, CO: Lynne Rienner Publishers, 2003): 90.

63 Kathleen Knight Abowitz and Jason Harnish, "Contemporary Discourses of Citizenship," *Review of Educational Research* 76, no. 4 (2006): 653–90. https://doi.org/10.3102/00346543076004653

64 Thea Renda Abu El-Haj and Sally Wesley Bonet, "Education, Citizenship, and the Politics of Belonging: Youth from Muslim Transnational Communities and the 'War on Terror'," *Review of Research in Education* 35, no. 1 (2011): 29–59. https://doi.org/10.3102/0091732X10383209

65 Post, "Reframing of Martyrdom and Jihad," 381–5.

66 Robert Wuthnow, *The Restructuring of American Religion* (Princeton, NJ: Princeton University Press, 1988); Robert Wuthnow, *The Struggle for America's Soul: Evangelicals, Liberals, and Secularism* (Grand Rapids, MI: Eerdmans, 1989).

67 Os Guinness, *The American Hour* (New York: Free Press, 1993).

68 Richard John Neuhaus, *America against Itself: Moral Vision and the Public Order* (Notre Dame, IN: Notre Dame University Press, 1992).

69 Scott C. Flanagan and Aie-Rie Lee, "The New Politics, Culture Wars, and the Authoritarian-Libertarian Value Change in Advanced Industrial Democracies," *Comparative Political Studies* 36, no. 3 (2003): 235–70. https://doi.org/10.1177/0010414002250664

70 Abdel Aziz Mi, "Changing Policy for Female Genital Mutilation and the Case for Change: A Consensus Treatment," *Sudanese Journal of Public Health* 4, no. 2 (2009): 236–41.

71 Emma Varley, "Islamic Logics, Reproductive Rationalities: Family Planning in Northern Pakistan," *Anthropology & Medicine* 19, no. 2 (2012): 189–206. https://doi.org/10.1080/13648470.2012.675044

72 Alexander Caeiro, "Transnational Ulama, European Fatwas, and Islamic Authority: A Case Study of the European Council for Fatwa and Research," in *Producing Islamic Knowledge: Transmission and Dissemination in Western Europe*, ed. Martin van Bruinessen and Stefano Allievi (New York: Routledge, 2011): 121–42.

73 Sabine Damir-Geilsdorf and Leslie Tramontini, "Renegotiating Shari'a-Based Normative Guidelines in Cyberspace: The Case of Women's 'Awra," *Heidelberg Journal of Religions on the Internet* 9 (2015): 19–44.

74 Iain McLean and Alistair McMillan, *The Concise Oxford Dictionary of Politics* (3rd ed.) (Oxford: Oxford University Press, 2003): 373.

75 Gabriel Weimann, "Cyber-Fatwas and Terrorism," *Studies in Conflict & Terrorism* 34, no. 10 (2011): 765–81, 774. https://doi.org/10.1080/1057610X.2011.604831

76 Michaelle Browers, "Official Islam and the Limits of Communicative Action: the paradox of the Amman Message," *Third World Quarterly* 32, no. 5 (2011): 943–58. https://doi.org/10.1080/01436597.2011.578969

77 Rohan Gunaratna, "Al Qaeda's Ideology," *Current Trends in Islamist Ideology* 1 (2005): 59–83.

78 Ali Albarghouthi, "Authority and Representation in North America: The Ijtihad Criteria and the Construction of New Religious Authority," *Journal of Islamic Law and Culture* 13, no. 1 (2011): 18–33. https://doi.org/10.1080/1528817X.2012.693388

79 Paul Ricoeur, *Hermeneutics and the Human Sciences* (Cambridge: Cambridge University Press, 1981).

80 Wilna A. J. Meijer, "Fanaticism, Fundamentalism and the Promotion of Reflexivity in Religious Education," in *International Handbook of Inter-Religious Education*, ed. Kath Engebretson, Marian de Souza, Gloria Durka, and Liam Gearon (New York: Springer, 2010): 729–41.

81 William L. Reese, *Dictionary of Philosophy and Religion* (Brighton, Sussex: Harvester Press, 1980).

82 Robert A. Traina, *Methodical Bible Study* (Grand Rapids, MI: Francis Asbury Press, 1985).

83 Peter J. Leithart, *Deep Exegesis: The Mystery of Reading Scripture* (Baylor, TX: Baylor University Press, 2009).

84 Peter Crisp, "Allegory, Blending, and Possible Situations," *Metaphor and Symbol* 20, no. 2 (2005): 115–31. https://doi.org/10.1207/s15327868ms2002_2

85 James Barr, "The Literal, the Allegorical, and Modern Biblical Scholarship," *Journal for the Study of the Old Testament* 44 (1989): 3–17. https://doi/pdf/10.1177/030908928901404401
86 Milton Terry, *Biblical Hermeneutics: A Treatise on the Interpretation of the Old and New Testaments* (Grand Rapids, MI: Zondervan, 1974).
87 Ibid., 205.
88 Howard G. Hendricks, *Living by the Book* (Chicago: Moody Press, 1991).
89 Martin Heidegger, *Being and Time* (New York: Harper & Row, 1962).
90 Richard Palmer, *Hermeneutics: Interpretation Theory in Schleiermacher, Dilthey, Heidegger, and Gadamer* (Evanston: Northwestern University Press, 1969).
91 Martin Heidegger, *Poetry, Language, Thought* (New York: Harper Collins, 1971).
92 Charles Bazerman, *The Informed Writer: Using Sources in the Disciplines* (5th ed.) (Boston: Houghton Mifflin Company, 1994).
93 Umberto Eco, *Interpretation and Overinterpretation* (Cambridge: Cambridge University Press, 1992).
94 Peter Ekegren, *The Reading of Theoretical Texts. A Critique of Criticism in the Social Sciences* (London: Routledge, 1999).
95 Haleh Afshar, "Can I See Your Hair? Choice, Agency and Attitudes: The Dilemma of Faith and Feminism for Muslim Women Who Cover," *Ethnic and Racial Studies* 31, no. 2 (2008): 411–27. https://doi.org/10.1080/01419870701710930; Iqbal Jhazbhay, "The Politics of Interpretation: The Call of Islam and Ulama Disciplinary Power in South Africa," *Journal of Muslim Minority Affairs* 22, no. 2 (2002): 457–67. https://doi.org/10.1080/1360200022000027401
96 Sulaiman Musa, "The Influence of Tafsir Al-Jalalayn on Some Notable Nigerian Mufassirun in the Twentieth-Century Nigeria," *Journal of Muslim Minority Affairs* 20, no. 2 (2000): 323–8. https://doi.org/10.1080/713680358; Harry S. Neale, *Jihad in Premodern Sufi Writings* (New York: Palgrave Macmillan, 2016).
97 Ahmad Von Denffer, *Ulum al Qur'an: An Introduction to the Sciences of the Qur'an* (Markfield: The Islamic Foundation, 2011).
98 Mustansir Mir, "Tafsir," in *The Oxford Encyclopedia of the Modern Islamic World*, ed. John L. Esposito (Oxford: Oxford University Press, 1995).
99 Imad Zeroual and Abdelhak Lakhouaja, "A New Quranic Corpus Rich in Morpho-syntactical Information," *International Journal of Speech Technology* 19, no. 2 (2016): 339–46. https://doi.org/10.1007/s10772-016-9335-7
100 Farag Ahmed and Andreas Nurnberger, "Arabic/English Word Translation Disambiguation Approach Based on Naive Bayesian Classifier," *International Multiconference on Computer Science and Information Technology* (October 20–22, 2008, Wisia, Poland). https://doi.org/10.1109/IMCSIT.2008.4747261
101 Zeroual and Lakhouaja, "A New Quranic Corpus," 339–46.
102 Von Denffer, *Ulum al Qur'an*, 4–9.
103 Devin Stewart, "Kecia Ali, Imam Shafi'i: Scholar and Saint (Oxford: Oneworld Press, 2011). Pp. 160. $32.69 cloth," *International Journal of Middle East Studies* 46, no. 2 (2014): 434–7. https://doi.org/10.1017/S0020743814000403
104 David G. Kibble, "*Dabiq*, the Islamic State's Magazine: A Critical Analysis," *Middle East Policy* 23, no. 3 (2016): 133–43. https://doi.org/10.1111/mepo.12222
105 Mohd Izhar Ariff Mohd Kashim and Ahmamd Muhammad Husni, "Maqasid Shariah in Modern Biotechnology Concerning Food Products," *International Journal of Islamic Thought* 12 (2017): 27–39. https://doi.org/10.24035/ijit.12.2017.00
106 Meijer, "Fanaticism, Fundamentalism," 732–8.
107 Intisar A. Rabb, "Ijtihād," in *The Oxford Encyclopedia of the Islamic World*, ed. John L. Esposito (Oxford: Oxford University Press, 2009).
108 Saim Kayadibi, "Ijtihad by *Ra'y*: The Main Sources of Inspiration behind *Istihsan*," *American Journal of Islamic Social Sciences* 24, no. 1 (2007): 73–95.

109 Abdullah Saeed, "Ijtihad and Innovation in Neo-Modernist Islamic Thought in Indonesia," *Islam and Christian-Muslim Relations* 8, no. 3 (1997): 279–95. https://doi.org/10.1080/09596419708721127

110 Michael Kemper, "Ijtihad into Philosophy: Islam as Cultural Heritage in Post-Stalinist Daghestan," *Central Asian Survey* 33, no. 3 (2014): 390–404. https://doi.org/10.1080/02634937.2014.942581

111 Haleh Afshar, "Muslim Women and Feminisms: Illustrations from the Iranian Experience," *Social Compass* 54, no. 3 (2007): 419–34. https://doi.org/10.1177/0037768607080838; Nimat Barazangi, *Woman's Identity and the Qur'an: A New Reading* (Gainesville: University Press of Florida, 2004).

112 Amanda Keddie, "Disrupting (Gendered) Islamophobia: The Practice of Feminist Ijtihad to Support the Agency of Young Muslim Women," *Journal of Gender Studies* 27, no. 5 (2018): 522–33. https://doi.org/10.1080/09589236.2016.1243047

113 Marium Jabyn, "Transformations in Shari'ah Family Law in the Republic of Maldives," *Jindal Global Law Review* 7, no. 1 (2016): 61–79. https://doi.org/10.1007/s41020-016-0022-y

114 Saeed, "Ijtihad and Innovation," 283–9.

115 Saim Kayadibi, *Principles of Islamic Law and the Methods of Interpretation of the Texts (Uṣūl al-Fiqh)* (Kuala Lumpur: Islamic Book Trust, 2017).

116 Michael Cahill, "Reader-Response Criticism and the Allegorizing Reader," *Theological Studies* 57, no. 1 (1996): 89–97. https://doi.org/10.1177/004056399605700105

117 Jane P. Tompkins, *Reader-Response Criticism: From Formalism to Post-Structuralism* (Baltimore: Johns Hopkins University Press, 1980).

118 Aznan Hasan, "An Introduction to Collective Ijtihad (Ijtihad Jama'i): Concept and Applications," *The American Journal of Islamic Social Sciences* 20, no. 2 (2003): 26–49.

119 Nadirsyah Hosen, "Nahdlatul Ulama and Collective Ijtihad," *New Zealand Journal of Asian Studies* 6, no. 1 (2004): 5–26.

References

Abowitz, Kathleen Knight, and Jason Harnish, "Contemporary Discourses of Citizenship," *Review of Educational Research* 76, no. 4 (2006): 653–690. https://doi.org/10.3102/00346543076004653.

Adraoui, Mohamed Ali, "Purist Salafism in France," *ISIM Review* 21, no. 1 (2008): 12–13.

Afshar, Haleh, "Muslim Women and Feminisms: Illustrations from the Iranian Experience," *Social Compass* 54, no. 3 (2007): 419–434. https://doi.org/10.1177/0037768607080838.

Afshar, Haleh, "Can I See Your Hair? Choice, Agency and Attitudes: The Dilemma of Faith and Feminism for Muslim Women Who Cover," *Ethnic and Racial Studies* 31, no. 2 (2008): 411–427. https://doi.org/10.1080/01419870701710930.

Ahmed, Farag, and Andreas Nurnberger, "*Arabic/English Word Translation Disambiguation Approach Based on Naive Bayesian Classifier*," International Multiconference on Computer Science and Information Technology (October 20–22, 2008, Wisia, Poland). https://doi.org/10.1109/IMCSIT.2008.4747261.

Albarghouthi, Ali, "Authority and Representation in North America: The Ijtihad Criteria and the Construction of New Religious Authority," *Journal of Islamic Law and Culture* 13, no. 1 (2011): 18–33. https://doi.org/10.1080/1528817X.2012.693388.

Allport, Gordon, *The Nature of Prejudice*. Reading, MA: Addison-Wesley Publishing, 1954.

Balchin, Cassandra, "The Network 'Women Living under Muslim Laws:' Strengthening Local Struggles through Cross-Boundary Networking," *Society for International Development* 45, no. 1 (2002): 126–131.

Bandow, Doug, "Obama's Interfaith Dialogue: Let's Talk Persecution," *Lebanon Daily Star* (2009, June 1): A1.

Baraldi, Claudio, "New Forms of Intercultural Communication in a Globalized World," *International Communication Gazette* 68, no. 1 (2006): 53–69. https://doi.org/10.1177/1748048506060115.

Barazangi, Nimat, *Woman's Identity and the Qur'an: A New Reading*. Gainesville, FL: University Press of Florida, 2004.

Barr, James, "The Literal, the Allegorical, and Modern Biblical Scholarship," *Journal for the Study of the Old Testament* 44 (1989): 3–17. https://doi/pdf/10.1177/030908928901404401.

Bazerman, Charles, *The Informed Writer: Using Sources in the Disciplines* (5th ed.). Boston, MA: Houghton Mifflin Company, 1994.

Benard, Cheryl, *Civil Democratic Islam: Partners, Resources, Strategies*. Santa Monica, CA: RAND Corporation, 2003.

Benavides, Abraham David, Laura M. Keyes, and Brittany Pulley, "Understanding the Recruitment Methods and Socialization Techniques of Terror Networks by Comparing Them to Youth Gangs: Similarities and Divergences," in *Countering Terrorist Recruitment in the Context of Armed Counter-Terrorism Operations*, edited by Siddik Ekici, Hüseyin Akdoğan, Eman Ragab, Ahmet Ekici, and Richard Warnes, 40–54. Washington, D.C.: IOS Press, 2016.

Bergin, Anthony, "Local Government and Australian Counter-Terrorism Strategy," *Journal of Policing, Intelligence and Counter Terrorism* 12, no. 1 (2017): 74–77. https://doi.org/10.1080/18335330.2017.1295510.

Berman, Paul, *Terror and Liberalism*. New York: W. W. Norton & Company, 2003.

Beyer, Peter F., *Religion and Globalization*. London: Sage, 1994.

Browers, Michaelle, "Official Islam and the Limits of Communicative Action: the paradox of the Amman Message," *Third World Quarterly* 32, no. 5 (2011): 943–958. https://doi.org/10.1080/01436597.2011.578969.

Burgen, Stephen, and Ian Cobain, "Barcelona Attack: Four Suspects Face Court after Van Driver Is Shot Dead," *The Guardian* (2017, August 22): A1.

Caeiro, Alexander, "Transnational Ulama, European Fatwas, and Islamic Authority: A Case Study of the European Council for Fatwa and Research," in *Producing Islamic Knowledge: Transmission and Dissemination in Western Europe*, edited by Martin van Bruinessen and Stefano Allievi, 121–142. New York: Routledge, 2011.

Cahill, Michael, "Reader-Response Criticism and the Allegorizing Reader," *Theological Studies* 57, no. 1 (1996): 89–97. https://doi.org/10.1177/004056399605700105.

Cesari, Jocelyne, *Why the West Fear Islam: An Exploration of Muslims in Liberal Democracies*. New York: Palgrave Macmillan, 2013.

Chesler, Phyllis, "Are Honor Killings Simply Domestic Violence?" *Middle East Quarterly* 16, no. 2 (2009): 61–69.

Crisp, Peter "Allegory, Blending, and Possible Situations," *Metaphor and Symbol* 20, no. 2 (2005): 115–131. https://doi.org/10.1207/s15327868ms2002_2.

Damir-Geilsdorf, Sabine, and Leslie Tramontini, "Renegotiating Shari'a-Based Normative Guidelines in Cyberspace: The Case of Women's 'Awra," *Heidelberg Journal of Religions on the Internet* 9 (2015): 19–44.

Eco, Umberto, *Interpretation and Overinterpretation*. Cambridge: Cambridge University Press, 1992.

Ekegren, Peter, *The Reading of Theoretical Texts. A Critique of Criticism in the Social Sciences*. London: Routledge, 1999.

El-Haj, Thea Renda Abu, and Sally Wesley Bonet, "Education, Citizenship, and the Politics of Belonging: Youth from Muslim Transnational Communities and the 'War on

Terror'," *Review of Research in Education* 35, no. 1 (2011): 29–59. https://doi.org/10.3102/0091732X10383209.

Ensalaco, Mark, *Middle Eastern Terrorism: From Black September to September 11.* Philadelphia, PA: University of Pennsylvania Press, 2008.

Flanagan, Scott C., and Aie-Rie Lee, "The New Politics, Culture Wars, and the Authoritarian-Libertarian Value Change in Advanced Industrial Democracies," *Comparative Political Studies* 36, no. 3 (2003): 235–270. https://doi.org/10.1177/0010414002250664.

Freeman, Michael, "Democracy, Al Qaeda, and the Causes of Terrorism: A Strategic Analysis of U.S. Policy," *Studies in Conflict & Terrorism* 31, no. 1 (2008): 40–59. https://doi.org/10.1080/10576100701759996.

Gettleman, Jeffrey, and Dharisha Bastians, "Sri Lanka Authorities Were Warned, in Detail, 12 Days before Attack," *The New York Times* (2019, April 29): A1.

Gettleman, Jeffrey, Mujib Mashal, and Dharisha Bastians, "Sri Lanka Was Warned of Possible Attacks. Why Didn't It Stop Them?" *The New York Times* (2019, April 22): A1.

Goddard, Hugh, "Islam and Democracy," *The Political Quarterly* 73, no. 1 (2002): 3–9. https://doi.org/10.1111/1467-923X.00435.

Government of Canada, *2018 Public Report on the Terrorism Threat to Canada.* Ottawa: Government of Canada, 2019. Retrieved on May 3, 2019 from www.publicsafety.gc.ca/cnt/rsrcs/pblctns/pblc-rprt-trrrsm-thrt-cnd-2018/index-en.aspx.

Guinness, Os, *The American Hour.* New York: Free Press, 1993.

Gunaratna, Rohan, "Al Qaeda's Ideology," *Current Trends in Islamist Ideology* 1 (2005): 59–83.

Hafez, Mohammed, *Why Muslims Rebel: Repression and Resistance in the Islamic World.* Boulder, CO: Lynne Rienner Publishers, 2003.

Harris, Sam, *Letter to a Christian Nation.* New York: Vintage, 2006.

Hasan, Aznan, "An Introduction to Collective Ijtihad (Ijtihad Jama'i): Concept and Applications," *The American Journal of Islamic Social Sciences* 20, no. 2 (2003): 26–49.

Heidegger, Martin, *Being and Time.* New York: Harper & Row, 1962.

Heidegger, Martin, *Poetry, Language, Thought.* New York: HarperCollins, 1971.

Hendricks, Howard G., *Living by the Book.* Chicago, IL: Moody Press, 1991.

Hosen, Nadirsyah, "Nahdlatul Ulama and Collective Ijtihad," *New Zealand Journal of Asian Studies* 6, no. 1 (2004): 5–26.

Huntington, Samuel P., "The Clash of Civilizations?" *Foreign Affairs* 72, no. 3 (1993): 22–49.

Jabyn, Marium, "*Transformations in Shari'ah Family Law in the Republic of Maldives,*" Jindal Global Law Review 7, no. 1 (2016): 61–79. https://doi.org/10.1007/s41020-016-0022-y.

Jhazbhay, Iqbal, "The Politics of Interpretation: The Call of Islam and Ulama Disciplinary Power in South Africa," *Journal of Muslim Minority Affairs* 22, no. 2 (2002): 457–467. https://doi.org/10.1080/1360200022000027401.

Johnson, Stephen, "'We've Bought into the Lie That Is Tolerance and Diversity': Inside Radical Muslim Group Hizb Ut-Tahrir's Sydney Conference—Where Gender Segregated Members Heard Children Should Not Sing the National Anthem," *Daily Mail* (2019, April 28): A1.

Karmon, Ely, "Central Asian Jihadists in the Front Line," *Perspectives on Terrorism* 11, no. 4 (2017): 78–86.

Kashim, Mohd Izhar AriffMohd, and Ahmamd Muhammad Husni, "Maqasid Shariah in Modern Biotechnology Concerning Food Products," *International Journal of Islamic Thought* 12 (2017): 27–39. https://doi.org/10.24035/ijit.12.2017.00.

Kathman, Jacob D., "Civil War Contagion and Neighboring Interventions," *International Studies Quarterly* 54, no. 4 (2010): 989–1012.

Kayadibi, Saim, "Ijtihad by *Ra'y*: The Main Sources of Inspiration behind *Istihsan*," *American Journal of Islamic Social Sciences* 24, no. 1 (2007): 73–95.

Kayadibi, Saim, *Principles of Islamic Law and the Methods of Interpretation of the Texts (Uṣūl al-Fiqh)*. Kuala Lumpur: Islamic Book Trust, 2017.

Keddie, Amanda, "Disrupting (Gendered) Islamophobia: The Practice of Feminist Ijtihad to Support the Agency of Young Muslim Women," *Journal of Gender Studies* 27, no. 5 (2018): 522–533. https://doi.org/10.1080/09589236.2016.1243047.

Kemper, Michael, "Ijtihad into Philosophy: Islam as Cultural Heritage in Post-Stalinist Daghestan," *Central Asian Survey* 33, no. 3 (2014): 390–404. https://doi.org/10.1080/02634937.2014.942581.

Kibble, David G., "*Dabiq*, the Islamic State's Magazine: A Critical Analysis," *Middle East Policy* 23, no. 3 (2016): 133–143. https://doi.org/10.1111/mepo.12222.

Köchler, Hans, "Kulturelles Selbstverständnis und Koexistenz: Voraussetzungen für einen fundamentalen Dialog" [Cultural Identity and Co-existence: Preconditions for a Fundamental Dialogue], in *Philosophie und Politik. Dokumentation eines interdisziplinären Seminars*, 75–78. Innsbruck, Austria: Arbeitsgemeinschaft für Wissenschaft und Politik, 1973.

Leithart, Peter J., *Deep Exegesis: The Mystery of Reading Scripture*. Baylor, TX: Baylor University Press, 2009.

Lupovici, Amir, "Ontological Dissonance, Clashing Identities, and Israel's Unilateral Steps towards the Palestinians," *Review of International Studies* 38, no. 4 (2012): 809–833. https://doi.org/10.1017/S0260210511000222.

Mashal, Mujib, Dharisha Bastians, and Jeffrey Gettleman, "Errors Raise Questions About Sri Lankan Response to Bombing," *The New York Times* (2019, April 26): A1.

Matusitz, Jonathan, "The Implications of the Internet for Human Communication," *Journal of Information Technology Impact* 7, no. 1 (2007): 21–34. https://doi.org/10.1.1.99.5597&rep=rep1&type=pdf.

Matusitz, Jonathan, *Terrorism & Communication: A Critical Introduction*. Thousand Oaks, CA: Sage, 2013.

Matusitz, Jonathan, "Euphemisms for Terrorism: How Dangerous Are They?" *Empedocles: European Journal for the Philosophy of Communication* 7, no. 2 (2016): 225–237. https://doi.org/10.1386/ejpc.7.2.225_1.

McDonnell, Patrick J., and Alexandra Zavis, "Slain Paris Plotter's Europe Ties Facilitated Travel from Syria," *Los Angeles Times* (2015, November 29): A1.

McLean, Iain, and Alistair McMillan, *The Concise Oxford Dictionary of Politics* (3rd ed.). Oxford: Oxford University Press, 2003.

McNair, Brian, "From Control to Chaos, and Back Again," *Journalism Studies* 19, no. 4 (2018): 499–511. https://doi.org/10.1080/1461670X.2017.1389297.

Meijer, Wilna A. J., "Fanaticism, Fundamentalism and the Promotion of Reflexivity in Religious Education," in *International Handbook of Inter-Religious Education*, edited by Kath Engebretson, Marian de Souza, Gloria Durka, and Liam Gearon, 729–741. New York: Springer, 2010.

Mi, Abdel Aziz, "Changing Policy for Female Genital Mutilation and the Case for Change: A Consensus Treatment," *Sudanese Journal of Public Health* 4, no. 2 (2009): 236–241.

Mir, Mustansir, "Tafsir," in *The Oxford Encyclopedia of the Modern Islamic World*, edited by John L. Esposito. Oxford: Oxford University Press, 1995.

Moghaddam, Fathali M., "The Staircase to Terrorism: A Psychological Explanation," *American Psychologist* 60, no. 2 (2005): 161–169. http://dx.doi.org/10.1037/0003-066X.60.2.161.

Mullins, Sam, *Jihadist Infiltration of Migrant Flows to Europe: Perpetrators, Modus Operandi and Policy Implications*. New York: Palgrave Macmillan, 2019.

Musa, Sulaiman, "The Influence of Tafsir Al-Jalalayn on Some Notable Nigerian Mufassirun in the Twentieth-Century Nigeria," *Journal of Muslim Minority Affairs* 20, no. 2 (2000): 323–328. https://doi.org/10.1080/713680358.

Nacos, Brigitte, *Mass-Mediated Terrorism: The Central Role of the Media in Terrorism and Counterterrorism*. Lanham, MD: Rowman & Littlefield, 2002.

Neale, Harry S., *Jihad in Premodern Sufi Writings*. New York: Palgrave Macmillan, 2016.

Neuhaus, Richard John, *America against Itself: Moral Vision and the Public Order*. Notre Dame, IN: Notre Dame University Press, 1992.

Oberschall, Anthony, "Explaining Terrorism: The Contribution of Collective Action Theory," *Sociological Theory* 22, no. 1 (2004): 26–37. https://doi.org/10.1111/j.1467-9558.2004.00202.x.

Palmer, Richard, *Hermeneutics: Interpretation Theory in Schleiermacher, Dilthey, Heidegger, and Gadamer*. Evanston: Northwestern University Press, 1969.

Plattner, Marc F., "Globalization and Self-Government," *Journal of Democracy* 13, no. 3 (2002): 54–67. https://doi.org/doi/10.1353/jod.2002.0054.

Post, Jerrold M., "Reframing of Martyrdom and Jihad and the Socialization of Suicide Terrorists," *Political Psychology* 30, no. 3 (2009): 381–385. https://doi.org/10.1111/j.1467-9221.2009.00702.x.

Putnam, Michael T., "Music as a Weapon: Reactions and Responses to RAF Terrorism in the Music of Ton Steine Scherben and Their Successors in Post-9/11 Music," *Popular Music and Society* 32, no. 5 (2009): 595–606. https://doi.org/10.1080/03007760903251417.

Rabb, Intisar A., "Ijtihād," in *The Oxford Encyclopedia of the Islamic World*, edited by John L. Esposito. Oxford: Oxford University Press, 2009.

Reese, William L. *Dictionary of Philosophy and Religion*. Brighton: Harvester Press, 1980.

Ricoeur, Paul, *Hermeneutics and the Human Sciences*. Cambridge: Cambridge University Press, 1981.

Saeed, Abdullah, "Ijtihad and Innovation in Neo-Modernist Islamic Thought in Indonesia," *Islam and Christian-Muslim Relations* 8, no. 3 (1997): 279–295. https://doi.org/10.1080/09596419708721127.

Smale, Alison, Gaia Pianigiani, and Carlotta Gall, "Anis Amri, Suspect in the Berlin Truck Attack: What We Know," *The New York Times* (2016, December 22): A1.

Smith, Claire, Rosslyn von der Borch, Benjamin Isakhan, Sukendar Sukendar, Priyambudi Sulistiyanto, Ian Ravenscroft, Ida Widianingsih, and Cherrie de Leiuen, "The Manipulation of Social, Cultural and Religious Values in Socially Mediated Terrorism," *Religions* 9 (168): 1–19. https://doi.org/10.3390/rel9050168.

Stewart, Devin, "Kecia Ali, Imam Shafi'i: Scholar and Saint (Oxford: Oneworld Press, 2011). Pp. 160. $32.69 cloth," *International Journal of Middle East Studies* 46, no. 2 (2014): 434–437. https://doi.org/10.1017/S0020743814000403.

Suler, John, "The Online Disinhibition Effect," *International Journal of Applied Psychoanalytic Studies* 2, no. 2 (2005): 184–188. https://doi.org/10.1002/aps.42.

Sun Tzu, *The Art of War*. London: Oxford University Press, 1963.

Teitelbaum, Viviane, "The European Veil Debate," *Israel Journal of Foreign Affairs* 5, no. 1 (2011): 89–99.

Terry, Milton, *Biblical Hermeneutics: A Treatise on the Interpretation of the Old and New Testaments*. Grand Rapids, MI: Zondervan, 1974.

Tompkins, Jane P., *Reader-Response Criticism: From Formalism to Post-Structuralism*. Baltimore, MD: Johns Hopkins University Press, 1980.

Traina, Robert A., *Methodical Bible Study*. Grand Rapids, MI: Francis Asbury Press, 1985.

Tyler, Tom, and Steven Blader, "The Group Engagement Model: Procedural Justice, Social Identity, and Cooperative Behavior," *Personality and Social Psychology Review* 7, no. 4 (2003): 349–361. https://doi.org/10.1207/s15327957pspr0704_07.

Varley, Emma, "Islamic Logics, Reproductive Rationalities: Family Planning in Northern Pakistan," *Anthropology & Medicine* 19, no. 2 (2012): 189–206. https://doi.org/10.1080/13648470.2012.675044.

Vidino, Lorenzo, "Islamism and the West: Europe as a Battlefield," *Totalitarian Movements and Political Religions* 10, no. 2 (2009): 165–176. https://doi.org/10.1080/14690760903192081.

Volkmer, Ingrid, *The Global Public Sphere, Public Communication in the Age of Reflective Interdependence*. Cambridge: Polity Press, 2014.

Von Denffer, Ahmad, *Ulum al Qur'an: An Introduction to the Sciences of the Qur'an*. Markfield: The Islamic Foundation, 2011.

Walter, Barbara F., "The New New Civil Wars," *Annual Review of Political Science* 20 (2017): 469–486. https://doi.org/10.1146/annurev-polisci-060415-093921.

Weidmann, Nils B., "Communication Networks and the Transnational Spread of Ethnic Conflict," *Journal of Peace Research* 52, no. 3 (2015): 285–296. https://doi.org/10.1177/0022343314554670.

Weimann, Gabriel, "Cyber-Fatwas and Terrorism," *Studies in Conflict & Terrorism* 34, no. 10 (2011): 765–781. https://doi.org/10.1080/1057610X.2011.604831.

Wesch, Michael, "YouTube and You: Experiences of Self-Awareness in the Context Collapse of the Recording Webcam," *Explorations in Media Ecology* 8, no. 2 (2009): 19–34.

Wilkinson, Paul, *Terrorism and the Liberal State*. London: Macmillan Press, 1977.

Windsor, Jennifer L., "Promoting Democratization Can Combat Terrorism," *The Washington Quarterly* 26, no. 3 (2003): 43–58. https://doi.org/10.1162/016366003765609561.

Wuthnow, Robert, *The Restructuring of American Religion*. Princeton, NJ: Princeton University Press, 1988.

Wuthnow, Robert, *The Struggle for America's Soul: Evangelicals, Liberals, and Secularism*. Grand Rapids, MI: Eerdmans, 1989.

Yarchi, Moran, "ISIS's Media Strategy as Image Warfare: Strategic Messaging over Time and across Platforms," *Communication and the Public* 4, no. 1 (2019): 53–67. https://doi.org/10.1177/2057047319829587.

Zeroual, Imad, and Abdelhak Lakhouaja, "A New Quranic Corpus Rich in Morphosyntactical Information," *International Journal of Speech Technology* 19, no. 2 (2016): 339–346. https://doi.org/10.1007/s10772-016-9335-7.

Zgryziewicz, Rafał, *Violent Extremism and Communications*. Riga, Latvia: NATO Strategic Communications Centre of Excellence, 2018.

INDEX

For Product Safety Concerns and Information please contact our EU
representative GPSR@taylorandfrancis.com
Taylor & Francis Verlag GmbH, Kaufingerstraße 24, 80331 München, Germany

www.ingramcontent.com/pod-product-compliance
Lightning Source LLC
Chambersburg PA
CBHW070359270326
41926CB00014B/2623